DOCTORS OF MEDICINE
IN NEW MEXICO

DOCTORS OF MEDICINE
◆ IN ◆
NEW MEXICO

A History of Health and Medical Practice, 1886–1986

Jake W. Spidle, Jr.

THE UNIVERSITY OF NEW MEXICO PRESS
Albuquerque

To Mary Anna, with love and appreciation

Design by Milenda Nan Ok Lee

Library of Congress Cataloguing-in-Publication Data

Spidle, Jake W., 1941–
Doctors of medicine in New Mexico, 1886–1986.

Bibliography: p.
Includes index.
1. Medicine—New Mexico—History—19th century.
2. Medicine—New Mexico—History—20th century.
3. Public health—New Mexico—History—19th century.
4. Public health—New Mexico—History—20th century.
I. Title. [DNLM. 1. History of Medicine—New Mexico.
2. Physicians—biography. 3. Public Health—history—New Mexico.
WZ 70 S7d] R287.S65 1986 362.1'09789 86-11428
ISBN 0-8263-0909-7

Manufactured in the United States of America

First edition

Contents

Illustrations

Plates

Maps

Figures

Tables

Foreword

DURING THIS CENTENNIAL YEAR, WE ARE CHALLENGED TO reflect on the past through a written document for future generations. Many longtime practicing physicians throughout the state of New Mexico were interviewed and have shared in the preparation of *Doctors of Medicine in New Mexico.* All who were interviewed during the compilation of this history were practicing during the great technological revolution in medicine which started in the period following World War II. Their experience and recollections are invaluable.

The second revolution involving method of payment for medical care is in its infancy at the present time. Future historians will record this activity, also. Thus, those who participated in the "golden era of Medicine" await the outcome of this revolutionary phase with great concern for their patients.

Physicians who are responsible for the very high standard of medical care rendered in the past have every reason to be proud. Their diligence and dedication have etched a permanent place in the history of medicine in New Mexico. Physicians in this state have always been recognized for their interest in improving their professional ability and the quality of care for their patients. The Society has been in the forefront with the development of a number of programs that have assisted both the members and their patients.

In 1949, the statewide Board of Supervisors (later to be known as the Grievance Committee) was formed to continuously investigate the ethical deportment of the members of the medical profession in the state of

New Mexico. Its existence was advertised extensively in order to let the public know that there was a mechanism for handling complaints. In 1958, the President of the New Mexico Medical Society notified the New Mexico Department of Welfare that all members of the Medical Society would be asked to furnish essential care for medically indigent persons in the state requesting care, without charge to the state. This policy was terminated when sufficient funds were made available to pay physicians in accordance with the Department's fee schedule.

The first statewide Medico-legal panel for Screening Malpractice suits was established by the New Mexico Medical Society in 1964 when the first case was considered. The panel has served as a model throughout the nation and continues under the statutory name of the Medical Review Commission. In 1985, the Commission considered 118 cases involving 174 health-care providers and hospitals. The New Mexico Foundation for Medical Care was established by the New Mexico Medical Society in 1970. It was the first statewide professional peer review organization formed in the United States. A contract for professional review of the Medicaid program was awarded in June 1971.

The year 1975 proved to be one of crisis. All casualty companies licensed in New Mexico withdrew from underwriting medical malpractice insurance. Once again, the New Mexico Medical Society organized a statewide effort to have tort reform legislation adopted and also organized the New Mexico Physicians Mutual Liability Company. Today, this company continues as the major carrier of malpractice insurance in New Mexico and insures almost ninety percent of the practicing physicians in the state.

Many times during the past thirty-six years, I have been asked how so many first-time endeavors were accomplished. One of the reasons, in my opinion, is that the leadership of the New Mexico Medical Society has been able to agree on goals, and the membership has been willing to expend the time, money, and effort to bring about successful conclusions. It has been my very great pleasure to be a part of this successful story since 1949. No employee could have enjoyed a more satisfactory relationship with his "bosses." Sharing in the heartaches and pleasures with the best friends a man could have, has been a tremendously rewarding experience for me.

Ralph R. Marshall
Executive Director
New Mexico Medical Society
Spring 1986

Preface

AT THE 1910 ANNUAL MEETING OF THE NEW MEXICO MEDICAL Society held in Albuquerque, the society's president, Dr. J. W. Elder of the host city, made the following suggestion:

> The collection of data for a history of physicians who have been located in New Mexico should be undertaken. There are many whose record should be preserved. They were men of ability and force, men fitted to deal with the conditions of pioneer days. . . . This should be done while we still have with us those whose acquaintance and knowledge extend back to early days and who have themselves been important factors in the development and growth of New Mexico. This is the time for the appointment of an energetic committee to collect all information possible, which can later be edited and published.

In early 1982, a scant seventy-two years after Dr. Elder's appeal, a medical history program was established in the University of New Mexico Medical Center Library to do the work he sketched out. (Yes, now and again New Mexico is truly the land of *mañana.*) The idea for such a project originated in the library, but the cooperation and support of the New Mexico Medical Society was quickly enlisted. I was asked to join the effort as project historian in April 1982.

This book is the first fruit of the New Mexico Medical History Program's labors. It is based, first and foremost, on the ninety-plus oral history interviews done under the project's aegis and on the various materials already collected and assembled in the Medical History Archives housed in the Medical Center Library. From the program's start in 1982, we aimed at production of a book to help the New Mexico Medical Society celebrate its centennial in 1986, but this volume is in no way an end to the program's efforts. Rather, it is our hope that this book will kindle interest in the general subject and encourage broader participation in our work. New Mexico's medical heritage is a grand, multifaceted one, and the task of recapturing and preserving as much of it as possible has just begun.

The rationale for this book ought to be clearly spelled out. As noted, it is in part intended to focus some attention on New Mexico's doctors of medicine as they celebrate the 100th anniversary of the birth of organized medicine in this region. More importantly, however, it is meant to provide a starting point for filling in one of the larger holes in the study of New Mexico's past, namely its health and medical care history. There is perhaps no other major sphere of the state's heritage that has been so little studied by historians and other students of the region's culture. Historians are most comfortable writing a book like this one—a broad, sweeping survey exploring a complex subject over a long period of time—at the very end of a lengthy period of study and research in archival materials and on the foundation of extensive monographic literature. Alternatively, a book of this kind may be written close to the start of detailed investigation, to provide a framework for further work. I have tried to do this latter service and trust this book will prove a solid, reliable introduction to the subject.

In the research for this book and then in its writing, I have been the happy beneficiary of the assistance, good advice, and support of many people. Pride of place on that list must go to Mrs. Erika Love and her splendid staff of the University of New Mexico Medical Center Library. It is no exaggeration to say that without Erika Love there would have been no book. She has inspired the History Program and this book from their very start, providing a large share of the confidence, courage, and energy necessary to keep the Program and the book preparation moving forward. She has afforded far more than just the institutional support essential to a project of this scope. She has also provided the good judgment to help keep us on the rails and pointed in the right direction and an unwavering commitment to this work—Program and book—which lightened the load immeasurably for those of us engaged in this effort.

After Mrs. Love, my special thanks go to Janet Johnson and Theresa Haynes of the Medical Center Library staff. For more than two years Janet has served ably as Manager of the New Mexico Medical History Program and as Manager of the History Archives in the Medical Center Library. She has been a full partner in the work to recover what we can of New Mexico's medical heritage and in the preparation of this book. The same can be said of Theresa Haynes, Assistant to the Director of the Library. Theresa has been particularly important in the history program's oral history work, transcribing and editing the many taped hours of reminiscences with skill and discernment. Susan Chamberlin was centrally important in getting the History Program started, and Swanee Wilson and Stephen Pla contributed their energies and assistance in terms as managers of the program. Others at the Library who have cheerfully given their time, expertise, and encouragement to the History Program generally and to me personally include Cecile Quintal, Sandy Brantley, Patricia Campbell, Lillian Croghan, Judith DuCharme, Nina Garcia, Kathy Mondragon, Dave Percival, Herldine Radley, and Pat Standing. To all these professionals of the Medical Center Library I extend my thanks and the hope that they will regard this book, to the degree it has merit, as their own.

Outside the Library, the leadership and staff of the New Mexico Medical Society have been the strongest supporters of this effort. I have profited enormously from the wise counsel and encouragement of Ralph Marshall in this work, and the members of his staff, Dorothy Welby and Betty Edwards in particular, have often gone out of their way—with a smile, too—to help me when I've encountered problems. To the doctors of the Society's Medical History Committee I also extend my thanks and high regard, especially to the two physicians who have so ably chaired the committee and helped to steer our work, Drs. Robert Friedenberg and Fred Hanold, both of Albuquerque. I am also appreciative of the special help of Dr. Douglas Layman, who helped the program get started, and of the fruitful service of two veteran New Mexico doctors on the committee, the late Dr. C. Pardue Bunch of Artesia and Dr. William J. Hossley of Deming. If this book has anything of the solidity of these men, then it is strong indeed. The help of the personnel of the Board of Medical Examiners was also critical to the success of our efforts. Dr. Robert C. Derbyshire, head of the agency for more than thirty years, graciously offered his assistance in helping us understand the Board's files and how we might make good use of them; after Dr. Derbyshire retired, Michelle McGinnis was indispensably helpful. Animated by a firm sense of the historical significance of the Board's files, she faithfully protected them through the miscellaneous personnel changes, organizational realignments, and what-not of the last several years, and went far beyond the call of mere duty in helping us with our work.

Others around the state and region who have contributed in one way or another to this book include (in no special order) Charlie Cullin and Jane Knowles of Santa Fe's St. Vincent's Hospital; Stan Hordes, Don Lavash, and Richard Salazar of the State Records Center and Archives; Richard Rudisill and Art Olivas of the Museum of New Mexico; Tom Bodnar of the Greater Albuquerque Medical Association; Carolyn Tinker of the University of New Mexico School of Medicine; Ann Mossman, Lou Shields, and Liz Hendryson, who worked on our Medical History Committee; Professor Dorothy Beimer of New Mexico Highlands University; Pam Salmon of Southwestern Community Health Services; Merle Tucker of the Lovelace Medical Center, Inc.; Dottie Stevenson of the Menaul Historical Library; Lou Hibe of the University of Arizona Library, Special Collections; Mark Rosenthal of the University of New Mexico School of Medicine; and Judith DeMark and Judie Johnson of the University of New Mexico History Department. Special thanks also to friends and colleagues Richard Ellis, John Johnson, Alan Minge, and Noel Pugach, all of whom patiently listened to more about New Mexico medicine than they ever wished to hear. And I am particularly grateful for the encouragement and support of Dr. Peter Olch of Bethesda, Maryland, physician and historian extraordinaire, who graciously shared with me his expertise in oral history as well as his enthusiasm for the history of medicine in the West.

Finally, a special acknowledgement of the help provided by the nearly one hundred doctors of medicine whom I met and interviewed during the research for this book. I could not have asked for a more congenial or cooperative group with which to work. I emerged from the process with the greatest of respect for them and hope they will find this work a worthy celebration of their contribution to New Mexico society and the well-being of its people.

CHAPTER 1

"Regular" Medicine Comes to Las Vegas

IN 1882, LAS VEGAS, NEW MEXICO TERRITORY, WAS IN MANY ways the archetypal Wild West boomtown. Its busy, rutted streets still reflected the legendary rough and ready frontier West, but there were also the unmistakable signs of change arriving with the advance of civilization. The old coexisted uneasily with the new.

The derrick in Old Town plaza was an example of the town's split personality. In the center of that still crude and graceless square, where once the wagons of the Santa Fe Trail commerce had clustered, there stood a forty-foot-tall windmill derrick. It had been erected six years earlier by the plaza's merchants as a kind of community action project to power a well that would provide a good, reliable water supply to the residents and merchants of the vicinity. The ambitious citizenry of Old Town was looking to the future. As a matter of sad fact, the well had quickly gone dry, but the windmill derrick, an eyesore of considerable proportions, had remained to serve other social purposes. In February 1880, for example, it had been used by vigilantes, comprised of many of the town's leading citizens, as a gallows to hang three outlaws, with the mob peppering their writhing bodies with bullets to expedite the job. Later that year the derrick was again pressed into service, this time as a grisly display case for the bodies of four other miscreants who had been killed by pursuing vigilantes at a village near Las Vegas. The corpses were dumped on the derrick's platform as a warning to other undesirables, and it was difficult to ignore. Those who were slow to take heed or still unconvinced were given a final warning in a notice posted on the derrick and elsewhere around town on 24 March 1882:

> Notice to thieves, thugs, fakirs, and bunko-steerers among whom are J. J. Martin, alias "off Wheeler," Saw Dust Charlie, William Hedges, Billy the Kid, Billy Mullin, Little Jack the Cutter, Pockmarked Kid and about twenty others; if found within the limits of this city after ten o'clock P.M. this night you will be invited to attend a grand necktie party, the expense of which will be borne by 100 substantial citizens.[1]

One mile east of the Old Town plaza was the railroad depot and the bustling New Town that had sprung up around it. The Atchison, Topeka and Santa Fe railroad had reached Las Vegas in 1879—the first train had chugged into town on the Fourth of July with appropriate fanfare—and the already rough frontier town was besieged by new waves of "tough customers." The rowdy railroad construction crews and their assorted camp followers had been followed by other types notoriously on the make, and the action in the swollen town was little short of dazzling. More than two dozen saloons or dance halls existed for the comfort of the weary traveler in search of relaxation or the cowboy or sheepherder too long on the range. Painted ladies—Sadie, Big Hattie, Lazy Liz, Nervous Jessie, Careless Ida—were available in abundance to soothe the jangled nerves or to pep up the jaded existences of their customers, whichever the case might be. The sign over the bar at Close and Patterson's dance hall near the railroad track boasted, "Everybody entertained in the best possible manner"; and "the girls" did their best to live up to such promise.

Some among the good citizens of Las Vegas—and there were many—were disturbed by the corruption, loose living, and degradation of their town, and fearful that their community was taking on the dimensions of a Sodom or Gomorrah of the Southwest. They decried as disgraceful the "low, mud dance house[s] thick with tobacco smoke, rum breath, fumes of perspiration, and adobe dust,"[2] where unattached (and sometimes unwary) men paid fifty cents for two drinks and a dance with a "Mexican girl." To make matters worse, nearly all the saloon–dance halls had gambling rooms, too, most with two to four tables, all crowded. Indeed, the

[1]Lynn Perrigo, *Gateway to Glorieta: A History of Las Vegas, New Mexico* (Boulder, Colo.: Pruett Publishing Co., 1982), pp. 75–76. Perrigo is the source for most of the background material on Las Vegas in this chapter.

[2]Ibid., p. 69.

gambling fervor in the town was so powerful that even the citadels of respectability could not remain utterly unaffected. Miguel Otero, Jr., remembered the Exchange Hotel on the Old Town plaza (proudly? regretfully?) as the "poker capital of New Mexico."

But though there was much in the spirit of Las Vegas in 1882 which smacked of the raw frontier, there was also much that presaged the future. The coming of the railroad had ushered in a boom period for the town. For more than half a century Las Vegas had been an important trading center on the Santa Fe Trail, but the first few years after the arrival of the railroad witnessed a period of unprecedented growth. Its population mushroomed so rapidly that within a very few years the town, which counted 5,238 residents in 1886, was at least the second largest in New Mexico. Population figures for that period are uncertain at best, but Santa Fe with perhaps 5,500 to 6,000 people was probably larger. Albuquerque, with around 5,000 to 5,200, and Socorro, at 4,200, rounded out the roster of "big" towns in the territory. In Las Vegas new buildings were flying up, both in New Town around the railroad track and on the plaza in Old Town. Plenty of money was evident, not only in the gambling rooms, but also in the commercial segment of the town's economy. Las Vegas was a powerful commercial hub serving communities as far away as Carlsbad. In 1882 the town boasted numerous well-stocked mercantile stores, a brewery, a brick kiln, an iron foundry, a slaughterhouse, a flour mill, and even a factory for the manufacture of carriages and wagons. A few years later the abundant prosperity of the town was reflected in the total resources (1.3 million dollars) of its two banks and the ready deposits (600,000 dollars) on hand in them. For comparative purposes, the two banks in Albuquerque at the same time had only 700,000 dollars and 300,000 dollars respectively.

The disappointing well of Old Town plaza had quickly been succeeded by a modern water company; a volunteer hook and ladder company was available for firefighting duties; and an electric company was literally just around the corner. On a regularly scheduled basis, horsedrawn streetcars moved cumbersomely over the mile of track linking the railroad depot to the plaza, and other signs of progressive change were evident everywhere. Perhaps the most startling sign of the town's modernity, however, was its impressive, new telephone system. A telephone company had been founded in Las Vegas in 1879—only three years after physician Alexander Graham Bell had taken out the basic telephone patent—and by 1882 lines were strung all over town, tying together a total of 173 phones. A long-distance line ran the five miles out to the luxurious resort hotel established a few years earlier at the hot springs northwest of town. Company shareholders, however, were supposedly worried about the slow expansion of business among the town's Spanish-Americans, who were said to doubt "that that American machine could speak Spanish."[3] The derrick-gallows on Old Town plaza represented the Las Vegas of 1882, but so, too, did the telephone poles.

The evening of 31 December 1881 was a fairly typical New Year's Eve in old Las Vegas. Near the Old Town plaza, "a dance hall senorita named Cyentia" became involved in a nasty disagreement with one of her customers and to underscore her point stabbed him with a stiletto. (No charges were filed.) Over in New Town, according to the *Las Vegas Daily Optic,*

> a Kansas City siren whose short name is Mineola feasted on morphine at an east side dance hall and assayed to climb the golden stairs. A physician assayed her stomach and the powers that be may pull her through all right.[4]

The normal Saturday night hubbub was accompanied that evening by the boom of cannon fire as happy celebrants ushered in 1882, and the town was periodically brightened by the flash of what the newspaper called "a very creditable display of fireworks." The streets of both Old and New towns were filled with revelers, as the holiday spirit temporarily washed aside all serious business—or nearly all. As the newspaper succinctly noted, "The average young man was carried home on the traditional shingle."[5]

There was serious business conducted that evening, howeve[illegible] While the merrymakers caroused on Old Town plaza, a handful of fro[illegible]c-tors, perhaps six or seven, sat down in the offices of Don An[illegible]old on the plaza to try to form a medical society. Why they chose that night, of all nights, for their serious discussions, we do not know. Nor are we sure how many doctors participated in the meeting, nor exactly who was present, for the minutes of that evening's proceedings are mute on these points. Why had they chosen the offices of don Andrés, there on the noisy plaza, as the site for their assembly? The don was a highly respected merchant of the town, one of its leading citizens, and perhaps it was just

[3]Ibid., p. 31.
[4]*Las Vegas Daily Optic,* 3 January 1882.
[5]Ibid.

a matter of space and comfort and the don's graciousness; but a passing newspaper reference to the high quality of "old man Dold's Rhine wine"[6] may suggest other explanations. The noise outside may have complicated their exchange of views; we do not know. In the middle of negotiations, perhaps it was one of these doctors who was called away to assay the stomach of siren Mineola.

Las Vegas in 1882 had by far the largest contingent of physicians in the territory. In all of New Mexico there were fewer than one hundred physicians, and Las Vegas alone counted fifteen, perhaps as many as twenty, doctors among its citizenry. Not until the first years of the twentieth century would Albuquerque draw even and then pass Las Vegas in its supply of physicians. Given the boom in the town's economy and its location astride the railroad, new physicians arrived on an almost daily basis. Most were heading farther west, but many chose to spend a few days, weeks, or even months in the bustling town. Why push on before sampling, at least, the prospects of practice in Las Vegas? There was no form whatsoever of licensing regulation in the territory; so setting up practice meant simply announcing the fact, renting an office (or just working from a hotel room), and hoping for the best.

Many names with a "Dr." before them appeared once or twice in the local paper and then were seen no more, for it seems that the oversupply of physicians made Las Vegas a tough place for newcomers despite its boomtown nature. Among these peripatetic physicians on the make, there were approximately fifteen or so who could be said to have established roots in Las Vegas by 1882. Senior among them was Dr. John H. Shout, a forty-eight-year-old veteran of medical practice in the territory. A native New Yorker, Dr. Shout had graduated in 1854,[7] at age twenty, from tiny Castleton Medical College in Vermont. He practiced for a time in Iowa, and then, suffering from gold fever, moved on to Colorado. He was among the great majority who did not get rich quickly, moving south to Taos in 1859 or 1860, where two years later he was appointed regimental surgeon in Kit Carson's regiment, the First New Mexico Volunteers, stationed at Fort Union. Leaving the army at the end of the Civil War, Dr. Shout set up private practice in 1865 in Las Vegas and was the town's first per-

[6]Ibid.

[7]Medical schools of the nineteenth century did not often require extensive premedical preparation—often not even a high school education—and the curricula at most of them could be handled in two years or less. Thus, a twenty-year-old M.D. was not as rare as we might think. See below, pp. 55–59.

manent physician.[8] He was a "regular" physician—meaning that he practiced mainline, scientific medicine and did not subscribe to any of the specialized philosophies or therapeutics so prominent in the nineteenth century, such as homeopathy or Thomsonian medicine or eclecticism[9]—and he quickly established himself as the most prominent and respected physician of the entire territory. In 1882 Dr. Shout enjoyed the town's largest practice by far and was generally regarded as the "dean" of the Las Vegas medical community. To no one's surprise, he was selected to chair that New Year's Eve meeting held to discuss the formation of a medical society, and a month later he was chosen as the first president of the Las Vegas Medical Society.

The only other doctor in town with a reputation and practice approaching that of Dr. Shout was Dr. Joseph M. Cunningham, who had originally come to Las Vegas in 1873 and served continuously there for forty-nine years, both as a physician and a civic leader. For many years he was president of one of the local banks, served on the school board, and was a delegate to the New Mexico constitutional convention in 1910. However, despite his success as a practicing physician and his obvious respectability, Dr. Cunningham was *not* among the stalwarts of the Las Vegas medical community who banded together that New Year's Eve to form a medical society. It is fairly certain that his colleagues consciously excluded him, for Dr. Cunningham, an 1870 graduate of Chicago's Hahnemann Medical College and Hospital, practiced homeopathy, a prominent nineteenth-century medical sect or cult whose use of drugs was significantly different from mainline or "regular" doctors. One of the main reasons for the foundation of the medical society in Las Vegas was to distinguish between legitimate, respectable physicians and the potpourri of charlatans, quacks, and pretenders who were commonplace in the frontier West. Since it was the regulars who were defining "legitimate, respectable physicians" in banding together to form the Las Vegas Medical Society, Cunningham as a homeopath was thrust into the wilderness along with the other poseurs. However, he was so much a fixture of the medical scene and so clearly different from the run-of-the-mill mounte-

[8]*Las Vegas Daily Optic,* 18 January 1884, contains Shout's obituary.

[9]For good summaries of the divisions within American medicine in the nineteenth century, see William G. Rothstein, *American Physicians in the Nineteenth Century: From Sects to Science* (Baltimore and London: Johns Hopkins University Press, 1972), pp. 125–74, 217–46; and John Duffy, *The Healers: A History of American Medicine* (Urbana, Ill.: University of Illinois Press, 1979), pp. 109–28.

banks that his colleagues at the 28 January 1882 charter meeting of the Las Vegas Medical Society passed a special resolution inviting him "to attend and to be entitled to a seat during the proceedings of the society."[10] Given his obvious talents and solidity, Dr. Cunningham was welcome to attend the meetings of the new organization, but as a homeopath he was not acceptable as a full member.[11]

If Drs. Shout and Cunningham were the senior members of the Las Vegas medical corps in 1882 with seventeen and seven years' residence, respectively, all the other doctors in town were relative newcomers with no more than two or three years in the community. Most had come with the railroad boom, hoping to capitalize on the population explosion and the relative shortage of entrenched practitioners. They were a mixed lot as physicians. Some of them were neophytes fresh from medical school, eager to start off their careers with a flourish. Others were seasoned professionals at midcareer or approaching it, who for one reason or another had journeyed to the West after a decade or more of practice in the East or, more commonly, the Midwest. There were also physicians already in their fifties and even sixties who, in the latter stages of their careers, had pulled up stakes and headed to the West, most often for reasons of health or to seek semiretirement in balmier climes.

The fourteen doctors who signed the constitution and bylaws of the Las Vegas Medical Society at a special meeting on the evening of 28 January 1882, and thus became the charter members of the association, represented this variety of physicians in frontier Las Vegas. Four of them were newly graduated physicians with degrees only a year or two old. Three others were practitioners close to midcareer who had already served at least a decade in practice elsewhere before coming to Las Vegas, and the other seven charter signers were veteran doctors, each with more than twenty years of experience. A quick glance at each of these founding fathers may serve both to honor them and to provide a clearer perspective on New Mexico physicians of a century ago.

The presence of the four neophyte physicians—Drs. Russell Bayly, Er-

[10]Las Vegas Medical Society, Minutes, 28 January 1882.

[11]Dr. Cunningham did not accept the second-class citizenship offered him and played no role in the local or territorial medical societies during their first thirty years of existence. There is some evidence that he had become a member of both county and territorial medical societies by 1910—after 1902 he no longer identified himself as a homeopath—and at the time of his death, in 1922, he was definitely a full member of the New Mexico Medical Society.

nest L. Epperson, W. H. Ashley, and William R. Tipton—on the New Mexico frontier is relatively easy to understand. They were all young men in their twenties, just starting their medical careers. Where better to establish themselves than on the wide-open frontier? Russell Bayly, for example, an 1877 graduate of St. Louis Medical College (later, Washington University School of Medicine), had come to town in 1879 with the railroad. Not much is known about him, but he may simply have come to the West for the sake of adventure before settling down to a more traditional, staid practice in the East. He spent almost ten years in Las Vegas and was a loyal, active member of the infant medical society from its foundation until his departure from the territory in 1889. He was not only active in the medical community, but was also mentioned frequently in the *Las Vegas Daily Optic* as one of the town's bon vivants, and in 1886 he was hauled before the county commissioners for prescribing whiskey for an inmate (a friend?) of the county jail.[12] Bayly left New Mexico in 1889 for New York City, practicing for a time at the city mental institution on Blackwell's Island, then setting up private practice in general medicine on New York's East Side. He was the last surviving member of the charter group of the Las Vegas Medical Society at the time of his death in 1934 in New York at age eighty-two.

Young Dr. Ernest L. Epperson, who proudly announced himself in the local paper as a specialist "in diseases of the eye, ear, and rectum," was only twenty-one years old when he came to Las Vegas sometime in 1881. His tenure in town was rather brief, for it appears that in his haste to get started on his medical career he had neglected one very important thing, namely, to finish his medical education. In signing the Las Vegas Medical Society's charter he passed himself off as a bona fide, regular physician. However, Epperson was formally dropped from the society's membership roll in July of that same year when he failed to produce evidence of his graduation from a proper medical school,[13] and he apparently left town shortly thereafter. From his abortive practice in Las Vegas he went to the College of Physicians and Surgeons in Keokuk, Iowa, earning his degree there in 1883. Despite this shaky start in the profession, Dr. Epperson made a solid career for himself, serving more than fifty years as a general practitioner in St. Louis.

[12]For this reference I am grateful to Professor Dorothy Beimer, New Mexico Highlands University, Las Vegas.

[13]Las Vegas Medical Society, Minutes, 1 July 1882.

Dr. W. H. Ashley, an 1880 graduate of Kansas City Medical College, likewise spent relatively little time in Las Vegas. He came to town in either 1880 or 1881 to serve as principal of the Las Vegas Academy, a new school established by the Congregational church. Direction of the new school was his basic responsibility, but Dr. Ashley found time to build a large practice in general medicine as well. He was held in high regard by his medical colleagues and was one of the more frequent essayists and discussants at the medical society's meetings. He was obviously a man of many talents, for alongside his medical and pedagogical labors he added service as a part-time clergyman. In the community he was respectfully called the Reverend Dr. Ashley, and when he and his family left Las Vegas in 1889 for Connecticut, the town mourned the loss of one of its more versatile citizens and the medical society another of its charter members.

Though young Drs. Bayly, Epperson, and Ashley each played interesting roles within the medical community of Las Vegas, none of them approached Dr. William Reuben Tipton in long-term impact on the development of medicine in Las Vegas and in New Mexico generally. Over his lifetime of service, Dr. Tipton earned recognition as one of the three or four most influential New Mexico physicians of the past century. He was among a tiny minority—no more than three or four—of New Mexico doctors of the pioneer period who were actually native to the territory. Though born in Missouri in 1854, Tipton came to Watrous, New Mexico, with his family in 1860 as a six year old. Reared in the territory, he grew up familiar with its various cultures and the character of its society. He was, for instance, perfectly fluent in Spanish and frequently used his command of that language and his familiarity with the Spanish culture of the region as a lobbyist for the medical society at the territorial legislature in Santa Fe and as a simultaneous translator for Spanish-speaking guests at medical society functions. Tipton received his preliminary education at St. Michael's College in Santa Fe, and then went east for undergraduate and medical education at the University of Missouri, earning his M.D. there in 1876. Still young and apparently not completely satisfied with the solidity of his medical preparation, he enrolled in Philadelphia's Jefferson Medical College and took a second degree from that more prestigious institution in 1877. In the following year he returned to New Mexico and practiced in Las Vegas and its environs for forty-six years until his death in 1924.

During his half-century of service in New Mexico, Dr. Tipton contributed directly as a practicing physician to the well-being of thousands of its people. Just as importantly, he was a tower of strength and a champion of high standards within the medical profession, working tirelessly to improve the caliber of the physicians in the territory and to enhance the image and esteem enjoyed by them. He was one of the guiding spirits in the foundation of the Las Vegas Medical Society in 1882 and in its transition (see below, pages 26–29) to the New Mexico Medical Society in 1885. In the early, unsettled years of the Territorial Medical Society, Dr. Tipton served three separate terms (in 1885–86, 1888–89, and 1893–94) as the organization's president, more than any other physician in its history.[14] He was for years a member of the Territorial and then State Board of Medical Examiners, president of the local county medical society, and a recognized spokesman for organized medicine throughout the territory and state. His service to the profession was capped in 1911 by his election as a vice-president of the American Medical Association, the first of only two New Mexico physicians ever so honored.[15]

As a practicing physician, Dr. Tipton was one of New Mexico's most active and respected surgeons during the first quarter-century or so of his practice, specializing in the trauma surgery so common in a railroad town of the frontier West. The minutes of the meetings of the New Mexico Medical Society are liberally dotted with his case reports on repair of gunshot wounds, railroad injuries, congenital deformities, and much else. Around the turn of the century, however, his interest began to shift to neuropsychiatry, a new area of specialization undoubtedly stimulated by his years of service as medical superintendent of the state hospital for the mentally ill in Las Vegas.[16] Somehow, he also found time for service

[14]Five other doctors served two terms each as president of the society: Drs. W. H. Page (in 1883–84 and 1884–85), M. W. Robbins (in 1886–87 and 1887–88), and Francis H. Atkins (in 1890–91 and 1891–92), all of Las Vegas; Dr. George W. Harrison (in 1894–95 and 1901–2) of Albuquerque; and Valmora's Dr. Carl Gellenthien (in 1944–45 and 1945–46).

[15]Dr. Carl Gellenthien of Valmora was the other, chosen as AMA vice-president in 1953–54.

[16]The only whisper of scandal ever to sully the name of this eminent New Mexico doctor came through his association with the state hospital. In 1903, a local newspaper reported that the bones of a patient had been found scattered about the grounds of the institution and alleged general mistreatment of the patients by the hospital's staff. An investigating committee was appointed by the governor, and a nasty, public furor ensued. Dr. Tipton did admit that when a patient without relatives had died, he had first performed an autopsy, then had scraped the flesh from the bones in order to have a skeleton for study. Those bones had apparently been scattered about the grounds by a staff member eager to get Dr. Tipton removed. The committee absolved the doctor, but did scold him for careless handling of bones. See Perrigo, *Gateway to Glorieta*, pp. 39–40.

to his community as a private citizen. He was a longtime regent of New Mexico Normal University (later, Highlands University) and a devoted communicant and worker in the local Catholic church. When he died in 1924, the state's medical profession lost one of its most distinguished members. At the time of his election to the vice-presidency of the AMA, his colleagues had written of him, "No movement for the betterment of his profession and no movement for the betterment of the people of New Mexico ever failed to have his active support."[17]

Alongside these younger members of the charter group of the Las Vegas Medical Society stood three physicians of middle age, doctors who had established second practices in Las Vegas after a decade or so of service elsewhere. For instance, Dr. H. B. Peebles, had graduated in 1872 from Miami Medical College in Cincinnati, Ohio, and practiced in the Midwest for almost ten years before coming to Las Vegas in the early 1880s. He was one of the founders of the new medical society in 1882, but left the territory for California only two years later, after New Mexico's salubrious climate had failed to ease his wife's illness. Dr. E. C. Henriques practiced somewhat longer in the town. A graduate of the University of Michigan's medical department in 1871, Henriques came to Las Vegas in 1880 after a decade of practice in Connecticut. Little is known of him, but he earned sufficient respect among his peers to be elected president of the New Mexico Medical Society in 1889–90. He died in Las Vegas in 1894, after a decade-and-a-half sojourn in the community.

The third of the middle group, the patriotically named Dr. Madison Monroe Milligan, was the only one among them to leave a solid record in the annals of New Mexico's medical history. Another midwesterner from southern Illinois, Milligan got his M.D. at St. Louis Medical College in 1872, practiced seven years in rural Illinois, and then resettled in Las Vegas in 1879. From that year until his death in 1925, he served the health needs of thousands in Las Vegas and the area surrounding it. For most of his forty-six years in the area, Milligan practiced in Las Vegas itself, delivering babies, tending childhood illnesses, sewing up wounds, and doing the various things associated with the old-time country doctor. Nevertheless, his practice, like those of many of his peers in the late 1890s and 1900s, began to take on special focus with the arrival of large numbers of tuberculars in the territory at the turn of the century. (See Chapter 3.) By the first years of the new century, Dr. Milligan had become something

[17]*New Mexico Medical Journal* 6 (1911):222.

of a tuberculosis specialist and ran a sanatorium north of town. He ended his years of practice as a country doctor once again, with a nine-year stay in Stanley, New Mexico, and spent the last two years of his life in semi-retirement in Santa Fe. As a devoted country practitioner, M. M. Milligan earned the respect and appreciation of all those whose lives he touched.

Most influential in the early months and years of the infant medical society in Las Vegas were the seven veteran physicians among the charter group. They were veterans indeed, averaging more than twenty-five years each in medical practice as of the time of the society's foundation. With the exception of Dr. Shout, they were all newcomers to Las Vegas, with most of them having come to the territory for their health or to seek comfortable surroundings for semiretirement. One of them, Dr. Francis Reiger (M.D., Jefferson Medical College, Philadelphia, 1854), was so ill with lung problems as to be invalided—he died in Las Vegas in November 1883—and several others were only marginally active as practitioners. Nevertheless, they were critically important as counselors and consultants to the younger men, advising them on problems in their practices; they were also instrumental in getting the new medical society established and under way.

Dr. John Shout, the first president of the society, has already been profiled. His successor as president, a man serving two terms from 1883 to 1885, was considerably more influential than Shout in setting the new organization on firm rails. He was Dr. W. Hussey Page, clearly the most distinguished among these senior physicians. An 1853 medical graduate of Harvard University, Dr. Page had come to Las Vegas in 1881 as physician in residence for the hotel-spa operation at the hot springs north of town. After twenty-eight years of practice in his native New England, Page had been forced by increasingly severe lung problems to seek a better climate, and had selected the special opportunity afforded him at the Las Vegas Hot Springs. A cultivated gentleman of variegated interests and talents, W. Hussey Page was highly respected by his colleagues in the Las Vegas medical community. Informed by extensive experience with medical organizations in his native East, Dr. Page was the mainstay of the Las Vegas Medical Society in its formative years. When he left Las Vegas in the early spring of 1886 for the still sunnier climes of southern California—he died in Los Angeles in December 1888—he left his medical library to the tiny organization in Las Vegas that he had done so much to shape.[18]

[18]The size of this library and its ultimate fate are unknown.

He also left a powerful impress on his friends and colleagues. At an elegant dinner held in his honor on the occasion of his departure from town, an elaborate testimonial was passed by the society:

> Be it resolved that we hereby express our regret at losing the amiable society and judicious counsels of this our senior member; that we recall with marked gratitude his distinguished services in building up this medical society in its days of early weakness; that we trust he will meet with the approbation in his new home that his excellent attainments in our profession merit; and that he will take with him the warm esteem and best wishes of the New Mexico Medical Society.[19]

Three others among the older doctors involved in founding the medical society played much less glorious roles in the early phases of the organization's history. For example, Dr. Charles C. Gordon, an army surgeon who had settled in Las Vegas after a tour of duty at Fort Union, was elected the first treasurer of the new organization, but resigned after only a few months, explaining that "he did not like clubs."[20] Gordon, an 1860 graduate of Long Island College Hospital in Brooklyn, New York, practiced in Las Vegas for some forty-four years until his death at age eighty-seven in 1924. For much of that period he served as City Physician, but remained true to his dislike of clubs and never again played a part in medical organizations. The separation of two other charter members from the medical society, only a few months after its formation, was considerably more unpleasant. Like the young and not-quite-doctor Epperson mentioned earlier, veteran doctors E. H. Skipwith and N. J. Pettijohn were formally drummed out of the organization, only six months after its start, when they failed to produce proper credentials, namely, evidence that they had indeed graduated from medical school.[21]

This first great cause célèbre of the medical society was a stern test of the young association's principles—only "legitimate," regular professionals could belong—and involved considerable personal strain and embarrassment. In the case of Dr. Skipwith, in particular, the situation was terribly awkward and unpleasant, for he was one of the busiest and most popular doctors in town. He not only commanded the respect of his patients, but also enjoyed enough esteem among his professional col-

[19]New Mexico Medical Society, Minutes, 13 March 1886.

[20]Dorothy Beimer, "Pioneer Physicians in Las Vegas, New Mexico, 1880–1911," mimeographed, n.d.

[21]Las Vegas Medical Society, Minutes, 1 July 1882.

leagues to have won election as the new medical society's first vice-president. Skipwith claimed to be an 1861 graduate of the University of Louisiana Medical School, but was unable to produce any kind of evidence to support that claim. He accepted the professional embarrassment of dismissal from the medical society with apparent good grace, and went on about his business. His busy practice, incidentally, does not seem to have been affected at all by these unfortunate circumstances, and Skipwith continued medical practice in Las Vegas for another six years. He then moved to Roswell, practicing there with great success for another decade or so before dropping from sight. Pettijohn insisted that he had graduated in 1862 from George Town [*sic*] Medical College in Washington, D.C., but like Skipwith he was unable to produce any proof. After his expulsion from the medical association, he remained in Las Vegas at least another year, and, for unknown reasons, he became a special target of the regular physicians leagued in the medical society. Organization minutes from 1883 note that Pettijohn was under investigation so "that the Society might know whether he should be recognized as a regular physician," and such scrutiny apparently resulted in a negative verdict. Society minutes make a final reference to him in May of that year: "Dr. Pettijohn's case was left in the hands of the legal fraternity."[22]

Only one of the senior physicians present at the birth of the Las Vegas Medical Society was a member for more than a few years. Drs. Shout and Reiger died; Page left town; Gordon resigned; and Skipwith and Pettijohn were disenrolled. This left Dr. Myron W. Robbins as the surviving graybeard of the group. Unfortunately, little is known of Dr. Robbins beyond a few, scattered facts. He was a graduate of Chicago's Rush Medical College in 1854 and had practiced some twenty-six years in the Midwest before arriving in Las Vegas in 1880. He was quite active in the formation and early years of the medical society, serving as president for two terms in 1886–87 and 1887–88. He was still in practice in Las Vegas as late as 1897, when he must have been around seventy years old; but his name is missing from all medical directories thereafter.

Though the fourteen charter members of the Las Vegas Medical Society were dissimilar in age, experience, background, and much else, they were united in their conviction of the importance of a formal professional organization in linking the "respectable" physicians of the area. What

[22]Las Vegas Medical Society, Minutes, 7 April and 5 May 1883.

were their objectives in founding their tiny society in January 1882? What purposes did they expect it to serve?

To some degree the Las Vegas pioneers were simply transposing to their frontier setting an institution with which they had grown familiar in the eastern and midwestern cities from which they had come. One of the more prominent developments within nineteenth-century American medicine was the effort to professionalize the practice of medicine, to establish clear lines of demarcation between specially educated practitioners of medicine and the potpourri of irregulars who clogged the medical scene. This term included a broad variety of practitioners—root and herb doctors; "grannies" skilled in home remedies and perhaps also midwifery; "empirics," self-designated as doctors who learned mostly by doing; and a frightening mélange of out-and-out quacks, mountebanks, and miscellaneous poseurs. The foundation of medical societies was part of a rising self-consciousness and alarm within the ranks of regular practitioners and a step toward self-regulation of the medical marketplace. Considering the primitive nature of nineteenth-century therapeutics, it was not at all certain that "real" doctors, that is, those formally trained for the profession, could simply drive their competitors from the field by the superior results they produced; therefore, other means to achieve that victory were sought. By midcentury all the states of the East, Midwest, and South had their state medical societies, usually born from the merger of local ones, and a national organization, the American Medical Association, had been created in 1847 to speak for the regulars of the entire country in their battle for recognition vis-à-vis their competitors.[23]

As the trans-Mississippi West was settled and the war among the practitioners added frontier theaters, medical associations began to appear there, too. In the spring of 1871 the Denver Medical Society was created, and in July of that year it invited the other doctors of Colorado Territory to form the Colorado Medical Society. In 1879 the Montana Medical Association was founded; in 1892, the Arizona Medical Society; in 1895, the Utah Medical Society; and so on. There was nothing really exceptional in the organizational impulse of the Las Vegas group. Nor were they the first doctors in New Mexico to experiment with formal organization. In 1875 some New Mexico doctors of the extreme north of the territory had

[23]On the development of professional societies and the crowded health-care delivery spectrum of the nineteenth century, see Rothstein and Duffy as well as Paul Starr, *The Social Transformation of American Medicine* (New York: Basic Books, 1982).

been involved, though apparently peripherally, in the short-lived Rocky Mountain Medical Association, an enterprise which made little headway.[24]

The founders intended their medical association to serve a number of different objectives. First of all, they undoubtedly hoped that it would provide them with a special legitimacy and even with a competitive edge in the turbulent medical marketplace of the area. With physicians of all descriptions moving through town on the road westward, and with some stopping over for more or less lengthy periods of time, society membership might help prospective patients differentiate medical sheep and goats. Consequently, in the constitution of the fledgling society the founders were careful to insert provisions restricting membership to physicians holding degrees from "some respectable medical school" or to those doctors already members of some other medical society formally recognized by the American Medical Association. Such credentials were the minimum necessary to qualify a candidate for consideration, but prospective members had to pass further scrutiny by members already installed through ballot.[25] Additionally, the constitution was explicit about practitioners not welcome within the new organization:

> No persons holding patents for secret remedies or who shall by publication in newspapers or otherwise announce his superior qualifications in any particular disease or diseases, or publish cases of operation in daily print, or invite laymen to be present at operations, or boast of cases or remedies, or other similar acts shall be eligible to membership in this Society.[26]

Inclusion within the new organization would thus constitute a badge of legitimacy and respectability for its members, while exclusion, it was hoped, might have the opposite effect. The sketches already presented of the fourteen charter members testify to the rigidity with which eligibility standards were enforced. Even solid, respectable members of the medical community, such as Drs. Cunningham and Skipwith, found themselves on the outside when they could not produce the legitimizing credentials.

The new medical organization was intended to confer a kind of order

[24]Marcus J. Smith (M.D.), "The Rocky Mountain Medical Association and New Mexico Territorial Society," *Newsletter* (New Mexico Medical Society) 24, no. 1 (1981):2.

[25]Las Vegas Medical Society, Minutes, Constitution.

[26]Ibid. Standards of behavior were regularized by adoption of the AMA's 1847 Code of Ethics as Article XI of the constitution's bylaws.

on the Las Vegas medical community as well. Although we do not have hard evidence, we can speculate that the rapid growth of the physician supply in Las Vegas had produced uncertain economic conditions for the doctors in the town, perhaps even including fee competition among them. We know for sure that at that New Year's Eve organizational meeting in don Andrés's office, that subject was very much on the founders' minds. To the committees appointed that night to draft a constitution and bylaws and to nominate a slate of officers, a third task was added—to draft a fee-bill. This was, of course, a consistent element in the foundation of early medical societies across the nation. When the Colorado Medical Society, for example, had been founded eleven years earlier, its very first action was passage of a fee-bill.[27] It is clear that, given the unsettled nature of New Mexico medicine, the regulars of Las Vegas were eager to control competition to the degree practicable. The guidelines they eventually approved were hammered out through earnest debate and considerable disagreement—it was necessary to appoint a second committee to "revise and correct" the draft of the first—but agreement within fairly broad parameters was finally attained.[28]

Though the struggle against irregular practitioners and the desire to control competition within their own ranks were powerful determinants in the coalescence of the town's regulars, they were moved by other considerations as well. A few years earlier, their Colorado colleagues had given the following reasons for formation of their society:

> the improvement of the scientific and professional knowledge of its members; mutual recognition and fellowship; the promotion of the character, interests, and honor of the fraternity; and the elevation of standards in medical education.[29]

The Las Vegas group was more terse; it spoke only generally of "the advancement of Medical Science and the improvement of the Medical Profession among its members and in the territory generally," but there

[27]Judith Hannemann, "Birth of the Colorado Medical Society," *Rocky Mountain Medical Journal* (Colorado edition) 68, no. 4 (1971):29.

[28]Las Vegas Medical Society, Minutes, 14 January and 4 March 1882; *Las Vegas Daily Optic*, 19 January 1882. The charges detailed in the fee-bill are relatively high for the times and suggest the "boom" nature of the Las Vegas economy of the time. The fee-bill also reflects the range and texture of medical practice of the era as well.

[29]Hannemann, "Birth of the Colorado Medical Society":28.

is ample evidence that they shared the hopes and aspirations spelled out more precisely by their Colorado peers. They clearly intended, for example, that their medical organization should serve as an agency for the dissemination and exchange of professional information among its members. There is no more consistent element within the early records of the society than its focus on what we would call today "continuing education."

It is not surprising that New Mexico's pioneer physicians, far removed from the mainstream of American medical thought and practice, might feel with special keenness the necessity for strong, special efforts to "keep up." If medical journals, scientific meetings, and the like were becoming increasingly important to their brethren in the more settled, medically sophisticated parts of the country, how much more so to these physicians of a town located at the railroad's end? The commitment of the Las Vegas pioneers to using their medical association as a vehicle for continuing education was evident even at the group's charter meeting. The first order of business at that initial meeting, just after election of officers, was the appointment of a committee to study the idea of establishing a journal, which was a very progressive idea for its time.[30] In the short term that proposal came to nothing, for the committee reported that such an enterprise was not feasible, given the tiny base of the society, the limited number of physicians in the territory to support such a venture, the lack of financial resources, and so forth. However, the idea did not disappear entirely, and a *New Mexico Medical Journal* was established twenty years later. (See below, pp. 67–71.) For the short term the group agreed to make continuing education a basic part of its regular, monthly meetings, with at least one medical essay or clinical report presented by a member at each gathering. The expectation was that the special expertise or clinical experiences of individual members might be shared to the advantage of all through these presentations. At the charter meeting, for example, Dr. Epperson was asked to prepare a paper for the next meeting on variola (smallpox), "a subject that is now attracting universal attention and being

[30]Las Vegas Medical Society, Minutes, 28 January 1882. As a matter of fact, the Las Vegas planners were about a generation ahead of their time. As of January 1882 the *Journal of the American Medical Association* itself had not yet been founded—it was born in 1883—and the first state medical journal did not appear until 1896, when Pennsylvania blazed a trail followed by twenty-seven other state societies over the subsequent two decades. See James G. Burrow, *Organized Medicine in the Progressive Era: The Move toward Monopoly* (Baltimore and London: Johns Hopkins Press, 1977), pp. 168–69.

declared by the national Board of Health as epidemic."[31] It is no exaggeration to say that the monthly essay or, more often, the clinical report was the central agenda item during the society's early years. Almost no monthly meeting was held without at least one paper being presented, and that communication of information undoubtedly contributed significantly to the quality of medical care in the region.

Along with establishing these specific regulative and educational objectives in creating the society, the founders also recognized the general professional and even social values of such an organization. They hoped their society would be perceived as the corporate spokesman of the "better" class of physicians in the territory, a recognition which would strengthen their lobbying power with political agencies such as the territorial legislature or the Las Vegas City Council; they clearly intended to use the organization as a political instrument to protect the best interests of the profession as they saw them. They were political sophisticates, aware of the necessity and the mechanics of safe-guarding and advancing their professional interests. In addition, they hoped that by increasing professional and social interaction among the regulars, they might enhance professional solidarity and cooperation, resolving differences internally without allowing an opportunity for external parties to intervene. Even outsiders like the press respected the profession's efforts to organize itself and acknowledged the difficulty of the task. Two days after the charter meeting, the *Daily Optic* reported,

> The Las Vegas medical society held a most satisfactory and sugar-coated meeting at the office of Dr. Shout on Saturday evening. There were a few rebellious spirits in the association but they were lashed into line and pulled on the traces as steady as the wheel horses. . . . We are glad that the saw-bones are working in unity and hope they will continue in a fraternal pathway.[32]

A glance at the early history of the organization established by the Las

[31]Las Vegas Medical Society, Minutes, 28 January 1882. This is the same young Dr. Epperson whose medical education later came into question and who was eventually thrown out of the society. Did some of the members already have doubts about him? Was the variola assignment a kind of public test? We do not know, but the record does show that Dr. Epperson demurred, explaining vaguely that he could not accept the assignment because he was already busy on other subjects.

[32]*Las Vegas Daily Optic*, 30 January 1882.

Vegas pioneers suggests that their reach exceeded their grasp. Few of the high expectations they entertained were realized, and the successes claimed by the institution were limited and modest. Despite the enthusiasm and strong commitment of a number of the society's principals, its growth in size and influence was slow and disappointing. Within a very few months of its foundation, it had settled into an uninspiring routine and low-profile existence, far removed from the founders' intentions.

The most obvious weakness of the young society was its tiny size and its almost imperceptible growth and outreach. As already noted, the original charter group of fourteen members quickly shrank to eight in the first few months of the society's operation through expulsions, resignations, death, and other factors. These losses were particularly significant since the addition of new members was such a rare occurrence: the society admitted no more than two or three newcomers per year during the first three years of its operation. This was partially a matter of fewer physicians settling in the town after the large influx of the railroad boom, but it was also the result of a kind of lethargy or lack of aggressiveness on the part of the society's members. The small size of their organization concerned them, but there seems to have been little impulse to expand their numbers by relaxing qualifications for membership. The exclusivity of the association was preserved, and new applicants for membership were rigidly evaluated to ensure their suitability.[33] Nor was there any apparent interest in boosting numbers by expanding the geographic scope of the institution, perhaps because of the still primitive communications of the territory. As a consequence, the Las Vegas Medical Society remained a quiet, "clubby," and almost quaint institution throughout its existence. Its size and the scale of its operations were reflected in its budgets: When the group's treasurer presented his report for 1883 expenditures, the sum total of the

[33]One new member not a part of the charter group—he joined in February 1885—deserves special mention. Dr. Francis H. Atkins, an 1865 graduate of Long Island College Hospital in Brooklyn, had come to New Mexico Territory as an army surgeon assigned to Fort Stanton. He served several years at that post before settling in Las Vegas in early 1885. He quickly became one of the most active and influential members of the medical society, a regular essayist or discussant in the educational part of its meetings, a respected consultant on a broad variety of medical subjects, and a regular contributor to national medical journals like the AMA *Journal.* His service in the medical society and his belief in it were recognized by his election to two terms as its president, in 1890–91 and in 1891–92. Dr. Atkins left Las Vegas after the turn of the century for retirement in Los Angeles, where he died soon after 1912.

society's yearly outlay came to ten dollars, the cost of printing up membership certificates for each member.[34]

This is not to suggest that the Las Vegas Medical Society quickly lapsed into somnolence, for there was extensive activity within the small circle of the group's membership. Meeting at one or another of the town's hotels—most often at the Plaza, but on occasion at the St. Nicholas Hotel, the Hot Springs Spa hotel, or the railroad hotel—the organization became an important part of the schedule of those doctors committed to it. There were, in fact, many meetings, no fewer than nineteen in the first year of the association's existence, with most of them occasioned by the miscellaneous and sundry problems associated with the establishment of the institution. However, attendance at all those meetings was limited, stabilizing after a few months at a half-dozen or so loyalists. (Three other meetings had to be postponed for lack of a quorum, even though the constitution prudently designated the low quorum figure of five; that figure was later revised downward to three.)

Considerable charm marked those intimate, early meetings of the society. The complete minutes for the meeting of 6 September 1884, for example, read:

> The Society met according to call at the Hot Springs. Present: Page, Robbins, and Ashley. After a short discussion on contagious diseases, the three members spent the time in exploring the ruins of Pompeii from the charts of Dr. Page.[35]

Minutes of the meeting of 1 December 1883 note that the evening ended with a paper by Dr. Bayly on "Plaster of Paris in Fractures," which was followed by a motion "to adjourn to the residence of Dr. Ashley to finish the discussion over a dish of oysters."[36] Camaraderie of that sort was, of course, desirable and helped to cement good relationships within the society's membership; yet it was not, after all, among the main reasons for the group's formation. Two or three new members were added to the reduced charter group in 1882, none at all in 1883, and three more in 1884; but at the end of three years of operation, the Las Vegas Medical Society could still gather comfortably around one medium-size table. It was an organization of limited horizons and uninspiring prospects.

The failure of the society to develop anything that might vaguely re-

[34] Las Vegas Medical Society, Minutes, 5 January 1884.
[35] Las Vegas Medical Society, Minutes, 6 September 1884.
[36] Las Vegas Medical Society, Minutes, 1 December 1883.

semble momentum was reflected in a number of ways. Politically, for example, the society was unable to make any headway whatsoever in its number one priority, the tightening of the territory's legislation regulating the practice of medicine. As early as May 1883, an entire meeting of the Las Vegas organization was devoted to the discussion of the glaring inadequacies of the basic territorial medical law passed by the 1882 legislature (see pp. 41–44), and numerous suggestions were made for improving that statute. The same subject was the focus of the March 1884 meeting, but the society was unable to generate meaningful political pressure from its complaints. The meeting of 3 May 1884 ended with the angry charge that "under the existing conditions of the laws and courts of New Mexico quacks cannot be convicted."[37] Particularly offensive to the Las Vegas regulars was the significant role that medical quackery continued to play in their own hometown. The foundation of a professional medical society and its members' self-anointment as the only real, legitimate physicians in the town do not seem to have made much impression on the area's medical consumers. At their meetings, the members of the proper little medical society railed against the quacks, telling horror stories about their practices;[38] but the creation of a formal professional organization clearly had been no miracle cure for the problem, at least not for an organization so small and weak as theirs. Dr. Robbins somberly concluded in 1885 that "in regards to medical legislation there has been but little done for the profession and little or nothing of any consequence regulating the practice of medicine in the Territory."[39]

The society was a bit more successful in exercising supervision over the conduct of its own members, but even here its record was spotty. Consistent with the 1847 American Medical Association Code of Ethics, the Las Vegas group banned, in its constitution, any consultation by its members with irregulars. This issue proved a very real one in frontier Las Vegas, where so many suspect doctors flourished, including quite successful and respected ones like Drs. Cunningham and Skipwith. In September of the society's first year, its committee of ethics cited three of the organization's eleven members for violation of this principle, precipitating a severe test of the society's allegiance to professional rectitude. One of the accused, Dr. Robbins, was present at the meeting when the

[37]Las Vegas Medical Society, Minutes, 5 May 1883, 1 March 1884, and 3 May 1884.
[38]See, for example, Las Vegas Medical Society, Minutes, 4 October 1884.
[39]Las Vegas Medical Society, Minutes, 7 February 1885.

committee raised its rebuke and immediately made an explanation and an apology. (That explanation, unfortunately, is not recorded in the minutes of the meeting.) Dr. C. C. Gordon, another of the accused, made an explanation and apology at the next meeting (also unrecorded), but resigned shortly thereafter. His "dislike of clubs" (see page 13) was surely markedly stronger in the case of clubs that censured him and his practice. The third member of the society accused of violating its code of ethics was none other than the organization's president, Dr. John Shout.

One can only speculate about the dynamics of the Shout case, since the surviving information regarding it comes exclusively from the spotty, often cryptic minutes of the medical society. What we do know, however, strongly suggests the limited authority and significance of the medical society. Dr. Shout was not present at the meeting where he and the two other offenders were indicted, and he never bothered to attend again. The inference is that Shout, forced to choose between the infant society which had elected him as its president and his customary modes of practice (and maybe old friends), was more comfortable in giving up the former. When Shout failed to appear at either the October or November meetings to make explanation, the organization voted to notify him in writing—to warn him—that his unprofessional behavior would be discussed at its next meeting. He still refused to appear, and the society, clearly reluctant to confront its president and the town's most respected practitioner, deferred the whole issue to its next meeting. However, the minutes of 1883 contain no reference whatsoever to the Shout case, and the issue was apparently allowed to die as quietly as possible. As noted, Dr. Shout never again attended the society's meetings and died in early 1884.[40] The society's early instability and the problems occasioned by its attempts to regulate and control its membership are fully appreciated when it is realized that by the end of the first year of its operation the first president of the organization had been driven from the fold by charges of unethical behavior; its first treasurer (Dr. Gordon) had withdrawn, almost surely for the same reason; and its first vice-president (Dr. Skipwith) had been formally purged.

Though its weaknesses and failures were self-evident, the record of that pioneer medical society is not entirely negative. There is no question, for example, that the new organization did provide the forum for the exchange

[40]Las Vegas Medical Society, Minutes, 9 September, 7 October, 4 November, and 2 December 1882; and all meetings, 1883.

of information and discussion that its framers had envisioned, at least for those few members who attended. Through all the vagaries and problems of its infancy period, the Las Vegas Medical Society clung tenaciously to its continuing educational mission. A remarkable variety of subjects was discussed at its meetings, with the topics reflecting the range and challenge of frontier medical practice. Some of the papers read and discussed dealt with subjects of a broad or general nature and were often speculative in nature. In this category were essays examining the effects of climate on menstruation and sexual appetite (it was concluded there were essentially none); the general subject of necrosis; the length of pregnancies and the significance of divergences from the norm; disturbances of speech in general, and particularly after exposure to the hot sun; nerve stretching; public sanitation; and the relation of psychology to medicine.[41]

Over time, however, the focus of these scientific papers and discussions shifted emphatically from the more general and abstract subjects to the specific and precise. Case reports of particular disease entities became the norm—variola, diphtheria, scarlet fever, cholera, and appendicitis—with formal presentation followed by lively discussion of proper therapy, epidemiology, and the like. Such exchanges must have helped enormously the physicians involved, for the pooling of their experiences and expertise constituted a kind of crude consultation, a collegial approach to the problems of practice. After case reports on particular diseases, reports on surgical procedures, sometimes accompanied by anatomical specimens, were a commonplace at those early meetings. The repair of bones crushed in railroad accidents; the amputation of extremities injured in ranch mishaps; the lancing of abscesses; emergency tracheotomies in cases of diphtheria—the surgical reports presented at society meetings mirrored the everyday world of frontier medicine of the 1880s and undoubtedly represented for many members of the group all of the continuing education they could get. Some of these reports remind the late twentieth-century reader that Las Vegas, New Mexico, in the early 1880s was still very much the Old West of legend. At the 3 May 1884 meeting, for example, Dr. Tipton spiced a general discussion of necrosis with an example from his practice of a patient who had been scalped; Tipton was particularly interested in the long-term sequelae of the case. Almost no meeting passed without at least one report of repair of a gunshot wound. One

[41]These subjects are selected from the minutes of the first three years of the society's operation.

particularly striking example may serve to illustrate the genre. The presenter was again Dr. Tipton:

> I should like to speak of a case I was called to see a few nights ago, [a patient] who received a gunshot wound in the lower part of the abdomen, the case of whom you are all familiar. Upon holding autopsy, we found eleven distinct wounds in the ileum, but after a prolonged search could not find the ball which did not make an exit wound, remaining in the subject.[42]

This puzzling case was discussed further at the next meeting with Dr. Atkins, who had apparently assisted Dr. Tipton, at least in the autopsy, bringing along "a pathological specimen—the ileum in question—manifesting eleven different distinct wounds from a pistol ball, caliber no. 44."[43] Some within the society worried that the organization's requirement that every member present at least one paper or clinical report every year tended to discourage membership or active participation in the group, but a solid majority within the society refused consistently to modify the requirement. It was constantly emphasized that any good, conscientious practitioner could simply draw cases from his daily work to present to the group;[44] hence, this primitive effort at continuing education (and peer review) remained in place.

There were also some successes, at least on the local scale, in the society's dedication to claiming for itself the role of corporate spokesman for the medical profession of the region. Only months after its creation, for example, the society issued a press release, in the name of the medical profession in Las Vegas, denying reports of a smallpox epidemic in the town, a rumor that had already affected the town's economy and now threatened to do further damage. The medical association reported authoritatively that the town had only eleven smallpox cases, not the fifty to two hundred reported, and that the competent medical professionals of Las Vegas had the limited outbreak entirely under control.[45] A few months later, when the issue of establishing a city hospital was under discussion in the community, the medical society appointed a committee to study the matter. After receipt of the committee's report, the group addressed a formal memorial to the Las Vegas City Council supporting

[42]Las Vegas Medical Society, Minutes, 7 March 1885.
[43]Las Vegas Medical Society, Minutes, 2 May 1885.
[44]Las Vegas Medical Society, Minutes, 7 February and 7 March 1885.
[45]Las Vegas Medical Society, Minutes, 6 May 1882.

the idea and, most interestingly, presenting its views as those of "the medical profession in Las Vegas." The city fathers apparently accepted this claim, even though no more than six members had been present at either of the two meetings where the issue was discussed, and voted to make arrangements for the hospital.[46] Again in 1885, when questions were raised regarding the purity of the town water supply, it was the Las Vegas Medical Society as corporate authority of the medical profession which spearheaded the campaign to resolve the problem. The society was even "professional" enough to elect two official delegates to represent it at the 1883 annual meeting of the American Medical Association in Cleveland. Few of the other delegates there could have guessed that the representatives of this frontier medical association—Drs. M. M. Milligan and William R. Tipton[47]—comprised one-third of the total active membership of the organization! Still, it was another mark of the society's success in establishing some degree of credibility as the authentic voice of the medical profession in New Mexico Territory.

On balance, however, the initial four years of operation of the Las Vegas Medical Society had not produced the fruits its founders had expected of it. It is not too much to say that the organization had stagnated, and had settled into a comfortable routine which did not augur well for the future, particularly in a territory still experiencing rapid growth and looking confidently toward statehood. New enthusiasm and vision—and recruits—had to be found to lift the organization from its doldrums and set it moving forward again. While refusing to relax their standards regarding what constituted a true medical professional, the Las Vegas pioneers in early 1885 began to discuss the strengthening of their organization by its transformation from a local to a territorywide scale, and enlisting the support of legitimate physicians like themselves throughout New Mexico Territory.

The basic stimulus to that discussion may have been nothing more than the gradually dawning realization that the organization was going nowhere; but there seem to have been specific reasons as well: first of all, the irritating failure to make headway in securing tighter medical legislation for the territory. The possibility of broadening their base and thus enhancing their political clout was first discussed by the Las Vegas group at the 7 February 1885 meeting of the society; and the Nestor of

[46]Las Vegas Medical Society, Minutes, 12 August 1882.
[47]*Journal of the American Medical Association* 1 (1883):727.

the group, Dr. Page, tried to provide a broad frame of reference for the discussion. The minutes of that meeting paraphrase Page, as follows:

> In as much that the time was drawing near with the development and growth of the country together with the immigration and increase of population in our town and territory that necessity demands a Territorial Medical Society; and that to emerge from a local to general or New Mexico Territorial Medical Society would be in keeping with the general advancement of the other interests in the territory, . . .[48]

But the doctor concluded his general remarks with the comment that he "believed that a Territorial Medical Society would be influential in securing medical legislation," and several of the other doctors enthusiastically supported this practical judgment.[49]

This first discussion of the possible expansion of the society did not produce immediate action on the matter. Instead a three-month interlude of business as usual within the organization followed. Then, at its May meeting, Dr. Atkins proposed for membership the names of Drs. William B. Lyons of Albuquerque and George W. Harrison of Bernalillo (later of Albuquerque), and the expansion issue resurfaced in a kind of de facto fashion.[50] Atkins's motion also carried the rider that the normal rules of the society be suspended and that the out-of-town members be elected without the usual delay and scrutiny of credentials. He may have been emboldened to move so rapidly by the presence of both Drs. Lyons and Harrison at the meeting, believing that the seven regular members in attendance had already had ample opportunity to convince themselves of the outsiders' solidity and respectability. Incidentally, the presence of Drs. Lyons and Harrison in Las Vegas for the meeting cannot be explained. Was it just a matter of coincidence? Perhaps they were present in town on some other business, were invited to attend the society meeting as a simple gesture of courtesy, and then, having suitably impressed their hosts, were invited to join? Or could their presence have been contrived as part of a kind of power play to force the slow-moving organization to take action on the expansion question?

[48]Las Vegas Medical Society, Minutes, 7 February 1885.

[49]Ibid.

[50]Atkins's role in all this is especially interesting. He may very well have been consciously trying to breathe some new life into the organization. He himself was a new member, having been enrolled at the February meeting where Page first brought up the expansion question.

Whatever the proper explanation for the slightly irregular election of these first two out-of-towners, the meeting moved on to rationalize, so to speak, what it had just done by appointing a committee of three (again on the motion of Dr. Atkins) "to correspond with the profession in the different places in the northern part of the territory for the purpose of organizing a Northern New Mexico Medical Association."[51] That committee, composed of Drs. Atkins, Lyons, and Ashley, was strongly supportive of expansion, and its report one month later was largely pro forma. Without indicating how many doctors had been approached, the committee reported that five positive responses had been received, all from doctors in Albuquerque. Once more the regular rules of procedure were suspended, this time on Dr. Page's motion, and forthwith all the Albuquerque physicians who "had expressed a willingness to unite with us" were elected to membership in the society.[52] The speed of the whole business suggests the impatience of at least some within the organization to get on with it, and another committee was duly appointed to begin rewriting the society's constitution and bylaws.

That new committee presented its report on 14 November 1885, including its recommendation that the new name for the society be the New Mexico Medical Society. The motion carried by the unanimous vote of all seven—the old numbers problem again!—members present, and a new, grander (at least nominally) institution was born. A month later, the final details of the transition were worked out, and papers of incorporation of the new organization were transmitted to territorial authorities in Santa Fe. The decision was made to hold over for the interim the old officers of the Las Vegas Medical Society, but two new vice-presidents, Drs. Lyons of Albuquerque and Atkins of Las Vegas, were added to the list. The election of Lyons symbolically reflected the new, territorywide reach of the society and that of Atkins was probably an acknowledgment of his leading role in the whole reorganization. Plans called for the first official meeting of the new organization to be on 2 January 1886, coincident with the new year.[53] From the weak and tentative start in Las Vegas

[51]Las Vegas Medical Society, Minutes, 2 May 1885.

[52]Las Vegas Medical Society, Minutes, 6 June 1885. Drs. John F. Pearce and James H. Wroth were the most prominent among the Albuquerque men inducted in this first major expansion of the local society.

[53]This first assembly of the New Mexico Medical Society ought probably to be considered its official "birth" date, but the first annual meeting was not held until 7 and 8 July 1886 in Las Vegas. (See pp. 64–65).

had come a new institution which claimed, or hoped, to serve and speak for the legitimate medical profession of the whole territory. Like the useless water derrick in Old Town plaza, the little medical society founded four years earlier by some of Las Vegas's more progressive physicians did not produce much, but it did represent the firm commitment of New Mexico doctors to the future.

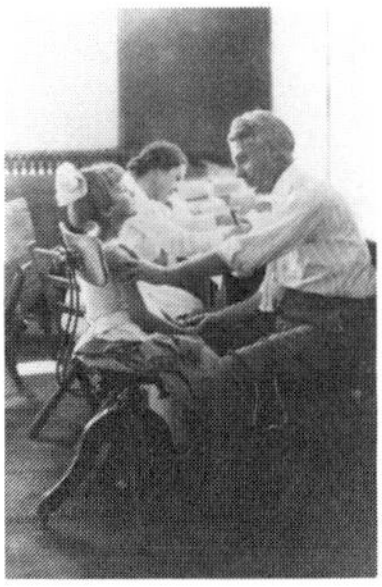

CHAPTER 2

Doctors in Swallow-tailed Coats

The Pioneers, 1886–1912

THE DOCTORS OF MEDICINE WHO FOUNDED THE LAS VEGAS Medical Society in 1882 were not, of course, the very first "regular" physicians in the territory. A handful of American doctors had preceded them in the new land. Several doctors, for example, had made brief visits to New Mexico as part of exploring parties, and a few others—among them the famous Dr. Josiah Gregg, a scantily trained physician who sought out the West for his health—came to know New Mexico through the Santa Fe trade. After American annexation in 1846, larger numbers were exposed to the rough frontier territory as contract surgeons serving with the U.S. Army, but as late as the 1870s their total number probably did not exceed a couple of dozen, and only a few of them actually settled in New Mexico Territory.[1]

With the increasing stabilization of the Indian frontier and the growing migration to the West after the Civil War, the Anglo-American population of New Mexico began to rise. Growing numbers of physicians began to trickle into the territory with the rising population of settlers. Some

[1]On these very first New Mexico regular physicians, see Victor K. Adams (M.D.), "The Medical Pioneers," *New Mexico Magazine* 28 (1950, 5):15ff.; George B. Anderson, ed., *History of New Mexico: Its Resources and Peoples*, vol. 1 (Los Angeles, Chicago, and New York: Pacific States Publishing Co., 1907), pp. 436–41; Stuart W. Adler (M.D.), "Biography of a Society," *Rocky Mountain Medical Journal* 64 (1967):33–35; Mildred S. Adler, "Early Military Medicine in New Mexico," typescript, History Archives, University of New Mexico Medical Center Library.

doctors became settlers as well, but more chose to move on than stayed. It was the arrival of the railroad in the late 1870s and the vigorous opening of mining activities in New Mexico that same decade which brought a surge of immigrants, doctors among them, to the developing land. The Las Vegas society-builders, then, were in fact part of the first sizable wave of doctors of medicine to seek their fortune in New Mexico.

Information regarding the numbers and distribution of New Mexico's pioneer physicians is relatively good, for publishers assembling medical directories made surveys of all the territory's doctors on several different occasions during the period from 1886 to statehood in 1912. The data developed in those efforts (by three different publishing houses) are fairly consistent and provide basic personal and professional information regarding the individual physicians practicing in New Mexico over that quarter-century; in the aggregate, the directories afford a reasonable picture of physician supply and distribution in the territory.[2] Adding material to that data base from the records of the New Mexico Medical Society and miscellaneous secondary sources produces a reliable overview of what New Mexico's old-time doctors were like and where they worked in the thinly settled region.

New Mexico was liberally supplied with physicians in that era. Our impulse may be to assume that in the unsettled, makeshift circumstances of frontier life, physicians were relatively rare birds, the products of a more orderly society in the East. In point of fact, Table 1 shows that by the time of statehood, at least, ample numbers of doctors had made their way to New Mexico, and the territory was better supplied with doctors than, say, South Carolina or Louisiana. Most clearly, the table shows a stunning growth in the number of physicians practicing in the territory over the quarter-century prior to statehood. While the area's total population grew from around 130,000 in 1885 to 327,301 in the 1910 census, an increase of approximately two and one-half times, its physician supply more than quadrupled. The increase was steady and broadly commensurate with the general population growth from 1886 to 1906. Physicians' exodus to New Mexico slightly exceeded the growth rate of the general

[2]On the basis of those directories, the records of the New Mexico Board of Medical Examiners office in Santa Fe, and other sources, I have assembled a basic index file which includes information on just over seven hundred New Mexico pioneer physicians. Unfortunately, the Board of Medical Examiners did not keep lists of the numbers of doctors practicing in the state, where they were located, and so forth; so no "official" data existed.

Table 1
Physician Supply in New Mexico, 1886–1912

Year	No. of Physicians	Population of Territory	Ratio
1886	99[1]	131,895	1:1,332
1897	117[2]	181,000 (est.)	1:1,547
1902	166[3]	206,000 (est.)	1:1,241
1906	221[4]	257,000 (est.)	1:1,163
1909	367[5]	308,000 (est.)	1: 839
1912	429[6]	350,000 (est.)	1: 816

Sources:
[1]*Polk's Medical and Surgical Directory of the United States, 1886.*
[2]*Flint's Medical and Surgical Directory, 1897.*
[3]*Polk's*, 7th ed. (1902).
[4]*American Medical Directory, 1906.*
[5]*American Medical Directory*, 2d ed. (1909).
[6]*American Medical Directory*, 3d ed. (1912).

populace, and the physician-to-population ratio declined from 1 doctor to every 1,332 people to 1 per every 1,163. Then, in the short period from 1906 to 1912, the number of doctors in the territory mushroomed, almost doubling in the span of six years.

The steady, general increase in the physician supply in the territory requires little explanation. At the most elementary level, New Mexico became more "civilized" year by year and less exotic to the East's potential emigrants. As the critical mass of Anglo-American settlers grew, they transplanted the essentials of their way of life to the plains and mountains of the Southwest, and New Mexico became a more familiar place for an eastern doctor to set up practice. Culture shock, in short, lessened each year, and it grew markedly easier for a doctor from Pittsburgh, say, to relocate and feel comfortable in Roswell or Las Cruces. Transportation improvements were an important part of the process, too, and railroad construction throughout the territory, particularly, opened broad new regions to settlement and development. The southeastern plains were especially noteworthy in this regard. With the railroad penetration of that region in the 1890s and early 1900s, and the irrigation farming opportunities associated with it, the whole southeastern part of the territory grew explosively. Towns like Clovis, Portales, Carlsbad, Artesia, and Roswell were born or, if already existent, given extraordinary new impetus for growth. Those five towns numbered no doctors at all in 1886, eight in 1897, eighteen in 1902, thirty-nine in 1906, and seventy in 1912. Much of New Mexico's special bulge in its physician population between 1906 and 1912 was directly related to this development of the eastern and southeastern plains or farming and ranching belt.

Some doctors undoubtedly came to New Mexico in response to "the lure of the frontier," attracted by the greater fluidity of frontier society and the relative weakness of entrenched interests. Many were excited by what they perceived to be the greater opportunities inherent in frontier practice. Others read the situation quite differently and were more impressed by the increasing stability and security of the region alluded to above, the fruit of a half-century of American administration and Anglo-American migration. The frontier could be different things to different people.

But alongside these general explanations for the rising numbers of New Mexico doctors, two particular and almost unique factors command special attention, for they played central roles in the process. One was the development of New Mexico's reputation as a haven for tuberculosis patients, a phenomenon discussed in detail in Chapter 3. Briefly, a large number of doctors who came to New Mexico Territory in the 1890s and early 1900s were themselves victims of tuberculosis, seeking the cure in the high deserts and mountains of this region; while others came as physician-entrepreneurs, hoping to fit themselves usefully (and profitably) into the region's newly developing tuberculosis industry. Though exact numbers do not exist, it is safe to estimate that perhaps as much as 50 percent of the physician influx at the turn of the century was tuberculosis-related. This exodus of physicians to New Mexico was part, then, of a general development within American medicine—specifically, the rise of altitude therapy for tuberculosis and the sanatorium movement—and was a great boon to the region's health-care system and economy. Far less positive and constructive was the second special reason for the large expansion in the number of doctors in New Mexico: the fact that medical licensure in New Mexico was much less strict than elsewhere in the nation. This was a sad reality which meant, in the words of one prominent New Mexico physician of the era, that New Mexico became "a veritable dumping ground of the least competent members of our profession, doctors who had not sufficient knowledge and ability to get by other State boards."[3] This charge is discussed in detail below; suffice it to say here that the relative ease of licensure in New Mexico undoubtedly contributed to the expansion of the territory's physician corps. Many doctors roosted in New Mexico Territory because the climate was nice and the region, quickly approaching statehood, was booming—and because they couldn't get licensed to practice elsewhere.

The most obvious immediate effect of this physician influx was the creation of a thoroughly "well-doctored" society in territorial New Mexico. At the time of statehood, New Mexico had 1 physician for every 816 of its citizens,[4] a ratio comparing not unreasonably with the national average at that time of approximately 1 doctor per every 568 citizens. In the more settled East and Midwest ratios were generally lower—in Illinois 1 to 586, in Indiana 1 to 558, in Massachusetts 1 to 567, and in Missouri 1 to 552—but New Mexico's physician supply was greater than in most other "frontier" areas. Minnesota, for instance, had only 1 doctor for every 981 people, North Dakota 1 for every 971, and Utah 1 per every 936. Of the Western states only California, with a ratio of 1 doctor per every 401 people, and Colorado, with a stunning ratio of 1 per 328, were more liberally supplied with physicians. Each of the latter, like New Mexico, had profited from the migration of health-seeking and/or otherwise "westering" physicians at the turn of the century; and each was, incidentally, badly overstocked with healers. Arizona's ratio of 1 per every 703 citizens was similar to that of New Mexico.

The argument can certainly be advanced that pioneer New Mexico, like most of American society in general, had far too many doctors for its limited population. Turn-of-the-century medical reformers, like Abraham Flexner, argued convincingly that American consumers suffered from an overabundance of poorly trained practitioners, with the effect that the cost of medical care in the United States was much higher than it needed to be and its quality significantly lower than it could or should have

[3]Evelyn Fisher Frisbie (M.D.), "Some of Our Problems in the Southwest," *New Mexico Medical Journal* 17 (1916):13.

[4]The comparable figure for 1985 was 1 to 565 with 2,522 physicians serving the state's 1,424,000 people.

been.[5] Medically sophisticated societies, like Germany with its much more mature health-delivery system, did very well with something like one doctor for every two thousand population; and that was the standard toward which contemporary medical reformers, Flexner and others, aimed. Such a ratio would surely not have worked for territorial New Mexico, where the population was spread across giant swaths of land; but it is clear that parts of New Mexico, at least, had far too many physicians. Artesia, for example, in 1912 had no fewer than 13 doctors to care for its 1,883 residents, plus a limited clientele of farm folk in the vicinity for a doctor-to-population ratio of 1 medico for every 145 people. Albuquerque's 11,020 residents were served by 43 physicians for a 1 to 256 ratio—less than the 1 to 460 ratio of New York City, the 1 to 580 of Chicago, or San Francisco's 1 to 370. In Roswell there were 29 doctors for the 6,172 people of the town; Tucumcari had 12 M.D.s serving 2,526 residents (a 1 to 211 ratio); Clovis 15 for 3,255 people (a 1 to 217 ratio); and so on. Smaller places like Estancia (5 doctors among its 517 people), Belen (673 people and 4 doctors), Cerrillos (110 people and 2 physicians), and Farmington (5 doctors among 785 people) showed the same phenomenon. Even villages like Columbus (population 10 in 1912), Dulce (40 souls in that year), and Mosquero (25 people) could boast their own doctor. Elk in Chaves County, population 20, had 2. Given such numbers, did doctors resort to buttonholing potential customers on the street? It seems that in some cases they did. At the December 1903 meeting of the Board of Medical Examiners the license of Dr. C. W. Hotchkiss of Alamogordo was challenged on the basis of his "unethical conduct in soliciting professional work on the street and otherwise."[6]

The question can be asked whether New Mexico suffered an absolute oversupply of physicians or whether the problem was a matter of maldistribution. (This issue, of course, continues to be a major one in contemporary New Mexico, where physicians tend to cluster in major population centers, leaving some rural areas underserved.) Maps 1 and 2 show the numbers and location of physicians in New Mexico in 1886 and 1912. Map 3 shows the physician-to-population ratio county-by-county in 1912 and lends some support to such a thesis, for New Mexico in 1912

[5]See Flexner's revolutionary Carnegie Foundation funded study, *Medical Education in the United States and Canada* (New York: Carnegie Foundation for the Advancement of Teaching, 1910). This study, a landmark in the history of American medicine, is the source for most of the figures and much of the argument in this section.

[6]New Mexico, Board of Medical Examiners, Minutes, 7 and 8 December 1903.

Map 1 PHYSICIAN DISTRIBUTION IN NEW MEXICO, 1886

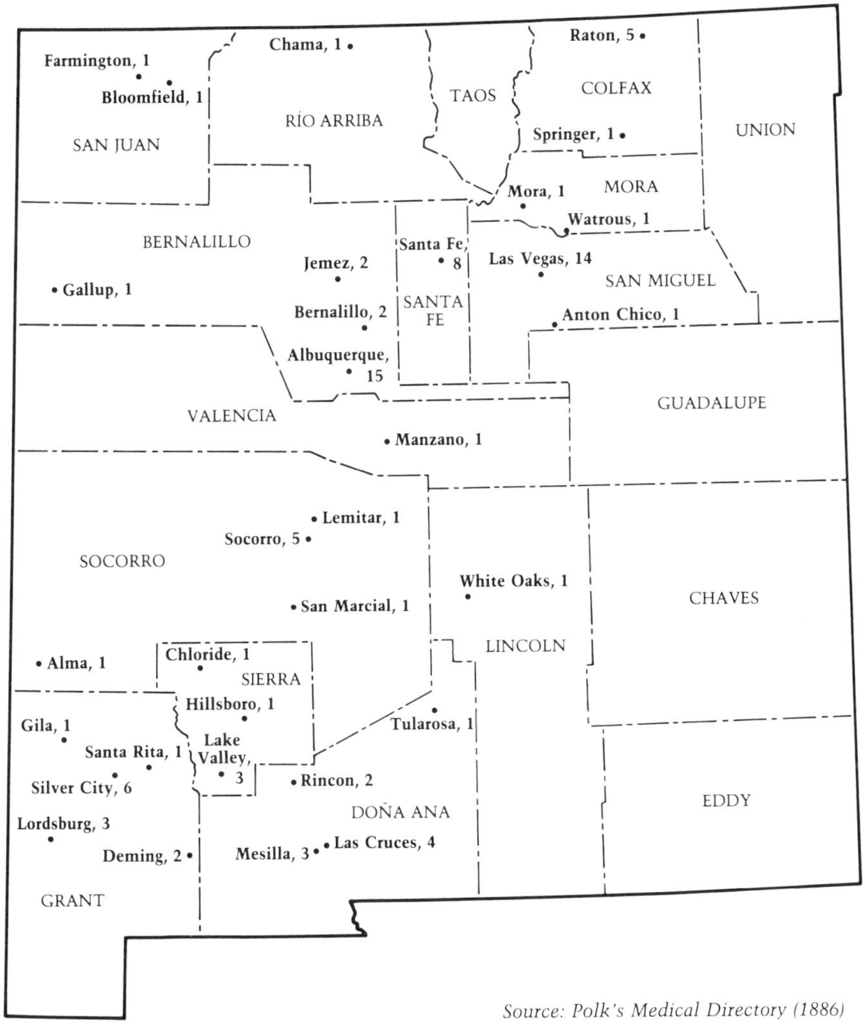

Source: Polk's Medical Directory (1886)

Map 2 NUMBER OF MEDICAL DOCTORS BY COUNTY, 1912

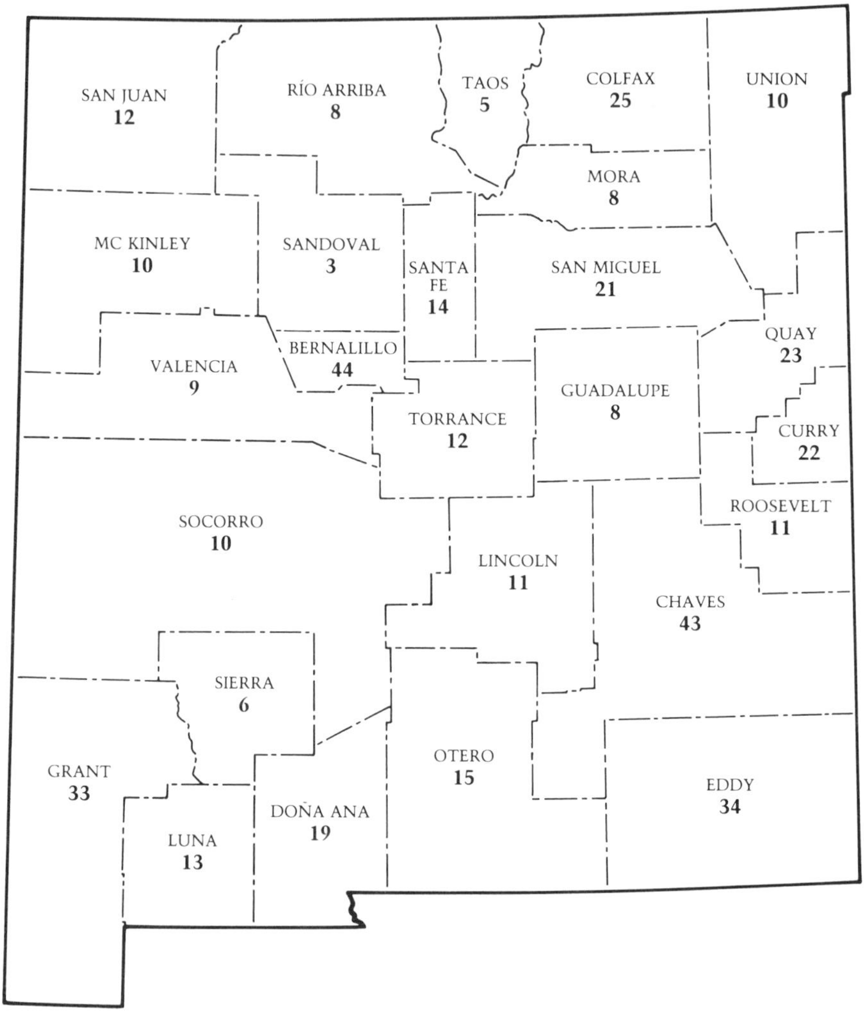

Map 3 RATIOS BY COUNTIES, MEDICAL DOCTORS TO POPULATION, 1912

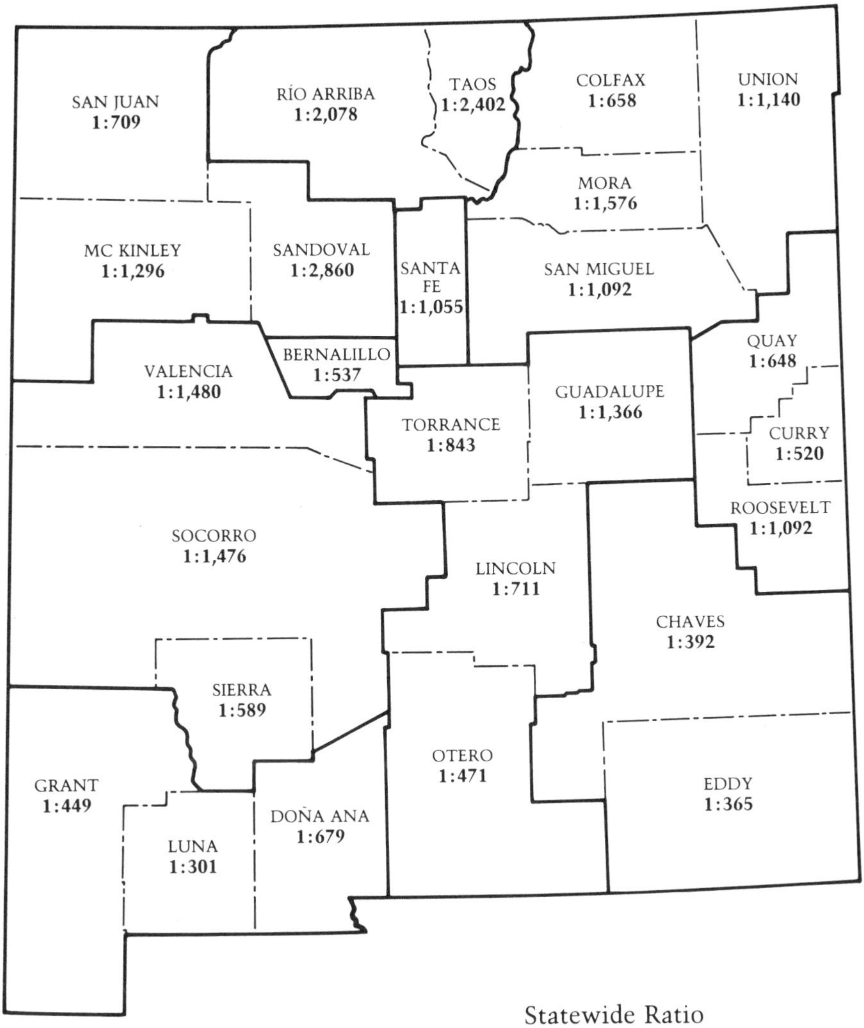

Statewide Ratio
1:816 (one MD for every 816 people)

did exhibit large differentials in physician supply. Looking at 1912, for example, and combining the new state's twenty-six counties (crudely) into ten regional groupings, a more accurate picture of the state's physician-availability emerges:

Chaves-Eddy	1:380
Grant-Luna–Doña Ana	1:486
Bernalillo	1:537
Quay-Curry-Roosevelt	1:686
Guadalupe-Torrance-Lincoln-Otero	1:765
Territory Average	**1:816**
Colfax-Mora-San Miguel–Union	1:991
Santa Fe	1:1,055
San Juan–McKinley	1:1,202
Valencia-Socorro-Sierra	1:1,265
Río Arriba–Taos	1:2,202

While the entire southern tier of New Mexico had ratios significantly lower than the 1 to 816 average, the entire north (with the exception of Colfax County) showed ratios higher than the average, and far higher in the mountainous areas of the extreme north.

The explanations for the disparities in these figures are various and include things so straightforward as population densities and the convenience and ease of transportation, but also more complex phenomena such as the cultural differences which often existed between the Anglo-American health-providers and their patients, as in the cases of the isolated, sometimes xenophobic Hispanic communities of the north or the Indian communities of Sandoval and McKinley counties. Perhaps most obvious of all, the economic underdevelopment of much of northern New Mexico discouraged physicians from setting up practice there. Then as now, doctors were concerned to establish themselves where they could make an acceptable living; hence, some parts of New Mexico were underserved while others fairly teemed with doctors. The problem of maldistribution only became acute with the filling-in of the eastern and southeastern farming territories, and the resultant concentration of so many doctors there after the turn of the century; but even earlier the same syndrome had existed. The map of physician distribution in 1886 shows a heavy concentration of medical men in the territory's commercial and transportation centers—Albuquerque, Las Vegas, Santa Fe, Socorro, and Raton—and in the territory's mining centers. Nevertheless, it seems clear that throughout the territorial period New Mexico's doctors, with some major exceptions, located where the need was. Distribution was skewed from place to place, but by and large the physicians were sprinkled reasonably across the land.

It has already been suggested that one reason for the abundance of physicians in New Mexico at the beginning of this century was the ease with which a doctor might secure licensure in the territory. The history of medical licensure in the territorial period is a tortuous one: six separate laws (or major amendments) were passed between 1882, the year of the first licensing law, and 1909; and at least as many others were introduced and fought through the territorial legislature without ultimate passage. The issue was, by far, the major legislative cause of the young New Mexico Medical Society throughout its first three decades. More broadly still, the fundamental question "Who may practice?" embroiled the New Mexico medical community in more social and political controversy than any other in the years before statehood. It was so intense an issue because it involved not merely the economic health of the medical establishment, but also the quality of health care rendered to the citizenry of the territory.

Prior to 1882, no form of medical licensure existed in New Mexico. Anyone who wished could declare himself a doctor, hang out a shingle, and hope for the best. Civil authorities had no responsibility in the matter; results, presumably, would show who really knew something about "doctoring" and who did not. Such a state of affairs was not unusual, for as late as the time of the American Civil War, there was almost free entry into the professional practice of medicine all over the country.[7] In the late 1860s and 1870s, states and territories around the country began to enact medical licensure laws ostensibly to help protect the public from incompetent medical practitioners and to force improvement in American medical education. The movement spread rapidly, and by 1881 half the nation's states and territories had such laws. As part of that national movement—neither especially early nor late—the New Mexico Territorial Legislature in March 1882 passed "An Act to Protect the Public Health

[7]For a convenient summary of this subject, see Samuel L. Baker, "Physician Licensure Laws in the United States, 1865–1915," *Journal of the History of Medicine and Allied Sciences* 39 (1984):173–97. For more comprehensive analysis of the subject and related matters, see the authoritative study written by New Mexico physician (and longtime Secretary of the Board of Medical Examiners) Robert C. Derbyshire, *Medical Licensure and Discipline in the United States* (Baltimore: Johns Hopkins University Press, 1969).

and Regulate the Practice of Medicine in the Territory of New Mexico."[8] This legislation created a seven-member Board of Medical Examiners, constituted of four "allopathic" or regular physicians, two homeopaths, and one eclectic, whose job it was to regulate through licensure the practice of medicine in the territory. The New Mexico law, like many others around the nation, was patterned on the 1877 Illinois law, but it was unique in legally specifying representation on a unitary board for the minority medical sects. It was a pioneering effort to resolve the sectarian conflict that had previously retarded regulation of the profession. The New Mexico law, in turn, became something of a model for handling the sectarian question, and over half the states that established unitary licensure boards followed the New Mexico example. Early on, then, New Mexico was something of a progressive pioneer or leader in medical licensure.[9]

New Mexico's law authorized its new Board of Medical Examiners to license practitioners who qualified in one of three ways. First of all, it could immediately license (upon payment of a five-dollar fee) all applicants who had "diplomas or licenses from legally chartered medical institutions in good standing."[10] Thus, the holder of a diploma from any medical school, even the most rotten and worthless of proprietary schools (see below) was entitled to claim immediate licensure in New Mexico. In addition, the Board at its discretion could examine applicants who lacked any degree or license and, if a majority of the panel so voted, grant licensure on the basis of a successful exam. Third, a grandfather clause authorized licensing, without further ado, all medical practitioners with more than ten years of service in the territory. This law, like those elsewhere in the nation, suffered from the major weakness that it recognized a medical diploma as a license to practice, providing no way to screen diplomas for the quality of the medical schools that issued them. When it is realized that no fewer than 457 medical schools had been established in the United States since the nation's first (the University of Pennsylvania in 1765), many of them for-profit schools of the weakest and most

[8]Twenty-seven states or territories preceded New Mexico in passing this kind of legislation, and twenty others followed. Western states were leaders of the movement. Wyoming enacted a physician-licensure law in 1871; Arizona followed in 1873, Nevada in 1875, Montana in 1876, and Colorado and Washington in 1881. After New Mexico came Idaho in 1887; Oregon in 1889; Utah in 1892; and California in 1896.

[9]Baker, "Physician Licensure Laws":182–83.

[10]Laws of New Mexico, 14th Legislative Assembly (1882), chapter 55, 2 March 1882.

venal sort, the problem becomes apparent. Many of the late nineteenth-century medical schools turning out "physicians" were housed in one or two dirty, ill-equipped rooms without laboratories or clinical facilities of any sort, but with a handful of "professors" willing to grant diplomas to farm boys who lacked a high school education yet had enough money to meet the medical school's fees.[11]

Under those circumstances, that first medical law in New Mexico excluded relatively few from practice. It did forbid practice to the self-taught doctor who lacked any semblance of formal training (and who was too scrupulous or impecunious to purchase a diploma), and it did limit the itinerant healers and outright charlatans who sold various health-giving nostrums and devices; but, at best, it was a modest start toward assuring the quality of medical care in the territory. The examination alternative for nongraduates further compromised its effectiveness. The act instructed the Board to devise its own examination for those seeking licensure in that way and defined carefully the fields which were to be examined. Questions were included on anatomy, physiology, chemistry, pathology, surgery, obstetrics, and the practice of medicine; but explicitly excluded were the basic fields of materia medica and therapeutics because those were the major areas of difference among the three medical philosophies represented on the Board.[12] The Board was also empowered to refuse licensure to individuals guilty of unprofessional or dishonorable conduct, with the American Medical Association Code of Ethics (1847) ordained by the act as the standard for determination of such things.

Another weakness of that first medical practice act should be mentioned here, both because it contributed to the undermining of the effectiveness of the law and because it proved to be one of the most enduring of all problems associated with medical licensure in New Mexico. From

[11]On the sorry state of medical education in the United States in the last half of the nineteenth century, see the famous Flexner report cited in n. 5, above; John Duffy, *The Healers: A History of American Medicine* (Urbana, Ill.: University of Illinois Press, 1979); and William G. Rothstein, *American Physicians in the Nineteenth Century: From Sects to Science* (Baltimore: Johns Hopkins University Press, 1972).

[12]By 1912 the Board's exam had evolved to cover the following areas: jurisprudence (5 percent), physical diagnosis (10 percent), anatomy and histology (10 percent), obstetrics (10 percent), gynecology (5 percent), surgery (10 percent), chemistry (5 percent), hygiene (5 percent), bacteriology (5 percent), materia medica (10 percent), therapeutics (10 percent), physiology (5 percent), and practice of medicine (10 percent). New Mexico, Board of Medical Examiners, Minutes, 8 July 1912.

the very start, New Mexico's licensing efforts were hamstrung by the problem of enforcement. It quickly proved difficult, if not impossible, to indict or convict unqualified practitioners when they had local popularity and/or political support and connections. The minutes of the New Mexico Medical Society, the chief proponent of tougher laws and tighter enforcement, and the records of the Board of Medical Examiners are replete with references to the failure of local authorities to prosecute unlicensed practitioners under the provisions of the law. Local district attorneys, for example, were "very busy men and not enthusiastic as a rule in enforcing this act,"[13] and, in general, local authorities were at least as likely to frustrate the Board in its efforts to insist on proper licensure as to help it. Unfortunately, the regulatory agency was entirely reliant on these unenthusiastic local authorities for meaningful enforcement, for it lacked any funds whatsoever to do that job by itself. It did adopt, from time to time, depending on the energy and commitment of its individual members, various expedients to deal with the problem. It could and did write to suspected offenders around the territory, directing them to appear before the Board and to make application for licensure, but rarely did such action have any effect.[14] Individual Board members sometimes took the initiative in their home areas of sniffing out "illegals" and prosecuting them as individual complainants.[15] The Board also tried to use local health officers, where they existed, as its agents in the assault on illegal practitioners. In 1905, for instance, it instructed Dr. Ora C. McEwen, county health officer in San Juan County, "that he proceed at once against [a suspected offender] for the illegal practice of medicine without a license," or else he, McEwen, would be replaced.[16] The Board even experimented briefly, from 1907 to 1909, with hiring its own Special Health Officer on a part-time basis, an official whose job would be to travel about the territory to root out and prosecute illegals. It hired the respected Albuquerque pharmacist Bernard Ruppe, then president of the New Mexico Board of Pharmacy, as its special agent; and Ruppe turned to the work with great

[13]New Mexico, Board of Medical Examiners, Annual Report to the Governor, 1 December 1923.

[14]See, for example, the summons to a Dr. Miller of Silver City in its minutes of 14 January 1908, or that to Dr. José Somellera of Park View, New Mexico, who had already been practicing in New Mexico *for five years.* New Mexico, Board of Medical Examiners, Minutes, 10 July 1916.

[15]New Mexico, Board of Medical Examiners, Minutes, 12 and 13 April 1909.

[16]New Mexico, Board of Medical Examiners, Minutes, 5 December 1905.

energy, prosecuting successfully several unlicensed physicians in Roosevelt and Quay counties. However, the project fizzled from lack of money to finance the officer's work.[17] In short, none of the makeshift arrangements that the Board devised for enforcement really worked, and that difficulty persisted into the forties and even fifties.

As a matter of sad fact, it was not only local politicos and law officers who refused to take the provisions of the law seriously. Many regular, properly licensed physicians were casual about it, too. When Dr. T. J. Webb of Texico, New Mexico, was hauled up before the Board in 1908 for practicing without a license, his defense emphasized the point. Board member Dr. William D. Radcliffe of Belen began the questioning:

> Radcliffe: Dr., Why didn't you come before this Board and apply for a license?
> Dr. Webb: Well, when I went there to Texico, I went to Dr. [Albert L.] Breeding and asked him about the law and asked him if I could practice and he said I could and asked me to go partners with him, and I went in partners, that was two years ago, in January, 1906, and then I asked about the Board and he says it was no use to go up before you, I will protect you. . . . [Later] Breeding told me, "If I were you, I would just wait until they notified you."[18]

Other evidence also suggests that even among doctors themselves respect for the new licensing law was not always strong. As late as 1911, the Bernalillo County Medical Society, that pillar of the medical establishment, formally requested the Board to ignore the law. It petitioned that the formalities of the law simply be waived and the Board issue immediately a license to a doctor resident in Albuquerque in whom the local medical society had taken special interest. The doctor and his wife had

[17]New Mexico, Board of Medical Examiners, Minutes, 14 October 1907, 14 April 1908, and 13 April 1909. It was originally hoped that funds for the investigative officer could be generated from fines collected through successful prosecutions, but the idea proved unrealistic.

[18]New Mexico, Board of Medical Examiners, Minutes, 13 January 1908. To follow the Webb case further, the Board was sympathetic to the confused and misled young doctor and agreed to let him stand for examination for licensure that very afternoon, but at the appointed time Dr. Webb did not appear. He did return to the next meeting: "Dr. Webb presented himself for examination and was given a set of the same questions as were given to other applicants; after looking over the questions, he refused to proceed with the examination and left the building." (New Mexico, Board of Medical Examiners, Minutes, 14 April 1908). Webb was no quitter, however. He showed up again at the Board's next meeting, took his exam, passed, and received his license (New Mexico, Board of Medical Examiners, Minutes, 13 July 1908). Presumably, these formalities were not allowed to interfere with his already two-year-old practice in Texico.

come to New Mexico as health-seekers several years earlier, had not made good progress physically, and now desired, according to the county society's petition, "only to go up to some small village and try to make a living by the practice of medicine."[19] Even though there were special circumstances in this case, the casual attitude toward the licensing law was evident in the request.

Consistently, throughout the territorial period, the New Mexico Medical Society fought for improvement of the 1882 licensing act, but progress was painfully slow in coming. Committees within the society studied the problem and prepared new draft legislation; physician-lobbyists were dispatched to Santa Fe to inform legislators of the difficulties with the old law; letters were sent, and delegations personally visited with the governors;[20] and public information campaigns were devised to get the reform message across to the public. The criticism of some of the regulars in the society was blunt to the point of rudeness. A resolution passed at the July 1888 annual meeting of the organization began: "Whereas the existing New Mexico statute regulating the practice of medicine is clumsily worded, a discredit to its framers, and an encumbrance to the statute book. . . ."[21]

The impression is strong that the basic reason for New Mexico's naggingly slow progress toward effective medical-licensure legislation lay in a combination of the medical society's weakness and simple legislative inertia. No dramatic difficulties with the existing law were obvious; and thus it was difficult to focus legislative attention on the matter, especially when only a few disgruntled regulars seemed interested in it. In addition, there were some elements of active opposition to any change in the 1882 law. First of all, the regular medical community seemed split on the question, with a faction in Santa Fe around Dr. Robert H. Longwill hostile to any reform,[22] and many other doctors around the territory blasé about it, as witnessed by the attitudes, already cited, of Dr. Breeding in Texico and the Bernalillo County Medical Society. More publicly, much of the press in the territory, especially the influential *Albuquerque Morning Journal,* was suspicious of the medical society's insistence on the need

[19]New Mexico, Board of Medical Examiners, Minutes, 10 April 1911. The Board acceded to the request and just issued a license, while insisting that the case constituted no precedent.

[20]For a lengthy, but extraordinarily interesting sample of the medical society's thinking on the issue, see Appendix A.

[21]New Mexico Medical Society, 3d Annual Meeting, Minutes, 11 July 1888.

[22]New Mexico Medical Society, Minutes, 5 January 1889.

for stronger licensing laws. Nationally, it was an era of trust-busting, and in New Mexico newspaper editors labeled the medical society reformers as "the medical trust." They were chastised as mere special pleaders intent on using the instrumentality of the state to guarantee them monopoly control over medical practice in the territory.[23] And it was not long before the medical society's agitation for tighter medical legislation roused an escalating chorus of criticism from other kinds of health practitioners—osteopaths, midwives, folk practitioners, homeopaths, and eclectics—all of whom worried that "the medical trust" was actually intent on squeezing them from the medical marketplace. Opposition by Christian Scientists was especially heated and important in 1912 in defeating a big push that year for a new law by the untiring advocates of the medical society.[24] The growing impatience and frustration of the reformers in the medical society at this opposition was manifest in a resolution passed at their 1909 annual meeting in Roswell:

> Resolved, that it is considered unethical for a physician to visit a patient who has been treated by an osteopath or Christian Scientist for the sole purpose of being in time to sign a death certificate.[25]

On several different occasions the New Mexico legislature did tinker with the medical practice law, and in piecemeal fashion a measure of improvement was achieved. Most notably, in 1907 progress was made in confronting the dilemma of differentiating among medical diplomas of greatly varying weight. By the terms of the 1907 "Act to Regulate the Practice of Medicine in New Mexico"[26] the territory's Board of Medical Examiners was instructed to license, by diploma alone, *only* those applicants who were graduates of one of the country's "Grade A" medical schools as determined by the respected Association of American Medical Colleges. This was a significant step forward, ending the automatic licensure of applicants who presented degrees from substandard medical schools. However, that improved law of 1907 still allowed for licensure by examination for graduates of nonapproved schools, and thus much of its effectiveness depended on the rigor of the Board's examination. Sadly,

[23]See the *Albuquerque Morning Journal* of early October 1913 for examples of this type of opposition.

[24]See the *New Mexico Medical Journal* 8 (1911–12):298–99, 331–32.

[25]*New Mexico Medical Journal* 5 (1909–10):6.

[26]Laws of New Mexico, 37th Legislative Assembly, chapter 34, 16 March 1907.

it never seemed particularly demanding in the setting and grading of its examinations. It gave a total of 126 exams between 1902 and 1923 and passed 106 of them, or 84 percent; and when it is remembered that it was testing only applicants with no degree whatsoever or, after 1907, only graduates of nonapproved schools, the figure is even more telling.[27] (For comparison, of 44 applicants who took the Illinois exam in the spring of 1909 only 21 passed; Oregon gave 52 exams at that time with 31 passing; in Massachusetts 19 of 32 applicants passed; and so forth.)[28]

By 1907 an unhappy and even dangerous situation had developed. New Mexico, which had been in the mainstream of medical progressivism with passage of its 1882 licensure law, had fallen well behind the rest of the nation in this sphere. As a consequence of legislative disinterest, strong opposition, and the weakness of the reformers, New Mexico's medical licensure law had become one of the weakest in the nation. Most notably, New Mexico had failed to adopt one of the most important of all the various reforms within the national movement, namely, the establishment of compulsory examinations for *all* applicants for medical licensure. In the 1890s and early 1900s, most states and territories around the country had stiffened their licensure requirements by adding this additional check on applicants' medical preparation. No longer was possession of a diploma, even from an "approved" school, sufficient; all applicants had to stand formal examination. In 1885 only three states or territories had such a requirement, but by 1906 only two lacked it. This movement toward requiring examination of all applicants was especially prominent in the period from 1900 to 1905, when sixteen states added that stipulation, joining the thirty others which had already established the policy. In only two places—New Mexico and Florida—could an applicant for licensure escape examination by appeal to the fact that he had a degree from an approved medical school.[29] The real significance of that fact is immediately evident in the figures. Between December 1902 and January 1923, New Mexico's Board of Medical Examiners issued a total of 1,360 licenses; 1,220 by mere endorsement of the applicants' medical diplomas (89.7 percent of the total), 106 by examination (7.8 percent), and 34 (2.5 percent) by reciprocity with other states.[30] New Mexico examined directly

[27]New Mexico, Board of Medical Examiners, Minutes, 1902–23.
[28]*Journal of the American Medical Association* 52 (26 June 1909):2127–28.
[29]Baker, "Physician Licensure Laws":187–90.
[30]New Mexico, Board of Medical Examiners, Minutes, 1902–23.

Table 2
Licenses Issued by New Mexico Board of Medical Examiners, 1896–1930

Year	No. of Licenses	Year	No. of Licenses
1896	15	1914	53
1897	15	1915	53
1898	10	1916	64
1899	30	1917	68
1900	35	1918	35
1901	30	1919	50
1902	30	1920	46
1903	44	1921	38
1904	51	1922	41
1905	56	1923	37
1906	102	1924	16
1907	79	1925	23
1908	138	1926	16
1909	95	1927	30
1910	100	1928	13
1911	80	1929	26
1912	97	1930	30
1913	47		

Source: New Mexico, Board of Medical Examiners, Minutes, 1902–30. The figures suggested for the period from 1896 to 1902 are estimates only, projected on the basis of other data. (Board records for the period before 1902 have been lost.)

about one doctor in thirteen who applied for licensure in the territory-state, while most other states and territories were demanding examination of essentially all their applicants.

The effect of the toughening requirements elsewhere can be seen in Table 2, which shows the number of licenses issued annually by New Mexico's Board of Medical Examiners between 1896 and 1930. The average number of licenses issued per year in the 1890s was probably around 10 or so, but that figure jumped to 61 per year between 1900 and 1923.

More startlingly, the average was a gigantic 99 new doctors licensed per year in the period from 1906 through 1912. What prompted that sudden fascination for New Mexico among so many doctors of the beginning of this century? Those high averages in the first two decades of the twentieth century reflect, to some degree, the arrival of "lunger" physicians, a phenomenon which began to escalate in that time frame. In addition, they were produced partially by increased compliance with the licensure law as public attention focused on the issue and as enforcement efforts grew more serious. But most clearly of all, the figures show a "rush" to New Mexico in those years by physicians who, for whatever reasons, sought a place of practice where they could set up their offices and begin business with a minimum of effort and, particularly, where they could get their licenses without confronting the uncertainty of examination. As a kind of confirmation of such an interpretation, it should be noted that the average number of physicians licensed in New Mexico plummeted from the 61-per-year average of the century's first two decades to 21 per year in the period from 1923 to 1930. *Not* coincidentally, 1923 was the year when New Mexico finally began requiring an examination of all who sought licensure in the state.[31] In his 1913 presidential address to the New Mexico Medical Society, Albuquerque's Dr. LeRoy Peters raged about the state of affairs:

> Before we go further let us draw a word picture of conditions as they exist in New Mexico today. As president of the organized profession of this state, I hang my head in shame. I feel that we are most humiliated. Our laws on matters of health and the laws regulating the practice of medicine are a disgrace. To think that a supposedly civilized unit of our nation should tolerate such conditions is unbelievable. Yet today New Mexico is the dumping ground of the medical profession of America, yes, even of the entire world. Graduates from a medical school, here or abroad, try to obtain a license in any state or territory in the United States, and if you fail, come to New Mexico, the land of sunshine, the land of opportunity. She will open her doors, and in the majority of cases—by far a big majority—you will secure your license to practice without an examination, merely by presenting so-called credentials and the payment of a license fee.[32]

[31]It should also be noted, in passing, that the absolute supply of new doctors churned out by American medical schools began to decline from the 5,000-plus per annum in the first decade of the century to considerably smaller numbers in the 1920s. This fact also had its impact on the New Mexico numbers.

[32]*Albuquerque Morning Journal*, 3 October 1913, p. 4.

Reform finally came to New Mexico in 1923 with passage of a new and far more effective medical-licensure law. The incessant criticism of the medical society, the gradual wearing down of opposition, a changed political atmosphere, and, most important of all, the spreading realization that New Mexico had indeed fallen behind the times finally produced the Medical Practice Act of 1923. That legislation included the crucial change of requiring examination for all seeking the right to practice in the state. Exception was made only for those already licensed in other states where they had been examined. The new law established a basic parity between New Mexico and the rest of the nation and eliminated some of the more egregious problems with regulation of the medical profession for a generation. The Board of Medical Examiners, in its 1927–28 annual report to the governor, proudly noted its effects:

> The present Medical Practice Act, taken as a whole, is the best that New Mexico has ever had. Insofar as it applies to regular practitioners of medicine, it has enabled us to keep out incompetents and to raise the standards of the medical practitioners within the state until today our Board is recognized by 42 other State Boards and the general average of medical ability within the state will compare favorably with any other state in the Union.[33]

That appraisal was probably accurate, but it is clear that New Mexico had reached that happy plateau only with great labor.

Implicit in all the discussion regarding New Mexico's backward medical-licensing standards was the suggestion that its negligence in the matter had resulted in significant numbers of substandard practitioners unleashed on the innocent medical consumers of the region. Only in rare outbursts, such as that of Dr. Peters, cited above, was the charge baldly made; but it percolated just beneath the surface whenever the issue was discussed. What evidence existed to support such a notion? Was the physician corps of New Mexico significantly inferior to those elsewhere? There was a certain logic inherent in the situation: Everybody else had higher standards, and that must mean that pretenders and weaklings flocked to New Mexico, and yes! the numbers of the licensure table confirm that interpretation. Was territorial New Mexico glutted with marginal (or worse) physicians?

One way of developing some sense of the quality of New Mexico's

[33]New Mexico, Board of Medical Examiners, Annual Report to the Governor, 1927–28.

pioneer physicians is to try, almost a century removed, to appraise their medical educations. Map 4 and Table 3 provide considerable information about 586 New Mexico doctors of the prestatehood era, for whom precise information regarding the place of their medical training is available.[34] The data indicate clearly that New Mexico's doctors came from the major medical education centers, good and bad, of turn-of-the-century America. The high figures for Missouri, Illinois, Kentucky, New York, Ohio, Pennsylvania, and Tennessee—together, these seven states provided 71 percent of the doctors in the total sample—reflect nothing more clearly than the fact that those states were the major (quantitatively, at least) locations of medical schools in that era. As late as 1910 Illinois still had eighteen separate medical colleges in operation, mostly in Chicago, and more than forty had operated in the state at one time or another in the period from 1837 (the chartering of Illinois's first medical school, Rush Medical College in Chicago) to 1907.[35] Nor is it at all surprising to find that large numbers of New Mexico physicians came from schools located in Missouri. That state had sheltered no fewer than forty-four medical schools in the period from 1840 to 1906, thirteen of which survived as of 1910. Similar explanations apply in the cases of the other five states so prominent in producing New Mexico physicians of the pioneer era. Either they had large numbers of medical schools turning out doctors, or, as in the case of Kentucky and one or two others, a limited number of schools, but large ones producing lots of medical graduates. There are, of course, additional reasons for the special prominence of Missouri and Illinois on the list. In the last half of the nineteenth century, St. Louis and Chicago were the traditional jumping-off points for migration farther to the West. Overland trails had long focused in St. Louis, trails to the Southwest in particular, and the development of the railroad gave Chicago a special prominence as a gateway to the West. New Orleans served a similar role

[34]It is my judgment that this 586-doctor sample constitutes between 2/3 and 3/4 of the total number who practiced in the territory in the period from 1886 to 1912.

[35]See the comprehensive list with short sketches of each institution in *Polk's Medical Register*, 12th ed. (1912–13), pp. 151–82. The *American Medical Directory*'s "History of Medical Schools" section, found in most of its early editions (see, for example, the 16th ed. [1940], pp. 86–96), lists forty-one medical schools in Illinois between 1837 and 1907, among them such ephemeral (and often patently fraudulent) places as College of Physicians and Surgeons of the Upper Mississippi; Scientific Medical College, Chicago (closed by postal authorities in 1900); and the German College of Gynecology, Pediatrics, and Obstetrics, which was both born and (mercifully) died in Chicago in 1892.

Map 4 STATES WHERE PIONEER PHYSICIANS RECEIVED MEDICAL EDUCATION

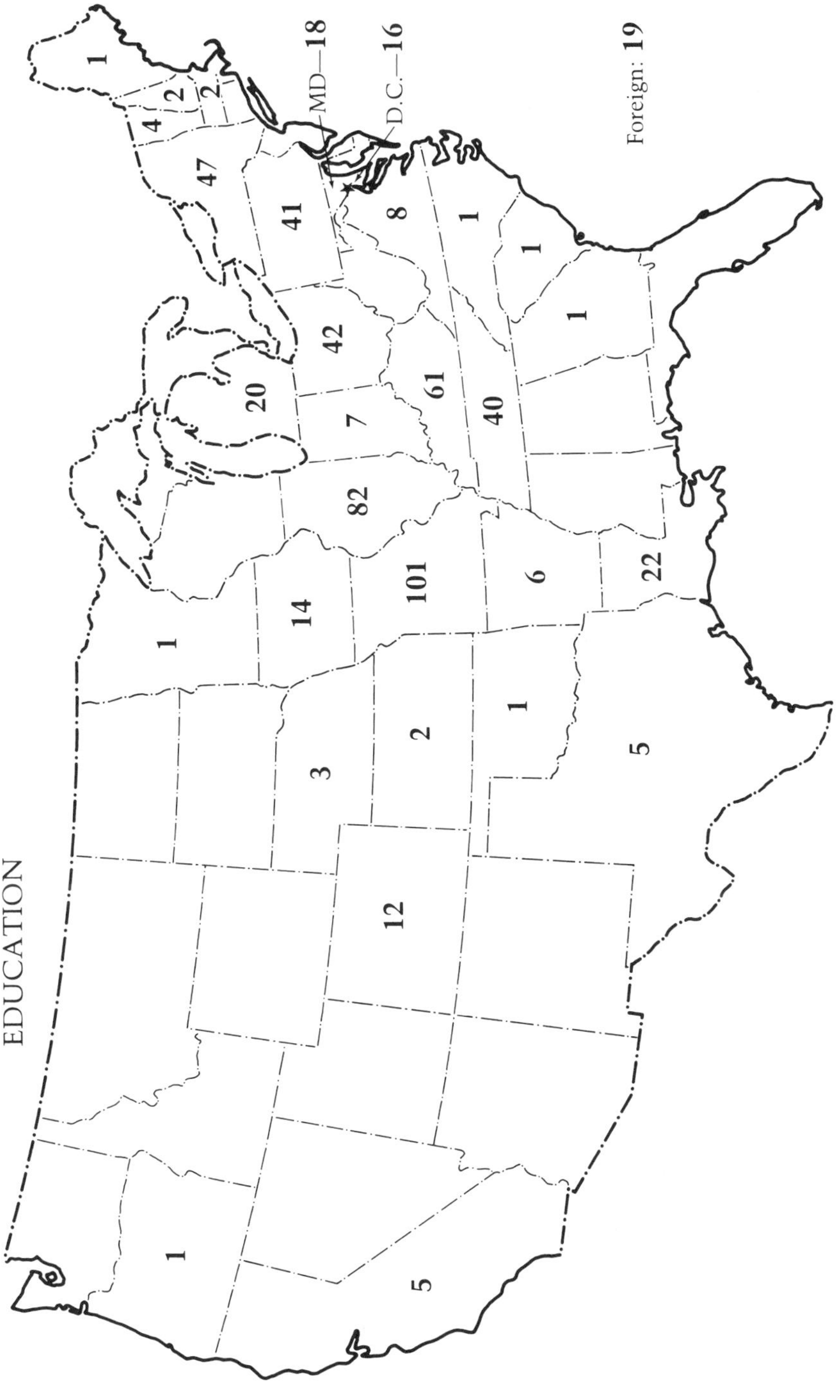

Table 3
Location of Medical Schools Attended
by New Mexico Pioneer Physicians

State	Number
Missouri	101
Illinois	82
Kentucky	61
New York	47
Ohio	42
Pennsylvania	41
Tennessee	40
	414 subtotal (71%)
Louisiana	22
Michigan	20
Foreign	19
Maryland	18
District of Columbia	16
Iowa	14
Colorado	12
Virginia	8
Indiana	7
Arkansas	6
Texas	5
California	5
Vermont	4
Nebraska	3
Kansas, Massachusetts, New Hampshire	2 each
Georgia, Maine, Minnesota, South Carolina, Oregon, Oklahoma, North Carolina	1 each
	586

for the lower Mississippi valley, and Tulane University alone provided twenty-one pioneer physicians to New Mexico, doctors who most likely filtered into the region across Texas.

At first glance, the relatively small number of doctors who came to New Mexico from western medical schools might seem surprising. Splitting the country down the middle, roughly along the Ninety-fifth Parallel or the eastern borders of the Dakotas, Nebraska, Kansas, Oklahoma, and Texas, only 29 doctors of the sample of 586, about 5 percent, came from schools in the western half of the country. This reflected nothing so much as the immaturity of medical education in the West, certainly by comparison with the East and Midwest, and that region's rapid growth. The relatively few schools which existed were producing physicians for a growing local market with few graduates left over for export to places like New Mexico. It might also be noted that relatively few physicians in pioneer New Mexico came from foreign medical schools. A total of nineteen of them had earned their degrees in foreign institutions, nine from Canadian schools, and one each from colleges in Austria, Germany, the Netherlands, Ireland, England, and Scotland. Only four Hispanic doctors with degrees from Mexican medical schools came north to practice across the Rio Grande, although there were originally no special barriers of any kind to limit them.

The quality of the medical schools in which New Mexico's first regular doctors got their educations ranged across a very broad spectrum. Table 4 shows the particular institutions from which they took their degrees, and the list includes some of the most august as well as some of the shabbiest of American medical colleges. There was certainly nothing wrong with Chicago's Rush Medical College, alma mater of twenty-six New Mexico practitioners, or Jefferson Medical College of Philadelphia, which followed close behind. They were each solid, if not spectacular, schools, and major producers of medical graduates over the last half of the nineteenth century. Tulane University's medical school, number three on the list, was rather weaker, at least until its reformation around the turn of the century; but the formal instruction it offered its students, especially in its clinical facilities, was at least adequate in turning out reasonably qualified practitioners. The same cannot be said about the University of Louisville Medical Department. It alone was alma mater to twenty New Mexico physicians; but in the first decade of the twentieth century, it had absorbed four other Louisville medical schools, which together had produced another thirty doctors who practiced in territorial New Mexico. Thus, a grand total of fifty pioneer New Mexico physicians got their

Table 4
Medical Schools Attended by New Mexico Pioneer Physicians

Rush Medical College, Chicago	26
Jefferson Medical College, Philadelphia	23
Tulane University School of Medicine, New Orleans	21
University of Louisville School of Medicine	20
St. Louis College of Physicians and Surgeons	17
University of Illinois College of Medicine, Chicago	16
University Medical College of Kansas City (Mo.)	16
Louisville Medical College	15
Hospital College of Medicine, Louisville	14
Northwestern University Medical School, Chicago	14
Vanderbilt University, Nashville	13
Memphis Hospital College of Medicine	12
Missouri Medical College, St. Louis	12
Washington University (St. Louis) School of Medicine	11
Columbia University (N.Y.) College of Physicians and Surgeons	10
George Washington University School of Medicine	10
Medical College of Ohio, Cincinnati	9
University of Michigan Medical School, Ann Arbor	9
University of Maryland School of Medicine	9
Barnes Medical College, St. Louis	9
Chicago Homeopathic Medical School	9
New York University Medical College	8
University of Pennsylvania School of Medicine	8
Kentucky School of Medicine, Louisville	8
Bellevue Hospital Medical College, New York City	7
St. Louis University School of Medicine	7
Kansas City (Mo.) Medical College	7
University of Nashville Medical Department	7
Eclectic Medical College, Cincinnati	7
University of Arkansas Medical Department	6
Long Island College Hospital, Brooklyn	6
Bennett Medical College, Chicago	5
Miami Medical College, Cincinnati	5
College of Physicians and Surgeons, Keokuk (Iowa)	5
Albany (N.Y.) Medical College; University of Pittsburgh Medical Department; Marion-Sims College of Medicine, St. Louis; Hahnemann Medical College and Hospital, Chicago; Cincinnati College of Medicine and Surgery; Detroit College of Medicine and Surgery; College of Physicians and Surgeons, Baltimore; State	

Table 4, continued

University of Iowa College of Medicine; Gross Medical College, Denver; Medical College of Virginia, Richmond; University of Virginia Department of Medicine, Charlottesville; Medical College of Indiana, Indianapolis	4 each
Cornell University School of Medicine; Illinois Medical College, Chicago; Hering Medical College, Chicago; University of Tennessee Medical Department, Memphis; Lincoln Memorial University Medical Department, Knoxville; Baltimore Medical College; University of Missouri School of Medicine, Columbia; Denver and Gross Medical College, Denver; Georgetown University School of Medicine, Washington, D.C.; Beaumont Hospital Medical School, St. Louis; University of Texas Medical Department, Galveston; University of Vermont College of Medicine; University of Toronto (Canada)	3 each
University of Buffalo Medical Department; Niagara University Medical Department, Buffalo; New York Homeopathic Medical College; Hahnemann Medical College and Hospital, Philadelphia; Medico-Chirurgical College of Philadelphia; American Medical College, St. Louis; Ensworth Medical College, St. Joseph; Homeopathic Medical College of Missouri, St. Louis; Kentucky University Medical Department, Louisville; Southwestern Homeopathic Medical College and Hospital, Louisville; Ohio Medical University, Columbus; Western Reserve University School of Medicine, Cleveland; Starling Medical College, Columbus; Toledo Medical College; Columbus Medical College; Cleveland Homeopathic Medical College; University of Wooster, Medical Department, Cleveland; Michigan College of Medicine and Surgery, Detroit; Detroit Medical College; Wayne University College of Medicine, Detroit; State University of Iowa, College of Homeopathic Medicine; Keokuk Medical College, College of Physicians and Surgeons; Denver College of Medicine; University of Colorado School of Medicine; Central College of Physicians and Surgeons, Indianapolis; Howard University School of Medicine; Fort Worth School of Medicine; Cooper Medical College, San Francisco; Creighton Medical College, Omaha; Dartmouth Medical College; Harvard University Medical School; College of Physicians and Surgeons, Kansas City (Kansas); McGill University Faculty of Medicine, Montreal	2 each
48 others	1 each

medical training in Louisville. That city was one of the snake pits of American medical education, a place (in the reformer Flexner's words) "to which crude boys thronged from the plantations."[36] One resident of the city during the 1890s, a time when the place was host to a horde of twelve to fifteen hundred medical students, insisted that it was customary at the time to classify Louisville's inhabitants in four categories: white persons, colored persons, dogs, and medical students, "in descending order of social acceptability."[37] Given what is known of the extremely low quality of Louisville medical schools of the late nineteenth century, it is doubtful that many of the fifty New Mexico pioneer doctors who got their medical degrees there learned much medicine in a formal way. This is not, of course, to say that they were poorly educated, for the assiduous student might very well have learned a great deal in self-study and in informal settings, but it is pretty sure that the Louisville graduates lacked the opportunities afforded more fortunate medical students elsewhere.

The same is true for the seventeen doctors on the list who traced their medical degrees to the number-five school on the list, the St. Louis College of Physicians and Surgeons. It, too, was a grossly unsatisfactory institution, a reality scathingly depicted in the brief report that Abraham Flexner wrote on the school after a 1909 visit. In a few terse words, he so captured the essence of what the phrase "a rotten medical school" really meant that his description bears full reproduction here:

(9) St. Louis College of Physicians and Surgeons. Organized 1869. An independent institution.

Entrance requirement: Nominal.

Attendance: 224.

Teaching staff: 49, of whom 25 are professors, 24 of other grade.

Resources available for maintenance: Fees only, amounting to $16,035 (estimated).

Laboratory facilities: The school occupies a badly kept building, the inner walls covered with huge advertisements. A single ordinary laboratory is provided for chemistry; there is a make-believe laboratory for experimental physiology; for the school owns the equipment stipulated by the state board, though the dust-covered tables do not indicate use. Rows of empty reagent bottles are also to

[36]Flexner, *Medical Education in the United States and Canada,* p. 230.

[37]Hampden C. Lawson, "The Early Medical Schools of Kentucky," *Bulletin of the History of Medicine* 24 (1950):174.

> be seen. The "museum" consists of some cheap photographs and drawings and a few badly preserved wet specimens,—all carefully arranged so as to occupy as much space as possible. Microscopes appear to indicate a laboratory of pathology or bacteriology; but the "individual lockers" were empty. It was explained that "students have to bring slides, holders, and cover-glasses with them, for they furnish their own and keep them at home." Anatomy was "over"—only empty tables were found in the dissecting-room, the sole access to which is by way of a fire-escape.
>
> *Clinical facilities:* A small, poorly lighted, badly ventilated, and overcrowded hospital is part of the school building. Its operating amphitheater is good. Clinics of slight value are also held at the City Hospital. A few other opportunities of inferior importance are obtained in the usual way.
>
> A dark and dingy suite of rooms serves for a dispensary. The room devoted to gynecology, for instance, is without a window, and contains no equipment except a deal table covered with a sheet.
>
> The school is one of the worst in the country.[38]

This school—"one of the worst in the country"—was alma mater, as noted, to no fewer than seventeen New Mexico doctors, and many of their peers were graduates of institutions equally bad and even in some cases worse.

This kind of evaluation could be extended through every school on the list, but the point should already be clear. New Mexico's pioneer physicians represented the broad spectrum of American medical education at the end of the nineteenth century and the beginning of the twentieth. At any given time in the territorial period, New Mexico had a mixed bag of medical graduates, doctors from good schools and those from bad ones, but the mix was not necessarily constant throughout the period. Although there is no good statistical study of the problem, there is reason to speculate that as time passed the proportion of graduates from inferior schools may have risen as a result of the licensure problem. As suggested earlier in this chapter, graduates from weak schools facing tough state board examinations elsewhere around the country—and in a growing number of jurisdictions not even permitted to stand the examination—naturally went to those places, like New Mexico, where they could hang out their shingles with the least effort. This phenomenon was mitigated to some degree by the flow of tubercular physicians, for tuberculosis was egali-

[38]Flexner, *Medical Education in the United States and Canada*, p. 256.

tarian, striking graduates of the Johns Hopkins University School of Medicine just as readily as those of the Knoxville Medical College (a truly dreadful institution for "colored" students in Knoxville, Tennessee).

As a way of developing some perspective on the caliber of New Mexico's early physicians, this "good school–poor school" discussion would not be complete without reference to a third group: the "no-school-at-all" practitioners who played a major role in health-care delivery in territorial New Mexico. Again, there are no good statistics available, but it is clear that there were substantial numbers of them, at least in the early days of the territorial period, and that they found plenty of room for their services in New Mexico's frontier society. The information available about them is scanty, but it does suggest that they were commonplace in the medical community. For example, Henry Hoyt, an old-time doctor who flitted through New Mexico in the late 1870s, told in his autobiography of falling ill in the town of Bernalillo in 1879:

> I was suddenly stricken with some kind of fever, was put to bed, and old Dr. Carroll was called in. He at once confided in me that he was not a physician; that all he ever gave was quinine, castor oil, and native wine. This wine, of very good quality, was made each year by most of the families, from the famous Mission grapes that are found everywhere in the Rio Grande Valley. Although the good old doctor's drug supply was limited, I found him to be a splendid nurse, and I was well cared for.[39]

(Dr. Carroll's quick, forthright confession may have been inspired by his fear that his hotshot, young physician-patient would surely recognize his lack of training. At that time, Hoyt's medical education consisted of the following: country schools in rural Minnesota followed by two semesters [perhaps] at Minnesota State University [*sic*], and then "a year or so" of medical apprenticeship with a physician-uncle, a year of desultory work in a St. Paul Hospital, and "some formal study at Chicago's Rush Medical College.")[40]

Santa Fe's Dr. Francis Crosson was not unlike Dr. Carroll. He was a pillar of the Santa Fe medical community from the 1880s until 1902 and served a large practice. However, he was apparently trained via apprenticeship alone, which was, of course, not at all uncommon as late as the

[39]Henry F. Hoyt, *A Frontier Doctor* (Boston and New York: Houghton Mifflin Co., 1929), p. 141.

[40]Ibid., pp. 17ff.

1870s or 1880s. Nevertheless, in 1894, when Dr. Crosson was proposed for membership in the New Mexico Medical Society, its executive committee reported archly that "the Committee feels that both the interests of the Society as well as the future of Dr. Crosson demand that he receive a diploma from a regular medical school."[41] Twelve years earlier, at the time of the formation of the Las Vegas Medical Society, three of its charter members, it will be remembered, were "excused" from the organization when they proved unable to produce diplomas from a medical school. But perhaps the most slyly gracious statement of this reality in New Mexico medicine of the territorial period is found in George B. Anderson's 1907 *History of New Mexico,* a kind of "booster" history of the territory featuring profiles of many prominent citizens designed to flatter them and inflate sales of the book. Eager to be delicate at a time when the absence of a formal medical degree was becoming strongly unacceptable, Anderson, in writing of one prominent Lincoln County physician, came up with the following:

> Dr. Melvin G. Paden began practicing in White Oaks in 1880, although it was not until 1886 that he had thoroughly equipped himself for the profession by continued study and graduation at Louisville, Kentucky.[42]

The Carrolls, Crossons, and many others who practiced in the territory without formal education gradually disappeared from the medical landscape through the territorial period. They were most common in the earlier years, not surprisingly, and for the 99 doctors listed in *Polk's Medical and Surgical Directory* of 1886, no medical school affiliation at all could be established for 56 of them.[43] *Flint's Medical and Surgical Directory* of 1897 lists 115 doctors practicing in New Mexico, 44 of whom carry no reference to medical school graduation.[44] They were increasingly replaced at the end of the century by doctors with diplomas, including those whose diplomas were virtually worthless, first in the larger cities

[41]New Mexico Medical Society, 10th Annual Meeting, Minutes, 11 September 1894.

[42]Anderson, *History of New Mexico,* vol. 1, p. 439.

[43]*Polk's Medical and Surgical Directory of the United States* (Detroit: R. L. Polk and Co., 1886), p. 616. Some of those for whom no medical school was listed may well have had degrees which did not get registered in the data-gathering process, but that correction of the figures might well be balanced (or overbalanced) by the number who may have "exaggerated" their formal schooling.

[44]A. L. Chatterton, comp., *Flint's Medical and Surgical Directory of the United States and Canada* (New York: J. B. Flint and Co., 1897), p. 633.

Table 5
Rate of Continuity of Physicians in New Mexico, 1886–1914

1886–1897	21 of 99 M.D.s stayed in same place	21%
	5 of 99 stayed in N.M., but different place	5%
		26%
1897–1902	46 of 117 M.D.s stayed in same place	39%
	8 of 117 stayed in N.M., but different place	7%
		46%
1902–6	68 of 166 M.D.s stayed in same place	41%
	13 of 166 stayed in N.M., but different place	8%
		49%
1906–14	98 of 221 M.D.s stayed in same place	44%
	18 of 221 stayed in N.M., but different place	8%
		52%

Source: Medical directories cited in Table 1.

and towns, then in the countryside as well. Nevertheless, their contributions to the well-being of large numbers of New Mexicans of the territorial era were considerable and deserving of respect.

Two other observations regarding New Mexico's pioneer physicians ought be made here since they, too, bear on the quality of care they rendered to the New Mexico populace. One has to do with the flux or instability which characterized New Mexico's physician corps of that era. It is only a small exaggeration to speak of the pioneer doctors as a group of transients. Much of the territory's population in that era could be labeled as transient—miners, entrepreneurs, adventurers, and other on-the-move and on-the-make types—and the physicians of the frontier society were no different. Of the ninety-nine New Mexico doctors listed in that 1886 edition of *Polk's*, only twenty-one were still in the same town eleven years later; another five were still in the territory, though at a different location. This 26 percent continuity rate improved significantly as New Mexico's frontier society matured, as Table 5 indicates, but the fact remains that there was a large and rapid turnover among New Mexico doctors of the frontier era. There were certainly doctors who put down firm roots in Albuquerque or Raton, or wherever, and stayed for decades; but the typical New Mexico physician, among the 700-plus for whom concrete information exists, practiced a much briefer time in the territory, many of them for a year or two, or for a few years at best. The explanations for that fact were various, but two major factors played dominant roles in the high turnover among New Mexico's pioneer physicians. Many among them simply moved on to other, less-crowded or otherwise more attractive practice opportunities. Either New Mexico did not measure up to their expectations in some way or other, or perhaps they had never perceived it as anything more than a temporary part of their careers. For others, however, practice tenure in New Mexico was brief simply because they retired or died.

This latter observation is related to the fact that at the end of the last century and the beginning of the twentieth many doctors sought out New Mexico either because they were seeking a comfortable, sunny retirement spot or hoped to win some respite from their own personal cases of tuberculosis, or both. The figures for the period from 1906 to 1923, for example (comparable figures for the period before 1906 do not exist), show that the doctors setting up practice in New Mexico were not, by and large, brand new doctors fresh from medical school, but rather seasoned practitioners at midcareer or even well beyond. Of the 1,193 physicians licensed in that period, 532 (44.6 percent) had medical degrees more than ten years old, indicating (in most cases) extensive practice prior to coming to the territory, and another 426 (35.7 percent) possessed medical diplomas between three and ten years old. Only 194 doctors, or 16.3 percent of the total, were less than three years out of medical school, indicating that they were more or less beginners.[45]

Study of the records of the Board of Medical Examiners for the pioneer period produces many case studies of physicians newly licensed in New Mexico when they were in their fifties, sixties, and even seventies. Those files are liberally sprinkled with new licensees whose medical school days lay thirty-five, forty, or, in at least one case, forty-nine years in the past.[46] As suggested, many of those doctors were ill themselves with tuberculosis and came to New Mexico seeking the cure. Others were in

[45]New Mexico, Board of Medical Examiners, Minutes, 1906–23.

[46]New Mexico, Board of Medical Examiners, Minutes, 14 July 1920.

search of pleasant retirement or semiretirement surroundings, but, given the ease of licensure in New Mexico, got their license to practice. These older and/or ill physicians contributed significantly to the oversupply of physicians in parts of the territory, even though the practices of many of them were severely limited. Their contributions to the caliber of New Mexico medicine may be variously evaluated. With their years of experience, many of them undoubtedly provided solid, top-quality care. At the same time, it ought be noted that they had trained in the "old days," during the era before germ theory, antiseptic surgery, the birth of bacteriology, the explosive development of the biomedical sciences, and the like; thus the effectiveness of the medicine they practiced is subject to question. Even state-of-the-art medicine at the end of the nineteenth century could be of dubious value to suffering patients, and it is pretty certain that some of the old-timers did not measure up to even that.

And what of that infant medical society whose birth and early growth pains were traced in Chapter 1? Giving it the benefit of every doubt, at best it might be said that it sputtered through its first quarter-century of existence. Its fortunes rose (though never to very high levels) and fell during the time from its birth in 1886 to statehood, and the down cycles were on the whole more common and emphatic than the contrary. Indeed, at one point early in the century, the New Mexico Medical Society almost faded entirely from existence, only to be resuscitated by reorganization and the licensure wars of the early 1900s.

The problem that had so chronically afflicted the old Las Vegas Medical Society—severely limited participation—continued to plague its successor. The very first annual meeting of the New Mexico Medical Society, held in Las Vegas on 7 and 8 July 1886, proved to be a painful reminder of the society's need to expand its base of support. Some within the organization had suggested that the inaugural meeting be held in Santa Fe or Albuquerque to emphasize the transition from a local to a territory-wide sphere of operations, but the proposal had been defeated, "lest we should lack a quorum and due interest in Santa Fe or Albuquerque."[47] The Las Vegas founders of the territorial society were reluctant to entrust it to the uncertain hospitality of Santa Fe or Albuquerque, but they did make plans on a grand scale to welcome out-of-town physicians to that first annual meeting in Las Vegas. They organized comprehensive sci-

[47]New Mexico Medical Society, Minutes, 6 March 1886.

entific sessions for the edification of their guests and planned a full array of ancillary activities, including an elaborate banquet complete with swallow-tailed coats, professional musicians to entertain, and the finest fare available in the territory. They intended and worked hard to make that first annual meeting a memorable one. At the opening session, on 7 July, a grand total of ten doctors attended, all of them from the host city. They gave a wonderful party, and no one came. Their disappointment is manifest in the minutes of the meeting, one section of which reads, "On motion of Dr. Henriques the Executive Committee were instructed to avoid all extra expenses as no guests were present from out of town."[48]

It was an uninspiring start. Five months later, as the second annual meeting began to loom on the horizon, the chagrin and uncertainty of the Las Vegas group were evident in their decision "that the preparations for the annual meeting this July should consist alone in sending out postal cards to all respectable regular physicians in New Mexico inviting them to the meeting."[49] Things were little better at that second annual meeting in 1887, where total attendees numbered eleven. However, two out-of-town doctors were present: Drs. Charles B. Kohlhousen of Raton and George W. Harrison of Bernalillo, later of Albuquerque. Through the remainder of the 1880s and into the 1890s, the society remained strictly limited to Las Vegas, with a hard core of perhaps six to eight local doctors showing up for monthly meetings and maybe one or two more for the annual gathering each July. In short, the change of name from the Las Vegas Medical Society to the New Mexico Medical Society had not produced any real change in the organization, and enthusiasm within it began to wane noticeably. At the sixth annual meeting in July 1891, the growing disinterest was evident in the passage of a resolution—"As the attendance was not large, Dr. Henriques moved that the present officers just hold over until an election be held"[50]—and over the next twelve months, just one meeting was held, a desultory affair convened merely to certify delegates to that year's AMA meeting in Detroit.

The torpor of the institution was broken in 1892 with the realization, finally, that fresh blood was imperative and that to achieve this objective the society was going to have to move out of Las Vegas and into the territory at large. Reluctantly, the decision was reached to hold 1892's

[48]New Mexico Medical Society, Minutes, 7 July 1886.

[49]New Mexico Medical Society, Minutes, 7 January 1887.

[50]New Mexico Medical Society, Minutes, 8 July 1891.

annual meeting in Albuquerque during Fair Week, a time chosen in hopes of improving interest and attendance and because the railroads would offer reduced fares for that week.[51] That seventh annual meeting was a grand success. Five doctors from Las Vegas made the trip down and were joined by no fewer than nineteen other doctors, most from Albuquerque and nearby towns such as Belen, Los Lunas, and Socorro, but also from places so distant as Deming. As the first order of business, the rules of the society were suspended and all nineteen of the new attendees were immediately elected members of the society.

It could certainly be argued that the 1892 annual meeting was in reality the first for a territorywide society. The Las Vegas faithful, who believed in the organization and had kept it alive over the preceding years, were encouraged to think that it had finally reached solid footing. They had to pay a price for that success, however. At that first Albuquerque meeting, Dr. James H. Wroth of Albuquerque was elected president of the organization, the first non–Las Vegan so honored; and Dr. Wroth's motion was passed "that the annual meeting be held at Albuquerque until further change should be decided."[52] Control of the organization they had created slipped from the hands of the Las Vegas founders in 1892, but it was a price gladly paid for the obvious strengthening of the institution. After a decade of standing still, the regulars seemed finally to have established some momentum in their effort to pull together the territory's "respectable" members of the profession.

Their hopes were quickly dashed, however, when the grand success of that first Albuquerque meeting of the society turned out to be a false spring. In 1893, again in Albuquerque, the boom attendance of the preceding year was not repeated, for only twelve doctors bothered to show (six from Albuquerque, two from Las Vegas, and four others), and the third meeting in the Duke City in 1894 produced even poorer results. By 1895 the New Mexico Medical Society seemed to have lapsed back into its old groove: physically it was back in Las Vegas, and once again attendance at the annual meeting failed to top ten. As yet another sign of the organization's inactivity, the treasurer reported the expenditure of no

[51]New Mexico Medical Society, Minutes, 9 July 1892.

[52]New Mexico Medical Society, Minutes, 14 September 1892. Incidentally, the first substantive business conducted at this "revival" meeting of the society was the appointment of a new committee on medical legislation, charged with the responsibility of drafting a new medical-licensure bill for presentation to the territorial legislature.

funds whatsoever during the preceding year.[53] Two years later, almost in desperation, the motion passed unanimously that the society's dues be dropped from three dollars per year to one, "and that this one dollar annual dues be collected,"[54] but that change, too, had little effect in stimulating membership. A nadir of sorts was reached at the thirteenth annual meeting held in Las Vegas in June 1898, when only eight members showed up, and the society's president, first vice-president, and second vice-president were *not* among them.

The tottering New Mexico Medical Society was saved from almost total oblivion by the revival of the medical-licensure question in the first years of the new century and by the immigration during that period of so many new doctors to the territory. These were developments that called for a strong response from the physicians already practicing in New Mexico, and the urgency of the situation prompted them to look to their medical society for organization and leadership in the effort to cope with the rapidly changing medical environment. In late 1904, an organizational transformation took place within the society with adoption of a new constitution and bylaws patterned on those of the better-established state societies in the East. The institution's old town-meeting style of operation, with the annually elected officers in full charge of day-to-day operations of the society, was replaced by the representative style of governance that is essentially still in place today. A House of Delegates was established by the new constitution to serve as the legislative body of the organization, and a Council was created to act as a kind of executive committee to oversee on a continuous basis the business and activities of the society. County societies were linked tightly to the central organization in the new constitution, and the new structure prepared the society organizationally for much more efficient operation.[55]

Although that constitutional reform was critical to the future success and prospects of the society, at least as important was the decision during that 1904–5 period of reform or revival to publish a medical periodical,

[53]New Mexico Medical Society, 10th Annual Meeting, Minutes, 10 July 1895. The 1895 meeting did distinguish itself, however, by its election—apparently with no controversy whatsoever—of its first woman member, Dr. Alice H. Rice of East Las Vegas.

[54]New Mexico Medical Society, 12th Annual Meeting, Minutes, 12 May 1897.

[55]For a copy of that new constitution, as modified slightly over the first few years of its existence, see *New Mexico Medical Journal* 8 (1911–12):303–12.

the *New Mexico Medical Journal*.[56] The new publication, one of the pioneer medical journals of the West, was a pivotal part of the overall effort to breathe some life into the society. It was designed to increase communication within the medical community and to serve as corporate voice of its sponsoring institution, but just as importantly it was hoped the new *Journal* would stimulate corporate consciousness and esprit de corps in the ranks of New Mexico's doctors. It was also intended that the new publication would underscore the weight and dignity of the parent organization and raise its public visibility.

For twelve years the tiny journal, edited for most of that time by the energetic Dr. Robert E. McBride of Las Cruces, rolled off the presses, carrying various kinds of news to its two or three hundred subscribers. It printed heated editorials and general-information pieces on the prominent professional questions of the times—medical licensure; the "perils" posed by Christian Science practitioners, osteopaths, and patent medicines; the shabby treatment (financially) of professional witnesses in the courts of the territory; and the like. Every issue included organizational news as well, such as the minutes of the annual meetings of the society, committee reports, and news of component county societies of the organization. Most issues also contained gossipy personal notes of interest regarding the activities, professional and otherwise, of the doctors of the territory, plus advertisements to bring in revenue and to help keep readers abreast of the latest things in the field. (See Plates 1 and 2.) Most interesting of all to modern readers, and presumably useful to its contemporary subscribers, are the clinicial reports and essays contained in each issue of the publication. Some titles may suggest the range and variety of those contributions: "Gastro-Enteric Intoxication in the New-Born," by Dr. J. R. Gilbert of Alamogordo; "Feeding in Typhoid," by Santa Fe's Dr. J. A. Rolls; "Care of the Stomach in Tuberculosis," by Dr. S. G. Sewell of Albuquerque; and "The Catholic Doctrine on Interruption of Pregnancy," by Dr. W. R. Tipton, Las Vegas. These case reports and essays provide extraordinary insight into the practice, thinking, and problems of the early twentieth-century practitioner, and may surprise the modern reader: they

[56]Originally entitled *The Journal of the New Mexico Medical Association* (for a brief while in 1904–5 the "Society" became the "Association"), the first issue appeared in June 1905. It was published without interruption, first as a quarterly, then as a bimonthly, and finally as a monthly, until its absorption by the newly created *Southwestern Medicine* in 1917.

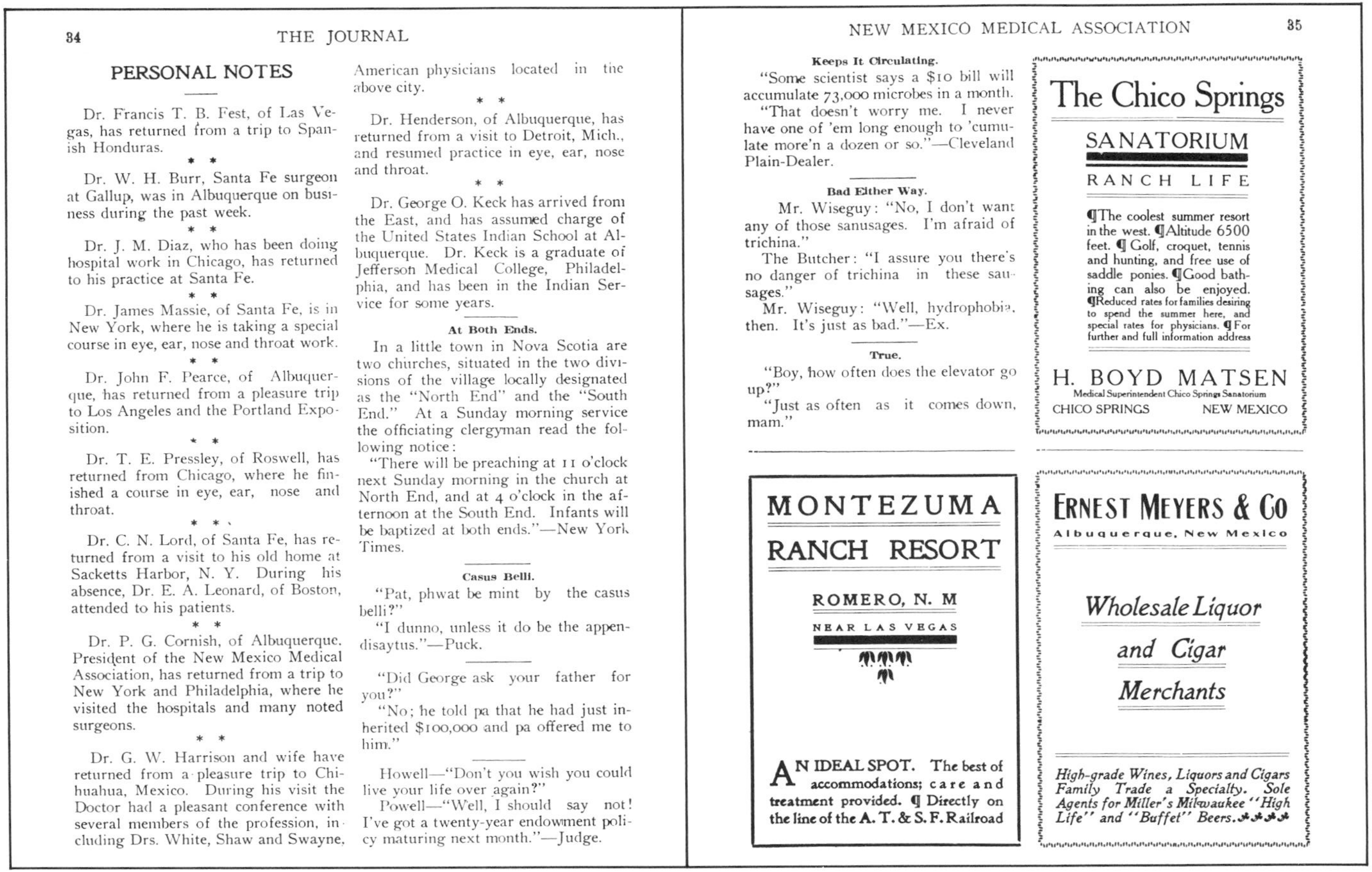

34 THE JOURNAL

PERSONAL NOTES

Dr. Francis T. B. Fest, of Las Vegas, has returned from a trip to Spanish Honduras.

* *

Dr. W. H. Burr, Santa Fe surgeon at Gallup, was in Albuquerque on business during the past week.

* *

Dr. J. M. Diaz, who has been doing hospital work in Chicago, has returned to his practice at Santa Fe.

* *

Dr. James Massie, of Santa Fe, is in New York, where he is taking a special course in eye, ear, nose and throat work.

* *

Dr. John F. Pearce, of Albuquerque, has returned from a pleasure trip to Los Angeles and the Portland Exposition.

* *

Dr. T. E. Pressley, of Roswell, has returned from Chicago, where he finished a course in eye, ear, nose and throat.

* *

Dr. C. N. Lord, of Santa Fe, has returned from a visit to his old home at Sacketts Harbor, N. Y. During his absence, Dr. E. A. Leonard, of Boston, attended to his patients.

* *

Dr. P. G. Cornish, of Albuquerque, President of the New Mexico Medical Association, has returned from a trip to New York and Philadelphia, where he visited the hospitals and many noted surgeons.

* *

Dr. G. W. Harrison and wife have returned from a pleasure trip to Chihuahua, Mexico. During his visit the Doctor had a pleasant conference with several members of the profession, including Drs. White, Shaw and Swayne, American physicians located in the above city.

* *

Dr. Henderson, of Albuquerque, has returned from a visit to Detroit, Mich., and resumed practice in eye, ear, nose and throat.

* *

Dr. George O. Keck has arrived from the East, and has assumed charge of the United States Indian School at Albuquerque. Dr. Keck is a graduate of Jefferson Medical College, Philadelphia, and has been in the Indian Service for some years.

At Both Ends.

In a little town in Nova Scotia are two churches, situated in the two divisions of the village locally designated as the "North End" and the "South End." At a Sunday morning service the officiating clergyman read the following notice:

"There will be preaching at 11 o'clock next Sunday morning in the church at North End, and at 4 o'clock in the afternoon at the South End. Infants will be baptized at both ends."—New York Times.

Casus Belli.

"Pat, phwat be mint by the casus belli?"

"I dunno, unless it do be the appendisaytus."—Puck.

"Did George ask your father for you?"

"No; he told pa that he had just inherited $100,000 and pa offered me to him."

Howell—"Don't you wish you could live your life over again?"

Powell—"Well, I should say not! I've got a twenty-year endowment policy maturing next month."—Judge.

NEW MEXICO MEDICAL ASSOCIATION 35

Keeps It Circulating.

"Some scientist says a $10 bill will accumulate 73,000 microbes in a month.

"That doesn't worry me. I never have one of 'em long enough to 'cumulate more'n a dozen or so."—Cleveland Plain-Dealer.

Bad Either Way.

Mr. Wiseguy: "No, I don't want any of those sanusages. I'm afraid of trichina."

The Butcher: "I assure you there's no danger of trichina in these sausages."

Mr. Wiseguy: "Well, hydrophobia, then. It's just as bad."—Ex.

True.

"Boy, how often does the elevator go up?"

"Just as often as it comes down, mam."

Plate 1. Pages from the *New Mexico Medical Journal,* including some advertisement for sanatoria.

Plate 2. Pages with advertisements from the *New Mexico Medical Journal.*

are far more often testimonials to the skills and sophistication of the old-time doctors than evidence to the contrary.

If the birth and success of the *New Mexico Medical Journal* contributed enormously to the revitalization of the Territorial Medical Society in the first two decades of the century, so too did the foundation of county societies across the territory in the 1890s and early 1900s. Beginning with the Bernalillo County Medical Society, founded in 1893–94,[57] county organizations cropped up all across New Mexico. They were small—usually no larger than a dozen or so members—and sporadic in their operations, but they were positive and lively additions to the medical landscape. The impression is strong that county societies were more important and meaningful to many, perhaps most, pioneer physicians than the more distant Territorial Medical Society. The local county society was the most convenient and comfortable place to share information, to iron out professional and personal disagreements, and to unwind among peers. The scale of the county groups meant that they could cater more immediately and directly to the interests and needs of their members, and as a result, they were far more "personal" institutions than the territorial one. As one homespun example, the newly founded Santa Fe County Medical Society chose to meet in 1909 "on the first Thursday of the month or before the full of the moon" to make easier attendance by doctors in outlying places like Golden or Cerrillos who would have to drive into Santa Fe by team.[58] The intimacy of the county organizations also led to difficulties, of course. Two brief references, selected from the pages of the *New Mexico Medical Journal,* illustrate the point. The April 1910 issue included a report on the good progress of the Chaves County Society—"The Chaves County Medical Society is now, since ridding itself of all disturbing elements, doing good and scientific work in peace and harmony"[59]—and a 1909 report from Luna County testifies to the apparently spirited internal life of the county oganizations:

> The Luna County Medical Society is in excellent condition. Our field is not large, we are few in number, but a most fraternal feeling exists for each other. We can

[57]New Mexico Medical Society, 9th Annual Meeting, Minutes, 11 September 1894; Adler, "Biography of a Society":36.

[58]Santa Fe County Medical Society, Minutes, 27 March 1909; *Southwestern Medicine* 10 (1926):77.

[59]*New Mexico Medical Journal* 5 (1909–10):182.

boast of having had no troubles or friction during the existence of the Society. So may it ever be. What other medical society can boast of the same?[60]

The stronger organizational structure created by the new constitution in 1904, the birth of the *New Mexico Medical Journal,* and the elaboration of the county societies all combined to produce a much stronger Territorial Medical Society by the time of statehood in 1912. Membership statistics attest to this. As late as 1905, the New Mexico Medical Society had only 76 members, not many of them active, but the number swelled steadily thereafter as did member participation in the organization. By 1914 the society had 153 "members-in-good-standing"—that is, those who had paid their dues—and another 50 to 75 who were on the rolls but were temporarily derelict in squaring their accounts.[61] This doubling of membership in less than a decade was noteworthy, but it ought be remembered that this was the time of large-scale physician immigration to New Mexico. The point is that the roughly 200 members of the New Mexico Medical Society in 1914 probably represented no more than 50 percent of the eligible physicians in the new state. That was a fact of life which continued to worry those who committed their energies to making the society work. The pages of the *New Mexico Medical Journal* were filled with editorials and essays stressing the necessity for energetic recruitment of all eligible doctors in New Mexico. Some of those pieces could become quite heated and even intemperate:

Every practitioner in New Mexico ought to belong to us. It is an honor to belong to the affiliated societies. It is a sign of good standing. Not always, but as a rule, whenever a man refuses to join, keeps himself aloft [*sic*] of his fellow practitioners,

[60]*New Mexico Medical Journal* 4 (1908–9):24.

[61]*New Mexico Medical Journal* 12 (1913–14):5–8. The distribution of those 153 members was:

Bernalillo County Medical Society	42
Chaves County Medical Society	16
Doña Ana County Medical Society	9
Las Vegas Medical Society	16
Luna County Medical Society	12
Santa Fe County Medical Society	16
Quay County Medical Society	8
Otero County Medical Society	8
Grant County Medical Society	17
Not affiliated with any county society	9

has no desire to improve himself with and through them, there is a nigger in the woodpile somewhere. As a rule the nigger is in the very man's heart.[62]

At the height of the physician influx of the first decade of the new century, the New Mexico Medical Society's House of Delegates hoped to do something about the recruitment problem by hiring a professional executive to recruit as well as organize and administer the society's affairs. The plan was to pay this official by making the society's annual banquet a subscription affair with the funds received used to pay the salary of the Organizer (such was the bland title selected for him). That proposal passed the House of Delegates and the society's General Session at the 1908 annual meeting, but for whatever reason it was never implemented.[63] It was to be another forty years before the society finally got around to hiring a professional manager.

As the society grew in size and strength in the early years of the century, its annual meetings finally began to take on some real significance. On the eve of statehood in 1911, the last annual meeting of the Territorial Medical Society (held, appropriately, in Las Vegas) drew 51 registrants, two-thirds of whom came from outside the host city, plus another dozen or so who informally participated in one component or another of the meeting's program. One explanation for the growing size and success of these annual gatherings was the decision to shake loose from the society's narrow Albuquerque–Las Vegas axis and to move the annual meetings around the territory. Roswell, Taos, Gallup, and Las Cruces, among others, were selected to host the annual conclave, even though the still primitive nature of transportation in New Mexico sometimes made such divergence from the center of the territory difficult. As examples, when the society in 1909 made its first visit to the southeast to meet in Roswell, it was felt expedient to wangle special discount fares from the railroads to encourage attendance; and for those progressive members of the organization eager to try their new horseless carriages, the *New Mexico Medical Journal* announced that "permission to use the private automobile road between Torrance and Roswell had also been secured . . . but the management requests that, should the road be wet, the mailcar leaving Torrance at 5:30 A.M. be allowed to pilot the private cars to Roswell."[64]

[62]*New Mexico Medical Journal* 5 (1909–10):231.
[63]*New Mexico Medical Journal* 4 (1908–9):4.
[64]*New Mexico Medical Journal* 5 (1909–10):3.

Movement away from the comfortable and familiar presented all kinds of unexpected difficulties. Two years prior to the Roswell convention, when the annual meeting had first been held in Las Cruces, the opening of the House of Delegates meeting and the society's General Session itself had been delayed several hours "by the tardiness of the train bearing the president and several members."[65]

Despite the logistical problems involved, it is certain that the society's travels around the territory paid handsome public relations benefits and helped to free the organization from the suspicion that it was exclusively an Albuquerque–Las Vegas institution. It was also an opportunity for doctors to get away from their practices and familiar surroundings for a few days and enjoy the fellowship of their colleagues. Then, as now, for some hardworking physicians the annual meeting was a chance to let their hair down and relax a bit. A report from the 1909 meeting in Roswell charmingly made that point clear:

> After the masses had gone to bed, after the mass had sifted down by the survival of the fittest, a conclave was held and some scientific tests were made regarding the vibrations of the eardrums of the natives. They stood the pressure well and we have all reason to assure the world that the citizens of Roswell are a peace-loving community and not easily disturbed after reaching once the post-somnolent stage. Sonorous sonorificity at the soniferous cult of Bacchus seems to increase the condition.[66]

It was clear that many among the Roswell conventioneers had enjoyed themselves and their fellows, and their apparent boisterousness reflected the spirit of the newly reinvigorated society. After tenuous beginnings, by the time of statehood in 1912 the New Mexico Medical Society was becoming an imposing and increasingly vigorous institution. Few of the Las Vegas pioneers from thirty years earlier were still around, but their spirit, especially their commitment to high professional standards, still animated the institution they had created.

No account of New Mexico's pioneer physicians, even one so broad and general as this, could pretend to be adequate without some effort to sketch at least the general lines of their workaday world. Unfortunately, very little information remains to us of those first New Mexico doctors

[65]*New Mexico Medical Journal* 3 (1907–8):6.
[66]*New Mexico Medical Journal* 5 (1909–10):1.

of medicine, either as individuals or as practitioners. For even the most prominent among them, few records exist beyond basic biographical materials, some usually quite limited scraps of personal information and "color," and perhaps an encomium or two. For the average New Mexico practitioner of those early days, a few bare lines on a notecard are commonly all that survive. However, from the scattered materials available, especially their own testimony as presented in the pages of the *New Mexico Medical Journal* and the minutes of their territorial and local medical societies, we can reconstruct something of their character and the essentials of their practice of medicine.

They were, first of all, a hardy breed physically, for the practice of medicine in frontier New Mexico absolutely required it. The really good ones among them were on the move day and night, whenever duty called. Often called upon to travel long distances over the most primitive roads and trails, their practice placed a premium on physical stamina. Of course, there were a number of them, especially the "lunger" physicians of the turn of the century and afterward, who necessarily established limited practices; for most of New Mexico's pioneer doctors, however, the physical demands of everyday practice were enormous. Much of that pressure stemmed directly from the long days and nights they worked, and a major part of that reality was the traveling required in the course of practicing medicine. Early in the territorial period, when physicians were scattered across broad expanses, it was not uncommon for a frontier doctor to bounce—by buggy or horseback—more than a hundred miles to make a call. Dr. Howard Thompson, who practiced some years in Mescalero, New Mexico, before moving on to city practice in El Paso, recalled years later having traveled more than 200 miles in one case, to attend a rancher's wife in confinement, and 140 miles in another, to take care of a young man with peritonitis. Trips on horseback of 50 miles or more were too common to elicit any special mention.[67] Even as late as the early days of the twentieth century, such treks remained a part of the service of many country doctors. Dr. L. H. Pate, longtime and much-beloved general practitioner in Carlsbad, traveled by buggy into the tough ranch country east of town for more than a hundred miles to tend sick patients. The round trip required five days, and the doctor charged a total of sixty-five dol-

[67]Howard Thompson (M.D.), "Pioneer Practice in the Southwest," *Southwestern Medicine* 1 (1917):47.

lars.[68] Very often, given the distances traveled, the doctor arrived "only in time to tell what the man died of."[69] Drs. Jacob S. and George S. Easterday, brothers practicing in Albuquerque in the 1890s, were famous for their iron constitutions, which made it possible for them "to work in the town all day and country all night."[70] In addition to the Easterday brothers, Albuquerque around the turn of the century had its "Four Horsemen"—Drs. Walter G. Hope, John F. Pearce, James H. Wroth, and P. G. Cornish, Sr.—so-called because one or another of them could always be seen dashing around the town or countryside in their buggies.[71] In a brief article written in 1913, Dr. Hope vividly captured the essence of country house calls:

> In those days there were practically no physicians in the country within 100 miles of Albuquerque, the profession here did all the practice within this radius and a consultation practice far beyond this distance. No blizzard of sand or snow, or other storm was too severe to prevent those then young men from facing it across valley, mesa, and over mountains when the appeal came. There was no cut-off nor Santa Fe Central, no automobiles, no hospitals, no trained nurses. It was just get a pole team at Trimble's, button up your ulster, and try to follow the trail. If you lost your trail in the darkness, draw the drapery of your Navajo blankets around you and wait for daylight to guide you back. How good the electric lights on Central Avenue looked to us, say from University Hill, at two o'clock in the morning after an eighty to one hundred mile drive over Rocky mountains to San Pedro, Chilili, or Ponto de Aqua [*sic*]. With what relish the ready order meal at Sturges' or Zeigers' was eaten, when the team was stabled, and with cramped limbs we arrived at those havens.[72]

[68]*Pageant of Progress, The Carlsbad Story* (Carlsbad, N.M.: n.p., n.d. [1972]), p. 25. Dr. Catherine Armstrong-Seward, who has invested almost forty years of practice in Carlsbad, recalls seeing the elderly Dr. Pate making a house call in the poorest part of town on the day before he died in 1953. "He was deaf as a post then," she remembered, "but I can still see him solemnly and with great dignity pulling out his stethoscope and putting it up to his ears, though I can't imagine he heard a thing." Dr. Catherine Armstrong-Seward, interview with author, Carlsbad, N.M., 13 March 1985.

[69]*Southwestern Medicine* 1 (1917):42. This doctor also observed that consultation was unusual, "for the patient usually died before the second doctor could be fetched." (ibid.:43.)

[70]Walter G. Hope (M.D.), "Reminiscences of Medical Men and Matters in Albuquerque," *New Mexico Medical Journal* 10 (1913–14):156.

[71]Mrs. Myrl Hope Sisk, interview with author, Albuquerque, N.M., 4 April 1984. Mrs. Sisk, daughter of Dr. Hope, was eighty-eight years old at the time of the interview and could remember going on calls with her father and holding his horse for him.

[72]Hope, "Reminiscences":157.

There was, of course, danger associated with those cross-country mercy calls. Dr. George Easterday was thrown from his buggy on one such trip and sustained a fractured femur, and respiratory problems from exposure and assorted scrapes and bruises all too often were simply occupational hazards.[73] Also, long-distance journeys through country sometimes only tenuously "civilized" required prudent men to take precautions. Dr. Thompson of Mescalero carried a Colt .45 revolver, "sawed off," and a belt full of cartridges on his horseback pilgrimages through the rough Lincoln County countryside, with that heavy auxiliary medical appliance dangling from the horn of the saddle.[74] The same kind of preparation was exercised by young Dr. William Randolph Lovelace—later famous as the founder of the Albuquerque clinic named after him—when he began his New Mexico tenure in 1906 as a country doctor in Fort Sumner. Years after his country-doctor experience, he remembered the Iver Johnson revolver, which he had purchased for $2.50 in St. Louis before heading off to the wilds of New Mexico, as "a comforting possession" on his long buggy rides through the Pecos Valley countryside.[75]

But the strain imposed on the pioneer physicians was just as much, or more, psychic as physical. On a country house call a doctor was usually entirely on his own, for miles separated him from any kind of advice or support. In the cities and towns the opportunity to consult with colleagues or to resort to rudimentary hospitals existed, but even there a difficult home delivery by gaslight in the dead of the night could be a daunting prospect. Sometimes the pressure simply became too much to bear. The minutes of the New Mexico Medical Society meeting in Las Vegas in 1889 laconically report one such case:

> Dr. Tipton reported a case of transverse presentation, arm and funis in vagina, the first medical attendant having fled in dismay, the second having remained in same state, while Dr. Tipton—the child being dead—removed the arm and delivered.[76]

Nerves sometimes cracked, but more often the old-time physician simply reached down inside himself and summoned all the courage he could

[73]Ibid.

[74]Thompson, "Pioneer Practice in the Southwest":47.

[75]Lovelace Medical Foundation for Medical Education and Research, Board of Trustees, Minutes, 25 September 1947.

[76]New Mexico Medical Society, Minutes, 2 February 1889.

muster, and usually, even in the worst of circumstances, it was enough. Dr. J. H. Laws, a country doctor in Lincoln from 1901 until his relocation in El Paso in 1918, was illustrative of the breed. His account of the treatment of a particularly tough and cantankerous old man whom he had first treated some time earlier for a hip fracture—for which he had not been paid—is lengthy, but it captures graphically the tension and primitiveness of pioneer practice:

About one year later [after treatment for the hip fracture], about ten o'clock at night, a young Dr. S. telephoned, stating that he had a case of strangulated hernia in the person of Uncle Thomas H., that reduction under anaesthetic had been impossible and that there was stercoracious vomiting. Notwithstanding the natural inclination to send word to Uncle Tom to go straight to a certain hot place, beginning with a capital H., Dr. S. was informed that under the circumstances help could not be refused a brother physician. A twenty-five mile trip at night over mountain roads, an operation on an old man addicted to drink, in a two room log house, with no skilled assistance, was not a very cheerful prospect; nevertheless duty called. A folding operating table, and a suitcase of sterilized dressings, kept in readiness for such emergencies, were loaded in and Uncle Tom's bedside reached about one o'clock at night. Neighbors rustled a large store lamp and managed to fasten it to the building-paper covered ceiling. Instruments were boiled over a small cook stove, Dr. S. gave the anaesthetic, and with the assistance of a medical student the writer began dissection over inguinal hernia. On opening the hernial sack the strangulated loop of intestines was black and the hernial sack filled with prune-colored fluid. Having relieved the constricting rings with successive nicks of the bistoury, hot towels were applied to the strangulated loop for a few minutes and perceiving a slight return of color, resection was considered unnecessary, and the loop of intestines was returned to the abdomen. While dissecting out a portion of the hernial sack, Dr. S. became more interested in the operation than in noticing the anaesthetic and Old Tom stopped breathing.

This necessitated in lowering the patient's head and in the operator performing artificial respiration. While performing artificial respiration, the wife and friends entered, took one look and left with loud lamentations. Finally respiration was restored, but the chain of asepsis attempted was broken. Fortunately an extra pair of gloves had been boiled and were available, so that operation for radical cure of hernia was finally completed, sewing tissues layer by layer, closing without drainage. Patient was returned to bed. He soon began to come out from under the anaesthetic. Wife and friends entered the room with renewed hope, to let out one wild shriek that the house was on fire, the heat of the lamp having set fire to the building-paper of the ceiling. Despite the fact that Uncle Tom was instructed to remain in bed for at least ten days, Dr. S. found him sitting on the door step of his cabin on the third day. However, union was perfect and cure of hernia absolute.[77]

This vignette from country practice suggests much about the requirements for success (or even survival) in that tough arena. In addition to physical stamina and good nerves, resourcefulness was a critical attribute of the pioneer physician, for he lacked most of the adjuncts—reliable, effective drugs; good equipment; clean, well-lighted facilities; trained technical help—which play so large a part in modern practice. The store lamp crudely fastened to the ceiling in Uncle Tom H.'s cabin did its job nicely before beginning to burn a little too brightly, and the sterilizing pan on the small cookstove worked effectively, too. Though Dr. Laws apparently worked on a portable operating table, the kitchen table served that purpose for most frontier surgeries. The procedure was well established: First came a quick scrubdown with soap and bichloride, and the table was fitted with a blanket or quilt to provide a modicum of comfort. Next came a clean oilcloth, brought along by the doctor; a clean sheet; and the surgeon was in business.[78] The same kind of rough-and-ready resourcefulness was reflected in the trauma work of Bernalillo's Dr. Hoyt, who would ride to some outlying ranch, or sheep or cow camp, find a fractured arm or leg, and "with absolutely none of the ordinary materials available that I could use as splints, I would order a panful of adobe mud and use it exactly as we use plaster of Paris and had fine results."[79]

The pioneer doctors also needed resourcefulness and imagination in searching for and using medications to ease their patients' ills. While possessing very few drugs of proven effectiveness and safety (by modern standards), they did the best they could within their limitations. Castor oil and calomel were among the basic standbys of their armamentarium

[77]J. H. Laws (M.D.), "Observations of a Country Physician," *New Mexico Medical Journal* 13 (1914–15):90–91.

[78]J. S. Perkins (M.D.), "How to Do Clean Surgery at Small Cost," *Transactions of the Rocky Mountain Inter-State Medical Association,* 3d Annual Meeting (1901), p. 122. Dr. Carroll Womack, longtime general surgeon in Artesia and Carlsbad and Veterans Administration physician in Albuquerque, remembered doing surgery on kitchen tables in the environs of Artesia as late as the 1930s. His strongest memory regarding practical arrangements was of making sure that the patient's head was kept as far as possible from the stove, for the dripping of ether anesthetic in such circumstances could literally prove to be a matter of playing with fire! Dr. Carroll Womack, interview with author, Carlsbad, N.M., 12 March 1985.

[79]Hoyt, *Frontier Doctor,* p. 144.

and were used liberally in purging the system.[80] Mercury drugs, little improved since their introduction by Paracelsus in the sixteenth century, were used for everything from diphtheria to dysentery. Tartar emetic, ipecac, opium, copper and iron salts, and turpentine, among others, played prominent roles in the prescriptions they wrote (and very often filled from their own bags). Whiskey, which found a large number of medicinal applications, was employed predominantly as an antiseptic, but could also be used as a crude anesthetic or to steady the doctor's nerves.[81] Dr. Laws of Lincoln, confronted with a teenage boy in convulsions from eating something poisonous, saved his patient by injecting two ounces of whiskey beneath the skin and administering ether.[82] Whiskey was also considered useful in cases of diphtheria, although the exact mechanism of its workings was vague. For his nine- and ten-year-old diphtheria patients in Las Vegas, Dr. William H. Page recommended as much as a pint of one-hundred-proof spirits in a twelve-hour span, for he thought the spirits "were destructive to the existence of the germ."[83] The liberality of Santa Fe doctors in prescribing whiskey, especially on Sundays when regular commercial sales were forbidden, brought charges of unethical behavior, a canard indignantly rejected by resolution of the Santa Fe County Medical Society.[84]

Some among the pioneer doctors invented their own medicines, and particularly successful ones eventually claimed widespread folk renown. The potency and all-around utility of Dr. Chester Russell's "brown drops," the ingredients of which remained known only to him, were legendary in the farm country around Artesia.[85] Years after the death of Dr. Lysander Black of Carlsbad, residents continued to call at the druggists' emporiums for Dr. Black's Remedy No. 1 or No. 2, as well as other potions.[86] The

[80]For an affectionate portrait of one of the pioneer doctors who believed firmly in castor oil, calomel, and other medications, see Alice Bullock, "Memories of Doc Hobbs," *Impact* (*Albuquerque Journal Magazine*) 4, no. 9 (1980):10–11. When young Dr. I. J. Marshall set up his practice in Roswell in 1933, calomel was still king of the medicine satchel for many old doctors of the area. Dr. I. J. Marshall, interview with author, Roswell, N.M., 15 August 1983.

[81]Richard Dunlop, *Doctors of the American Frontier* (Garden City, N.Y.: Doubleday and Co., 1965), *passim*.

[82]Laws, "Observations of a Country Physician":89.

[83]Las Vegas Medical Society, Minutes, 21 February 1885.

[84]Santa Fe County Medical Society, Minutes, 26 May 1910.

[85]Dr. Pardue Bunch, interview with author, Artesia, N.M., 4 June 1984.

[86]*Pageant of Progress, The Carlsbad Story*, p. 25.

forced inventiveness of the pioneer doctors and the casualness of their pharmacy are encapsulated in the following story told by Alamogordo's Dr. J. R. Gilbert. In the summer of 1909, Dr. Gilbert treated a young man whose hand had been terribly mangled in a rifle accident. Sepsis had set in, and despite Dr. Gilbert's use of conventional antiseptics the infection began to spread:

> Temperature went to 105 and patient raving with pain and fever. . . . the swelling and redness progressed until it had reached the insertion of the deltoid. The septic condition of my patient was becoming very alarming. . . .
>
> I announced to patient and family that I would go over to the drug store and fix some medicine with which to dress the arm, without the least idea as to what that medicine would be. I went gazing about through the prescription case for inspiration [when] my eyes happened to catch the guaiacol and ichthyol bottles at the same glance, so I decided to mix the two, which was done and then glycerine appealed to me as a suitable menstrum, so. . . .[87]

It need not be said, but Dr. Gilbert's patient, of course, quickly got well.

Stories like this one ought not leave the reader with the impression that New Mexico's early doctors were exclusively empirics or just primitives insofar as their drug therapy was concerned. Their case reports, published in their own medical journal, make it clear that they as a group were fully attuned to the strengths and weaknesses of the pharmacopoeia of their day and the developments within it. For example, as early as December 1910, a country doctor in Las Cruces was publishing a paean of praise to salvarsan, Paul Ehrlich's "magic-bullet" treatment for syphilis, which had been announced to the world only a few months before;[88] the speed suggests the keenness with which New Mexico's frontier doctors—some of them, at least—kept up with developments in that field.

If the drug arsenal of New Mexico's pioneer physicians was limited in its range and questionable in its reliability and effectiveness, so, too, did the hospitals of territorial New Mexico give only limited assistance and support to its early-day doctors. The territory's larger cities—Albuquerque, Santa Fe, Las Vegas, and Roswell—had, for the times, adequate general hospitals, most of them built around the turn of the century, but

[87] J. R. Gilbert (M.D.), "Some Experience with Guaiacol and Ichthyol as a Local Antiseptic," *New Mexico Medical Journal* 6 (1911):274.

[88] Troy C. Sexton (M.D.), communication in ibid.:47–48. See, also, Henry Ingals (M.D.) [Roswell], "606," *New Mexico Medical Journal* 7 (1911):3–4.

beyond those few, hospital facilities were primitive to nonexistent. In Carlsbad, for instance, when the good ladies of the Literary Club decided in 1897 to focus on health care instead of literary pursuits, they discovered that facilities in the town for the care of the sick were sorely limited. Broadly speaking, there were four options: (1) patients could go as paying guests to the Hagerman Hotel for forty dollars a month, and friends could call and wait on them; (2) the sick could remain at home under family care, by far the most common thing; (3) the Railroad Hospital (three rooms), built by and for the use of the Pecos Valley Railroad, would admit private patients if it had room; and (4) the patient could become an honored inmate of the jail under the sheriff's care, presumably the least-favored option.[89]

Private physicians very often sought to fill the gap by developing small "hospitals," usually six to eight beds or smaller, in private homes or even in rooms adjacent to their own homes or offices; such facilities, however, were in reality little different from home care. But it ought not to be assumed from this description that New Mexico's hospitals were especially "backward" for the times, for it must be remembered that before the twentieth century hospitals all over American were very narrow institutions. They were fundamentally concerned with protecting the healthy public outside their walls—hence the establishment of "pest-houses" in Albuquerque and Las Vegas at the time of an outbreak of smallpox in 1882—rather than serving as places for the constructive treatment of the unwanted or the mentally, contagiously, or incurably ill who were confined within them. Only recently have hospitals become houses of healing instead of houses of dying, and certainly the New Mexico doctors of the territorial period were little aided by them.[90]

Given the frailty of the drug weapons available to New Mexico's pioneer doctors; the frequent casualness of their educational preparation for the life-and-death business of medicine; the primitive conditions under which they commonly had to work; and the physical weariness that was so inescapably a part of medical practice in territorial New Mexico, it is, after all, the raw courage, the nerves, of the old-time physicians which most impressively characterizes them. That courage or equanimity in the

[89]Delia Jenkins Clayton, "Pioneer Hospitals of Eddy County," in *Eddy County, New Mexico, to 1981* (Carlsbad, N.M.: Southeastern New Mexico Historical Society, 1982), p. 112.

[90]For the special-use hospitals called "sanatoria," designed specifically for the cure of tuberculosis victims, see Chapter 4.

face of great challenges and frequent defeats is strikingly manifest in a report presented in February 1885, by Dr. William R. Tipton to his colleagues of the Las Vegas Medical Society. Las Vegas and the country surrounding it were in the throes of a severe, midwinter diphtheria epidemic at that time; and in his report Dr. Tipton calmly, unemotionally, and with scientific exactness described his experiences with it:

> Gentlemen of the Society, since the last regular meeting I have had some experience in the treatment of diphtheria. On 3rd of last month I was called to Watrous, New Mexico. Patient nine years old under treatment of another physician. Upon consultation I performed the operation of tracheotomy, removed some membrane. Patient's breathing much relieved. Left patient in care of physician. Upon neglect of physician removing tube and cleaning it (from timidity or otherwise), found a new membrane formed, difficult respiration which continued until midnight and patient died.
>
> Case 2. Was called to bedside on Saturday. Found difficult respiration and suppression of urine. On introduction of catheter, no urine was found in bladder. Performed tracheotomy; breathing very difficult; death in about 24 hours.
> Case 2 in second family [Case 3], about a five-year-old. Operated tracheotomy; lamp went out, cut the jugular vein. Operated under difficulties taking about 1/2 hour. Insertion of catheter, found no urine; spasms, died in about 12 hours. Last two cases died of diphtheritic nephritis.
>
> Case 4, found a few patches on throat; could not decide its being diphtheritic membrane. Was called again and found a complete membrane. Operated tracheotomy. While operating membrane formed a coagulum of blood. Used alkaline solutions, bi-tartrate of pottassium and bi-carbonate of soda, etc. Membrane became detached, reformed. Patient lived about 48 hours.
>
> After this I changed theory in treatment of the disease.[91]

(Tipton essentially had concluded that he simply needed to operate earlier, before the patient weakened too much.)

What motivated and sustained New Mexico's pioneer doctors in the face of horrors such as these? It surely was not money, for there is ample evidence that no physicians got rich in territorial New Mexico through the practice of medicine alone. In fact, early in the period it was difficult for a doctor simply to make a living. In the late 1870s and early 1880s, frontier doctor Edwin Hoyt shifted back and forth from "doctoring" to

[91] Las Vegas Medical Society, Minutes, 21 February 1885.

bartending, to punching cows, to working as an assistant postmaster—all as market conditions dictated.[92] While practicing medicine, he found himself most of the time (in his words) "in that financial condition commonly known as flat broke."[93] Carlsbad's Dr. Black worked as a blacksmith at the Dog Canyon copper mine when he first came to New Mexico, and only when the mine shut down did he hesitantly turn to doctoring.[94] In the 1870s, Dr. John Symington arrived in Albuquerque as a mule skinner with a wagon train, and only after that business slowed did he hang out his shingle.[95] Silver City's first doctor, Myers H. Casson, was fundamentally interested in getting rich quickly through prospecting. In 1870 he moved to Silver City, "where he had little success at mining, but was well thought of as a physician."[96] Dr. Joseph Kornitzer of Socorro ran a dairy and a drugstore to supplement his practice, and San Marcial's Dr. Charles G. Cruickshank ran a meat market in that town and a ranch near Socorro to help support his family.[97]

As time wore on, and especially as decent-sized cities developed, some of the frontier doctors became prosperous, especially some of the city doctors who managed well the money produced in their practices. As late as the dawn of statehood, however, rural physicians still struggled to make ends meet. Most of them found their reward elsewhere. Dr. Thompson of Mescalero spoke for many of them when, in describing the long journeys he made by horseback to care for sick people, he wrote:

> But the people were (in the main) so grateful, so honest, and so kind; the mountains and plains so beautiful; the food, be it never so plain, was so seasoned with the hunger of youth and exercise in the open air that life was worth living, and sleep was sweet and dreamless.[98]

Probably the best way to close this survey of New Mexico's pioneer

[92]Hoyt, *Frontier Doctor*, pp. 63ff.

[93]Ibid., p. 63.

[94]*Pageant of Progress, The Carlsbad Story*, p. 25.

[95]Adler, "Biography of a Society":34.

[96]Helen J. Lundwall, ed., *Pioneering in Territorial Silver City: H. B. Ailman's Recollections of Silver City and the Southwest, 1871–1892* (Albuquerque: University of New Mexico Press, 1983), p. 151.

[97]Anderson, *History of New Mexico*, pp. 454, 451–52. On the difficult economics of medical practice in frontier New Mexico, see, also, Will Harrison, "Anything but Medicine," *Southwestern Medicine* 44 (1963):252–54.

[98]Thompson, "Pioneer Practice in the Southwest,":47.

doctors is to cite one who knew them well. Dr. J. W. Hannett came to New Mexico in 1919 and was first exposed to some of the old-timers when he set up practice as a railroad surgeon in Gallup. He also got to know well the old guard in Albuquerque when he moved to that city in 1929. In a 1950 speech, given at the end of a distinguished career that included, among other honors, election as president of the New Mexico Medical Society, he remembered the pioneer doctors with respect and affection:

> The day of the doctor with the sideburns, swallow-tail coat and capacious medicine case is gone forever. A small percentage of them were pompous and sometimes pious frauds; yet they delivered babies, reduced compound fractures, removed an occasional tonsil, sat up all night at the period of an expected crisis in lobar pneumonias, diagnosed appendicitis as inflammation of the bowels, cancer of the uterus as change of life, and effectively covered a multitude of errors with profound dignity, unfailing patience and a gentle, kindly comprehension of their people. The home folks loved and respected them. Some of the better ones played poker on Saturday nights and went fishing on Sundays, while some equally righteous attended choir practice and were seen in church with their families at the Sabbath. They loved their horses and their dogs in those days, and they were better psychologists than we are and perhaps lived a fuller and richer life.[99]

[99] J. W. Hannett (M.D.), "The Public Health Officer and the Average Doctor," *New Mexico Health Officer* 18 (1950, 1):3–4.

CHAPTER 3

"An Army of Tubercular Invalids"

New Mexico and the Birth of a Tuberculosis Industry

THE SEARCH FOR THE MAIN THEME OR THE MOST STRIKING feature of New Mexico medicine at the end of the nineteenth century and during the first decades of the twentieth is a short, easy task. The White Plague, or tuberculosis, dominated New Mexico medicine during that era and cast a long shadow into the future as well. It was one of the central factors in the foundation and development of hospitals across the state; it was the main reason for the migration of hundreds of physicians to the state; and it heavily influenced the basic structure and differentiation of the state's medical profession. But the importance of the tuberculosis industry (for such it swiftly became) hardly stopped there. Simply put, it was one of the basic factors in the peopling and development of the state, in general, in the critical decades just before and after statehood.

New Mexicans are keenly aware of the importance of the cattle and mining industries in the early history of their state. They are not so conscious of the central role played by the tuberculosis business. It was nothing less than coequal in importance to the other two. Erna Fergusson wrote of Albuquerque in the 1920s and 1930s that the town had only two industries, the Santa Fe railroad and tuberculosis; and a Roswell physician observed of his hometown in 1910, "Were it not for this reputation [as a haven for lung patients], Roswell today would still be only a cow-camp."[1]

[1]Erna Fergusson, *Our Southwest* (New York: Alfred Knopf, 1940), p. 228; Charles M. Yater, M.D., "Therapetitic [*sic*] Notes—Status of Tuberculosis in Roswell," *New Mexico Medical Journal* 5 (1909–10):270.

At the end of the nineteenth century New Mexico became known as "nature's sanatorium for consumptives,"[2] and a flood of pulmonary invalids sought it out for refuge. A Santa Fe physician of the modern era, himself a tuberculosis victim in his youth, summarized the phenomenon:

> The Spaniards had gone North and West, seeking golden cities to loot and pagan souls to save. The Anglo-Saxons went West to seek land and gold and to save their health.[3]

For most Americans of the twentieth century tuberculosis is a faintly anachronistic term, something that smacks more of the history book than of our everyday world. To the degree that it enters our consciousness at all, it is largely an unpleasant historical memory. Some few Americans are aware of its continued significance in the developing countries around the globe, where it remains a major public health problem, and, of course, it constitutes a surprisingly resilient, worrisome menace among our own Native American peoples.[4] But, fundamentally, we are disinterested in tuberculosis, even faintly contemptuous. That attitude is a very recent phenomenon, however. It stretches back no further than a generation or so, to the advent of effective drug therapy against the disease in the late 1940s and the early 1950s. Prior to that discovery, tuberculosis—most commonly called "consumption" in the English-speaking world because it seemed literally to eat away its victim's flesh—was one of the most dreaded and historically momentous of human-disease foes.

The White Plague has been a tragically familiar companion of humankind so far back as we can see in human history. Bone lesions in Egyptian skeletal remains dating back to 3000 B.C. testify to the disease's presence then, and various kinds of evidence confirm its existence in ancient Chinese and Indian societies as well. The Greeks of the ancient world suffered its ravages, as did the Romans of the imperial era.[5] Steadily,

[2]Paul M. Carrington, M.D., "The Climate of New Mexico, Nature's Sanatorium for Consumptives," *New York Medical Journal* 86 (1907):1.

[3]Julius Lane Wilson, M.D., "The Western Frontier and Climate Therapy," *The Journal-Lancet* 86 (1966):564.

[4]For an appraisal of the continuing impact of tuberculosis on the American Indian, see J. M. Samet et al., "Respiratory Disease Mortality in New Mexico's American Indians and Hispanics," *American Journal of Public Health* 70 (1980):492–97.

[5]Henry A. Sigerist, *A History of Medicine*, 2 vols. (New York: Oxford University Press, 1951, 1961), vol. 1: *Primitive and Archaic Medicine*, pp. 53–54.

throughout the medieval and Renaissance periods of Western history, the affliction exacted a punishing toll in human misery and mortality. It reached a terrible climax from the seventeenth through the nineteenth centuries when it was the most fearsome killer of Western society. In the seventeenth century, John Bunyan called it "the captain of the men of death," the respectful label enshrined ever since in medical history textbooks. In America the nineteenth century was called "the century of tuberculosis,"[6] for it was the leading cause of death throughout that century and into our own. The mortality figures associated with the disease were frightening—at the end of the century tuberculosis consistently claimed 150,000 lives in the United States year in and year out—but these statistics only begin to suggest its full impact. For every death attributed to the malady, there were another ten to twenty victims suffering in some stage of the disease. Nor was it any respecter of persons. Among the famous tuberculars of Western history were Keats, Shelley, Schiller, Elizabeth Browning, Thoreau, the Brontë sisters, Chopin, Balzac, Robert Louis Stevenson, Cecil Rhodes, Niccolo Paganini, and Ralph Waldo Emerson.

The special horror of tuberculosis was the slow, lingering death so characteristic of it and the futility of the treatments available for it. As late as the end of the nineteenth century therapy for this dread ailment was little better than at the time of Hippocrates, and in many ways it was worse. Some of the fourth century B.C. contemporaries of Hippocrates had been on the right track, prescribing good food, mild exercise, and change of climate for the problem. Other antique remedies were less savory, involving medicines with ingredients such as liver of wolf, boiled in wine; lard of a thin sow fed on herbs; bouillon made from the flesh of an ass; dried rosin from the lung of deer; and the eating and drinking of filth, based on the logic that the more offensive the remedy, the more likely it was to drive from the patient's body the malignant substances that caused the disease.[7] Certainly, the so-called heroic therapy employed against the disease in the eighteenth and early nineteenth centuries—purging, vomiting, sweating, diuresis, blistering, and bleeding—was utterly ineffective and undoubtedly sped the disease's progress in many cases. The great American physician and signer of the Declaration of

[6]Esmond R. Long, "Tuberculosis in Modern Society," *Bulletin of the History of Medicine* 27 (1953):302.

[7]Julius H. Comroe, "T.B. or Not T.B.? Part II: The Treatment of Tuberculosis," *American Review of Respiratory Disease* 117 (1978):379.

Independence, Benjamin Rush, reported bleeding his consumption patients two or three times a week, taking six to eight ounces at a sitting, and recommended long journeys on horseback between bleedings![8] The second half of the nineteenth century, however, witnessed the gradual abandonment of heroic therapy and the substitution of more moderate, conservative treatment of the disease. Even so, a century ago a tuberculosis diagnosis sent a chill down the anxious patient's spine, and was regarded as something akin to a death sentence. Upon the development of his first pulmonary hemorrhage, the poet Keats, trained as a physician, observed with resignation, "That drop of blood is my death warrant, I must die,"[9] and a year later he was indeed dead, at age twenty-five. So grim was the prognosis for the disease, and so ineffectual all therapies for it, that the great French physician Sigismond Jaccoud lamented, "The treatment of tuberculosis is but a meditation on death."[10] Within that depressing scenario a new form of tuberculosis treatment called "altitude therapy" developed in the middle of the nineteenth century; and New Mexico and the Rocky Mountain West, in general, suddenly took on special, new prominence as a great natural spa.

Even before tuberculosis patients began to look to the mountains for salvation, New Mexico began to enjoy a reputation for the special salubrity of its climate, particularly for its beneficent effects on people with "weak lungs." As the exploration of the Rockies proceeded, accounts of the special healthiness of the region began to appear. Zebulon Pike in 1810, Dr. Edwin James of the Long expedition in 1823, Josiah Gregg in 1844, and Captain James Fremont in 1845 all noted the unusual healthiness of the region. Gregg was particularly influential in establishing the reputation of the area as a health sufferers' paradise. William Bucknell and party had opened the sixty-year-long history of the Santa Fe Trail in 1821, and Gregg made the first of several treks to Santa Fe ten years later. In his famous *Commerce of the Prairies: Or the Journal of a Santa Fe Trader during Eight Expeditions across the Great Western Prairies, and a Residence of Nearly Nine Years in Northern Mexico,* first published in

[8]Ibid.

[9]Cited in Harry F. Dowling, *Fighting Infection: Conquests of the Twentieth Century* (Cambridge, Mass.: Harvard University Press, 1977), p. 70.

[10]Selman A. Waksman, *The Conquest of Tuberculosis* (Berkeley: University of California Press, 1964), p. 96.

1844, Gregg testified to the curative properties of the wagon-train trek down the trail and of the upland region, which was its goal:

Among the concourse of travelers at this starting point [Independence, Missouri], besides traders and tourists a number of pale-faced invalids are generally to be met with. The prairies have, in fact, become very celebrated for their sanitative effects . . . owing, no doubt, to the peculiarities of diet and the regular exercise incident to prairie life, as well as to the purity of the atmosphere of those elevated unembarrassed regions. An invalid myself, I can answer for the efficacy of the remedy, at least in my own case.[11]

More emphatic still, and explicit in linking the glorious climate of the Rockies and relief from pulmonary ailments, was the account published in 1847 by the young English adventurer George Frederick Ruxton, describing his explorations of the area around Pikes Peak:

It is an extraordinary fact that the air of the mountains has a wonderfully restorative effect upon constitutions enfeebled by pulmonary disease; and of my own knowledge I could mention a hundred instances where persons whose cases have been pronounced by eminent practitioners as perfectly hopeless have been restored to comparatively sound health by a sojourn in the pure and bracing air of the Rockey Mountains, and are now alive to testify to the effects of the reinvigorating climate.[12]

Reports similar to these multiplied as increasing numbers of people traveled down the Santa Fe Trail, with almost all accounts insisting on the curative properties of the West's pristine air, its glorious sunshine (especially in the Southwest), and the generally tonic effects of the region's altitude and its outdoor life. The response to such tidings was rapid. As both Gregg's and Ruxton's accounts observe, as early as the 1830s and the 1840s pale-faced invalids were beginning to trickle across the prairies, seeking deliverance in the favored mountain country of the West.

In New Mexico the stream of health-seekers was accelerated by the annexation of the region to the United States in 1846. The presence of the U.S. Army afforded at least a modicum of security and stability for would-be immigrants, and, just as importantly, the reports of army officers

[11]Josiah Gregg, *Commerce of the Prairies*, ed. by Milo Milton Quaife (Lincoln: University of Nebraska Press, 1967), p. 21.

[12]Cited in Frank B. Rogers, "The Rise and Decline of the Altitude Therapy of Tuberculosis," *Bulletin of the History of Medicine* 43 (1969):3.

and medical men stationed in the new territory lent a vital boost to the region's growing reputation for salubrity. Army surgeons, for example, reported glowingly on the health conditions of the region and particularly emphasized the virtual freedom from tuberculosis of soldiers stationed in the area.[13] These army reports, coupled with those of the Santa Fe Trail pilgrims, contributed enormously to the relatively quick emergence of New Mexico as a "salubrious El Dorado."[14] More basic still, however, was the rise of new medical doctrines in the latter half of the nineteenth century.

The second half of the nineteenth century was arguably the most creative and revolutionary epoch in the entire history of Western medicine. Among the major developments of that period were Pasteur's germ theory and the bacteriological revolution that it initiated; the discovery and development of both general and local anesthesia for surgical purposes; the pioneering work in antiseptic surgery; the birth of modern chemotherapeutics; the root-and-branch reform of nursing effected by the inestimable Florence Nightingale; the discovery of the X-ray; and much else that is fundamental to modern medical science and health-care delivery. In that fertile milieu of radical thought and experimentation, ideas achieved a prominence that greatly boosted New Mexico's growing acclaim as a convalescent's haven. One such idea was the notion, supported by an increasingly convincing body of evidence, that altitude possessed special curative power in the treatment or relief of miscellaneous and sundry human ills, and lung problems in particular. The basic logic of altitude therapy rested on the assumption of good, or at least better, air at high altitudes—cleaner, fresher air without the pollutants of lower climes—and on the ostensibly beneficial effects of reduced air pressure.

At least as early as Hippocrates, of course, Western medicine had preached the therapeutic value of good air, but it remained for the nineteenth century to elaborate that homespun wisdom into a science. Particularly

[13]Julius L. Wilson, "Pikes Peak or Bust: An Historical Note on the Search for Health in the Rockies," *Rocky Mountain Medical Journal* 64 (1967, 9):59. The strength and consistency of those reports ultimately led the federal government to choose New Mexico as the site for the first two federal sanatoria in the country—one at Fort Bayard, in October 1899, and the second at Fort Stanton, in November of that year.

[14]This felicitous phrase is that of Karen Shane, in "New Mexico: Salubrious El Dorado," *New Mexico Historical Review* 56 (1981):387–99. This is the best general account of New Mexico's emergence as a kind of gigantic natural spa.

important in that process were the contributions of two European physician-researchers, the German tuberculosis specialist Dr. Hermann Brehmer and a London chest-doctor Hermann Weber. In 1854, Brehmer opened an experimental hospital for tuberculosis patients in the central Germany village of Göbersdorf. Through his doctoral research, Brehmer had become convinced of the therapeutic effects of altitude in cases of early tuberculosis, and the institution at Göbersdorf was designed to test his theory. He also preached the importance of abundant, rich food and regular exercise for victims of the disease, and in the 1870s Brehmer's theories and results began to attract wide attention.[15] The publication of two important essays—"On the influence of Alpine climates on pulmonary consumption" and "On the treatment of phthisis by prolonged residence in elevated regions"—by the Londoner Weber was particularly important in drawing attention to Brehmer's work and in promoting the advocacy of convalescence at high altitudes for tuberculars.[16] Weber had worked and studied in the Swiss Alpine resorts of Davos and St. Moritz, and from his experience there, he was persuaded of the importance of altitude therapy for the victims of a wide variety of lung diseases, especially tuberculosis. In his work, he catalogued a half-dozen advantages associated with high altitude: the diminished humidity of the air; the dryness of the soil; low temperature; the relative absence of manmade and natural pollution; the greater number of clear days; and the higher percentage of ozone in the air. Weber made very little effort to correlate his observations with hard physiological data, but argued basically from empirical observation and the tenets of common sense. His work, combined with that of Brehmer, attracted widespread interest, most of it quite favorable, and won general acceptance within influential medical circles. Among the reasons for its attractiveness, of course, was the fact that it provided a patina of scientific

[15]R. Y. Keers, *Pulmonary Tuberculosis: A Journey Down the Centuries* (London: Baillière Tindall, 1978), pp. 75–77. One of Brehmer's patients, Peter Dettweiler, who became his pupil, opened a similar institution at Falkenstein in Germany's Taunus Mountains in 1876. Dettweiler, however, was less convinced than his teacher of the salutary effect of altitude itself; instead, he was persuaded that it was the fresh air which was the critical factor. Exposure to fresh air, whatever the altitude, was the absolutely indispensable or essential element for recovery. This uncertainty—what, exactly, was it that most benefited the consumptive: altitude, fresh air, abundant food, exercise, rest?—was much disputed well into the twentieth century.

[16]On Weber and the history of altitude therapy in general, see Rogers, "Rise and Decline," especially pp. 5–6.

respectability or logic to the traditional belief in the power of mountain air.

The development of this formal altitude therapy in Europe immediately imparted renewed vigor and enhanced credibility to the arguments of those who had already, for some decades, insisted on the special salubrity of the mountain West. In linking their arguments to the work of Weber and the school he established, American physicians in both the East and the West began to explain the special health advantages of the Rockies by reference to the new "science." Several Colorado and New Mexico doctors, for example, became advocates of the theory that a line of immunity from tuberculosis existed at approximately five thousand feet above sea level. This notion was dressed up in full scientific regalia (including capital letters—The Line of Immunity) and was explained as "that elevation of some particular locality or country at which the atmospheric air is free of germs and enjoys the unobstructed effects of heat, light, and electricity."[17] For many Rocky Mountain physicians, the explanation for the special salubrity of their home environs became elementary: Above the five-thousand-foot line germs simply found it hard to exist. One Chicago enthusiast pushed this idea so far as to argue that in the Rocky Mountain country putrefaction of meat was a rare phenomenon, with meat curing naturally in the open air![18]

The Line-of-Immunity thesis was just one of a broad variety of explanations for the special power of mountain climes. The dryness of the air at high altitude, for example, was frequently cited as the critical element in ensuring the special salubrity of the highlands, as was the equability of temperature, and particularly the absence of severe extremes. According to some, the "rarefaction" or thinness of the air was the key determinant, for "the patient is obliged to breathe more fully and deeply than in low-lying localities, and in this manner the lungs are expanded and stimulated to healthy development."[19] A Colorado physician-theorist was impressed with what he called the "diathermancy" of the mountain air, by which he meant its increased capacity to transmit radiant heat, and by the atmospheric electricity of the mountain country: "You get up in

[17]Wilson, "Pikes Peak":59–60, citing Dr. J. Hilgard Tyndale, *Home and Climatic Treatment of Pulmonary Tuberculosis* (1882).

[18]George M. Kellogg (M.D.), "New Mexico as a Health Resort," *Journal of the American Medical Association* 27 (12 September 1896):583.

[19]E. H. Ruddock, *On Consumption and Tuberculosis of the Lungs* (1873), cited in Rogers, "Rise and Decline":7.

the morning from your negative electric bed to stretch yourself in the positive electric air."[20] Buttressed by powerful "scientific" arguments such as these, altitude therapy became firmly rooted in the armamentarium of ninteenth-century American medical thought and practice, reaching an apogee at the end of the century and slowly fading thereafter. For obvious reasons, it especially charmed physicians and lay boosters of the mountain West, even though very little hard evidence was ever adduced to support it. It proved a potent factor in the growing attractiveness of New Mexico as a health resort particularly suited to the recovery of tuberculars.

But there was more to New Mexico's appeal than just its mountains. Its climate, in general, was held up by medical men in the territory and elsewhere as extraordinarily well suited to the treatment of invalids with bad lungs. An eastern physician enumerated an entire laundry list of the territory's climatic advantages:

> The climate of New Mexico, though far from ideal, can only be understood and appreciated by comparison with that of other states and countries. A survey of its climatic conditions, such as its altitude, its southerly latitude, its even average temperature, its low humidity, the small amount of precipitation, its excess of sunshine, the minute amounts of aqueous vapor contained in its atmosphere, its isolation from large population centers, its great distance from large bodies of water, its immunity from high winds and sandstorms [*sic*], and its freedom from unsanitary surroundings, should convince the reader that there does not exist a better or more ideal climate for the elimination of disease and the restoration of health.[21]

The hymns of praise to the New Mexico climate sometimes reached surprising levels of exaggeration. For example, a French scientist-physician, a Parisian M.D., and a member of the *Sociète Medicale de Paris* no less, claimed to have spent more than two years traveling across North, Central, and South America seeking the absolutely best possible spot to establish a sanatorium for consumptives. In a letter to the editor of the *Journal of the American Medical Association,* he spelled out the desi-

[20]Charles Denison, "The Influence of High Altitude on the Progress of Phthisis," *Transactions of the International Medical Congress, Philadelphia* (1876), cited in Rogers, "Rise and Decline":8–9.

[21]Dr. Curtis Bailey, quoted in "New Mexico as a Health Resort," *Journal of the American Medical Association* 31 (12 November 1898):1179.

derata: altitude between four and five thousand feet; not too hot nor too cold; minimal rain; no fog; limited snow; pure air; and so forth. After traipsing all across the Western Hemisphere, he finally found his perfect spot—the San Agustin plains of central New Mexico. It met all of his demanding climate criteria, and he noted: "There is a peculiarity in this country. No sooner does any one get there than he feels happy!"[22] Such effusions became almost a commonplace in medical literature at the end of the century, reaching a climax in the judgment of an eminent Toronto physician, Dr. J. F. Danter. Danter visited New Mexico Territory in 1891 as the officially deputized Special Commissioner of the American Health Resort Association. He was charged with responsibility for evaluating the region's claims as a tubercular's haven, and he left the territory a true believer. His report asserted that New Mexico was superior "to any other part of the United States *or the world* in helping to cure the consumptive."[23]

Among the general chorus of praise, there were a few naysayers or discordant voices, who insisted that there was another side to the territory's rosy image. For example, a Virginia physician, who had brought his sick wife out to Carrizozo, complained in a public letter about the exaggerated claims made on behalf of New Mexico:

> It is true that we have only about twelve rainy days a year, that the sun shines all the time and that the temperature is seldom too hot or too cold. But there are many disadvantages to which attention should be called. During the past four months the wind has blown two-thirds of the time so hard that my wife has not been able to stay outdoors, and during the entire year the wind and dust have kept her more closely housed than the rain did in Virginia. Often for two months at a time we do not have enough rain to dampen the ground. In 1903 it did not rain for nine months. The dust is as fine as meal and very irritating on account of its excessive alkalinity. Four days at a time I have seen the wind raise so much of this dust that the view was obstructed as completely as in a fierce snowstorm. There are a few towns high up in the mountains or in small ravines where there is more rain or where the wind is not so bad, but I have described the conditions prevailing in 75 per cent of New Mexican towns.[24]

Such criticism was rare, however, and informed medical opinion at the end of the century emphatically shared the judgment of one of New

[22]*Journal of the American Medical Association* 18 (27 February 1892):274.

[23]Cited in Shane, "Salubrious El Dorado":391. (Emphasis added.)

[24]Dr. Bathurst Browne Bagby, Letter to the Editor, *Journal of the American Medical Association* 50 (6 June 1908):1918.

Mexico's tuberculosis specialists, Dr. H. B. Masten, that "New Mexico possesses a climate that is not surpassed, even if it is equalled, by that of any other part of the world."[25] With such acclaim, it is not surprising that the tide of pale-faced invalids seeking healing in New Mexico began to swell.

The trickle of weak-lunged travelers heading toward the Southwest in the years after the opening of the Santa Fe Trail accelerated with every passing decade, and particularly as altitude therapy and the spreading reputation of the region for salubrity took hold. Sizable numbers of tuberculars were settled in Albuquerque and Santa Fe as early as the 1850s and 1860s.[26] But the hard journey across the prairies by horseback or wagon took from two to three months to complete, and it demanded considerable physical strength and resiliency of those who traveled it. Stagecoaches were somewhat quicker, but they were expensive and physically draining as well. Getting to the "Well Country" (a term often used by local boosters of New Mexico) remained a major problem long after the region's reputation was solidly established. It was a very real bottleneck limiting utilization by suffering consumptives of the region's pristine air and abundant sunshine. The arrival of the railroad in New Mexico at the very end of the 1870s and the early 1880s finally resolved the difficulty, and the trickle of health-seekers swelled to a flood. Within a very brief time, care of the tuberculars became big business in New Mexico, for from the 1880s until the start of the Second World War the "lungers" came by the thousands.

The question of exact numbers is an exasperating one. Most of the estimates made by those who lived through New Mexico's tuberculosis era and by students of the subject are frustratingly vague and subjective. Words like "numerous," "large," "significant," "thousands," and even "enormous" are bandied about, but there were of course no census-takers stationed at the borders demanding sputum samples of every immigrant to the region. Though indisputably accurate statistics do not exist, it is nevertheless possible to make reasonably solid judgments about the numbers of people involved. It is almost surely safe, for example, to conclude that around 1920, approximately 10 percent of the state's total population

[25] H. B. Masten, "New Mexico as a Health Resort," *New York Medical Journal* 76 (1902):414.

[26] Billy M. Jones, *Health-Seekers in the Southwest, 1817–1900* (Norman: University of Oklahoma Press, 1967), p. 87.

consisted of health-seekers, and to that number should be added their dependents. From town to town the percentage of tuberculars varied widely with many towns made up predominantly of "lungers" and their families, while others for various reasons remained largely unaffected by the influx. The first attempts at estimating the numbers of the health-seekers were made during the height of the phenomenon by contemporaries impressed with the scale of the immigration. For example, an eastern journalist writing in 1910 about Colorado, Arizona, and New Mexico suggested that "if the health-seekers and their families were to leave, the country would probably lose more than half of its population."[27] Though there was certainly a good measure of hyperbole in that judgment—and the journalist gave no evidence for his estimate—he was probably right, at least for some New Mexico communities. That was definitely the conclusion of the best contemporary study of the health-seeker migration, a detailed investigation carried out in 1913 by a United States Public Health Service physician named Ernest Sweet.[28] Sweet concluded that in the *majority* of New Mexico towns (except for the mining communities) anywhere from 20 percent to 60 percent of all households had at least one family member who was tubercular, and his investigation proved that approximately 90 percent of those consumptives were nonnative.[29] Silver City was the most extreme case, and, in Sweet's opinion, "Were all the consumptives to leave . . . Silver City would become a mere spot in the desert."[30] He calculated that 80 percent of the families of that Grant County town sheltered at least one tubercular.

Several other New Mexico towns were not far behind. Socorro, Las Vegas, Raton, Las Cruces, Roswell, and others were all heavily influenced by the migration, each of them with a strong majority of their families including at least one "lunger." Even so large a town (comparatively) as Albuquerque bore distinctly the impress of the phenomenon, with perhaps as much as 50 percent of its citizenry consisting of consumptives and their relatives.[31] Dr. LeRoy Peters, one of the state's most prominent

[27]Cited in Francis T. B. Fest, "The Consumptive's Holy Grail," *New Mexico Medical Journal* 5 (1909–10):117.

[28]Ernest A. Sweet, "Interstate Migration of Tuberculous Persons, Its Bearing on the Public Health, with Special Reference to the States of Texas and New Mexico," *Public Health Reports* 30 (1915):1059–91, 1147–73, 1225–55.

[29]Ibid.:1071, 1066–67.

[30]Ibid.:1250.

[31]Ibid.:1071.

tuberculosis specialists, estimated that in 1915 Albuquerque had more than 2,500 consumptives among its 11,020 citizens, with his figures comparing very closely to those of Sweet.[32] For the state in general, there were in 1913 probably around 30,000 resident health-seekers within its total population of 330,000; hence, one of every eleven New Mexicans of that era had come seeking the cure.[33] Large numbers came, and the migration was still increasing as of 1913. The flight of health-seekers to New Mexico and the West generally began to slow somewhat in the 1920s (for reasons discussed below), but throughout the twenties and thirties and into the forties their numbers remained significant. The Albuquerque Civic Council estimated that for that city alone at least 350 to 500 health-seekers (plus families, in the case of many) were arriving every year as late as the end of the thirties.[34] Given the state's limited population base in the first half of this century, it was a population influx of enormous significance.

What kind of people were these health pilgrims of the tuberculosis era, and how did New Mexicans react to these particular strangers in their midst? The refugees were mostly young people in their twenties and thirties, for its was part of the special savagery of tuberculosis that it struck down young adults in the prime of their lives with special frequency. At the beginning of this century, pulmonary tuberculosis claimed in any given year fully one-third of all the young adults who died in the productive years between fifteen and forty-four years of age. The New Mexico health-seekers fit that national pattern, for most of them were young people, with the over-forty group rarely represented.[35] And they were predominantly male. A sample of a thousand health-seekers in El Paso, made around the start of the First World War, produced 715 males and 285 females,[36] and figures for New Mexico would surely be little different. Pulmonary tuberculosis itself showed no such marked sex preference; hence, the great predominance of men in the health-seeker sample is merely a reflection of the greater independence and mobility among American males of that era than among females. Sociologically, they represented the spectrum of America's populace, although there was a

[32]LeRoy Peters, "What New Mexico Needs Most in Tuberculosis Legislation," *New Mexico Medical Journal* 15 (1915–16):230.

[33]Sweet, "Interstate Migration,":1071.

[34]Fergusson, *Our Southwest*, p. 229.

[35]Fest, "The Consumptive's Holy Grail":118.

[36]Sweet, "Interstate Migration":1245.

slight tilt toward the upper end of the social ladder. One authority has called the "lunger" exodus "a selective process" that stocked western cities "with educated, upper-middle-class, professional people, often the fathers or grandfathers of today's civic leaders";[37] and that judgment seems, by and large, accurate. The other end of the social spectrum, however, was also represented in New Mexico. Silver City doctors, for example, certainly judged the clientele at the two federal sanatoria in the state harshly:

> Without a doubt no other institutions, outside those of a penal character, or insane asylums, can show quite so inferior a class of patients as these two have to accept. Their patients are mostly soldiers and sailors: equally improvident, thoughtless, dissipated, ungrateful, and to a great extent syphilized.[38]

There may indeed have been something to that unequivocal indictment of the patients at the federal institutions, but, in general terms, the health-seekers were important contributors and valuable additions to New Mexico society (as will be demonstrated below).

For their part, New Mexicans were generally inclined to welcome the health-seekers, greeting them with sympathy and encouragement. To their great credit, simple compassion and concern for their stricken brothers and sisters seem to have been the controlling elements in the reactions of most New Mexicans. If their glorious sunshine and magnificent mountain air might ease the physical ills of these unfortunate health-seekers, then so be it and welcome! However, there were also many who were quick to appreciate the economic opportunities inherent in the phenomenon. There was an immediate need, of course, for hospital construction to take care of the more desperately ill among the invalids, and the very great majority of them would have to seek out local physicians for proper medical supervision while they "chased the cure,"[39] but the economic impact did not vaguely stop there. Hotels and boardinghouses profited from the steady tide of "lungers" and their families; real-estate agencies,

[37]Wilson, "The Western Frontier and Climate Therapy":566.

[38]Earl S. Bullock and C. T. Sands, "Twelve Years of Pulmonary Tuberculosis Treatment in the West," *Journal of the American Medical Association* 52 (19 June 1909):1975.

[39]This superficially curious phrase was ubiquitous during the era of the "lungers," but I do not know of any formal study of its origins. It surely had something to do with the flight of tuberculars from their homes in quest of recovery, chasing the will-o'-the-wisp of good health. It may also have had to do with the most prominent physical symbol of sanatorium life, the chaise lounge on which tubercular patients took their daily rest.

moving and storage companies, and service industries, in general, were beneficiaries of the influx; and other spinoff businesses (including funeral homes for the unsuccessful or for those who came too late) were boosted by the growth of the migration.

State and local governmental agencies and business circles quickly organized themselves to respond to the opportunities and responsibilities associated with the tuberculosis industry. As early as 1880, the arrival of the railroad had prompted the territorial government to establish a Bureau of Immigration to help promote the territory and encourage the investment of money and people in it. Over the subsequent years the Bureau issued reams of promotional material, with much of it emphasizing the state's special salubrity. An explicit appeal to consumptives and to physicians caring for them was very commonly a part of that propaganda. As an example, one of the Bureau's 1881 publications wrote of Grant County: "For all pulmonary complaints there is not a more congenial spot on the top of the earth. Here you inhale the pure, fresh, life-giving and invigorating air."[40] Other official and nonofficial agencies also played a part in boosting the territory. Albuquerque's Commercial Club, forerunner of the Chamber of Commerce, encouraged its members to take advantage of all opportunities to publicize their city as a health-sufferer's paradise, and promoted the health industry in other ways as well. It organized and financed advertising campaigns—its secretary in 1915 coined a new slogan for the city: "Albuquerque, New Mexico, where the sick get well and the well get prosperous!"[41]—and directly invested some of its funds in helping tuberculosis-related enterprises get off the ground. One prominent example reveals that in 1907–8, when the Presbyterian church was considering Albuquerque and a number of other Southwest cities as a possible site for a church-sponsored tuberculosis sanatorium, the Commercial Club offered to raise two thousand dollars to help purchase a site for the institution.[42]

Similarly, both state and local governments offered various incentives to facilitate the development of the health industry. The territorial leg-

[40]Cited in Shane, "Salubrious El Dorado":388–89.

[41]*Journal of the American Medical Association* 65 (2 October 1915):1194.

[42]Marion Woodham, *A History of Presbyterian Hospital, 1908 to 1976, with an Update through 1979* (Albuquerque: Presbyterian Hospital Center, 1980), p. 2. It appears, however, that the club did *not* deliver on its pledge. See Stephany Wilson, "The Passing of an Era: Presbyterian Sanatorium Coming Down," *Inside: The Presbyterian Hospital Center Magazine* 1 (1967):4.

islature in 1903 offered exemption from taxation for a period of six years to any company willing to invest one hundred thousand dollars in construction of a sanatorium.[43] City governments tried various stratagems to encourage this kind of development. When foundation of a sanatorium by the Methodist church was under discussion in 1917, the city of Albuquerque was eager to help, offering to waive sewer-connection charges for the new facility, for example. (However, in the very next year the city fathers could not see their way clear to deal expeditiously with a request for the city's cooperation in the establishment of a "Booker T. Washington Memorial Sanatorium," and the proposed institution came to naught, with the plan essentially killed by delays.[44] There were obvious limits to what *kinds* of tuberculosis-related enterprises should be encouraged!) This entrepreneurial response to the influx of health-seekers ought not to be considered callous or heartless exploitation of the unfortunates flocking to New Mexico. Although it was indeed opportunistic and hardheaded, there is virtually no evidence of flagrant exploitation of the tuberculars over the half-century span of the health-seeker era. However, it would be foolish to ignore the pragmatism that certainly accompanied the honest desire to help in the reaction of New Mexico and its citizens to the development.

New Mexico's doctors joined enthusiastically in the promotion of their home as a haven for consumptives. For example, they made sure that the territory was prominently represented in national organizations and conferences associated with the war against tuberculosis. No fewer than seven New Mexico tuberculosis specialists from around the territory trekked to New York City in 1901 to represent their territory at a meeting of the American Congress of Tuberculosis, and Dr. Francis Crosson of Albuquerque delivered a paper on "The Sanatorium Treatment of Tuberculosis in New Mexico."[45] Additionally, they pounded away at their typewriters, producing numerous articles for both local and national journals. Much of that writing was straightforward boosterism, touting the advantages of New Mexico for consumptives;[46] but they also published quite respect-

[43]*Journal of the American Medical Association* 41 (5 December 1903):1432.

[44]Shane, "Salubrious El Dorado":394–95.

[45]*Journal of the American Medical Association* 36 (18 May 1901):1405.

[46]See, for example, Bullock and Sands, "Twelve Years of Pulmonary Tuberculosis Treatment":1973–80, for a good example of the genre. Drs. Bullock and Sands, who were themselves "lungers," practiced in Silver City at the Cottage Sanatorium. Bullock was one of the grand old men of New Mexico tuberculosis specialists, practicing in Silver City from

able research reports and clinical studies, an activity which at least indirectly served to emphasize the fact that New Mexico and its physicians were in the forefront of research and treatment of the disease.[47] And they cultivated and preserved an extensive network of medical contacts around the nation in order to keep in touch with ongoing research and study in their field and to keep themselves and their region in the mainstream of the burgeoning tuberculosis industry.

Consistently through the half-century of the "lunger" era, New Mexico welcomed and encouraged pulmonary immigrants. As late as 1932 the Albuquerque Civic Council, especially created to boost the city's renown as a health center and funded by a special tax levy, was still billing Albuquerque as "the heart of the health country."[48] However, there was definitely another side to that coin, for a kind of backlash to the flood of tuberculars, at least to some elements among them, did in time develop. The objections voiced against the health-seekers were broadly of two types. First, some New Mexicans began to fear the spread of the disease, to worry about the effects on healthy natives of so many pulmonary patients coughing, wheezing, and spitting invisible death all about them. And second, while tuberculars flocking to the state with sufficient money to take care of themselves in their exile were one thing, impecunious consumptives, sitting on the curbsides, spitting in the roadway, and depending on the largess and goodwill of New Mexicans for their care were quite another.

Although the basic studies in the 1860s of the French army surgeon Jean Villemin had strongly suggested the contagiousness of tuberculosis, it was not until after the discovery of the tubercle bacillus in 1882 by the great German bacteriologist Robert Koch that the idea began to take firm root in the public consciousness. Initially, there was relatively little worry about the communicability of the disease, but shortly after the turn of the century the general public grew increasingly concerned about

1899 until 1926, when he returned to his native Michigan. He published numerous papers and personally taught and influenced several waves of New Mexico lung specialists. Dr. Sands was one of those bright young men who worked, studied, and sought to recover from their own cases of tuberculosis with Bullock's help. Sands left Silver City for Las Cruces, but he died there of pulmonary tuberculosis at age thirty-three in 1916.

47 On this point and on the old tuberculosis specialists in general, see Chapter 4, pp. 155–59.

48 See its publication, *Sunshine and Health in Albuquerque* (Albuquerque: Civic Council, 1932), p. 3.

the spread of the germ by spitting, sneezing, and coughing. That increasing anxiety took form in different ways, with the passage of restrictive public-health legislation as one of its more conspicuous and constructive manifestations. One of the major reasons for the formation of the New Mexico Society for the Study and Prevention of Tuberculosis, organized at the 1909 annual meeting of the New Mexico Medical Society, was "to promote interest in the fight against tuberculosis and to stimulate on the part of the people a desire for laws offering some degree of protection against the large number of alien consumptives who annually flock to our doors."[49] In his 1908 presidential address to the New Mexico Medical Society, Dr. Robert E. McBride, a distinguished Las Cruces physician who, incidentally, had come to New Mexico in 1904 for the sake of his wife's health, expressed the growing alarm felt by many in the territory and hinted at the prospect of strong measures:

> The army of tubercular invalids should be brought under some sort of control; promiscuous expectoration should be stopped and every possible means taken to prevent these unfortunates from becoming a danger to the population. I would not have you understand that I advocate the plan that forbids them the right to search for health in this glorious climate, but I most assuredly do believe that in return for the health-giving properties of our glorious climate they should be willing to submit to some legal regulation. Just what, is the question, but if we put our heads together I am sure that we can evolve some plan whereby they may be made comfortable and yet not be a source of danger.[50]

President McBride's mention of "the plan that forbids them the right to search for health in this glorious climate" referred to the fact that there already existed widespread public sentiment, not only in New Mexico but also in other areas strongly affected by the "lunger" migration, in favor of legal barriers to control the influx. The suggestion was already bruited about that the federal government should step in and regulate the traffic by a system of inspection and by requiring the issuance of a permit to all infected interstate travelers. This was considerably more than just citizen grousing. The governor of Texas had already convened an interstate conference in Waco, Texas, to which delegates from Kansas, Utah, Colorado,

[49]Peters, "What New Mexico Needs Most in Tuberculosis Legislation":229.

[50]Dr. Robert E. McBride, "The New Mexico Medical Society: Some Duties and Opportunities" (Presidential Address to the New Mexico Medical Society, 2 September 1908), *New Mexico Medical Journal* 4, no. 2 (1908–9):13.

Arizona, Oklahoma, and New Mexico had been invited to discuss the possibility of establishing a quarantine at state boundaries, which would permit passage only to special classes of health-seekers.[51] Such discussion eventually came to naught, but it was important in building public sensitivity to the issue and consensus on the necessity for public-health legislation to cope with the situation.

Despite its intensive exposure to the problem, New Mexico lagged behind most of the nation in establishing public-health laws for the control of tuberculosis. A law prohibiting public spitting was passed in 1907, slightly later than similar legislation elsewhere, but New Mexico officials were slow to see the wisdom of basic steps like making tuberculosis a notifiable disease or requiring the fumigation of quarters vacated by tuberculars. Their dilatoriness was partially a function of the territory's general backwardness in the sphere of public health (see Chapter 6), but it was also a result of the concern of vested interests not to overreact and scare away the health-seekers by a frenzy of restrictive legislation. Sadly, New Mexico was "ahead" in only one area of public-health legislation—its well-intentioned but ill-conceived 1901 law forbidding teaching in the public schools by tuberculars.[52]

The growing concern about the large numbers of tuberculars in New Mexico cities and towns was reflected also in the significant discrimination against health-seekers. Paradoxically, hospitals certainly held them at arm's length. In his 1913 tour through New Mexico and Texas, Sweet found that "the majority of privately owned institutions, unless of course they are conducted for that purpose, absolutely refuse admission to such cases."[53] Viewed from the perspective of the hospital administrator, a tuberculosis case was the same as one of diphtheria or scarlet fever. It was dangerous to handle, the other patients very commonly objected, and nurses often refused to care for tuberculars. Under such circumstances, the seriously ill "lunger" newly arrived in Albuquerque or Las Vegas might indeed encounter problems in finding a hospital bed. Similarly, hotels and boardinghouses could be flagrantly discriminatory. The better hotels frequently would not take consumptives at all. When the great Colorado

[51]Sweet, "Interstate Migration":1086–87, 1160.

[52]I can find no record of any other state enacting such a law, at least not so early as New Mexico. On the whole subject of public-health laws against tuberculosis, see Philip P. Jacobs, comp., *The Campaign against Tuberculosis in the United States* (New York: National Association for the Study and Prevention of Tuberculosis, 1908), pp. 347–414.

[53]Sweet, "Interstate Migration":1154.

internist James J. Waring arrived in Colorado Springs in 1908, then a young physician seeking the cure for his case of pulmonary tuberculosis, the famous Antlers Hotel reluctantly agreed to take him, but made him promise to use the freight elevator.[54] Rejected by first-class hotels, the tubercular might find a modicum of comfort at a third-rate one, but even that might be only temporary. Sometimes, "having once passed muster, he finds that a more discerning clerk appears, or that another guest has complained of his presence, and he is politely informed that his room must be vacated."[55] Often the only lodging available to the newly arrived health-seeker was the boardinghouse, and access to it might require quiet negotiation and perhaps even a small bribe for the owner, who would then introduce the new guest to his fellow boarders as a victim of "hay fever" or nervous trouble. A "lunger" who first sought refuge in Colorado wrote that he had to leave his first boardinghouse after three days when ten of his fellow boarders objected to his presence, but had better luck at a second:

> As I entered the dining-room for the first time, I was introduced by the landlady to the assembled boarders as the gentleman whom she had told them about—the one who came to Denver for his rheumatism. . . . It was surprising the number of diseases I found represented in that rooming house. But it was more surprising that everyone coughed—dyspeptics, rheumatics, nervous wrecks, heart patients, kidney patients, ear patients, Keely cure patients—all coughed.[56]

Not all hotels and boardinghouses reacted to consumptives in the same way, and within particular businesses attitudes changed over time; but the growth of "phthisiophobia"[57] in the Southwest was definitely reflected in the lodging industry. It was also expressed in employment discrimination against the health-seekers. The New Mexico territorial law barring tuberculars from the teaching profession has already been mentioned, and in Arizona ranchers and businessmen put up signs declaring consumptives unwelcome, at least as jobseekers.[58] The fear of the

[54]Rogers, "Rise and Decline of Altitude Therapy":13.

[55]Sweet, "Interstate Migration":1152–53.

[56]Thomas Galbreath, *Chasing the Cure in Colorado* (1907), quoted in Rogers, "Rise and Decline":13.

[57]This is Sweet's term, coined from his observations on his 1913 tour of Texas and New Mexico. "Phthisis," of course, was from the old Greek word for "wearing away" and was a synonym in the nineteenth century for consumption. See "Interstate Migration":1149.

[58]Clyde L. Gittings, "Arizona's Reputation as a Health Spa," *Arizona Medicine* 40 (1983):153.

contagion spread by the consumptives was compounded by economic resentment among a substantial segment of the working class in New Mexico. The influx of "lungers," especially those who had to look for work, drove the wages of labor down. One labor leader commented, "Between the Mexicans and lungers conditions are frightful."[59]

Fear of the spread of the disease by the army of immigrant consumptives was clearly the major factor in the growth of a backlash against the "lungers" in the Southwest, and, regrettably, not all tuberculars exercised precautions to protect others. Those who had spent some time in government sanatoria or in one or another of the better eastern institutions had been well trained and carried sputum cups, but the vast majority of the consumptives, as well as healthy persons—turn-of-the-century America was a society which spat—were careless with their sputum.[60] But fear of the bacillus broadcast about by the "lungers" was often accompanied and magnified by the sad fact that among the swarm of health-seekers debarking from railroad coaches all over the Southwest were many who had spent their savings for the ticket to the West.

The evidence regarding the dimensions of the indigent consumptives' problem is conflicting. Certainly, the descent of large numbers of moneyless health-seekers was a major problem in Colorado, California, and Arizona as early as the 1880s and 1890s, presenting significant medical and social problems.[61] New Mexico was apparently not affected so severely as those regions, but there were surely enough indigent "lungers" around to cause concern. Undoubtedly, the numbers and their impact varied greatly from place to place. Dr. C. M. Mayes of Roswell was worried enough about the number of indigent "lungers" in his town in 1909 to advocate a state-line quarantine to keep health-seekers out if they lacked sufficient resources to care for themselves. His concern was mixed with compassion, however:

> From a viewpoint of humanity or charity, if you like, there is no sadder picture anywhere than the indigent consumptive patient, and the picture becomes many times more sorrowful when they are cast among strangers, especially when the strangers (as we are) are overburdened with this class. They are sent to us or drift here in all stages of the disease, and only too often without income or friends,

[59]Sweet, "Interstate Migration":1248.

[60]Ibid.:1083.

[61]Gittings, "Arizona's Reputation":152–53; Peters, "What New Mexico Needs Most in Tuberculosis Legislation":230.

and for the most part unable to perform the manual labor necessary for their support. They sit about our parks, on our curbs, in our places of amusement and recreation. They are in the saloons, breathing tobacco smoke and air otherwise contaminated. Friendless, homesick, and only too often poorly clad, badly housed and hungry. . . .[62]

Dr. C. M. Yater, his Roswell colleague, agreed about the severity of the problem, claiming that only 25 percent of those who arrived in Roswell chasing the cure were financially able to take care of themselves.[63] Over in Silver City, Drs. Bullock and Sands thought their situation was almost as bad, judging that 50 percent of Silver City's arrivals were unable to bear the essential costs of convalescence.[64] In Albuquerque the problem was serious enough in 1905 to prompt a special meeting of the town's associated charities to pass an indignant resolution of protest:

Resolved, that the physicians and authorities in other sections [of the country] be strongly censured for sending health seekers to Albuquerque and New Mexico when they have reached the stage where they are beyond help from climatical advantages or are without sufficient funds to support themselves for a period of at least six months, and that the press be urgently requested to give this resolution the greatest publicity.[65]

In light of this growing problem, the advertising campaigns boosting New Mexico as the "Well Country" were modified to contain strong language that prospective health-seekers had better not come without being able to finance a year's sanatorium care at from fifty to one hundred dollars per month, but little dent was made in the numbers. As late as 1934 doctors in the Southwest were still complaining that "people [have yet to] learn that climate is valueless unless it is backed up by a healthy appetite, a contented soul, and an adequate pocket-book."[66]

Facilities for the care of the indigent sick were virtually nonexistent in New Mexico during the era of the health-seekers. For example, there was no state tuberculosis sanatorium until 1936, and it was intended properly for the care of New Mexico natives only and not for immigrants

[62]C. M. Mayes, "The Indigent Consumptive Proposition," *New Mexico Medical Journal* 5, no. 2 (1909–10):18–19.

[63]Yater, "Therapetitic Notes":271.

[64]Bullock and Sands, "Twelve Years of Pulmonary Tuberculosis Treatment":1978.

[65]*Journal of the American Medical Association* 45 (16 December 1905):1880.

[66]*Southwestern Medicine* 18 (1934):33–34.

to the state. Private hospitals and sanatoria did what they could, but there were clear limits to the number of charity cases they could handle. Given these circumstances, an insidious, if understandable, practice called "passing on" became common in New Mexico and throughout the Southwest. Communities simply unloaded indigent consumptives on one another. It became common practice for charity organizations as well as for city and county agencies to dump their paupers, their insane, their criminals, and other undesirables, indigent consumptives included, upon neighboring cities.[67] City officials of, say, Raton might "help out" a penniless "lunger" from the East by buying him a railroad ticket to Las Vegas. Southwestern city, county, and state officials complained bitterly that their part of the country had become "the dumping ground for the tuberculous poor of other states,"[68] but the problem was definitely an intrastate as well as interstate one.

Other factors also played at least minor roles in the growth of "phthisiophobia" among some New Mexicans. There were those, for example, who were already dreaming of the development of a gigantic tourism industry for the state and were fearful that tourists would not want to go where hordes of tuberculars crowded the countryside, scattering bacilli broadcast. Others were persuaded that western cities and towns by the end of the century simply did not need the tuberculars as badly as they once had, for the flow of healthy immigrants had grown sufficiently to provide for the developmental needs of the region.[69] The full dimensions of this antitubercular sentiment, however, are difficult to gauge. The Public Health Service researcher who toured the state in 1913 thought it substantial, claiming there was no doubt that the majority of citizens thought the movement was harmful.[70] What is certain is that the worriers and naysayers never generated any serious attempt to do anything about the tubercular traffic beyond innocuous (and largely unenforced) anti-spitting laws. The bulk of opinion seems actually to have rested with those who, while aware of the problems associated with the phenomenon, nevertheless were more impressed with its positive aspects or at least its unavoidability. Many also simply believed that a helping hand held out to these unfortunates was, after all, just the right thing to do.

[67]Sweet, "Interstate Migration":1167–68.
[68]Ibid.:1160.
[69]Ibid.:1149–51.
[70]Ibid.:1245.

Whether they were welcomed or not, this army of tubercular invalids claimed tough, frontier New Mexico as their own, changing it fundamentally in the process. The territory and then new state adjusted to accommodate these new citizens who came to it with special needs and interests.

1

2

Figure 1. Dr. Myers H. Casson, first physician in Silver City. Dr. Casson came to Silver City in the 1870s hoping to get rich in the hunt for silver. He had little success as a miner, but left his mark as a doctor. He died in 1891. (Photo courtesy of Museum of New Mexico, Photo Archives. Hereafter MNM, PA.)
Figure 2. Kingpin of Santa Fe doctors for thirty years, Dr. John H. Sloan was President of the New Mexico Medical Society, 1900–1901. One lifelong Santa Fe resident remembered oldtimers observing, "I'd rather have John Sloan drunk than any other doctor sober . . . and that's usually the way you got him!" (Photo courtesy of MNM, PA.)

3

4

5

Figure 3. Dr. Walter G. Hope (President, New Mexico Medical Society, 1902–3) was one of Albuquerque's "Four Horsemen," flitting around the city and its environs from 1890 until his retirement in the early 1930s. This 1891 photograph, taken on Albuquerque's east mesa, shows the Sandia Mountains in the background. (Photo courtesy of Mrs. Myrl Hope Sisk.)
Figure 4. Tucumcari's Dr. James M. Doughty was no horse-and-buggy doctor, but a man of the twentieth century. From 1912 until the early 1940s, he bounced along Quay County roads, often using his spiffy Harley-Davidson. (Photo courtesy of Judge Robert M. Doughty II.)
Figure 5. Dr. Samuel D. Swope (President, New Mexico Medical Society, 1898–99) rode the countryside around Deming from 1895 until 1925. This picture was taken at a National Guard encampment ca. 1920. (Photo courtesy of Deming-Luna-Mimbres Museum of the Luna County Historical Society, Inc.)

6

7

Figure 6. A Raton area physician (Dr. George N. Fleming?) in his office around 1906. (Photo courtesy of MNM, PA.)
Figure 7. A mainstay of the Santa Fe medical community from 1881 to 1919, Dr. William S. Harroun was an 1865 graduate of Georgetown University School of Medicine. Shown here around 1896, he was very proud of his Bartlett pears. (Photo courtesy of MNM, PA.)
Figure 8. Dr. Lucien G. Rice, Sr., was one of the many "lunger" physicians who sought out the Southwest for relief from their own lung ailments. He practiced in Albuquerque for more than four decades. Here he is examining a young girl, probably at a public school clinic. (Photo courtesy of University of New Mexico Medical Center Library, Medical History Archives. Hereafter UNM-MCL.)

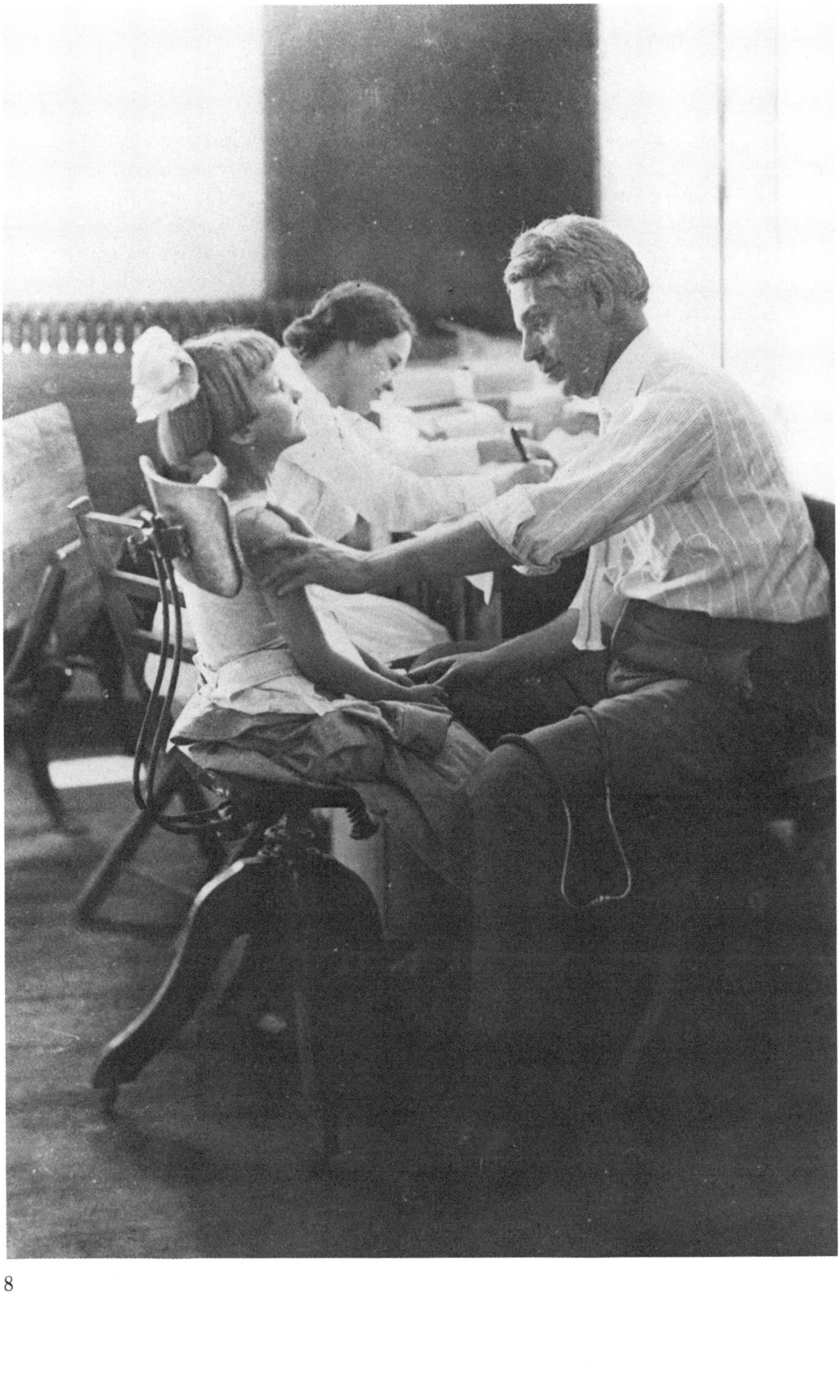

8

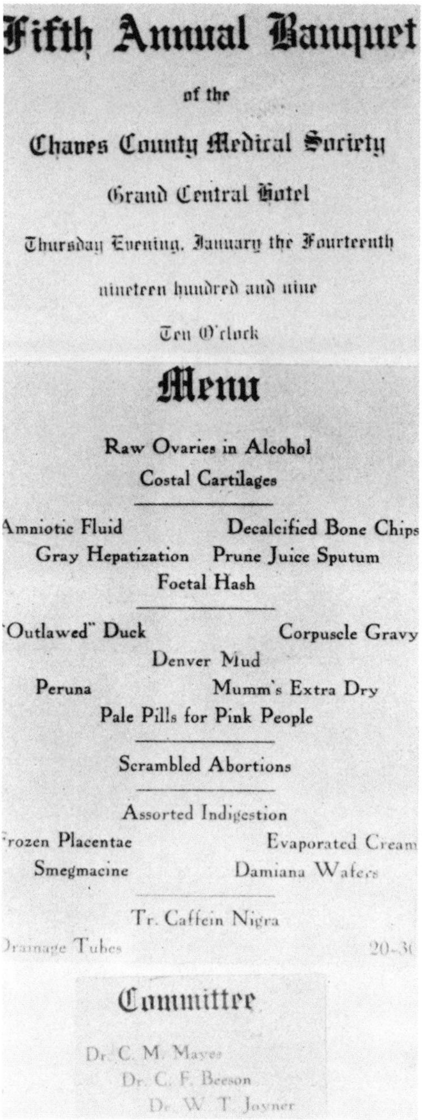

Fifth Annual Banquet

of the

Chaves County Medical Society

Grand Central Hotel

Thursday Evening, January the Fourteenth

nineteen hundred and nine

Ten O'clock

Menu

Raw Ovaries in Alcohol
Costal Cartilages

mniotic Fluid — Decalcified Bone Chips
Gray Hepatization — Prune Juice Sputum
Foetal Hash

"Outlawed" Duck — Corpuscle Gravy
Denver Mud
Peruna — Mumm's Extra Dry
Pale Pills for Pink People

Scrambled Abortions

Assorted Indigestion
rozen Placentae — Evaporated Cream
Smegmacine — Damiana Wafers

Tr. Caffein Nigra
rainage Tubes — 20-3

Committee

Dr. C. M. Mayes
Dr. C. F. Beeson
Dr. W. T. Joyner

9

Figure 9. This example of medical society humor(?) from 1909 produced an embarrassing public scandal in Roswell. Dr. David Galloway, who had been drummed out of the Chaves County Medical Society in a bitter split, latched onto this banquet invitation and filed criminal charges against its authors, accusing them of sending pornographic material through the mails. (Courtesy of Chaves County Historical Museum.)

Figure 10. Dr. James I. Dunham was Chama's physician from 1917 until his death in 1970—and was undaunted by its winter weather. (Photo courtesy of Mr. Dewey Tidwell, Las Cruces.)

Figure 11. Dr. Melvin Paden, center, practiced in White Oaks and Carrizozo for more than fifty years, 1880s into the 1930s. This 1895 photograph was taken in his White Oaks drugstore. (Photo courtesy of MNM, PA.)

10

11

12

13

14

Figure 12. Before his move to Albuquerque and his foundation of the Lovelace Clinic, Dr. William Randolph Lovelace I was a country surgeon. In this 1908 photograph he is shown in his neatly organized Fort Sumner office. Notice especially the medicines on the wall; country doctors were their own pharmacists. (Photo courtesy of Lovelace Foundation.)

Figure 13. Albuquerque's Southwestern Presbyterian Sanatorium around 1911 (looking south). The main Administration Building, left, and Brockmeier Cottage, right, flank the tent cottages in the center. The street in front of the sanatorium is Railroad (Central) Avenue. (Photo courtesy of Southwest Community Health Services.)

Figure 14. A cottage at Santa Fe's Sunmount Sanatorium, 1913. The openness, of course, was to ensure the patient plenty of fresh air, even in winter. (Photo courtesy of MNM, PA.)

15

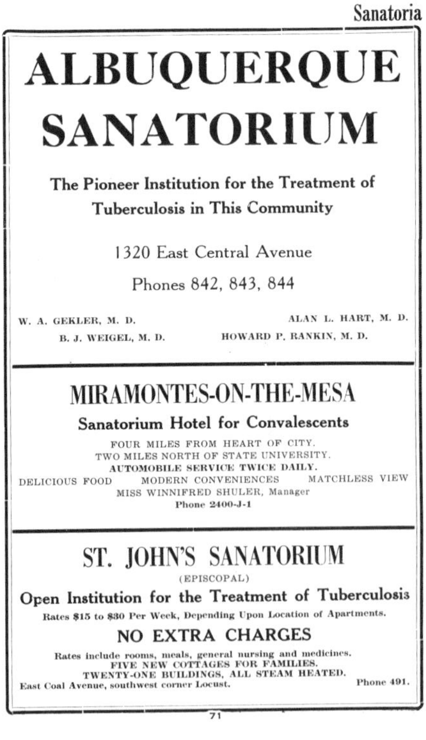
Sanatoria
ALBUQUERQUE SANATORIUM
The Pioneer Institution for the Treatment of Tuberculosis in This Community
1320 East Central Avenue
Phones 842, 843, 844
W. A. GEKLER, M. D.
ALAN L. HART, M. D.
B. J. WEIGEL, M. D.
HOWARD P. RANKIN, M. D.
MIRAMONTES-ON-THE-MESA
Sanatorium Hotel for Convalescents
FOUR MILES FROM HEART OF CITY.
TWO MILES NORTH OF STATE UNIVERSITY.
AUTOMOBILE SERVICE TWICE DAILY.
DELICIOUS FOOD
MODERN CONVENIENCES
MATCHLESS VIEW
MISS WINNIFRED SHULER, Manager
Phone 2400-J-1
ST. JOHN'S SANATORIUM
(EPISCOPAL)
Open Institution for the Treatment of Tuberculosis
Rates $15 to $30 Per Week, Depending Upon Location of Apartments.
NO EXTRA CHARGES
Rates include rooms, meals, general nursing and medicines.
FIVE NEW COTTAGES FOR FAMILIES.
TWENTY-ONE BUILDINGS, ALL STEAM HEATED.
East Coal Avenue, southwest corner Locust.
Phone 491.
71

16

17

Figure 15. St. Vincent's Sanatorium in Santa Fe, ca. 1895. This hospital-sanatorium was founded in 1865 and was the oldest in the Territory. The main building, center in this photo, burned in 1896. (Photo courtesy of St. Vincent's Hospital, Santa Fe.)
Figure 16. An advertisement page from the 1923 *Albuquerque City Directory.* Miramontes-on-the-Mesa, far out in the country but linked to the city by automobile service, was located approximately where Menaul Boulevard and Carlisle presently meet.
Figure 17. Patients "chasing the cure" in 1918 at Valmora Sanatorium. The building at the extreme right in the picture has its canvas-flap window down. (Photo courtesy of Dr. Carl H. Gellenthien, Valmora.)

18

Figure 18. Since tedium was so great a problem in the the old tuberculosis sanatoria, light exercise was often encouraged for recovering patients. These croquet players were patients of Santa Fe's Sunmount Sanatorium around 1900–1910. (Photo courtesy of MNM, PA.)

Figure 19. A picnic outing for Valmora Sanatorium patients in 1937. The physician-accordionist, Dr. Carl H. Gellenthien, cheerfully took requests, but everything came out "Home on the Range." Dr. Gellenthien still (1986) lives and practices at Valmora. (Photo courtesy of Dr. Gellenthien.)

Figure 20. Dr. William T. Brown, shown here in a 1931 photo, was one of the old tuberculosis specialists who originally came to New Mexico for their own health. In 1904 he founded Valmora Sanatorium near Watrous. (Photo courtesy of Dr. Carl H. Gellenthien, Valmora.)

20

21

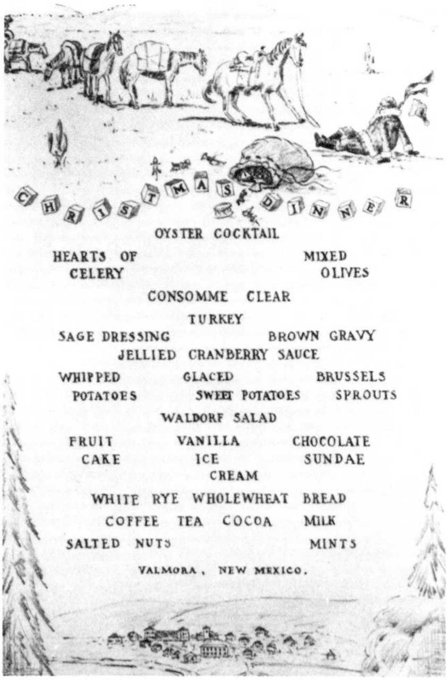
CHRISTMAS DINNER
OYSTER COCKTAIL
HEARTS OF CELERY
MIXED OLIVES
CONSOMME CLEAR
TURKEY
SAGE DRESSING
BROWN GRAVY
JELLIED CRANBERRY SAUCE
WHIPPED POTATOES
GLACED SWEET POTATOES
BRUSSELS SPROUTS
WALDORF SALAD
FRUIT CAKE
VANILLA ICE CREAM
CHOCOLATE SUNDAE
WHITE RYE WHOLEWHEAT BREAD
COFFEE TEA COCOA MILK
SALTED NUTS
MINTS
VALMORA, NEW MEXICO.

22

23

Figure 21. A sunny, airy room at Santa Fe's Sunmount Sanatorium, ca. 1900–1910. (Photo courtesy of MNM, PA.)
Figure 22. Good food—and lots of it—was part of the sanatorium cure for tuberculars. This meal was, of course, special: Christmas dinner at Valmora Sanatorium, 1934. (Photo courtesy of Dr. Carl H. Gellenthien, Valmora.)
Figure 23. The emphatically Southwestern lobby of St. Vincent's Hospital, Santa Fe, around 1925. (Photo courtesy of St. Vincent's Hospital, Santa Fe.)

Figures 24 through 27. Publicity photos taken at Valmora Sanatorium in 1928. (Photos courtesy of Dr. Carl H. Gellenthien, Valmora.)

24

25

Figure 24. Patient on arrival at the sanatorium.
Figure 25. Beginning the cure.

26

27

Figure 26. After two months.
Figure 27. After three months.

Figures 28 through 31. Varieties of tuberculosis therapy at Valmora Sanatorium, 1931–35. (Photos courtesy of Dr. Gellenthien.)

28

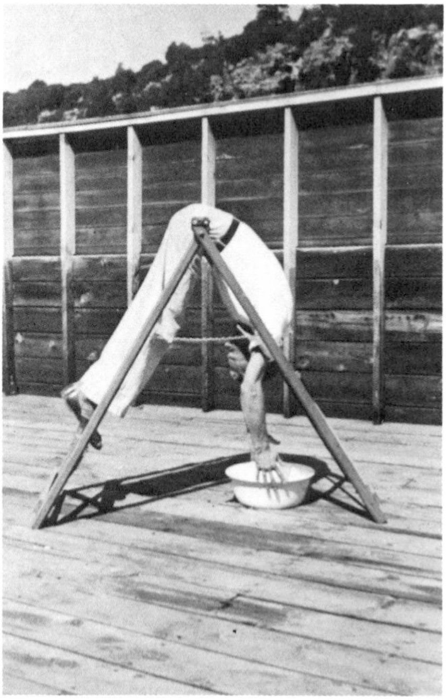

29

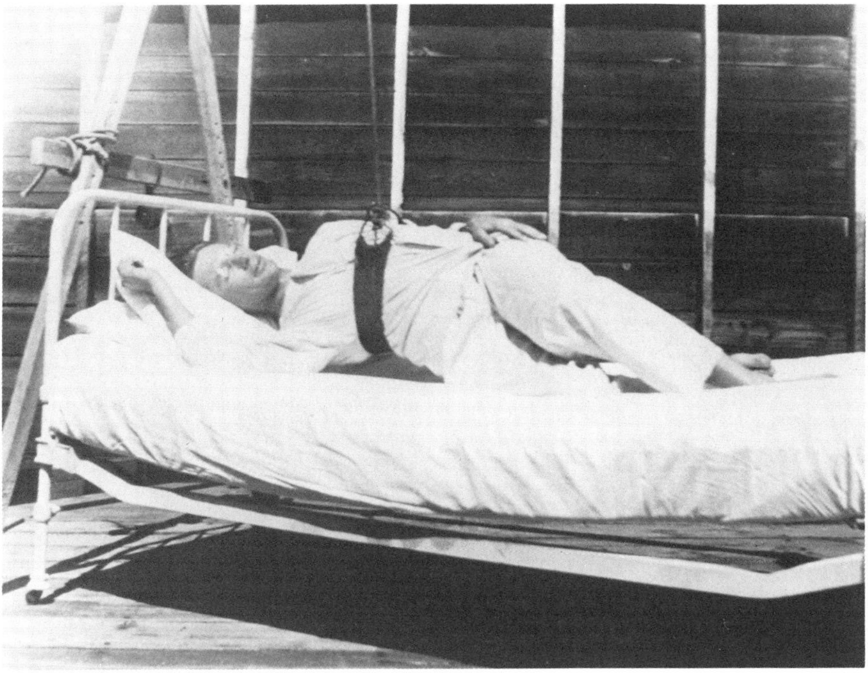

30

Figure 28. This young woman, a victim of tuberculosis of the larynx, is holding her tongue down with the implement in her left hand, while using the mirror before her to focus the sun's rays on her ailing throat. This treatment was called heliotherapy.

Figure 29. This patient, suffering from a suppurative disease of the lung, is trying to drain fluid from his lungs. The technique was called postural drainage. (This patient died a few weeks after this photo was made.)

Figure 30. The belt hoist slung around this patient's thorax was intended to limit the chest's motion, providing opportunity for his lungs to rest.

31

32

Figure 31. Another form of heliotherapy for tuberculars: simple sunbathing. This young woman, who had been a model in Chicago before falling ill with tuberculosis, agreed to pose for publicity photos for Valmora Sanatorium. Dr. Carl H. Gellenthien, Medical Director of the sanatorium at the time, remembers that the photos were never used, for none of them looked sufficiently "clinical." Note the Indian rugs used to help provide some privacy!

Figure 32. A panoramic view of a cottage sanatorium out in the fresh air of the countryside, in this case Valmora Sanatorium, ca. 1935. The main building is partially obscured in the grove of trees, center left, with cottages scattered all around. (Photo courtesy of Dr. Carl H. Gellenthien, Valmora.)

Figure 33. Dr. Paul M. Carrington was a chest specialist sent by the Army to New Mexico's Fort Stanton in 1899. This 1902 photograph shows him with prize(?) trout. (Photo courtesy of New Mexico State Records Center and Archives. Hereafter State Archives.)

33

34

35

Figure 34. Appearances to the contrary, the nattily attired Dr. Arthur J. Evans was a hard-working country doctor. He practiced in Elida (Roosevelt County) from 1908 until 1938, then in Magdalena until his death in 1952. (Photo courtesy of New Mexico Board of Medical Examiners, Santa Fe. Hereafter BME.)

Figure 35. Dr. James F. Scott lived in a dugout when setting up his practice in 1906 in the plains region around Texico and Clovis. He became one of the leading physicians of the area and served a large constituency before his death in 1923. (Photo courtesy of BME.)

36

37

Figure 36. Albuquerque's Dr. Abraham Shortle, who practiced in the city from 1908 until his death in 1922, was a nationally known specialist in tuberculosis. He founded one of the city's largest and best known sanatoria in 1908. (Photo courtesy of BME.)

Figure 37. Dr. Chester Russell was the much-loved town doctor for Artesia from 1910 until his death in 1958. He served as president of the New Mexico Medical Society, 1921–22. (Photo courtesy of BME.)

38

HEALTH MOBILE
AUTOMOVIL DE LA SALUD
NEW MEXICO PUBLIC
HEALTH ASSOCIATION
ASOCIACION DE SANIDAD
PUBLICA DE NUEVO MEXICO

39

40

Figure 38. Deming's Dr. Fred D. Vickers practiced in the town from 1912 until his death in 1939. He was one of the state's many general practitioners who developed special expertise in treating tuberculosis. He was president of the state medical society in 1932–33. (Photo courtesy of BME.)

Figure 39. A 1920 photograph of the "Health Mobile" financed privately by the New Mexico Public Health Association and used as a kind of traveling laboratory. It was more important for the public attention it garnered to the Association's campaign for a state board of health. (Photo courtesy of UNM-MCL.)

Figure 40. Before the health mobile, three prominent physicians are identifiable. Second from the left is Dr. Lucien G. Rice, Sr.; the woman in the center is Dr. Evelyn Fisher Frisbie (President of the New Mexico Medical Society, 1915–16); and Dr. J. E. J. Harris, President of the Society in 1943–44, stands third from the right. (Photo courtesy of UNM-MCL.)

CHAPTER 4

The Sanatorium Movement and New Mexico Medicine

THE ARRIVAL IN SUCH LARGE NUMBERS OF THE HEALTH-seekers quickly made an enormous and indelible impact on the structure and practice of medicine in New Mexico. Its effects were manifest in numerous ways, but most obviously in the rapid proliferation of sanatoria around the state. Many of them became permanent fixtures within the health-care delivery system of New Mexico, and they remain, if in modified form, important institutions today.

In the last quarter of the nineteenth century, at the very acme of the emphasis on altitude therapy for pulmonary tuberculosis, an old therapeutic regimen, refined and elaborated, rose to dominate the field, sweeping aside almost all other approaches to treating the disease. This was what has come to be called the sanatorium movement,[1] and New Mexico was one of the major citadels of it. A brief sketch of the background to the sanatorium movement may provide a useful perspective on this striking aspect of modern medicine.

As with most of the major medical discoveries of the nineteenth century—general anesthesia is a conspicuous exception—European medicine pioneered in the creation of the sanatorium treatment of tuberculosis. Special hospitals for pulmonary patients were founded first in England—the Royal Hospital for Diseases of the Chest (1814) and the Brompton

[1]There are various spellings of the noun "sanatorium" and its plural form. Since the word stems from the Latin verb "sanare," meaning "to heal or to cure," I prefer the form used and the proper Latin plural, "sanatoria."

Hospital for Consumption and Diseases of the Chest (1841), both in London—and later spread to the continent and North America.[2] Hospitals devoted exclusively to the care of tuberculars became relatively common during the last half of the century, and many general hospitals added special wards, wings, or annexes for the care of tuberculars. More specific yet, hospitals for pulmonary patients located in mountain regions, consistent with altitude-therapy doctrine, became fixtures of the medical landscape by the last quarter of the century.

The properly conceived and operated sanatorium, however, was much more than just an institution limited to chest patients and did not necessarily require location in the mountains. Rather, it was a therapy *regimen,* first and foremost, requiring scrupulous respect for certain basic therapeutic principles, chief among which was rest. The ideas and work of Hermann Brehmer in the 1850s and 1860s have already been mentioned for their importance in the emergence of altitude therapy. But in his treatment of tuberculars, Brehmer always insisted that there was much more to it than just deep breathing of the life-restorative air of the mountains. He emphasized as well the importance of good and abundant food, a modicum of exercise, close medical supervision, and, perhaps most important of all—he was after all a good nineteenth-century German—an orderly, controlled, and moderate daily routine. To these fundamental doctrines his pupil Peter Dettweiler both added and subtracted. Dettweiler accepted most of his mentor's principles, but he was more convinced than his teacher that rest outdoors in the bracing air of the countryside was the key element that was essential for recovery from lung disease. It was Dettweiler who started the tradition or practice of bundling up his patients and propping them up outdoors on chaise lounges for lengthy periods of absolute rest, and he was utterly inflexible in the execution of his cure. Despite rain, fog, winds, and snow, his patients chased the cure outside. Even when the thermometer sank as low as

[2]Julius Wilson identifies Boston's Channing Home (1857) and House of the Good Samaritan (1861) as this country's first hospitals for the care of tuberculars ("The Western Frontier and Climate Therapy," *The Journal-Lancet* 86 [1966]:564–65) and St. Vincent's Hospital in Santa Fe, established in 1865, as the third ("Pikes Peak or Bust," *Rocky Mountain Medical Journal* 64 [1967]:59). St. Vincent's certainly did the bulk of its business in caring for consumptives, but whether it could be called a hospital exclusively for tuberculars in the first decades of its existence is questionable. See Clark Kimball and Marcus Smith, M.D., *The Hospital at the End of the Santa Fe Trail: A Pictorial History of St. Vincent Hospital, Santa Fe, New Mexico* (Santa Fe: Rydal Press, 1977).

twelve degrees, and very commonly in the complete absence of the sun, his wards took their daily rest treatments of seven to ten hours, sometimes as much as twelve, outdoors.[3]

While Brehmer, Dettweiler, and other European physicians experimented with tuberculosis therapy involving the principles mentioned above, American pioneers joined in the investigation. The first American sanatorium for tuberculars was the short-lived American Mountain Sanatorium for Pulmonary Diseases established in Asheville, North Carolina, in 1875 by an emigrant doctor from Bavaria, Josef Gleitsmann. Though this institution apparently got good medical results, it was not so fortunate economically, closing after three years of operation. Much more successful was a second sanatorium established in Asheville ten years later, an institution important in shaping the sanatorium movement in that city and in the country generally.[4] The North Carolina physicians were the earliest in the United States to employ sanatorium treatment for tuberculosis, but a young New York doctor named Edward Trudeau was ultimately far more influential. Stricken himself with pulmonary tuberculosis in the 1870s while nursing his sick brother, Dr. Trudeau went off into the Adirondack Mountains to spend his declining years in peace. But despite his own expectations and those of his doctors, Trudeau got well, learning firsthand the restorative effects of the outdoor life, rest, good food, and close medical attention to the needs of a frail constitution. Using his own experience as a guide, he founded the Adirondack Cottage Sanatorium, later called the Trudeau Sanatorium, at Saranac Lake, New York, and dedicated himself and the institution to the care of tuberculosis victims. Within a brief period of time, Trudeau and his work attained worldwide fame, and his institution became an exemplar for the sanatorium movement in general.

It was the Saranac Lake pioneers, particularly Trudeau and his able associate Dr. Lawrason Brown, who established the basic principles of the American sanatorium movement. Sanatorium therapy was initially, and to some extent remained, an idiosyncratic thing, dependent to a considerable degree on the individual preferences and prejudices of the doctors and administrators who ran the institutions; but Saranac was a special Mecca of the movement. The fundamentals of its therapy regimen

[3]R. Y. Keers, *Pulmonary Tuberculosis: A Journey Down the Centuries* (London: Baillière Tindall, 1978), pp. 75–78.

[4]Wilson, "Western Frontier":564–65.

involved five basic requirements: rest, hyperalimentation (a term meaning, simply, "plenty of food"), "outdoor life"—lots of fresh air, sunshine, light exercise, and so forth—moderate and regular habits, and good medical care.

Rest was by far the most important among these basic principles of sanatorium therapy and meant much more than just "taking it easy." It meant reduction of the body's physical activity to the absolute minimum possible, on the premise that the sick lungs needed the greatest possible opportunity to heal themselves. They could not achieve that objective while straining to provide oxygen to fuel physical or mental activity, even those so relatively nontaxing as chatting with a friend or sitting up in bed reading a book. Cecil's great *Textbook of Medicine,* in its very first edition (1927), stressed the rigorous medical meaning of the word *rest:*

> Of the countless remedies for tuberculosis, complete rest is the only one which has proved eminently successful. This means not what is generally considered rest, but absolute quiet in bed as long as the fever persists. Even sitting up in a chair or reclining in a chaise-lounge must be regarded as exercise. Since it is undesirable for the patient to walk even as far as the toilet, a bedpan or commode should be used. . . . After the temperature has remained normal *for several months,* exercise should begin by degrees. Part of the day may be spent in a chaise-lounge.[5]

Most sanatorium theorists also believed strongly in the necessity for good nutrition in treating the consumptive. The tubercular, whose body was being literally consumed by the disease process, was obviously in need of large quantities of nutritious food to compensate and limit the damage and to build the victim's resistance to the basic disease as well as to opportunistic infections. The first commandant of the new United States Army Sanatorium at Fort Bayard, New Mexico, a physician who firmly believed in the efficacy of sanatorium therapy, contended that "the problem in the treatment of tuberculosis is essentially one of nutrition," and no less an authority than the great Sir William Osler concurred: "The cure of tuberculosis is a question of nutrition; digestion and assimilation control the situation; make a patient grow fat and the local

[5]Russell L. Cecil, ed., *A Text-Book of Medicine by American Authors* (Philadelphia and London: W. B. Saunders Co., 1927), p. 294.

disease may be left to take care of itself."[6] As with the concept of "rest," sanatorium therapy meant by "good food and lots of it" far more than just three square meals a day. An old "lunger," Dr. Esmond Long, who survived to become director of medical research for the National Tuberculosis Association, remembered that when he was a sanatorium patient in 1915 he drank four quarts of milk and sometimes ate a dozen eggs a day *plus* three full meals under the "grow fat" regimen.[7] (He also remembered gaining forty pounds and marveled at the cholesterol load he placed on his system.) At the same time, patients in some New Mexico sanatoria were fed six times a day;[8] and authorities at the Fort Bayard Sanatorium, believers in the "get 'em fat" school and concerned about their soldier-patients "eating too rapidly and bolting their food, [found it] necessary to direct that ambulant patients must remain in the dining-room for at least twenty minutes during each meal."[9]

The other basic elements of sanatorium therapy were only slightly less important. The efficacy of good air—clean, unpolluted, and dry—was taken over into sanatorium therapy from the older altitude or climate therapy schools, and remained a basic part of sanatorium treatment. Rest was the really critical thing, but rest outside in fresh air and dazzling sunshine was best of all. Sanatoria all over the country preached the virtues of good air, but that message was especially prominent in the advertising by New Mexico sanatoria for self-evident reasons. At Fort Bayard the belief in the efficacy of clean, outdoors air was so strong that patients were not allowed in their dormitories from eight in the morning until eight at night, and all dormitory windows were always open year-round.[10]

The positive effects of rest, good food, and fresh air were ensured in the

[6]Major D. M. Appel, "United States General Hospital for Tuberculosis at Ft. Bayard, N.M.," *Journal of the American Medical Association* 35 (20 October 1900):1003; William Osler, *The Principles and Practice of Medicine,* 3d ed. (New York: D. Appleton and Co., 1898), p. 332.

[7]Julius H. Comroe, Jr., "T.B. or Not T.B.?: The Treatment of Tuberculosis," *American Review of Respiratory Diseases* 117 (1978):382.

[8]Francis T. B. Fest, M.D., "The Consumptive's Holy Grail," *New Mexico Medical Journal* 5 (1909–10):118.

[9]Major D. M. Appel, "The Army Hospital and Sanatorium for the Treatment of Pulmonary Tuberculosis, at Fort Bayard, New Mexico," *Journal of the American Medical Association* 39 (24 November 1902):1376.

[10]Appel, "United States General Hospital":1003.

sanatoria by rigid insistence on routine and by schedules designed to incorporate them in the patients' lives in fundamental ways. The daily life of the sanatoria was an exercise in sociomedical engineering, and there was in many cases an almost military or penal-institution rigidity associated with it. Sanatoria physicians and administrators believed so firmly in that basic triad of tuberculosis therapy (already discussed) that their patients were almost dragooned into respecting the treatment regimen. Without respect for the schedule, there could be no cure; it was that simple. The following schedule of an Albuquerque sanatorium reflects the effort to maximize regular habits and the other elements of the sanatorium cure:

7:00 A.M.	Glass hot water
7:30 A.M.	Prepare for breakfast
8:00 A.M.	Breakfast
9:00 A.M.	Chase[11]
10:00 A.M.	Temperature and pulse; glass hot milk; recreation, such as reading, writing, visiting, or writing letters
11:15 A.M.	Chase
12:15 P.M.	Prepare for dinner
12:30 P.M.	Dinner
1:00 P.M.	Chasing
3:00 P.M.	Temperature and pulse
3:15 P.M.	Glass hot milk; one hour recreation
4:15 P.M.	Chasing
5:15 P.M.	Prepare for supper
5:30 P.M.	Supper
6:00 P.M.	Chasing
8:00 P.M.	Temperature and pulse
8:15 P.M.	Glass hot milk
8:30 P.M.	Retire for the night[12]

On such a schedule the patient slept $10^1/_2$ hours and rested or chased another 7 hours per day, spent around 2 hours at table, and the other $4^1/_2$ hours of his day in very light exercise and miscellaneous nontaxing activities. Despite the tedium, everything depended on adherence to the

[11]Note the formal incorporation of this casual term used for resting outside, usually in a chaise lounge.

[12]"The 'Rest Cure' in the Treatment of Tuberculosis," *The Herald of the Well Country* 1, no. 5 (1915):6.

schedule. A prominent Las Vegas tuberculosis specialist was adamant about it: "It is the enforcement of the routine—life in the open air all the time; absolute, continuous rest; the very best of food, and as much of it as possible—together with the scientific care of the sanatorium which makes it valuable."[13] One of the most eminent of New Mexico's old-time tuberculosis specialists, Dr. Earl S. Bullock of Silver City, believed so strongly in the sanatorium routine that he was even willing to surrender the special salubrity of his beloved New Mexico—in which he also strongly believed—if it were necessary to choose between the one or the other. Bullock taught that it was the sanatorium discipline which was the indispensable element in recovery: Better to stay home in a sanatorium than to go to the West and try to live outside one.[14]

One of the main reasons, surely, for the physicians' stern insistence on the importance of sanatorium routine was the difficulty in getting patients to follow it. As the schedule cited above suggests, it was an extraordinarily confining, tedious regimen which required unusual discipline of those subjected to it. Given the fact that the average length of stay in a New Mexico sanatorium was just over nine months,[15] the fever of pathologic tuberculosis was very often accompanied by "cabin fever," and sanatoria doctors, nurses, and other officials were hard put to maintain the rigor of the cure. Fort Bayard physicians, whose patients had been ordered to the sanatorium, understood well the psychological demands of sanatorium therapy: "In fact, very few Americans, especially of the class to which our patients belong, will voluntarily submit to a constant supervision and regulation of every detail of their lives, even to a lesser extent than is in vogue in the German sanatoria."[16] It is not surprising, then, that the especially relaxed life-style of the Southwest leaked over into its sanatoria, for as an eastern visitor noted, "In no community in the Southwest, with the possible exception of Silver City, does one witness the enthusiasm and attention to details with which patients follow the cure at Saranac."[17]

[13]Fest, "Holy Grail":118.

[14]Earl S. Bullock, M.D., and C. T. Sands, M.D., "Twelve Years of Pulmonary Tuberculosis Treatment in the West," *Journal of the American Medical Association* 52 (19 June 1909):1978.

[15]Ibid.:1977.

[16]Appel, "Fort Bayard, 1902":1375.

[17]Ernest A. Sweet, "Interstate Migration of Tuberculous Persons, Its Bearing on the Public Health, with Special Reference to the States of Texas and New Mexico," *Public Health Reports* 30 (1915):1253.

There were various kinds of reinforcement to make the dreary existence of sanatorium patients more tolerable, ranging from some quite harsh and unpleasant ones through attractive inducements. In the first category, a patient at Albuquerque's Methodist Sanatorium on East Central Avenue, known as "San Alley" in the 1910s and 1920s, recalled one of the more sobering reminders of the importance of sanatorium routine: "From my window all I could see were the ambulances that drove up to take someone away to die. That made a believer out of me."[18] Given the inherently unpleasant, though necessary, restrictions of sanatorium life, everything possible was done to ease the burdens of the patients. At Fort Bayard, for example, the physicians and staff endeavored "to reduce the irksomeness of the daily life of the patients to a minimum"[19] by encouraging light exercise, particularly sports like croquet and quoits, and by sponsoring singing groups and hobby clubs. Almost all sanatoria had their musicians and musical diversions and cardplaying, and all encouraged their fitter patients to visit and walk in the bracing outdoor air with one another. This was partially just common sense, an effort to relieve the tedium, but it was also the sign of a broad consensus that a good part of the recovery from tuberculosis depended on the will to do so. An Albuquerque patient wrote:

> Worry and despondency are self-poisoning to the tubercular, and the antidote is cheerfulness. The class of patient who get along the best are the ones who can adopt cheerfulness at all times. Mental despondency causes tubercular activity, upsets the digestive system, causes a nervous hacking cough and a rise in temperature.[20]

Sanatoria officials definitely encouraged an upbeat, cheerful, and optimistic mood within their walls, and one prominent medical historian credits them with being one of the first groups to stimulate interest in psychosomatic cures and relationships.[21] By and large, they seem to have been successful in blunting or at least reducing the negative aspects of sanatorium life. An Albuquerque physician and sanatorium owner–direc-

[18]Toby Smith, "They Were Called 'Lungers,'" *Albuquerque Journal,* 16 March 1980.

[19]Appel, "Fort Bayard, 1902":1377–78.

[20]"The 'Rest Cure,'" *Herald of the Well Country:*6.

[21]Richard H. Shryock, *The National Tuberculosis Association, 1904–1954: A Study of the Voluntary Health Movement in the United States* (New York: National Tuberculosis Association, 1957), p. 154.

tor, Dr. Abraham G. Shortle, claimed that he had patients "who were cured and back at their old vocations" returning each year to spend their vacations at his sanatorium.[22] There may have been something to that, for strong bonds certainly developed among the tuberculars. The shared discomfort, fear, boredom, and hopefulness, coupled with the concern, hard work, and compassion of their doctors, very often produced at least a grudging toleration of the sanatorium routine and sometimes even a pronounced esprit de corps. Shortle noted this latter phenomenon at his East Central Avenue sanatorium:

> For instance, on a cold, blustery, unpleasant morning you will see one of your oldest and best trained patients come out, well bundled up and lie down on his cot on the porch and soon, one by one, like burros following their leader over a mountain, the rest of the patients emulate his good example.[23]

Along with rest, good food, fresh air and sunshine, and regular habits, close medical attention was also basic to the sanatorium patient's treatment and his prospects for recovery. Daily medical evaluation was the direct means for determining progress or, in its absence, a change in therapy. The close watch on pulse rates, weight-levels, temperature, and other physical signs exercised by the sanatoria doctors and other medical staff undoubtedly made the difference in the recovery from the disease's ravages for many sanatoria patients. The skills, the standing in their field, and the compassion of New Mexico's tuberculosis specialists are appraised below. Suffice it to say here that the top-quality medical attention afforded by most of New Mexico's sanatoria physicians was fully within the best traditions of the sanatoria movement nationwide.

One crude measure of New Mexico's prominence in the sanatorium movement nationally was the sheer number of institutions established in the state and the number of beds available within them. Although the sanatorium movement had begun in the 1880s under the influence of Trudeau's successful sanatorium at Saranac Lake, the real boom period of the phenomenon was the first two decades of the twentieth century. Sanatoria, most of them privately owned and operated, proliferated around the country, and the growth of the industry was startlingly rapid. In 1904 it is estimated there were 96 sanatoria around the country with a total

[22] Abraham G. Shortle, "Home Treatment vs. Sanitarium Treatment of Tuberculosis," *New Mexico Medical Journal* 5 (1909–10):222.

[23] Ibid.

capacity of 9,000 beds, but the numbers leaped to 393 institutions with 26,000 beds within a mere six years. By 1920 there were 550 sanatoria with bed space for more than 56,000 patients, an expansion over a sixteen-year period of approximately 600 percent.[24]

New Mexico's experience paralleled that of the nation, with its major burst of sanatorium construction falling in the period from 1900 to 1920. As already noted, the first sanatorium in the Southwest was probably St. Vincent's in Santa Fe, originally opened in 1865. Treating consumptives from the beginning, the hospital set aside space exclusively for the use of lung patients as early as the 1880s. Sanatoria devoted entirely to the care of tuberculosis began to spring up in all quadrants of the state around the turn of the century. Table 6 suggests the chronology, geography, and character of that process, but it is incomplete and restricted to the larger, more prominent, or otherwise easily identifiable institutions. Numerous small-scale and less formal sanatoria flourished in the Mesilla Valley, Deming, Roswell, Raton, Las Vegas, Santa Fe, and Albuquerque—there was no kind of regulation of the industry—without ever earning mention in the directories and miscellaneous lists on which Table 6 is based.

Table 6 documents the coextension of New Mexico's sanatorium construction boom with that of the nation at large. Between the late 1890s and the mid-1920s, more than forty-four separate institutions were founded in the state. The movement was so ubiquitous that even the state penitentiary at Santa Fe established its minisanatorium, setting up a separate five-bed pavilion for tubercular inmates where a modified sanatorium regimen was practiced, modified basically by the fact that "some [patients] are sent out to work on the roads."[25] Virtually the entire state was affected, though there were special concentrations of sanatoria, notably in Albuquerque and Silver City. Indeed, because of its climate, railroad connections, and the facilities available, Albuquerque by 1915 was conventionally cited as one of the chief resort cities of the country for tuberculars, along with El Paso, Asheville, Colorado Springs, San Antonio, Denver, San Diego, and Los Angeles.[26] But all regions of the state shared in the development, and one study done in 1908 placed New Mexico fifth

[24]Shryock, *National Tuberculosis Association*, p. 116.

[25]Philip P. Jacobs, comp., *The Campaign Against Tuberculosis in the United States* (New York: National Association for the Study and Prevention of Tuberculosis, 1908), p. 167.

[26]Sweet, "Interstate Migration":1064. The omission of Phoenix and Tucson from this list is perhaps explained by the fact that they developed slightly later than Denver or Albuquerque because of the somewhat slower pace of railroad development in that state.

Table 6
Sanatoria in New Mexico, 1865–1937

Year Established	Name and Place	Ownership	Capacity	Other
1865	St. Vincent Sanatorium, Santa Fe	Sisters of Charity	75 (1912)	
1896	St. Anthony's Sanatorium, Las Vegas	Sisters of Charity	70 (1914)	
1897	Mountain Camp, Dripping Springs Canyon (Las Cruces)	Private	?	
1899	U.S. Army General Hospital, Ft. Bayard	U.S. Government	400 (1899)	
1899	U.S. Public Health Service Sanatorium, Ft. Stanton	U.S. Government	250 (1899)	
1901	Plaza Sanatorium, Las Vegas	Private	45	Dr. W. C. Bailey, Physician
	Sunmount Sanatorium, Santa Fe	Private	50	Dr. F. E. Mera, Prop.
	St. Joseph Sanatorium, Silver City	Sisters of Mercy	50	
1902	St. Joseph Sanatorium, Albuquerque	Sisters of Charity	40 (TB Annex)	
1903	Chico Springs Sanatorium, Chico Springs	Private	35 (1912)	Dr. H. B. Masten, Physician
1904	Mesa Ranch Resort, Las Vegas	Private	?	Dr. M. M. Milligan, Physician
	McBride Sanatorium, Las Cruces	Private	?	Dr. R. E. McBride, Physician
1905	Ranch Sanatorium, Lincoln	Private	25 (1912)	Dr. J. W. Laws, Physician
	New Mexico Cottage Sanatorium, Silver City	Private	80 (1912)	Dr. E. S. Bullock, Medical Director
	St. Mary's Hospital, Roswell	Sisters of the Most Precious Blood	15 (1914)	
	Valmora Ranch Sanatorium, Watrous	Private	20 (1905) 100 (1923)	Dr. W. T. Brown, Physician
	The Home, Las Vegas	Private	?	Dr. W. E. Kaser, Physician
	Montezuma Ranch Resort, Romero	Private	25 (1909)	Dr. P. J. Farmer, Physician
	Roswell Tent City and Sanatorium, Roswell	Private	?	Dr. Z. T. Martin, Physician

Table 6, continued

Year Established	Name and Place	Ownership	Capacity	Other
1906	Alamogordo Sanatorium, Alamogordo	Private	60 (1912)	Dr. W. S. Saltzgaber, Physician
	Diaz Sanitarium, Santa Fe	Private	30 (1909)	Dr. J. M. Diaz, Physician
1907	Home Sanatorium, Tucumcari	Private	20 (1912)	Dr. John E. Manney, Physician
	Fraternal City Sanatorium, Alamogordo	Private	100 (1908)	Dr. O. M. Miller, Physician
	The West Sanatorium, Silver City	Private	20 (1912)	P. P. West, Prop.
1908	Alamo Cottage Sanatorium, Alamogordo	Private	10 (1912)	
	Carlsbad Tuberculosis Sanatorium, Carlsbad	Private	16 (1909)	Dr. J. D. Pettet, Physician
	Southwestern Presbyterian Sanatorium, Albuquerque	Presbyterian Church	60 (1912)	Rev. Hugh Cooper, Superintendent
1909	Albuquerque Sanatorium, Albuquerque	Private	50 (1914)	Dr. A. G. Shortle, Physician
	Sunnyside Ranch Sanatorium, Silver City	Private	25 (1909)	Dr. LeRoy Peters, Medical Director
1910	Laguna Sanatorium, Laguna	U.S. Indian Service	40 (1921)	Dr. P. A. Slatter, Physician
1911	Aztec Sanatorium, Aztec	Private	10 (1914)	Dr. T. J. West, Physician
1912	Rest Haven Sanatorium, Silver City	Private	?	Dr. G. S. Milligan, Physician
	Alamogordo Sanatorium, Alamogordo	Private	10 (1914)	Dr. E. D. McKinley, Physician
	Murphy Sanatorium, Albuquerque	Private	28 (1916)	Dr. W. T. Murphy, Physician
	Cipes Sanatorium, Albuquerque	Private	25 (1916)	Dr. Joseph Cipes, Medical Director
	St. John's Sanatorium, Albuquerque	Episcopal Church	100 (1923)	
	Methodist Deaconess Sanatorium, Albuquerque	Methodist Church	65 (1923)	
1913	Black Rock Sanatorium for Indians, Black Rock (Zuñi)	U.S. Indian Service	16 (1931)	
1914	Children's National Tuberculosis Sanatorium, Silver City	?	30 (1916)	
	Deming Cottage Sanatorium, Deming	Private	9 (1916)	F. J. Reid, Superintendent

Table 6, continued

Year Established	Name and Place	Ownership	Capacity	Other
1915	National Methodist Sanatorium, Silver City	Methodist Church	45 (1916)	
1916	Mescalero Indian Hospital, Mescalero	U.S. Indian Service	44 (1931)	not all beds TB
	Civic Betterment League Sanatorium, Albuquerque	Private	?	
1918	Jameson Sanatorium, Albuquerque	Private	?	
1921	Jicarilla Southern Mountain Sanatorium, Dulce	U.S. Indian Service	100 (1921)	Dr. J. S. Ruoff, Medical Director
	Miramontes on the Mesa, Albuquerque	Private	22 (1923)	
	E. S. Marshall Sanatorium, Albuquerque	Private	12 (1923)	
1922	White Cross Sanatorium, Silver City	Private	14 (1925)	Mrs. E. M. Flynn, R.N., Supervisor
1923	Holy Cross Sanatorium, Deming	Catholic Church	180 (1931)	Dr. M. A. Cunningham, Medical Director
1926	Monkbridge Sanatorium, Albuquerque	Private	25 (1927)	Dr. M. K. Wylder, President
1927	Hillcrest Sanatorium, Albuquerque	Private	85 (1931)	
	Sunshine Sanatorium, Albuquerque	Private	?	
1931	National Lutheran Sanatorium, Albuquerque	Lutheran Church	?	
1934	Albuquerque Indian Sanatorium, Albuquerque	U.S. Indian Service	104 (1934)	
1936	State Tuberculosis Sanatorium, Socorro	State government	86 (1940)	
1937	AHEPA National Sanatorium, Albuquerque	Fraternal	46 (1940)	Dr. W. A. Gekler, Medical Director

in the nation in the number of beds available for the care of tuberculars, behind only New York, Pennsylvania, Colorado, and Massachusetts,[27] a remarkable record by comparison with the others, given the tiny population and economic base of the territory.

Ownership of the sanatoria varied across a fairly broad spectrum. Agencies of the federal government, such as the United States Army, the Public Health Service, and the Indian Service, were heavily involved during the construction boom of the first two decades of the century, followed closely by various Catholic and Protestant church groups. Prominently represented, however, were the private, for-profit institutions, many of them founded by private physicians or nurses and others by nonmedically connected businessmen. It is clear that private individuals sought to capitalize on the sanatorium boom, but it does not appear that the business was a very profitable one. The rise and oftentimes rapid disappearance of private institutions suggests as much, as do the extant records of some of the larger institutions, Southwestern Presbyterian Sanatorium and Methodist Deaconess Sanatorium, for example, both of which had to struggle very hard to make ends meet.[28] Many of the physician-owned and -operated private sanatoria were primarily for the convenience of the doctors with, surely, the hope that they would at least cover their own expenses and perhaps even turn a small profit.

Costs were a major and chronic problem for all the state's sanatoria, whatever their ownership. Since the essence of sanatorium care was prolonged rest—months at least, and for some patients years—sanatoria officials necessarily worked hard to keep their monthly costs and charges as low as possible. The charges levied by New Mexico institutions were generally low to average compared to similar institutions around the nation, but it ought to be remembered that even moderate rates projected over long periods of time became extremely burdensome. Silver City's New Mexico Cottage Sanatorium was one of the more expensive institutions in the state, charging as much as 90 to 100 dollars per month for its patients, but most of the facilities around the state were significantly

[27]Jacobs, *Campaign Against Tuberculosis*, pp. 3–143, is a list of "Sanatoria, Hospitals, and Day Camps for the Treatment of Tuberculosis."

[28]This impression is confirmed in the case of one of the larger and better-funded institutions, Valmora Industrial Sanatorium in Watrous or Valmora, New Mexico. Dr. Carl Gellenthien, interview with author, Valmora, N.M., 18 December 1984. See also Judith DeMark, "Chasing the Cure—A History of Health-Seekers to Albuquerque, 1902–1940," *Journal of the West* 21 (1982):49–58.

cheaper. In Albuquerque, for instance, Southwestern Presbyterian Sanatorium charged only 50 dollars per month in the 1920s and most of the other "sans" in the city charged about the same. The Methodist Deaconess Sanatorium on East Central Avenue offered a variety of options to potential patients. Cottages with sleeping porches cost 60 dollars per month, and those without them cost 50 dollars. For the more well-heeled a room in the sanatorium main building, with a sleeping porch and a private bath, could be had for 85 dollars per month. Those prices included board and general nursing and such amenities as steam heat and running water, but medical attention came extra.[29] To provide some perspective on those figures, it might be noted that a novice attorney starting out with one of Albuquerque's largest law firms was paid 75 dollars a month at that time, so even the relatively modest charges of New Mexico's sanatoria were not inconsequential. Certainly, they were high enough to force many "lungers" to forego sanatorium treatment entirely, to—in the phrase of the era—"make the cure on their feet," putting their trust exclusively in the climate.

The costs of sanatorium care varied according to the physical comforts of the facilities and the nature of the in-house medical care afforded their patients. Physically, the sanatoria ranged across a broad spectrum, although there were common elements among them. A large number of them, particularly in the first decade or so of this century, were simple tent cities. The first private sanatorium in Santa Fe, for instance, began as Sun Mount Tent Colony, before construction of more substantial buildings led to its renaming as Sunmount Sanatorium.[30] Dr. C. M. Yater of Roswell sank almost two thousand dollars of his personal savings in the construction of Roswell Tent City in the first years of the century, only to see the project die quickly since, he judged, too few consumptives were willing to accept the routine of the sanatorium; they preferred "to congregate in hotels, boarding-houses, rooming houses, or just throw up tents wherever."[31] When young Chester French came to Albuquerque in 1904 with his tubercular brother Jesse, the first residence for the young men was a tent city at Mountain Road and North Tenth Street.[32] These tent-

[29]"First Methodist Hospital Nothing Like Today's," *Albuquerque Tribune*, 24 May 1967.

[30]*Journal of the American Medical Association* 39 (27 September 1902):779.

[31]Charles M. Yater, M.D., "Therapetitic [*sic*] Notes—Status of Tuberculosis in the City of Roswell," *New Mexico Medical Journal* 5 (1909–10):271.

[32]Arthur N. Loveridge, *A Man Who Knew How to Live Among His Fellow Men: A Graphic Life Story of Chester T. French* (Boulder, Colo.: Old Trails Publishers, 1965), pp. 7–8.

city operations were largely ephemeral, but they were entirely consistent with the outdoor life and fresh air emphasis of the sanatorium movement.

From the tent cities the sanatoria ranged upward to considerably more elaborate and costly structures. Most common, at least among the larger institutions of forty or fifty beds and up, was what was called the cottage plan institution, modeled after the Trudeau Sanatorium at Saranac Lake. Cottage-plan sanatoria customarily consisted of a main building housing a dining room, kitchen, treatment rooms and facilities, offices for the staff, perhaps a recreation room, and a number of private or semiprivate rooms for the patients. Around this central building would be located a number of small cottages, normally housing no more than one or two patients.[33] The cottages were usually built as permanent structures, but they were hardly elaborate. Typically, they were modest, one-room structures with wooden floors and side walls made of wood and canvas, with the upper halves constructed of the tent material so that they could be easily raised to let in the healing air. Furnishings were simple and institutional—at least before patients added their personal touches—usually containing a single bed, a small dresser, chair, and table. Two cottages shared a common bath, although all cottages had running water for washing. Most of them were steam-heated and also had electricity. Most distinctively, almost all the cottages were fitted out with a small, screened porch at least large enough for a "chaser" or lounge chair. The screened-in porch became the architectural hallmark of New Mexico tuberculosis industry construction. The leitmotiv carried over to the design of the main buildings, which were characteristically built with broad, screened-in verandas or porches to facilitate taking the air. Cottages and bungalows almost always featured the screened-in porch—where patients often invited their fellow convalescents to "porch parties"—and even private residence construction was marked by the ubiquity of the sleeping porch. This was especially important since so many recovered or recovering "lungers" moved out of the sanatoria into the community to continue the cure in less expensive surroundings.

This discussion of sanatorium costs and construction should not obscure the fact that many "lungers," certainly a solid majority of those

[33]See the description of Sunmount Sanatorium in Beatrice Chauvenet, *Hewett and Friends: A Biography of Santa Fe's Vibrant Era* (Santa Fe: Museum of New Mexico Press, 1983), pp. 176–77, or that of St. Joseph's Sanatorium in Silver City in *Journal of the American Medical Association* 38 (31 May 1902):1451.

who sought out the desert Southwest for relief from the burden of their disease, never saw the inside of a sanatorium except possibly as visitors. Although we lack reliable figures on the subject, it is clear that most New Mexico health-seekers chased the cure without the benefit of sanatorium care, with costs barring the way for most of them. As a result, most of the state's tubercular havens were filled with "convalescing homes," where three or four boarders might rent basic accommodations, and many private homeowners rented out a room or two to "lungers" unable or unwilling to afford institutional care. A prominent Albuquerque real-estate broker remembered long after the fact that he had finally been forced to complain to Albuquerque chest specialist Dr. LeRoy "Pete" Peters about the doctor's standard advice to newly arrived patients that they find sunny, airy rooms with southern or eastern exposure. By the midtwenties there was not a vacant room in town with southern or eastern exposure, and the whole town tilted toward the southeast.[34] The pressure on Albuquerque's housing market was such that some invalids were forced to seek refuge in auto courts for extended periods of time,[35] and the "lungers" made a similar impact on the real-estate markets of Las Vegas, Roswell, Silver City, and Las Cruces, among others.

Whether the health-seekers sought treatment in the state's sanatoria or simply chased the cure on their feet, most of them turned to New Mexico's physicians for medical supervision, whether regular or spasmodic, of their struggle with the disease within them. What estimates can be made of the quality of care offered to the hopeful tuberculars who flocked to the state? New Mexico's altitude and climate were almost uniformly hailed as something approaching natural specifics for the lung-sick emigrant, but what about its doctors? Dr. Yater of Roswell grumbled (with surely a touch of exaggeration) that Roswell's streets were full of tuberculous refugees from the East, whose doctors had counseled them "to go west and eat all the milk and eggs they can and stay away from the doctors."[36] Were the doctors a weak link in the chain of elements that constituted the Southwestern cure? The available evidence would seem to indicate that exactly the opposite was true. At its worst, medical care for tuberculars in New Mexico seems to have been average, comparable

[34]George Savage, interview with author, Albuquerque, N.M., 8 February 1985.

[35]Walter I. Werner, "The Problem of Tuberculosis in New Mexico," *Southwestern Medicine* 24 (1940):406.

[36]*Southwestern Medicine* 10 (1926):15.

to care elsewhere, and at its best, it compared favorably with the best care available anywhere in the country.

Broadly speaking, there were two significantly different types of doctors treating tuberculosis in New Mexico—the general practitioner who took tuberculosis cases as he encountered them in the midst of his general practice, and the tuberculosis specialist whose practice was focused exclusively on treatment of the disease. There were superb practitioners within both categories. Almost all New Mexico physicians at the end of the nineteenth century and the beginning of the twentieth had extensive clinical experience with tuberculosis. This was largely because there were simply so many consumptives within the general populace, not all of whom (as noted) took refuge in the sanatoria. As a matter of course, general practitioners treated them for the miscellaneous and sundry ailments which afflicted them and their families, and kept a professional eye on their convalescence (or lack of it) from the lung disease as well. The physician of that prespecialization era was much less reluctant than doctors today to tackle whatever came along. He was accustomed to relying on his own resources and to taking responsibility for whatever problems presented themselves, for he lacked the extensive network of specialist support, expensive equipment, and complex tests on which modern doctors depend. The result is evident in the medical literature of the period, where articles and clinical reports by the tuberculosis specialists are liberally supplemented by contributions on tuberculosis treatment from the "country docs." For example, it is not surprising at all to find clinical articles entitled "Dietetic Treatment of Diarrhea in Babies" or "Inferior Midwifery: A Case Report,"[37] from the pen of a longtime Albuquerque family doctor like Meldrum K. Wylder, but it is at first blush surprising to find him—and many other general practitioners like him—engaged in detailed clinical discussion of tuberculosis cases with the chest specialists, and clearly holding his own in the exchange.[38] The explanation lay simply in the abundance of clinical tuberculosis among the New Mexico populace. A physician with a large practice, such as Wylder (or Dr. Robert E. McBride in Las Cruces, Dr. Thomas B. Martin in Taos, or Dr. William Wittwer in Los Lunas), encountered tuberculosis almost everywhere he turned and treated it himself, especially if it were

[37]*Southwestern Medicine* 6 (1922):301–4; *Southwestern Medicine* 20 (1936):178–79.

[38]See, for example, Wylder's article, "Childhood Tuberculosis: Discussed with Special Reference to Preventive Measures," *Southwestern Medicine* 18 (1934):120–22.

a mild or incipient case or if the victim were some poor mountain farmer physically and financially far away from the specialists of the larger towns. Also, there was a second, quite personal reason for the interest of so many general practitioners, like Wylder, in tuberculosis. Dr. Wylder originally came to New Mexico from Missouri in 1903 with a case of pulmonary tuberculosis himself, seeking the cure. There were many others like him (and the importance of this factor in liberally sprinkling the state with bright and well-trained young physicians will be examined below). For these reasons, the general practitioners of New Mexico—and they constituted at least 90 percent of all doctors—were busy in the war against tuberculosis. Well into the 1930s they did not hesitate to treat the disease and, given their familiarity with the problem, did a good job of it.

Alongside the general practitioners taking tuberculosis cases as they found them, the chest specialists very early appeared on the New Mexico scene, relatively few in number at first, but large in the scale of their practices and in prestige. They constituted something of an elite within the panoply of New Mexico medicine and ranked among the top echelons of tuberculosis specialists nationally. About a dozen of them stand out from their peers: Drs. Earl S. Bullock, Oliver T. Hyde, and LeRoy Peters of Silver City; Colonel George E. Bushnell of Fort Bayard; Drs. Abraham Shortle, Walter Gekler, Carl Mulky, J. E. J. Harris, and Peters in Albuquerque; Drs. Frank Mera and Robert O. Brown of Santa Fe; Dr. Francis T. B. Fest of Las Vegas; and Drs. W. T. Brown and Carl Gellenthien of Valmora, New Mexico. They command special mention here both as representatives of the "old-school" tuberculosis specialists and because of the special distinction of their individual careers and achievements.

As a group, they were distinguished by the high caliber of their educational backgrounds and attainments. They were impeccably trained physicians, graduates of some of the finest American and European medical institutions. They came from such places as Yale (Harris), Columbia (Hyde), Heidelberg (Fest), and Illinois (Peters and Gellenthien). No fewer than four of them (Shortle, Fest, Gekler, and Hyde) had done special work in tuberculosis therapy in German universities, world leaders at the end of the last and the start of this century. Dr. Shortle had even spent time in working with the eminent European chest specialist Dr. Carl Spengler in Davos, Switzerland, lodestar of the sanatorium movement. Both Mulky and Gellenthien made regular study pilgrimages to the Trudeau School of Tuberculosis at Saranac Lake, New York. All of them, in short, brought the finest of academic preparations to the New Mexico vineyard, and long before the advent of compulsory continuing education they were zealous in keeping their information and skills fresh. Their commitment to study and their contemporaneity were reflected in their prolific scholarship as well. Despite the time pressures and the demands of their extensive private practices, almost all of them were represented in the pages of regional and national journals that reported the results of their work and study. All of the thirteen mentioned had national reputations, primarily as a function of their publications.

They were also active and prominent in local, regional, and national medical organizations, another important vehicle for the dissemination of their information and influence. Without exception, they were loyal and active members of their local medical societies, and, without disparagement of the generality of doctors around the state, it is probably accurate to cite the tuberculosis specialists as the leaven of the county medical societies in the first part of this century. Six of the thirteen mentioned (Fest, Peters, Mulky, Harris, Robert O. Brown, and Gellenthien) were honored by election to the presidency of the New Mexico Medical Society, a measure of the esteem in which their colleagues held them. And their reputations definitely extended beyond the frontiers of New Mexico. They filled high offices in all of the prestigious national organizations of their field, including the National Tuberculosis Association, the American Trudeau Society, the American Sanatorium Association, the American Climatological Society, the American College of Chest Physicians, and others. Gellenthien was elected vice-president of the American Medical Association in 1953, and Fest was a Fellow of the Royal Society of Surgeons and vice-president of the 1908 International Congress of Tuberculosis, meeting in Washington. Drs. Fest and Gekler had truly international reputations, the former as developer of an operative procedure for the cure of enuresis in females, which came down in the surgical literature as "Fest's operation,"[39] and then later as a tuberculosis specialist. Gekler, who studied and practiced at the University of Marburg in Germany, the great municipal hospital in Frankfurt, and in the sanatoria of Asheville, North Carolina, after his basic medical education at Indiana Medical College, was a national and international expert on pneumothorax (see pp. 158–59) before the First World War.

Many of the old tuberculosis doctors shared something else in common:

[39]Francis T. B. Fest, "Eine neue Operation zur Heilung der Incontinentia Urinae bei Frauen," *Der Frauenarzt* 10 (1895):193.

firsthand experience with the White Plague. Seven of the thirteen singled out (Peters, W. T. Brown, Bullock, Hyde, Robert O. Brown, Harris, and Gellenthien) were tuberculars themselves, who came to New Mexico to get well and then to practice; and an eighth (Fest) came with a tuberculous wife. Victimization by the disease was very common among the first generation of chest specialists in the state, but less so as time passed. Bullock wrote in 1909:

> Most of us who have been long enough in the work [study and treatment of tuberculosis] rather lament the fate that made us specialists in the disease; for it really is fate and not choice that makes most of us tuberculosis specialists, nearly all having served time as consumptives before taking up the work.[40]

Dr. Bullock's story was typical of many in that first generation of chest specialists. Graduating from his hometown Detroit College of Medicine (later Wayne University) in 1893, he was quickly successful in establishing a growing private practice in general medicine in New York City's fashionable West Side. To do his patriotic duty, he enlisted in the Spanish-American War and came down with pulmonary tuberculosis during that conflict. He was sent out to New Mexico in 1899 with the original medical complement charged with establishing the U.S. General Hospital for Tuberculosis at Fort Bayard. He was both chasing the cure himself and serving as acting assistant surgeon and pathologist for the new hospital. He got better, moved from the army sanatorium to practice in the private sanatoria in Silver City, and quickly established himself as one of the pillars of the New Mexico medical community, especially among its chest doctors. After twenty-seven years in Silver City, and patient and skillful ministration to several thousand tuberculosis victims, he returned to his native Michigan to semiretirement, dying there, full of years and achievement, at age seventy-one in 1941.[41]

[40]Bullock and Sands, "Twelve Years":1973–74.

[41]Bullock's story might be quickly balanced, however, by that of the young doctor who was his colleague and coauthor of the paper cited immediately above. Charles Turner Sands, a native of Pittsburgh and a graduate of Philadelphia's Jefferson Medical College, came down with tuberculosis shortly after graduation and came out to Silver City in 1909, twenty-seven years old and disappointed, and chasing the cure like Bullock had done a decade before him. Sands took the cure with Bullock, stayed and worked with him at the New Mexico Cottage Sanatorium for a time, and then set up private practice in Las Cruces. He died there in 1916, thirty-three years old, of pulmonary tuberculosis. A few weeks earlier,

The distinction and even eminence of New Mexico's old-time tuberculosis specialists is confirmed also by their practices. Many of their former patients still alive in the 1970s and 1980s—a fact that in itself is a testimony to their skills—remembered their old doctors fondly and respectfully. They insisted on their skill and compassion, but also, and maybe more tellingly, they recollected that they originally came to New Mexico because their doctors back in Pennsylvania or Illinois had heard of Dr. Brown or Dr. Peters or Dr. Gekler.[42] Their high offices in national organizations also bore witness to their standing among their peers around the country, an indirect reflection of the solidity of their practices. Probably the most concrete evidence, however, of the high standard of their practice is the case reports that they published in local or regional journals like the *New Mexico Medical Journal* or *Southwestern Medicine,* but also in national ones like the *American Review of Tuberculosis, American Review of Respiratory Diseases, Bulletin of the National Tuberculosis Association,* and the *Journal of the American Medical Association.* Those reports indicate clearly that the "backwoods" doctors of New Mexico were in the forefront of research on tuberculosis and tuberculosis therapy, and among the national leaders of the field. As one example, the surgical treatment of pulmonary tuberculosis called artificial pneumothorax might be mentioned. That technique was first attempted experimentally in Europe in 1882, but it was still an obscure, dangerous, and unproven therapy for the disease until 1912. At the spring meeting in that year of the National Tuberculosis Association, Dr. Mary Lapham of Highlands, North Carolina, stunned the profession with the results that she had achieved in twenty-three cases of artificial pneumothorax. Through careful introduction of an inert gas into the pleural cavity, Dr. Lapham produced intentionally the collapse of a diseased lung, with the extended period of rest allowing the diseased organ the opportunity to heal itself. From that beginning grew the collapse therapy which dominated tuberculosis treatment from the 1920s to 1950. Initially, however, the proce-

Albuquerque newspapers had carried notices of the death of Dr. Emmanuel O. Stuckey, a Georgian who had come out to Dr. W. T. Brown at Valmora Sanatorium a few years earlier, hoping for redemption from his case of tuberculosis. It did not come, and Dr. Stuckey took his own life by overdosing himself with morphine, leaving a note that he would not "linger on in my wretchedness." (*New Mexico Medical Journal* 15 [1916]:206). Sands and Stuckey remind us that not all made the cure.

[42]Judith R. Johnson, "Health Seekers to Albuquerque, 1880–1940" (Master's thesis, University of New Mexico, 1983), pp. 63–83.

dure remained controversial and its efficacy suspect, and only a few brave physicians dared to explore the new treatment. The point of interest here is that by the end of 1912, a few scant months after Lapham's pioneering paper, Dr. Abraham Shortle had already operated 17 cases at his Albuquerque Sanatorium using the new procedure,[43] and Drs. LeRoy Peters and Earl Bullock in Silver City were experimenting with the procedure before the end of that year as well.[44] New Mexico's tuberculosis specialists may have been distant physically from the famed eastern and midwestern centers of American medical research and practice, but this illustration suggests that they were nevertheless part of the advance guard of their field. They earned and deserved the special respect accorded them by their peers nationally and by their friends and colleagues locally.

But did it all do any good? If it can be conceded that New Mexico possessed the kind of climate deemed most suited to recovery from tuberculosis; if it can be agreed that it quickly developed the modern physical facilities required for the care of tuberculars; and if the state's physicians can be recognized as first-rate and among the nation's leaders in treating the disease, did it all make any difference? What kind of results did the health-seekers receive for their flight to New Mexico? At first glance, the statistics bearing on this basic question are jolting. The national death rate from tuberculosis in the year 1910 was 153.8 deaths per 100,000 population. The death rate from the disease in Albuquerque that year was 1,133.1, more than seven times the national norm. And that year was better for the city than most; the mean death rate from tuberculosis in Albuquerque during the period from 1903 to 1912 was 1,404.6.[45] However, the raw figures require close consideration before their meaning emerges. Since it could be proven that natives of New Mexico had a tuberculosis death rate far below the national average—one reason, of course, for the state's reputation for salubrity—it follows that the stunningly high tuberculosis death rate had to be the result of a significant mortality among the health-seeker émigrés. Indeed, according to the calculations made in the U.S. Public Health Service study done in 1913, 91 percent of Albu-

[43]Abraham G. Shortle, "Artificial Pneumothorax," *New Mexico Medical Journal* 9 (1912–13):101.

[44]LeRoy Peters and Earl S. Bullock, "Artificial Pneumothorax in the Treatment of Pulmonary Tuberculosis," *New Mexico Medical Journal* 9 (1912–13):95–97.

[45]Sweet, "Interstate Migration":1064–65. Sweet argues convincingly that these figures were almost certainly *too low,* since health authorities, as well as families, were often unwilling to record tuberculosis deaths as such.

querque's tuberculosis deaths in the period from 1903 to 1912 were among new residents of the city. Of the 1,419 deaths definitely attributed to tuberculosis in that period, 222 (15.6 percent) were of people who had been in the town *less than thirty days,* 439 (30.9 percent) were resident for from thirty days to six months, and another 160 (11.3 percent) were residents of six-months to one-year duration. Thus, 58 percent of Albuquerque's very high tuberculosis mortality figure consisted of recent arrivals who had sought the cure in New Mexico in vain.[46]

These figures make it clear that for many consumptives Albuquerque was not the rainbow's-end of victory and healing, and the results could not have been much different elsewhere around the state. Beyond these limited statistics from the 1913 study, the numbers available to measure what happened to the health-seekers in New Mexico are slippery and sometimes contradictory. Although it is evident that many health-seekers died within a brief time of their arrival in New Mexico, what percentage of the total traffic did they represent? There is no clear answer to that question, but we do have scattered statistics that shed some light on the subject. These numbers refer to sanatoria-cure rates and provide some perspective on what happened to the most favored class of health-seekers, those able to afford to chase the cure in the sanatoria around the state.

Sanatoria-cure rates were approximately the same in New Mexico as in the better sanatoria elsewhere in the nation, and perhaps slightly better given the equability of the climate. But nowhere were the cure rates greatly encouraging. In 1911 the Adirondack Sanatorium of Trudeau, the institution almost uniformly hailed as the exemplar of the movement, did a follow-up study of its patients. It was able to trace 2,672 of the total 2,878 consumptives it had treated during the period from 1885 to 1909. Of that total, 1,512, or approximately 57 percent, were still alive at the time of the study, and 43 percent were dead.[47] Many variables were entirely uncontrolled within those raw numbers, but still the numbers were not encouraging. When it is realized that the Adirondack Sanatorium, like most others around the nation, had early on adopted a policy of admitting only patients who had the disease in the first stages and thus

[46]These figures from the USPHS study were generally accepted as accurate by local experts on the subject. Indeed, if they were questioned at all, the suggestion was that they were probably too low. See LeRoy Peters and P. G. Cornish, Jr., "The Cauterization of Adhesions by Closed Pneumolysis after the Jacobaeus–Unverricht Method," *Southwestern Medicine* 15 (1931):61.

[47]Comroe, "T.B. or Not T.B.?":383–84.

could be said to have a more favorable prognosis, and when it is acknowledged that the sanatoria were peopled largely by young adults and not older ones, then the statistics become more ominous indeed. The statistics of the Toronto Hospital for Tuberculosis were even more gloomy. That institution treated 7,181 adult patients over the quarter-century from 1904 to 1930. Of that number, 3,221 definitely died of tuberculosis, producing a case mortality rate of 44.9 percent. (The institution discharged another 31.1 percent of its patients with the cautious judgment "improved," and classified only a handful of its released patients as "apparently arrested" cases.)[48]

In New Mexico the situation was almost surely not much better. Albuquerque doctors LeRoy Peters and P. G. Cornish, Jr., gave even more dismal figures in a 1931 article, in which they referred to statistics from "one of the best institutions in the west" which purportedly showed that 80 percent of the institution's patients were dead within three years of discharge.[49] That figure is almost surely exaggerated, but there were other authorities whose judgments were just as negative or gloomy. For instance, a recent study of the "lunger" migration to Arizona cites an identical percentage, concluding that eight out of ten consumptives died more or less soon after their arrival in that state.[50] The death rate among sanatoria patients was surely not as bad as all that, but the fact that respected authorities could paint so grim a picture is clear evidence that cure rates in general were nothing to get excited about.

More concrete in many ways than any of the appraisals mentioned thus far are two good statistical studies surveying the first several years of operation of the federal government sanatoria at Fort Bayard and Fort Stanton. The study of the first 623 patients treated at Fort Bayard during its initial eighteen months of operation yielded the following results:

	623 patients admitted (first eighteen months)
–	174 still in the sanatorium as of 3/31/02
	449 discharged or died

Results of these 449 cases disposed of were summarized as follows:

[48]Godfrey Gale and Norman C. DeLarue, "Surgical History of Pulmonary Tuberculosis: The Rise and Fall of Various Technical Procedures," *Canadian Journal of Surgery* 12 (1969):381.

[49]Peters and Cornish, "Cauterization of Adhesions":61.

[50]Clyde L. Gittings, "Arizona's Reputation as a Health Spa," *Arizona Medicine* 40 (1983):153.

clinically cured	33	7.4%
convalescent	52	11.6%
improved	157	34.9%
unimproved	113	25.2%
died	94	20.9%[51]

A study done several years later at Fort Stanton produced similar results: 22 percent died and 10 percent unimproved.[52] A summary of results at the Valmora Industrial Sanatorium, published in the AMA *Journal,* purported to show much better results, possibly because its patients began sanatorium treatment in less advanced stages of the disease.[53] Whatever the exact success ratio of the sanatoria, it is clear that they could not help all those who turned to them for aid. And if the sanatoria could not help up to a quarter or more of their patients, what about the mortality rates among that larger number of victims who could not afford lengthy sanatorium stays? They must have been markedly higher, although statistics are not available. In short, the limited data available make it easy to understand the sweeping judgment of a Roswell physician: "Many, in a measure, regain their health, but it is a lamentable fact that far the greater number sooner or later succumb to the ravages of this dreadful disease."[54]

Many tuberculars simply came too late, with the plague inside them too far advanced for any cure to help. Others lost their battles for survival because they lacked the money necessary to buy the period of rest, good food, and competent medical care which afforded the best chance for recovery. Many came to New Mexico's sanatoria and medical specialists and, lacking the patience and discipline essential to get well, still died. Almost all New Mexicans as late as the 1970s and 1980s knew someone who had come to the state to chase the cure, someone who arrived ill but got well. The logic of that situation ought to be clear, however. By definition, we do not know the thousands who died. It ought surely to be remembered that for every Dr. Earl Bullock, who came to New Mexico seeking health and got well, there was a Dr. Charles Sands, who did not recover. Albert G. Simms, the brilliantly successful lawyer, congressman, and businessman of the middle half of the century, came to New Mexico

[51]Appel, "Fort Bayard, 1902":1374.

[52]Bullock and Sands, "Twelve Years":1974.

[53]*Journal of the American Medical Association* 60 (14 June 1913):1891.

[54]Yater, "Tuberculosis in Roswell":271.

seeking the cure and found it, but his first wife Kathryn, also a "lunger," did not. Clyde Tingley's tuberculous wife Carrie recovered, but Chester French's brother Jesse did not. In 1910, Dr. LeRoy Peters, recovering nicely from his own case of tuberculosis, enthusiastically hymned the praises of his new home:

> We recognize the fact that climate per se is not a specific in tuberculosis, but we also know from experience that more wonderful cures and far better results are obtained in the southwest in the treatment of this disease than in any other part of the United States. . . . The climatic controversy will no doubt remain unsettled, as long as there are doctors east and doctors west, but even so, as long as there are consumptives east there will be consumptives west because a certain percentage after chasing a will o' the wisp in the cold and damp eastern states will . . . cast their lot with the rest of us who would rather enjoy life in the sunshine of New Mexico's hills and plains than fill a grave in the frozen regions of the north.[55]

His almost belligerent exuberance is forgivable, for Peters was doing well indeed. (The disease left him with a quite distinctive "whiskey voice," however, and ultimately killed him.) But for many of the health-seekers there was no balm in the Southwest Gilead, and the sad end of their hopeful chase was nothing other than a grave "in the sunshine of New Mexico's hills and plains."

The onset of the Great Depression was the beginning of the end for the tuberculosis era in New Mexico. There had been some dwindling of the flood of health-seekers in the 1920s, even before the national economic catastrophe, for as the sanatorium movement developed, it had become increasingly clear that it was the sanatorium regimen, and not the location of the institution, which was critical. Therefore, eastern and midwestern states, counties, and municipalities had begun to build their own sanatoria locally to care for their tuberculosis residents; and, although New Mexico continued assiduously to tout its air and sunshine, increasing numbers of tuberculars concluded that its marginal advantages did not justify the costs of the long trek west, the uprootedness, the separation from family and friends, and so forth. Furthermore, the rise of collapse therapy, initially artificial pneumothorax and then thoracoplasty, reduced the sheer length of sanatorium care. Instead of forcing the whole organism

[55] *New Mexico Medical Journal* 5 (1909–10):88.

to rest in bed or on a chaise lounge, the diseased lung itself could be put at rest locally and allowed a chance to heal with the patient requiring much less extensive institutional care. But this deemphasis of sanatorium care was a relatively slow process until it accelerated markedly in the depression years. With the advent of hard times, fewer people could afford the "luxury" of extended rest and the significant costs associated with it. Peters wrote an obituary for the sanatorium phenomenon:

> Up to the crash of 1929, money was plentiful. The butcher, the baker, the candlestick maker, spent his along with the millionaire. Private sanatoria were filled and were happy with a long waiting list. People believed in climate and were willing to pay for the luxury. . . . Patients bought climate the way they bought Packards, Pierces, and Cadillacs. But all that changed with the depression.[56]

Marginally successful sanatoria began to close or to convert to other uses in the 1920s, but the more solid institutions hung on into the 1940s and even early 1950s. Dealt serious blows by the Great Depression, the rise of public sanatoria, and the spread of collapse therapy, the sanatoria ultimately became medical anachronisms with the discovery and development of effective drug therapy for the disease in the early post–World War II years. First streptomycin in 1944, then para-aminosalicylic acid (P.A.S.) in 1950, and isonicotinic acid hydrazide (or isoniazid) in 1952 were proven as effective chemotherapeutic agents arresting the disease; and it was not long before medical textbooks actually preached against the old, time-honored therapies for the problem:

> Chemotherapy is the essential factor in the treatment of tuberculosis—bed rest, nutritional supplements, surgery, and other auxiliary procedures have become unnecessary.[57]

And, more bluntly still, it was declared: "Bed rest, hospitalization, and sanatorium care are not beneficial."[58] In 1950 there had still been long waiting lists for the beds available in public sanatoria around the nation, but within a decade the U.S. Public Health Service was reporting that less than half the beds available in the country for tuberculosis patients

[56]LeRoy S. Peters, "Changing Concepts of Tuberculosis during Twenty-Five Years," *Southwestern Medicine* 24 (1940):48.
[57]*Current Therapy* (1983):132, 137.
[58]Ibid., p. 137.

were then in use.[59] An era of New Mexico and American medicine had passed very quickly.

It is difficult to exaggerate the impact made by that army of tuberculous invalids on the development of New Mexico medicine or on New Mexico history in general. It was by far the most dramatic single phenomenon of the past century of New Mexico medical history and left its imprint in indelible ways on the state, its society, and its medical institutions. In terms of its impact on the state's medical development, the era of the "lungers" was important most obviously in the fact that it brought hundreds of new doctors to the territory and then to the state. The figures cited in Chapter 2 testify to the dimensions of the physician influx. Between 1886 and 1906, the number of M.D.s in New Mexico Territory more than doubled from 99 to 221, while the total population was expanding by a little less than 80 percent; and between 1906 and 1914 a stunning number of new doctors was issued licenses to practice in the state—737. A large percentage of those doctors were "lungers" themselves, traveling west to chase the cure and, if all went well, to care for unfortunates like themselves. Others were on the move with a sick loved one, a wife or child. Still others were just bright young physicians heading where the action was, hoping to establish honorable names and solid practices for themselves. New Mexico's physician–patient ratio at the time of statehood compared very favorably with the more settled regions of the East and Midwest largely because of the doctor migration associated with the tuberculosis industry.

In particular places the visibility of the "lunger" physicians was especially startling. At one time almost all the doctors of Santa Fe were recovered "lungers": Drs. James A. Massie (president of the Territorial Board of Health), Leigh Patton (who eventually died of the disease), Robert O. Brown (president of the New Mexico Medical Society in 1930–31), Wallace Livingston, and Albert Lathrop (also president of the New Mexico Medical Society in 1953–54) prominent among them. The medical communities of both Las Vegas and Roswell in the 1930s still reflected clearly the emigration of the "lungers."[60] In Albuquerque the old chest doctors

[59]Selman Waksman, *The Conquest of Tuberculosis* (Berkeley and Los Angeles: University of California Press, 1964), pp. 190–92.

[60]Dr. Carl H. Gellenthien, interview with the author, Valmora, N.M., 18 December 1984; Dr. I. J. Marshall, interview with the author, Roswell, N.M., 15 August 1983.

themselves were mostly health-seekers, but so were many other prominent physicians practicing in other fields. Drs. William Randolph Lovelace I; Lucien Rice, Sr.; Edgar Lassetter, Sr.; William H. Woolston; and Meldrum Wylder all come immediately to mind. Prominent physicians of a younger generation—Drs. Robert C. Derbyshire, Harold "Monty" Mortimer, and William Badger, among others—also sought out the state in seeking relief from the lung trouble within them, and virtually no sizable community of the state was unaffected by the phenomenon.

In sum, the influx of health-seekers brought enormous changes to the medical corps of New Mexico society, both in numbers and in quality. It brought in far more doctors than the rough "foreign" territory might otherwise have been able to attract, but the qualitative impact was perhaps even more important. The tubercle bacillus was no respecter of persons, striking across the spectrum of medical students and practitioners. Many of its victims were young doctors of high ability and impeccable training, aiming, and reasonably so, at the very loftiest strata of the national profession. Many of these doctors of talent and limitless expectations would not have voluntarily chosen the relative backwater of frontier New Mexico as the site of their careers. The state reaped a harvest of medical brainpower that it would not otherwise have enjoyed. But for the mycobacterium which forced them to the salubrious Southwest, many of New Mexico's medical luminaries of the past half-century or so would have exercised their considerable talents elsewhere. And the impact was far from an ephemeral one. It was still evident long after the close of the tuberculosis era itself, and indeed its historical shadow still colored the seniority roster of the state's physicians as late as 1984. The four eldest of the state's doctors in length of service in that year were Drs. Carl Gellenthien of Valmora, who first set up practice in the state in 1927; Victor Berchtold of Santa Fe, in 1928; Joe Williams of Roswell, in 1931; and Harold "Monty" Mortimer of Las Vegas and Albuquerque. Both Gellenthien and Mortimer originally came to the state as tuberculars themselves, and Berchtold first came with his father who was chasing the cure (in vain, incidentally).

While shaping the size and texture of New Mexico's medical profession, the tuberculosis industry also powerfully affected the development of medical institutions in the state. Many of the major medical facilities of the present day were born or took on new focus and vitality in the tuberculosis era. For example, the state's largest hospital, Albuquerque's Presbyterian Medical Center, originated as a tuberculosis sanatorium, and such major institutions as St. Vincent's in Santa Fe, St. Joseph Hospital in Albuquerque, St. Mary's in Roswell, and others find their origins intertwined with the tuberculosis industry. There would be, for instance, no Lovelace Medical Center had not twenty-three-year-old Dr. William Randolph Lovelace I sought out Sunnyside, New Mexico for his ailing lungs in 1906.

But an accurate assessment of the historical significance of the tuberculosis era on the development of New Mexico and its society requires reaching beyond the relatively narrow confines of the world of medicine. As suggested earlier, there is no question of the centrality of the tuberculosis industry within the story of the general economic and social history of New Mexico in the first half of this century. Certainly, the economic significance of the flood of health-seekers was clear to the broad variety of New Mexico business interests and boosters of the period, who did all they could to stimulate the migration. The health-seekers and the physicians and institutions who ministered to them constituted an enormous commercial boost to the cities and towns where the tuberculars sought refuge. The large numbers of the "lungers" and their normal human needs—groceries had to be bought, new clothes were needed from time to time, hair had to be cut, entertainment needs had to be met, and so forth—were a pivotal element in the economic base of the territory and its growth and expansion. Without them, the development of commercial and business enterprises in New Mexico would undoubtedly have been significantly slower.

But clearly it was the extraordinary treasure of human capital brought to New Mexico within the crowds of health-seekers which was ultimately of the greatest long-term significance. The importance of the "lungers" in leavening and enriching the state's medical profession was paralleled in virtually every sphere of New Mexico life. The numbers were important, but even more so was the quality or caliber of the health-seeker populace seeking new lives in the state. The consumptives represented a cross-section of American society in terms of age, education, wealth, and talent, but there was a significant skewing within their ranks toward the upper end of all those scales. Although New Mexico was a cheaper health-resort area than many, it still drew disproportionately from the middle and even upper classes of American society. It took resources, after all, to finance the trip west, the extended period of rest and recuperation, and all the ancillary expenses associated with the sanatorium approach to tuberculosis therapy; and though there were poor and even indigent people among them, the lungers were generally a valuable addition, economically and socially, to the communities which sheltered them.

Even a short, selective listing of some of New Mexico's better-known "lungers" may suggest the range of their achievements and contributions to the state. Health-seekers, for example, played major roles in the development of educational institutions around the state. France Scholes, colonial New Mexico scholar, dean of the University of New Mexico Graduate School, and vice-president of that institution; Dudley Wynn, founder of the school's innovative American Studies program and also a vice-president of the institution; John Milne, superintendent of the Albuquerque public schools for no less than forty-five years; and Dr. John Weinzirl, pioneer in bacteriology and climatology at UNM, represent some of the talented educators who originally came to New Mexico not by free choice but as chasers of the cure. Such, too, were Grace Thompson Edmister, founder and longtime director of the Albuquerque Civic Symphony Orchestra, and Kathryn Kennedy O'Connor, who cofounded the Albuquerque Little Theater. New Mexico's most celebrated architect, John Gaw Meem, was an old "lunger" who made the cure. He came to New Mexico seriously ill in 1920 and died in 1983. The cofounders of *New Mexico* magazine, Willard Andrews and Ward Hicks, as well as that journal's editor for thirty-four years, George Fitzpatrick, all came to the state as health-seekers. "Lungers" have also played major roles in the development of political and legal institutions in the state, with Albert Fall of Teapot Dome scandal repute; Clinton Anderson, U.S. senator from New Mexico and member of President Truman's cabinet; Judge John Simms, Chief Justice of the State Supreme Court and political chieftain; Albert Simms, his brother and a U.S. congressman from New Mexico; and Don Dickason, cofounder of one of the state's largest and most prestigious law firms, just some of the more conspicuous among them. Chester French, civic leader and founder of French Mortuary, came to the Southwest with a suffering brother. Dr. Howard Raper, dental pioneer in the state; John Tombs, founding father of the state's health department; Irene Fisher, journalist and local-color writer; Holm Bursum; Bronson Cutting; and a legion of others might be added to the list. It is surely no exaggeration to say that the health-seekers constituted a bonanza of brainpower and talent from which New Mexico singularly profited, and that no other discrete group of settlers, save only the Spanish colonists of the sixteenth and seventeenth centuries, made a more significant impact on the area.

In the 1940s and 1950s, when the flood of health-seekers dried up to a trickle and the sanatoria began to close down or convert and the old guard of tuberculosis specialists began to fade away, a vitally important era of New Mexico medicine ended. But another revolution lay in store for the medical profession and health-care system of the state. With the Second World War came an epoch of basic change in the structure and organization of New Mexico medicine. The world of sanatoria, tuberculosis specialists, and country doctors was transformed into a new one of medical schools, nationally famous clinics and medical centers, and legions of young and progressive medical specialists.

CHAPTER 5

Las Doctoras

A Tradition of Excellence in New Mexico

THE WALLS OUTSIDE THE OFFICE OF THE DEAN OF THE UNIversity of New Mexico's School of Medicine proudly display the class photographs of that institution's first seventeen graduating classes. On the most recent of them (1984) the strong, attractive faces of twenty-nine new women doctors may be found, 37 percent of the total. The figure for the future is surely to be higher, for the class of 1988 is 46 percent female. The 1979 edition of the *Directory of Women Physicians in the United States* listed 205 women doctors practicing in New Mexico, and the figure has risen by almost 100 percent since that compilation.[1] Beginning in the 1960s and escalating through the 1970s and 1980s, women have claimed for themselves an ever larger role as physicians in the New Mexico health-care complex. These modern women practitioners, however, were heir to a surprisingly strong tradition of excellence and service to New Mexico built by women doctors. Given the "frontier" character of New Mexico through so much of its history, and the social and professional restrictions placed on women physicians prior to modern times, it would not be surprising to find that female physicians played little role in New Mexico's medical history at least until the contemporary era. That conclusion is certainly true, if sheer numbers alone are considered, for prior to 1960 no more than a handful of women doctors had

[1]Center for Health Services Research and Development (AMA), *Directory of Women Physicians in the United States* (Chicago: American Medical Association, 1979), pp. 359–60.

Table 7
Women Physicians in New Mexico, 1886–1985

Year	Total M.D.s	Women M.D.s	% of Total
1886	99	2	2.0
1897	117	1	0.9
1902	166	2	1.2
1906	221	5	2.5
1912	408	7	1.7
1921	529	6	1.1
1925	365	6	1.7
1931	374	5	1.3
1936	401	8	2.0
1940	439	11	2.5
1950	504	21	4.2
1956	635	32	5.0
1961	715	54	7.6
1965	820	64	7.8
1969	1,013	80	7.9
1973	1,348	111	8.2
1979	1,863	205	11.0
1985	2,522	382	15.1

Sources: The figures for 1886 are taken from *Polk's Medical and Surgical Directory* (1886); for 1897 from *Flint's Medical and Surgical Directory* (1897); and for 1902 from *Polk's* (1902). All others are from *American Medical Directory* for the respective years.

made contributions of any note whatsoever to New Mexico's medical development. A short list of perhaps two dozen would exhaust the roster. Yet among that select group were several extraordinary physicians whose stories justify telling and whose service earned for them places of high honor in the history of New Mexico medicine.

Table 7 testifies to the statistical insignificance of New Mexico's women doctors until very recent times. Nationally, women doctors constituted about 6 percent of the medical profession in 1910 and 5.1 percent in

1940;[2] thus, New Mexico lagged considerably behind the rest of the country. Not until after World War II did the state's percentage of women doctors begin to approximate nationwide norms. For any given year before 1945, the names of *all* the women doctors practicing in the state could be ticked off in about twenty seconds, for in no single year, as Table 7 shows, did the number rise so high as twelve. In fact, the grand total of all who practiced in New Mexico from 1886 to 1945 comes to just thirty-one.[3]

We know very little of the very earliest women doctors of medicine in New Mexico Territory. There was a Dr. Senvey (or Tenney) Clough practicing in Las Vegas in 1885, but beyond the facts that she had an office on Douglas Avenue and advertised herself as a specialist in obstetrics and diseases of women and children (the special focus one would expect of a woman doctor of that era), we know nothing about her.[4] She does appear in Polk's 1886 *Medical Directory,* but she is never mentioned in the records of the Las Vegas or New Mexico Medical Society, and her tenure in the territory was apparently brief. The same was almost certainly true of one Dr. Mary P. Sawtelle, who is listed as in practice in Albuquerque in 1886. Dr. Sawtelle was a homeopath and claimed to have received a medical degree in 1872 from New York Medical College and Hospital for Women; but she, too, was an ephemeral presence in early New Mexico medicine.

Of considerably greater significance and tangibility was the third documentable New Mexico woman physician, Dr. Alice H. Rice, who practiced in Las Vegas from 1895 to the mid-1920s. Dr. Rice was an 1893 graduate of Woman's Medical College of Chicago (later Northwestern University Woman's Medical School) and apparently came to Las Vegas with her family in 1894. She, too, focused her practice on "diseases of women and children" and had her office at her residence on Eighth Street.[5] She was elected as the first woman member of the New Mexico Medical Society in 1895 and was an active member. She read a paper entitled

[2]Richard H. Shryock, "Women in American Medicine," *Journal of the American Medical Women's Association* 5 (1950):377.

[3]Another dozen or so were issued licenses to practice in that six-decade period, but there is no evidence at all that they did so. New Mexico, Board of Medical Examiners, Minutes, 1902–45; and the medical directories cited in Table 7.

[4]Dorothy Beimer, "Pioneer Physicians in Las Vegas, 1880–1911," mimeographed, n.d., 13.

[5]*Las Vegas Daily Optic,* 1894.

"Nature, Our Schoolmaster" at the 1897 annual meeting, for example.[6] Dr. Rice remained in active practice in Las Vegas some thirty years until her death or retirement in the mid-1920s.

Even though their numbers were so limited, individual profiles of each of New Mexico's early women doctors cannot be attempted here. However, four other women doctors of the early years do merit at least brief mention. One of them, Dr. Celia W. Taylor-Goodman, an 1880 graduate of the Michigan Homeopathic Medical College in Lansing, Michigan, was the first female physician to carve out for herself a solid niche in the highly competitive Albuquerque medical community.[7] She came to Albuquerque in 1901, probably as a "lunger," after two decades of practice in Michigan and quickly earned the respect of her demanding Albuquerque peers. In 1907 they elected her as one of the two councillors representing their large, prestigious county organization in the territorial society, and in 1908 she was elected president of the Bernalillo County Medical Society, which was an honor not won lightly.[8] When she left Albuquerque for California in 1911 on account of failing health, her colleagues affectionately presented her with a silk umbrella at a banquet held especially in her honor.[9]

Similarly, Drs. Margaret Green Cartwright and Florence Janet Reid won full acceptance and the respect of their male colleagues by distinguished service as hardworking and astute clinicians, Cartwright in Albuquerque and Reid in Deming and Santa Fe. Dr. Cartwright, like Dr. Rice a graduate (1890) of Northwestern University Woman's Medical School, came to Albuquerque in 1908 after seventeen years of practice in the state of Nuevo León, Mexico.[10] For the subsequent thirty-four years she practiced in Albuquerque, with the exception of a brief interlude as college physician at New Mexico State College. She built and served a busy practice, mostly in obstetrics and gynecology, prior to her retirement in 1942 and

[6]New Mexico Medical Society, 12th Annual Meeting, Minutes, 12 May 1897. She was a good enough member to travel to Albuquerque to deliver her paper.

[7]She listed herself as a "regular" practitioner, despite her preparation in a homeopathic school (*Polk's Medical Directory* [1902], p. 1292). That *Directory* also identifies her as "formerly Prof., Sanitary Science and Preventive Medicine and Assoc. Prof., Diseases of Women, Saginaw Valley Medical College and Gynecologist to Woman's Hospital, Saginaw."

[8]*New Mexico Medical Journal* 3, no. 1 (1907–8):6; *New Mexico Medical Journal* 4, no. 3 (1908–9):19.

[9]*Journal of the American Medical Association* 57 (15 July 1911):226.

[10]New Mexico, Board of Medical Examiners, Minutes, 13 January 1908.

her death several years later in California. Dr. Janet Reid served New Mexicans not nearly as long as Dr. Cartwright—Reid practiced in the state only about a decade—but was unique in earning a place for herself alongside the state's old-guard tuberculosis specialists. An 1896 graduate of the College of Physicians and Surgeons in Keokuk, Iowa, Dr. Reid came to New Mexico in 1912 after a decade of practice in Missouri and four years in Grand Junction, Colorado.[11] (She, too, was probably one of those tuberculosis specialists who got interested in the disease through first-hand experience with it.) Like Dr. Goodman ten years earlier, Dr. Reid left New Mexico for California after a little more than a decade in the state, and was still in practice there as late as 1956.

Dr. Ada Chevaillier earned the grudging respect, or at least the toleration, of her Gallup colleagues in quite another way. She came to Albuquerque for her health in 1910, after a somewhat checkered medical career which included stints at two different medical schools, both of suspect quality, and twenty years of practice in Missouri, Colorado, Illinois, and British Honduras. She was unhappy in Albuquerque for unspecified reasons, and moved on to Gallup in 1915, where she quickly became involved in a bitter struggle with the entrenched physicians of the town. Whether they resented her attempt to horn in, her sex, or her ethics cannot be determined at this remove. What is certain is that she established her own hospital ("La Petite Hospital") and within a year found herself facing charges of miscellaneous and sundry wrongdoing, including performing abortions, filed against her by several of the other physicians in town. Dr. Chevaillier gave away nothing, fighting her accusers relentlessly in criminal court and in license-revocation proceedings before the Board of Medical Examiners. Her toughness prevailed, for eventually all charges against her were dropped and, as if to rub the faces of her antagonists in the dirt, she settled down for the first time in her life, remaining in Gallup for the next twenty-six years until her death in 1941.[12]

But on that short but impressive list of New Mexico's pioneer women physicians, one name clearly stands out from those of her sisters. It immediately comes up in any discussion of women doctors of the state, for Evelyn Fisher Frisbie stood for all that was good and strong within the state's medical tradition. In over a half-century of medical service to the state, forty-seven years in Albuquerque alone, Dr. Frisbie earned a special

[11]New Mexico, Board of Medical Examiners, Minutes, 8 April 1912.

[12]New Mexico, Board of Medical Examiners, Minutes, 11 October 1915, 10 January 1916.

place of honor. A close-up look at her career also has much to say about the lives and challenges faced, in general, by those early women doctors.

Like so many of New Mexico's physicians, Evelyn Frisbie was a native midwesterner, born in Grinnell, Iowa, in 1873. The daughter of a banker, she graduated from Grinnell College in her hometown, a member of the first wave of women students to push their way through the male-dominated American academic establishment. That accomplishment may have steeled her somewhat for the more daunting challenges before her, but it was not easy to push out from established channels. For example, she decided to devote her life to the healing arts, but for her generation that meant nursing for a young woman, not medicine. Following that convention, she enrolled in the nursing department of the Medical School of Iowa in 1898, and spent the subsequent two years preparing for a career in nursing.[13]

It is not clear why she chose to challenge the norms of her society by transferring to medical school. She later claimed it was largely a chance thing: on a visit to Chicago she overheard on a streetcar a casual reference to a woman physician practicing in the city, and that was the first time the country girl from Iowa realized such things were possible.[14] If that scene had any real substance, it was probably a matter of a passing reference crystallizing a growing restiveness or a discontent with conventionality. Evelyn Fisher's whole career was an exercise in pioneering, and her willingness to set out on new paths was manifest in her decision in 1900 to leave nursing school for medicine.

She looked beyond her native Iowa for her medical education, for female medical students were not encouraged in the medical schools of that conservative society. She chose the more cosmopolitan city of Chicago, a progressive and much more open society than Iowa and an important center of medical education at the turn of the century. The bland noun

[13]This profile of Dr. Frisbie is based largely on an unpublished University of New Mexico research paper done by Judith DeMark, "Evelyn Fisher Frisbie: Pioneer New Mexico Physician," and the materials—newspaper articles, court documents, interviews, and the like—collected in the process of her research. I am grateful to Dr. DeMark for sharing those materials with me. I have supplemented them with materials on Dr. Frisbie found in the files of the Board of Medical Examiners (Santa Fe); the Frisbie file in the Special Collections Department of the University of New Mexico's Zimmerman Library; the pages of the *New Mexico Medical Journal*; additional interviews; and other sources.

[14]*Albuquerque Tribune*, 4 June 1958, p. 1.

"center," however, fails to do Chicago justice. The Flexner Report of 1910 called the city "in respect to medical education the plague spot of the country."[15] There were no fewer than fourteen medical schools in the city, most of them proprietary schools offering scandalously inadequate medical instruction. There were, however, three schools of some quality in that "plague spot," and Fisher had the wit and courage to choose one of them. Chicago's College of Physicians and Surgeons had been founded in 1882, but in 1896 it had become linked to the University of Illinois so that the training received by young Fisher was respectable, if not truly distinguished. She was, of course, part of a small minority at the school—approximately ten women students among two hundred males—but finished with ease in 1902.

At some point in her preparation, she decided to focus her practice on the care of women and children. This was not surprising, for to the degree that women found any place comfortable in the world of turn-of-the-century medicine it was in the care of women and children ("women's work," if you will). Fisher did her internship in the Chicago Maternity Hospital, and throughout her almost six decades of active practice there was always a strong focus on obstetrics and gynecology and a lesser one on pediatrics. Like the very great majority of physicians of her generation, she was able to span the whole range of general practice and through most of her career did so, but she was always most comfortable and felt most rewarded when working in the fields of obstetrics and gynecology.

Her first years of private practice were spent in her native Iowa, where she established herself as a general practitioner in Des Moines. She quickly built a solid practice, while simultaneously serving on the faculty of Drake University's medical unit as a clinical instructor in obstetrics. There was also time to meet and marry Charles Bigelow Frisbie, a bright young physician specializing in the fields of urology and dermatology. The marriage, however, was a short and unsuccessful one, and Evelyn Frisbie remained single thereafter.

After six years of private practice in Des Moines and some exposure to the environment of a medical school faculty, Dr. Frisbie decided to move to the West in 1908. The failing health of her mother—perhaps a "lunger," although we cannot be sure—prompted the move, but the failed marriage may have had something to do with it as well. The initially chosen

[15]Abraham Flexner, *Medical Education in the United States and Canada* (New York: Carnegie Foundation for the Advancement of Teaching), p. 216.

destination for Dr. Frisbie and her parents was southern California, and she applied for a California license. While waiting for its processing, she visited friends in Las Vegas, New Mexico, who had established themselves in the area under the terms of the Homestead Act of 1862. Through their encouragement and the raw beauty and power of the area, Frisbie decided to stay. Las Vegas and its environs were still rough and ready territory as of 1908, but the young woman doctor was no hothouse flower. She welcomed the challenge posed by frontier New Mexico and moved her family to Wagon Mound at the end of 1908, filing claim on a one-hundred-and-fifty-acre tract of land in its vicinity. Living in town while building a crude cabin on her land and actually working the soil on the weekends, she took out a New Mexico license to practice in 1909.

Wagon Mound was a town of only eight hundred people in 1909 and already had a decent doctor—a Canadian-born and -educated physician who practiced in the town from 1898 until his return to Canada around 1920—so the new doctor had to fit herself in around the established practitioner. She did so by working the countryside, especially the farm and ranch area around Ocate, twenty-five miles distant from her home in Wagon Mound. For three years Dr. Frisbie was a horse-and-buggy doctor, bouncing across the gravel and dirt roads (trails, actually) of the area, delivering a baby here, taking out inflamed tonsils there, and perhaps losing a child now and then to diphtheria. The roads of the region quickly proved so bad that she made most of her longer tours through the countryside on horseback, reserving the fine buggy for shorter calls close to town. She became a confirmed New Mexican in those three years, her hands working the tough soils of the region at some times and holding medical instruments at others. During that time, she also made initial contact with the medical establishment of the territory, such as it was, for the record shows that she was a good member of the New Mexico Medical Society as early as 1910, and she definitely attended the 1911 annual meeting of the organization held in Las Vegas.[16]

She always remembered her rural practice and her experiment in homesteading with great fondness, but in 1911 she determined to move on, whether because of the needs and interests of her ailing parents or through her own choice. She selected Albuquerque as the site of her relocation and purchased the practice of Dr. Celia Taylor-Goodman, who was then

[16]At that meeting, she read a paper on "Gonorrhea in the Female," which greatly impressed her colleagues. *New Mexico Medical Journal* 7 (1911–12):128–32.

leaving for California. When she opened her first office at Third and Central, she doubled the growing town's population of women doctors. Dr. Margaret Cartwright was the other woman physician practicing in the town, though within a few months the peripatetic Dr. Chevaillier would join them.

Although the Albuquerque medical community was very much in flux in 1911 and rapidly expanding in numbers, an old guard of longtime physicians—P. G. Cornish, Sr.; Jacob Easterday; John Elder; Walter Hope; John Pearce; L. G. Rice, Sr.; and James Wroth prominent among them—dominated medical practice in the town. (Young Dr. Meldrum K. Wylder was still in the process of getting himself established, and Dr. William Randolph Lovelace would not move in to the town from Fort Sumner for two more years.) They were, all things considered, an impressive group and might not have been expected to greet newcomers with undue enthusiasm or warmth, especially, perhaps, female newcomers. Their quick and apparently complete acceptance of young Dr. Frisbie is, then, somewhat surprising and does them credit. The high esteem in which they held her predecessor, Dr. Taylor-Goodman, undoubtedly worked to her advantage, but she could trade on that connection only so far. Whether her acceptance was due to her obvious talent and skill, her strong commitment to her work, or both of these along with a gift for diplomacy, Dr. Frisbie quickly became a part of the Albuquerque establishment. Within three years she was president of the Bernalillo County Medical Society—her first vice-president and eventual successor was another newcomer to the town, Dr. Lovelace—a position of considerable honor and esteem within the profession. Even more august was the distinction that came her way in September 1915. At that year's annual meeting of the New Mexico Medical Society held in Las Vegas, Evelyn Frisbie was elected without opposition to the presidency of the group. She was not only the first woman to head the New Mexico Medical Society—and there has as yet been no second—but she was also the first woman to head any one of the nation's state medical societies.[17]

At first glance, her election seems surprising. She had only been practicing in the state for around five or six years, living several of these years in the isolation of the plains around Wagon Mound. She was relatively inexperienced in the sometimes intense skirmishing of New Mexico Med-

[17]Ralph R. Marshall, "The First Lady President of a State Medical Society," *Rocky Mountain Medical Journal* 59, no. 11 (1962):35–36.

ical Society politics. She was a member, at age forty-two, of the new, not the old guard of New Mexico medicine. And she was a woman; and the year was, after all, 1915. Despite these handicaps, she had obviously won the respect and confidence of her peers, and she knew how to operate in the man's world of early twentieth-century medicine. Dr. Samuel D. Swope, longtime practitioner in and around Deming and one of the grand old men of the New Mexico Medical Society, hinted as much in his introduction of her to the society as its new president:

> We have found a lady to serve us as our executive officer for the coming year, out of all her sisters in this great United States first to be elected to this important office. You are all gallant gentlemen. I cannot ask you to treat my friend, Dr. Evelyn Frisbie, kindly, for you could not do otherwise. And I want to say to you that if you feel like doing otherwise, you will find her thoroughly able to take care of herself under all circumstances.[18]

Her year as president was uneventful, dominated by discussion within the society of the necessity for more forceful state intervention in the sphere of public health and debate about the perennial licensure question. When her successor took her place at the end of 1916, Dr. Frisbie became one of the society's senior statesmen, a dignity she carried for the subsequent forty-nine years. Concentrating her attention on her practice, Frisbie in the 1920s and 1930s made herself one of the dominant figures of the Albuquerque medical community. She styled herself a general practitioner, like 90 percent of her peers, but concentrated her energies in obstetrics and gynecology. She delivered, literally, thousands of babies over the span of her practice, while keeping fully abreast of developments in her fields, as evidenced by her presentations of scientific papers.[19] She was also active in improving the institutional aspects of medical care in the city. Since regular hospital facilities for the care of sick women and children ranged from inadequate to nonexistent states,[20] Dr. Frisbie established and ran her own small maternity hospital in downtown Albu-

[18]*New Mexico Medical Journal* 15 (1915–16):15–16.

[19]See, for example, her "Obstetrical Anesthesia and Analgesia" (*New Mexico Medical Journal* 16 [1916]:77–81), published during her tenure as president of the state society. The information contained within the article and its citations indicate the currency of her knowledge.

[20]Dr. L. G. Rice, Jr., interview with the author, Albuquerque, N.M., 9 May 1984; Dr. Albert G. Simms II, interview with the author, Albuquerque, N.M., 17 and 18 May 1984.

querque, which she operated until Dr. Lucien G. Rice, Sr., built the Women's and Children's Hospital on East Central Avenue.

While building a large private practice, filling important positions in her city and state medical societies, and even dabbling in small-scale hospital construction and administration, Dr. Frisbie still found time to give of herself and her abilities to the advancement of public health in the state. She was a loyal member of the Congregational church in Albuquerque, and in the late 1920s she answered the call for medical assistance put out by missionaries of the church working in western New Mexico. From base operations at, first, Cubero, and then Grant, the missionaries were seeking to bring medical help to the isolated peoples of the region. There were no doctors for miles around—Grant (as it was called in the 1920s and 1930s) had a physician in town irregularly through the period—but the need for competent medical care was acute.

Frisbie took up the work in 1929, traveling to Cubero twice a month with stops at villages of the area such as Seboyetta, San Mateo, and Bluewater. To facilitate the work of the doctor, an old army commissary was used for the base clinic at Cubero, but conditions were primitive. There was no running water, for example; so Dr. Frisbie and her nurse hauled water for the clinic in fifty-gallon drums from the Cubero Trading Company, using an old Dodge ambulance to pack it. Nor were there telephones or electricity, and Frisbie had to stop at Presbyterian Hospital in Albuquerque on her way out to pick up sterlized implements. When the Cubero clinic was closed in 1932 and the missionaries opened a larger one in Grant, Frisbie remained the medical backbone of the effort, traveling to Grant over gravel and dirt roads.

This strenuous and demanding clinical work—for which she received no fees, incidentally—came hard on the heels of a great personal and professional tragedy, which marred her professional record and undoubtedly caused her great personal grief. In the late 1920s, Dr. Frisbie became associated with the New Mexico Girls' Welfare Home, a detention facility for problem girls located in Albuquerque. She served as the institution's attending physician, and this, too, was a part of her service to her community, at least for the first few years. By 1929 she was receiving a small retainer. In late January of that year, she was called to the home late one evening to help with four inmates who escaped from the institution, had "enjoyed" a cold January night outdoors wandering around on the mesa north of town, and had then been recaptured. Dr. Frisbie became involved in this tawdry scenario when four of the young women, all in their late teens, became noisy and hysterical in their isolation cells. The doctor did not examine them—she later said, quite reasonably, she feared for her safety, given their agitated condition—but did prescribe injections of "twilight sleep," a controversial sedative made up of morphine and scopolamine, to calm the young women. It was a drug with which Dr. Frisbie was thoroughly familiar, and indeed she had used it extensively in her practice with complete safety and good results.

This time, however, there were grave problems. On the day after administration of the drug, one of the girls, an eighteen-year-old from Portales, collapsed and died. Not long before, the Girls' Welfare Home had already been the target of allegations of maladministration and mistreatment of its inmates by institution personnel; so the mysterious death served as the spark to set off a thunderous hue and cry in the community. The press, a legislative investigative committee, and the local district attorney's office were all quickly involved, and the tragic situation grew especially unpleasant for Dr. Frisbie and the institution's superintendent, a registered nurse named Bertha Lips. (Lips had actually administered the drug prescribed by Dr. Frisbie.) Within days, both Frisbie and Lips found themselves under indictment for second-degree murder.

Not surprisingly, the incident became a cause célèbre within the community. Press headlines screamed the latest developments in the case day by day, and the years of self-sacrifice and service rendered to the community by Dr. Frisbie seemed to disappear in the din. Sadly, the case split the city's medical community, with at least two fellow physicians giving testimony as state's witnesses, testimony damaging to Dr. Frisbie. (One of them was the redoubtable Dr. Meldrum K. Wylder, always a fiercely independent and opinionated man.) Most of Albuquerque's physicians, however, fell into line behind their embattled colleague, and their support was reinforced by expert testimony of out-of-state witnesses. Eventually all charges against Dr. Frisbie were dropped, but not before she had suffered the indignities of arrest, formal indictment, and the start of a public trial. She was absolved of all guilt or responsibility for the unhappy incident,[21] but it was clearly a horribly scarring experience.

Dr. Frisbie was apparently able to recover personally from the shock of the Girls' Welfare Home incident and its aftermath with relative speed,

[21]The judge who dismissed all charges against Frisbie reduced those against Lips to manslaughter, but did allow her trial to continue. A jury quickly found the superintendent not guilty of all charges, but both Lips and Dr. Frisbie resigned from their posts at the home. For details of this sad incident, see the *Albuquerque Journal* for the period from January to April 1929.

and professionally the case seems to have done her no lasting damage. Through the 1930s and 1940s she was fully occupied with her large and busy private practice, while also undertaking the extensive charity work in western New Mexico mentioned earlier. She also made time for extensive nonmedical service to her community. For example, she was a charter member and first president of both the Duke City Business and Professional Women's Club and the Albuquerque branch of the American Association of University Women. She was also an active member of such organizations as the Mayflower Descendents Club, the Daughters of the American Revolution, Soroptomist, and the Congregational church. The range of her interests and accomplishments, plus her remarkable energy and ability to get things done, mocked all those who measured themselves against her.

She continued a full and active practice into the 1950s, well into her seventies. Dr. Eleanor Adler, a bright-eyed, young pediatrician newly arrived in Albuquerque in the late 1940s, has a particularly vivid memory of Frisbie. Adler tells with a little chagrin (and still more admiration) of being called out to a local hospital one night not long after her arrival, looking "frazzled and somewhat the worse for wear," and there encountering the venerable Dr. Frisbie, also on a middle-of-the-night call but "impeccably turned out, hat and earrings neatly in place."[22] But the encroachments of time did finally make their mark on her strong constitution, and she slowly began to wind down her practice. Her colleagues from Albuquerque and around the state did her the signal honor of naming her General Practitioner of the Year in 1955, forty years after the New Mexico Medical Society had first honored itself and her by electing her as its president; and her alma mater, Grinnell College, awarded its distinguished alumna a Doctor of Science degree in 1958.

A stroke suffered in the spring of 1958 finally forced her full retirement from practice at age eighty-five, and she died in Albuquerque in 1965. A Denver newspaper once quoted her as saying: "I know only by hearsay that prejudice against women as doctors sometimes exists. Being a physician is a most wonderful and interesting profession for a woman who is qualified. She can go just as far as her ability takes her."[23] Dr. Frisbie almost certainly did herself too little credit. There is ample evidence that women of her generation were indeed discriminated against and were the

[22]Dr. Eleanor Adler, interview with the author, Albuquerque, N.M., 18 April 1984.
[23]*Denver Post,* 28 July 1958.

victims of subtle and often not so subtle prejudice of various sorts. If indeed she did not perceive it, it was because her talents were so great, her commitment so intense, and her abilities so manifest as to steamroller aside even the most vigorous of benighted opposition.

The generation of Drs. Frisbie, Taylor-Goodman, Cartwright, and Reid was not followed by equally strong successors in the 1920s and 1930s. Relatively few new women physicians set up practice in the state during that period; fewer than twenty were licensed in the entire twenty-year period, and of them only six practiced for more than four years in the state. Most of them, like their predecessors of the pioneer generation, set up practice in New Mexico's cities and towns. Dr. Ly Werner, a pediatrician, and Dr. Lenna Clark, an obstetrician-gynecologist, came to New Mexico with their physician-husbands and set up practice in Albuquerque. Dr. Nancy Campbell (about whom more will be said later) originally practiced in Las Vegas, and then in Santa Fe; and Dr. Demarious Badger started her forty-plus year career in Hobbs at the end of the 1930s.

But it would be mistaken to identify New Mexico's women physicians exclusively with urban practice, for some among them made their marks in the especially demanding world of rural health-care delivery. Practice out in the countryside was largely a man's game, but a number of women physicians chose to accept the special challenges inherent in practicing medicine away from the support systems of city medicine. Especially prominent among them were several female missionary doctors who arrived in the 1930s to work in the mountain *plazas* of northern New Mexico's Sangre de Cristo Mountains. For a number of reasons, their story deserves to be told in some detail. First of all, their history may stand as a case study of those women doctors who hung out their shingles in rural New Mexico. That is, of course, the explicit reason for their inclusion here. But, just as importantly, the story of the women doctors serving in, first, Dixon, New Mexico, and then in Embudo, a few miles away, sheds light on the way in which modern, scientific medicine first reached the more out-of-the-way parts of the state, providing insight into the day-to-day realities of rural medicine. The portrait of the women doctors of Dixon and Embudo may be taken as representative, in many respects, of the life and work of New Mexico "country docs" in general.

Las doctoras of the Brooklyn Cottage Hospital (Dixon), Embudo Presbyterian Hospital, and, later, the Mora Valley Health Clinic (Cleveland) all came to their place of service as missionaries of the Presbyterian church. In the late nineteenth and early twentieth centuries, a number of Protestant missionary groups had begun work—usually educational or purely evangelicial—in New Mexico, focusing on the Indian and Hispanic peoples. The Presbyterians were particularly active in northern New Mexico, where their Board of National Missions in the 1870s and 1880s established a chain of day schools in such villages as Chacón, Holman, Embudo, Truchas, Chamisal, Peñasco, and others. Their work prospered, but typhoid epidemics, outbreaks of smallpox and malaria, horrifyingly high maternal and infant mortality rates, and a potpourri of other health problems bedeviled their efforts, exacting a high price in human misery from their tiny flocks. The missionary pioneers quickly concluded that tending the bodies of the disease-burdened people of the mountain *plazas* had to proceed hand in hand with tending their souls. Consequently, to their established work of proselytizing and education, the Presbyterians early in this century added a medical mission.[24]

The urgent need for skilled medical care in the region was obvious. At the turn of the century, there were no hospitals or clinics whatsoever, and only a handful of doctors, in the territory north of Santa Fe and west of Raton. *Flint's Medical and Surgical Directory*, published in 1897, listed a total of ten doctors in all of northcentral New Mexico—two each in Taos and Mora, and one each in Chama, Coyote, Dulce, Española, Hopewell, and Watrous.[25] The 1906 first edition of the *American Medical Directory* painted an even sadder picture, listing only eight.[26] Even that handful of physicians seems to have been very much of a transient population, with only one of the doctors listed in the 1897 compilation still in place nine years later, for example.

The Presbyterians began their medical mission by constructing a small cottage hospital in Dixon in 1914. This clinic-dispensary, initially staffed by two graduate nurses, was named Brooklyn Cottage Hospital after the women of the Brooklyn-Nassau Presbytery in New York who provided the money for it. The health services provided at the tiny clinic were limited to basic procedures—innoculations, first aid, obstetrical education and assistance, health education in general, and the like. Neverthe-

[24]Much of this account of the Presbyterian missionary doctors working in the mountain *plazas* of the Sangre de Cristo range is based on archival materials housed in the Menual Historical Library at Menaul School, Albuquerque. See, especially, the files on Brooklyn Cottage Hospital and Embudo Presbyterian Hospital and those on the physicians Sarah Bowen, Virginia Voorhies Milner, and Edith Millican.

[25]*Flint's Medical and Surgical Directory, 1897*, p. 633.

[26]*American Medical Directory, 1906*, pp. 594–95.

less, a tradition was established, and the confidence and support of the people of the area were slowly won. For seventeen years, the nurses of the clinic provided a vital service to the area; they were modern medicine's initial contact with the region. The arrival of Dr. Sarah Bowen in northern New Mexico in the winter of 1931, however, inaugurated a new era in the history of the tiny mission and a landmark in the history of rural health care in northern New Mexico.

Sarah Bowen was, in many ways, ideally suited to the task confronting her in New Mexico. Born in China in 1902 to missionary parents, she received a solid medical education, earning her medical degree at the University of Minnesota in 1929 and interning at San Francisco General Hospital and a small community hospital in upstate New York. Young Dr. Bowen intended to return to China as a medical missionary, and was formally under the charge of the Presbyterian Board of Foreign Missions, when the Japanese invasion of Manchuria in 1931 forced her to modify her plans, at least temporarily. While waiting for clearance to sail for China, she was asked by the Board of National Missions to make a survey of the medical needs and services available in northern New Mexico. Using Brooklyn Cottage Hospital as her base, the China-bound doctor thoroughly investigated health conditions in the broad area bounded by Santa Fe, Española, Taos, and Las Vegas. She was quickly convinced that the mountain people of that area—roughly the size of the state of Massachusetts—needed modern medical help almost as desperately as the millions in China; and this she reported to mission authorities in Philadelphia. The Board agreed with her judgment and promptly asked Dr. Bowen herself to accept the challenge. She later insisted—with tongue in cheek—that she just got stranded in northern New Mexico: "I was on my way to China, but there was a snow storm and I missed the train!" She did indeed miss her train and her boat for China, but found instead a place of honor in the history of medical service to the people of New Mexico.

For thirty years, Dr. Bowen worked in the villages of northern New Mexico. She was the guiding spirit behind the transformation of the useful, but limited, Presbyterian medical mission in the Sangre de Cristo Mountains from its modest beginnings into a frontier bastion of modern, scientific medicine. She started by expanding the facilities and services of the tiny cottage clinic at Dixon. In one of her early reports to Philadelphia, she noted that the 28′ × 34′ cottage hospital, divided into six different rooms, had held as many as twenty-seven patients at a time during the report period. Two or three new mothers might be crammed into one room; a tonsillectomy patient and a trauma victim might share another; and a suspected case of malaria might occupy a third. Babies might be found anywhere, stashed in apple boxes or bureau drawers. Babies were the special pride of Brooklyn Cottage Hospital; indeed, it was affectionately known to the people of the region as Baby Catcher Hospital.[27]

But there was much to do besides the ample workload of the rural hospital. While greatly expanding the range of modern medical services available and the patient traffic at the hospital, Dr. Bowen also established an enduring tradition of holding traveling clinics on a regular basis in the isolated communities of the region. If the people would not or could not, for whatever reason, come to her, then she would go to them. She held clinics weekly or monthly in nine different *plazas* scattered throughout the mountains, sharing her skills and information with their people. She was particularly conscious of the importance of protecting the young people of the area, and thus she concentrated on holding school health programs in the mountain villages, twenty-eight of them in the year 1934 alone.

Given her thirty years of tenure in the mountains, Dr. Bowen's personality, philosophy, and ways of doing things became firmly imprinted in the half-century history of the Presbyterian work in the Sangre de Cristos, and thus she deserves some special attention. She was an extremely able and well-rounded physician, and particularly strong as a diagnostician. Her special skills and interests lay in the spheres of obstetrics and pediatrics, fields of obvious utility given the nature of the work in the mountains. But she was well trained across the broad range of skills required in rural practice. And she was scrupulously conscientious in keeping current her information and abilities, constantly refining and improving what she already knew and exploring and developing new spheres. Her tenure in the mountains was interrupted from time to time by study leaves, sometimes for only a few days, but now and again for as much as a year. Together with the obstetrics and pediatrics which were her special joy, she also took formal training in basic anesthesiology and became fully competent in it. She was perhaps least happy in doing surgery. She and her colleagues at Dixon and Embudo did, of course, perform some surgery—appendectomies, tonsillectomies, and simple trauma work—and would undertake major surgery when circumstances demanded it,

[27]Dr. Virginia Milner, interview with the author, Albuquerque, N.M., 18 October 1983.

but she much preferred to rely on expert outside help when confronted with surgical problems. Santa Fe surgeons Phillip Travers and Robert C. Derbyshire were especially close to Dr. Bowen and her work in the mountains, and they made the trip to her hospital often, carrying the bulk of the surgical load for her and her associates.

It ought be noted that the efforts of Bowen and her colleagues at Dixon and Embudo commanded the full respect and admiration of their peer physicians. As mentioned, Drs. Travers and Derbyshire had close relationships, rooted in mutual respect, with Dr. Bowen and her assistants; and other prominent Santa Fe physicians, such as internist Eric Hausner, pathologist Aaron Margulis, radiologists Murray Friedman and Marcus Smith, and others were of great support to the mission doctors. Many of them served formally as consulting staff to the tiny hospital, and all respected the courage and achievement of the women doctors in the mountains.

Sarah Bowen was able to win the respect and cooperation of her physician peers, but perhaps more impressive was her success in winning the confidence of the sometimes remote, clannish, and mistrustful people of the mountain communities. Her patients grew to cherish her. A warm and expansive person, she reciprocated their affection, visiting in their homes, sharing their family trials of both medical and nonmedical nature, and earning their solid trust. The friendly *doctora* with the strong, open face and the auburn hair piled in braids on her head was fully responsive to them, genuinely cared for them, and they sensed it. But there was another element, simple yet fundamental, which helped her in winning their confidence. Bowen paid these mountain people the courtesy of learning their language. She spoke Spanish with her patients as a matter of course, and she did so with almost native fluency. Not surprisingly, many of her patients showed a fierce loyalty to her that extended beyond all norms. Dr. Milner, for example, remembers a young man of the area who, away working in Colorado and told he had an appendix in danger of rupturing, hitchhiked to Embudo for Dr. Bowen to care for him.[28]

Her diplomatic or interpersonal skills extended even to the establishment of amicable relations with the Catholic priests of the area. She and her Presbyterian "Anglo" medical mission were an intrusive element in the region, but she developed clear understandings with the Catholic church and its people working in the area. Her conception of her work

[28]Ibid.

facilitated mutual toleration and even tacit cooperation. Bowen saw her fundamental responsibility as ministering to the sick bodies of her patients. She was far too sensitive to seek to sell her particular brand of Christianity too aggressively. She was conscious of her responsibilities as a good Presbyterian missionary and established regular religious devotions at both Brooklyn Cottage Hospital and Embudo Presbyterian, but she definitely believed that her personal bearing, character, and way of life were the more important elements of her testimony or witness.

In addition to her demonstrable medical skills and the constructive effects of her personality and approach to her work, the final ingredient in Sarah Bowen's success was her vision and sense of the possible. Upon first seeing the poor, disease-ridden communities of the high mountains, she developed a clear sense of what was needed and an unshakable conviction of what was possible. The numerous uncertainties, impracticalities, difficulties, and hardships of the challenge never fazed her for long: The work was worth doing and she was willing to pay the price. She persisted and prevailed, but did indeed pay an enormous personal price in the process. Overwork that reached literally bone-wearying dimensions; the constant stress of too much responsibility; the day-to-day strains and exasperations of administration and personnel management; the depressive effect of stark loneliness for long periods of time—all took their toll. She was physically robust and full of energy when she came to the mountains, but the weight of her labors wore her down and she became subject to severe spells of nausea and vomiting when she grew overtired, which was frequently. The solution to her ills was obvious. As one of her colleagues noted, "She simply should have had a lot more help much earlier," but that was just one of the things she had to bear. She was conscious of the dimensions of her achievements and fiercely proud of her work, but the pressures of it sometimes reduced her to despair. Dr. Edith Millican, who worked with Bowen at Embudo, remembers that when she arrived in San Francisco in 1948, after five hard and draining years in China, there was an emergency telegram sent to her ship from Sarah Bowen, begging her to come as soon as possible to provide some relief. "She was pretty desperate, that's sure. She knew she had gone beyond her limit, working in a small, rather limited and isolated situation with few outlets."[29]

She was, after all, quite human and subject to periods of doubt and

[29]Dr. Edith Millican, interview with the author, Albuquerque, N.M., 30 August 1983.

despair, even if the dominant motif of her character and career was her strength. She did finally tire of the responsibilities she bore, retiring from her work at Embudo in October 1960. For a while, she practiced privately in Santa Fe, and then went into semiretirement in Las Vegas, near which she and her sister built a much-loved cabin in the mountains near Tres Ritos. Her Las Vegas practice was limited, however, for she was increasingly crippled by arthritis, and she was directly responsible for the care of her invalid sister. She gave up practice entirely in the late sixties. Increasingly frail, she and her sister were finally moved to a Presbyterian church home for retired missionaries in southern California, where Sarah Bowen died in 1982, just days after her eightieth birthday.

Though she was alone for lengthy periods of time during her tenure in the mountains, there were also periods when she was supported by able assistants. Early in her stay, Dr. Bowen petitioned mission authorities in the East for more doctors and nurses, and the first of a series of young doctors was sent out to Dixon to help her in the late 1930s. It was quickly apparent, however, that not just everyone was suited to the special circumstances of this particular mission field. The first young physician sent out to work with her was appalled at the circumstances—kerosene lanterns lighting tiny wards and living quarters; a *casita* at the end of a path; babies lying around in apple boxes—and left after a few days. A second doctor, having misread the situation entirely, showed up with golf clubs and tennis rackets and was also quickly back on the road to Santa Fe and "civilization."

But there were others like Sarah Bowen with the courage to tackle the special work at Dixon. One such person was Dr. Virginia Voorhies (later Milner), who arrived in early 1939, fresh from medical school preparation at Iowa State University and internship in Pittsburgh. Voorhies, daughter of a Presbyterian minister, had also prepared for a career abroad as a medical missionary, but she was "loaned" by the church's Board of Foreign Missions to go out to help Sarah Bowen "for a few months."[30] Like Bowen, Dr. Voorhies possessed the nerve and balance necessary for survival in the rigorous practice conditions of the Presbyterian mission. Her description of the cottage hospital, as she found it at the time of her arrival in 1939, captures the spirit of the place:

The front door of the cottage opened into what became the waiting room, recep-

[30]Milner, interview, Albuquerque, 18 October 1983.

> tion room, drug room, examining room, and, when we needed it, the operating room. One room was a medical/surgical ward with four beds. Your sex or age didn't matter; if you were medical or surgical, that was where you went. People didn't seem to mind; they sort of enjoyed being together. We also used one room as a maternity ward with six low-lying cots. . . . Another room was the pediatrics ward, the laboratory, the nurses' duty station, and the sterilizing room, all going at once. They ran the pressure steam sterilizers with kerosene burners which occasionally blew up, spouting soot all over the place. Off that room was the delivery room and, again, the bed was just a low-lying cot. It was also the newborn nursery. By the time I arrived, Dr. Bowen had made great strides from the days when she used to put babies in bureau drawers and apple boxes. She then had acquired laundry baskets lined with a sheet and placed in a row atop a plank on sawhorses. That was the newborn nursery, right in the delivery room. When we had complicated deliveries, we set up an old Army examining operating table to do obstetrical procedures. Most people, though, were delivered spontaneously without any anesthetic or anything. If an anesthetic were needed, we sent for the dietician to drip ether for us.[31]

The physical limits of Brooklyn Cottage Hospital are apparent from this description, but practical problems of that sort were not allowed to affect the service of the mission. Dr. Voorhies (Milner) remembers telling people with a sick child that there simply was no bed available in the cottage, to which the response was, "That's all right, we brought the bed."[32]

This medical mission was not charity work in the literal sense, for it was both the policy of the Presbyterian church and the conviction of the doctors working in Dixon and Embudo that patients ought to contribute to the support of the work. Adult patients at the hospital were charged three dollars a day, children one dollar, and babies fifty cents. An office visit to one of the doctors at the hospital brought a charge of fifty cents, and treatment at one of the clinics in the mountain villages was given at a cost of five cents per patient. Complete obstetrical care, which included ten days of hospitalization, cost a lump sum of thirty dollars. (Incidentally, mothers who delivered their babies at Brooklyn Cottage Hospital or at Embudo Presbyterian without prenatal care from their doctors were charged five dollars more than those who had received such care; this was a blunt but effective way of trying to avoid problems.) However, given the reality that in the 1930s 65 percent of the families

[31]Ibid.
[32]Ibid.

in the mountain region had a gross annual income of well under 250 dollars per year, the little hospital was flexible in its reckonings. Payment in kind was common—a load of wood, a homemade blanket, a hog, some chickens, or pumpkins—and labor was often offered and accepted in lieu of cash payment.

The arrival of Dr. Voorhies was a source of great relief for Sarah Bowen, for at last she had a skillful assistant to help bear the ever growing work load. Equally important was the opening in 1940 of a brand new hospital facility two miles west of Dixon in the community of Embudo, squarely astride the Española-Taos highway. The land for the new building was donated by members of the community, and much of the labor and material for the new hospital's construction was similarly contributed by local people. As one example, a group of men from Chimayo camped on the site for two weeks to make adobe bricks to be used in the new facility. The combined efforts of local people, the medical staff, and some external financing paid off with the opening of Embudo Presbyterian Hospital on 7 October 1940. It was a completely modern facility with twenty-five beds, twelve bassinets, operating room, X-ray facilities, and a medical laboratory. For almost a half-century that hospital afforded health care to the people of the region.

Even with the new facility, the medical challenge of Embudo remained intimidating. Dr. Voorhies, trained in the relatively sophisticated Midwest, saw her first cases of diphtheria, smallpox, typhoid, and malaria during her two-and-one-half years of service in the region. Especially painful to the doctors were the terrible intestinal infections that afflicted the children of the area with particular ferocity. (Those problems were caused fundamentally by the inadequate-to-nonexistent sanitation measures of the region.) And the medical problems were exacerbated by the logistics of mountain practice. There were, for example, no paved roads in the area, so house calls meant, at best, uncomfortable and often dangerous drives over dirt trails or through dry arroyos in automobiles not really built for conditions of that sort. Often, horseback was the only means of reaching patients, and when auto and horse failed, there was always walking. House calls or the holding of a clinic might involve the tricky job of balancing a doctor's bag while crossing the Rio Grande on a flimsy rope bridge. Nor were there telephones, reliable power nets, pharmacies, or ambulance services. There were surely moments when China must have looked like surcease to the women doctors in the mountains.

Given the pace of the work at Dixon and Embudo, the dimensions of the medical problems, and the difficulties of the logistics, the courage of even the strongest heart might have faded. But the doctors at the mission hospital persevered. Their special strength and tenacity is captured in the following recollection by Dr. Voorhies (Milner):

> An elder of the church came to conduct services one Sunday morning just after we had an emergency appendectomy, two deliveries, and a woman who had come in with a miscarriage and we hadn't even had time to look at her. When the elder suggested we sing "O Day of Rest and Gladness," I got so tickled I had to leave![33]

When the newly married Dr. Milner left the work at Embudo in 1941, the third of the remarkable women physicians of the Presbyterian mission arrived to take her place. This was Dr. Edith Millican, whose personal story parallels that of Dr. Bowen in several respects. Like Bowen, Dr. Millican was the child of Protestant missionaries working in China, and she spent all but a year or so of her childhood and adolescence in China's Hunan province, Shanghai, and Nanking. (At age thirteen, she was evacuated with the beleaguered American and European communities from that city in the famous Nanking Incident of 1927.) Millican, too, determined to return to China as a medical missionary, and after undergraduate training in Ohio, she got her medical degree at the famous Woman's Medical College in Philadelphia. Yet, as with Sarah Bowen before her, the exigencies of world politics conspired to thwart her plans. With the intensification of the Sino-Japanese War in the late 1930s and the slide toward U.S. involvement, it grew increasingly clear that Dr. Millican's China tour would have to be suspended, at least for a time. She was available, then, when Dr. Milner began her preparations for leaving Embudo. Millican, too, was "loaned" to National Missions to help Sarah Bowen.

Edith Millican's tenure in the medical-mission field of northern New Mexico was second only to that of Dr. Bowen. Her first tour at Embudo Hospital stretched from 1941 to 1943, where she served as assistant to the mission's founder. She was intrigued by the work and easily convinced of its importance, but the much-anticipated China opportunity came sooner than expected in 1943. Dr. Millican sailed for the Orient and served five turbulent, eventful years in China as the Second World War, and then the internal struggle for power between Nationalists and Communists, raged around her. A regularly scheduled furlough began in 1948, and that leave

[33]Ibid.

separated her forever from China. While considering her future options and waiting for the China situation to stabilize one way or another, she began residency training in obstetrics.

The takeover of China by Mao Tse-tung's Communists broke Dr. Millican's dream of returning to China, but it was good fortune for northern New Mexico. In 1951 Dr. Bowen was once again alone at Embudo, and again Dr. Millican answered her request for assistance. Her second tour in the mountains eventually stretched out over twenty-seven years, with limited segments of time off for advanced study, infrequent vacations, and episodes of illness-imposed hiatus. When she returned in 1951, the little hospital at Embudo was, of course, her base—it had, incidentally, been accorded full certification by the American College of Surgeons in 1948—but she was truly the peripatetic physician. She logged hundreds of miles on the rocky trails of the mountains, on her way to hold the *plaza* clinics that had become so central a part of the Presbyterian mission's service. Statistics provide a concrete idea of the dimensions of the work accomplished by the two women doctors and the team of nurses who assisted them at Embudo.[34] In the year 1957, for instance, they treated a grand total of 10,000 patients, admitting 898 of them to their hospital and performing just under a hundred surgeries. They also expanded their potential practice, as if that were needed, by delivering 243 babies.[35]

A significant portion of Dr. Millican's work in the mountains focused on the communities of the eastern slopes, particularly in the Mora Valley towns of Holman and Chacón where she held regular clinics. In the late 1950s, church authorities decided to try to simplify the logistics by establishing a permanent health clinic in the valley—that is, on the other side of the mountains from Embudo—and Edith Millican was the logical choice to get it established. It was a uniquely political as well as medical challenge. First, Presbyterian church officials had to be persuaded to reverse their traditional reluctance to accept government funds for support of their medical work, since Hill-Burton funds were the only practicable source of money for the new endeavor. Perhaps more difficult still, the traditionally strong political and family cleavages of the region had to be

[34]A fairly steady stream of temporary help came out to Embudo to assist Drs. Bowen and Millican, but usually these physicians were available for short periods of time only. Most prominent among these temporary staffers—and an exception to the rule of relatively short tenure—was Dr. Doris Schoon, who served more than two years in the mid-1950s. She went on from Embudo to a successful practice in ophthamology in southern California.

[35]*Española Valley News* (Española), 6 November 1957, p. 3.

smoothed over in order to secure the local support necessary to make the effort viable.[36]

In 1957, Dr. Millican moved across the mountains to the village of Cleveland, in the Mora Valley, to run the new clinic. She was successful in getting the experiment on its feet despite a grab bag of problems, medical and otherwise, and led the facility until the end of 1961. Her service in northern New Mexico concluded with a decade and a half of private practice in Las Vegas focused on obstetrics and gynecology, and she was also active in public-health work in the region, a logical extension of her earlier mission service. Severe eye problems and a pair of heart attacks finally forced her from active practice in 1978, and she died in Albuquerque in early 1985. Her work, however, along with that of Drs. Bowen and Milner and the nurses and temporary staffers who served in the Presbyterian mission in the mountains, constitutes a remarkable chapter in the story of the contributions made by women physicians in New Mexico.

As a part of the post–World War II economic and population expansion of New Mexico, larger numbers of women physicians began to come to the state, although their absolute numbers did not become significant until the 1960s. (As late as 1956 there were still fewer than three dozen female doctors in the state, and not all of them were in practice.) The newcomers of the forties and fifties included a number of talented women who served distinguished careers in the state: Drs. Eleanor Adler and Lucy McMurray of Albuquerque, Mary Waddell of Las Vegas, Catherine Armstrong-Seward of Carlsbad, and a sizable number in Santa Fe—Drs. Audrie Bobb, Anita Friedman, Marion Hotopp, Charlotte Jones, Alvina Looram, and Carol Smith. They built on the solid foundations established for them by the pioneer women doctors of the early days and by the dedicated missionary doctors who in the 1930s began their hard labors in the countryside. Without noticeable difficulty of any sort, they were fully integrated within the mainstream of New Mexico medicine and contributed their share to the well-being of the state's people.[37]

[36]Millican, interview, Albuquerque, 30 August 1983.

[37]Although the constructive work of New Mexico's women doctors of the forties and fifties received little public attention or acclaim, the private problems of one of them did. The name of the respected Santa Fe obstetrician-gynecologist Dr. Nancy DuVall Campbell was splashed across newspaper headlines around the state in November 1950, when she was arrested for the kidnapping for ransom of the daughter of a prominent Santa Fe family.

One special group among the women doctors of the modern era deserves special attention. These were the women physicians who played so important a role in the development of public health services in New Mexico, particularly in the fields of maternal and child health care. Since medicine remained so heavily male-dominated, many of the women physicians trained in the thirties and forties found it easiest to establish themselves in public health positions. Public health work was commonly the most poorly paid of medical careers and even, sadly, the least prestigious. Well into the middle part of the century, public health positions were frequently regarded as sinecures for aging male practitioners who could no longer keep up with the hurly-burly pace of private practice or for those who never could.[38] Given its poor pay, relatively low status, and comparatively regular hours, women physicians moved into public health work with comparative ease—and dignified it. Several of the physicians mentioned above—Drs. Hotopp, Looram, and Waddell, most prominently—spent the great bulk of their careers in public health service, and most of the others either began there, and then shifted to private practice (as did Jones and Campbell), or contributed large portions of their time to public health work.

Dr. Marion Hotopp stands out within this strong group. Over twenty-five years of service to New Mexico's mothers and children, she earned a place among the state's most distinguished physicians. She probably touched in direct fashion the lives of more New Mexicans than any other physician of the modern period. There are literally thousands of New Mexicans alive today who owe their strength of body and, in many cases, their lives themselves to her beneficient influence.

She first came to New Mexico as a forty-five-year-old public health specialist with strong credentials in the fields of maternal and child health care. Born in New Jersey at the turn of the century and educated at Mount

One year later, Dr. Campbell was tried and found guilty of the puzzling crime, and she eventually served a six-year prison sentence. Sadly, the two major scandals involving New Mexico doctors—the other being the murder trial of Dr. Frisbie—involved women doctors.

[38]Mrs. Beatrice Chauvenet, interview with the author, Albuquerque, N.M., 1 October 1984. (Mrs. Chauvenet was active in New Mexico public health work for more than three decades.) This judgment, of course, is not meant to disparage the service of the many male public health doctors of great energy, ability, and commitment in those early days. Many of New Mexico's public health doctors were capable, hardworking men, but there were many of the other variety as well. Mrs. Chauvenet's judgment was echoed in many of my interviews with veteran New Mexico physicians around the state.

Holyoke College in western Massachusetts, she entered Cornell University Medical School in 1930 and received her M.D. four years later. Hotopp flirted briefly with a career in bacteriology, but a residency at Philadelphia's Children's Hospital in 1936–37 focused her interest and career on pediatrics and obstetrics, especially the areas of proper nutrition for expectant mothers and infants and young children. After two years of practice as a physician at the New York State Training School for delinquent girls, she entered the Harvard School of Public Health and earned her Master's degree in 1940, concentrating her study and research in maternal and child hygiene. From 1941 to 1944 she headed the Crippled Children's and Maternal and Child Hygiene Service of the Delaware Board of Health. Working in that position, she quickly established a reputation as an expert on the needs of expectant mothers and small children through publication of a number of thoughtful and solidly researched articles on those subjects.[39] After a short stint as a consultant to the Children's Bureau of the U.S. Department of Labor working in Texas, she came to New Mexico in 1945 to serve as Director of the Maternal and Child Health Division of the state health department. She was board certified in both pediatrics and public health and enjoyed a growing national reputation, but she chose New Mexico in 1945 because of its critical need for her special expertise and the challenge it presented.[40] A warm, compassionate person with great empathy for suffering wherever she saw it, she devoted the rest of her life and career to New Mexico's mothers and infants.

In the 1940s, frontier New Mexico suffered from one of the highest infant mortality rates in the country as well as a frighteningly high loss rate among new mothers. These problems are discussed in detail in the following chapter, which describes the birth and elaboration of public health services in New Mexico. Suffice it to say here that Dr. Hotopp became the central figure in the state's attack on its infant and maternal mortality problems. Building on the solid foundations established by her predecessor in the Maternal and Child Health division of the state health department, Dr. Stuart Adler, Dr. Hotopp developed and executed programs and policies which steadily brought the death rates down. From 1945 until 1953, she coordinated all of the state's maternal and child

[39]See her articles in volumes 13, 14, and 15 (1941–43) of the *Delaware State Medical Journal* and *Medical Woman's Journal* 48 (1941):308–17.

[40]For biographical details on Dr. Hotopp, see her file in the University of New Mexico Medical Center Library, Medical History Archives.

health programs from her post in Santa Fe. But she was impatient with bureaucratic service—"hands-on" practice was always her forte, and she much preferred to lead by example—and from 1955 until her retirement from state service in 1967 she was a field practitioner, serving as District Health Officer for the counties of Santa Fe, Rio Arriba, and Taos. The need for her special talents and expertise was especially keen in those poor, mountainous counties, and she devoted the major part of her New Mexico career to them.

During her twenty-five years of practice in New Mexico, Dr. Hotopp was the architect and driving force behind an extensive network of public health clinics established around the state. Directing public health physicians and nurses and enlisting the aid of private practitioners all over the state, she took modern health care to expectant mothers, babies, and young children who otherwise had limited or no ready access to it. These well-baby and maternity clinics were the key element in her work, for they were the opportunity to deliver preventive health care to poor and isolated people around New Mexico and were the means of spreading the basic principles of public health. Dr. Hotopp personally developed clinics in Tierra Amarilla, Park View, Cuba, Vallecitos, and El Rito, among others, and her increasingly stooped figure—she suffered severely from degenerative spinal disease and spent her last years in a wheelchair—was a familiar one in crude adobe buildings all over northern New Mexico.

Though impeccably trained as a modern public health professional, Dr. Hotopp was a pragmatist who sought accommodation and convergence between the abstract principles of modern public health and the realities and traditions of rural New Mexico. She learned the Spanish of northern New Mexico's Hispanic communities and compiled a small dictionary of common Spanish terms, particularly those relating to health care and nutrition, and distributed them among the public health nurses working in rural service.[41] She accepted the cultural (and medical) importance of the midwives who delivered a high percentage of northern New Mexico's babies and did what she could to improve the quality of the service they rendered. Her flexibility and sensitivity to the culture of the people among whom she worked was legendary and is captured in the affectionate and respectful reminiscences of one of her private practice colleagues, Dr. Carol K. Smith of Santa Fe:

[41]Dr. Carol K. Smith, interview with the author, Santa Fe, N.M., 11 September 1985. Dr. Smith worked with Dr. Hotopp in her rural clinics.

She had beautifully developed nutrition programs underway, just using foods the people were accustomed to. This was, of course, largely a vegetarian diet back in the 1940s with the addition of some fish and venison and occasionally beef and chicken. She knew exactly what she was doing. She built on that base and put out all sorts of materials for use in the clinics, including various diets, and explained to mothers how to supplement their babies' diets. It was an interesting time, because during the war and just after a lot of Spanish women suddenly found that they could get out and work, so the young mothers didn't want to nurse their babies. Their mothers and grandmothers said, "Why do you want to stay home to breastfeed your baby? You can get out and work, and we'll take care of the babies." Northern New Mexico started to become a bottle-fed baby area, so Marion got busy explaining to the people about boiling the milk and teaching them to use canned evaporated milk. If they weren't already doing so, she tried to get them to supplement their diets with pinto beans and other reasonably high protein foods and advocated using rosehips as a source of vitamin C where people had a lot of roses around growing wild.[42]

As part of her many-sided campaign against needless maternal and infant deaths in New Mexico, Dr. Hotopp was also instrumental in spreading modern birth control information and techniques among those she served. One of her colleagues in the state health service emphasized her role and the work of other women doctors in this delicate sphere:

Male doctors by and large wouldn't touch it because of the political aspects of it, and women doctors just understood it better. They made birth control means available through their clinics quietly and without a lot of fanfare—for obvious reasons—basically because it was just obvious to them that a new mother couldn't take the best care possible of a new baby when she was already pregnant with the next one.[43]

Limited by her increasingly severe health problems, Dr. Hotopp retired from state service in 1967. She was hardly inactive in her last years, however, for her unique experience and expertise made her eagerly sought

[42]Ibid. Her strong advocacy of pinto beans, a staple food readily available to most New Mexicans, even the poorest, made a great impact around the state. One of her colleagues from the opposite end of New Mexico, Dr. James Sedgwick, who practiced in Las Cruces from 1938 to 1967, remembered "that lady public health doctor who preached so earnestly about mashed-up pinto beans," and emphasized the importance of Dr. Hotopp's nutritional programs in improving the health of the Spanish people, particularly, of his area. Dr. James C. Sedgwick, interview with the author, Albuquerque, N.M., 19 September 1983.

[43]Chauvenet, interview, Albuquerque, 1 October 1984.

as a consultant on maternal and child health care problems, particularly in poor, rural settings. Even before her retirement, public health nurses from Central and South America would come to Santa Fe to work with Dr. Hotopp and learn her techniques, and throughout the 1960s Peace Corps nurses training for service abroad came through her clinics as part of their training. Through the agency of the World Health Organization, she traveled and worked as a consultant in Guatemala, Honduras, and Bolivia in the late 1960s, helping those developing societies establish their maternal and infant health care services.[44] Her greatness and indelible service to New Mexico were appreciated by her peers, and in 1975, the year before her death, she was honored at a statewide public health conference held at Ghost Ranch in her beloved northern New Mexico. The plaque presented her there pronounced a fitting benediction on her life:

> In grateful recognition of a lifetime of service
> dedicated to the health and wholeness of others;
> Her children shall rise up and call her blessed.[45]

[44]Smith, interview, Santa Fe, 11 September 1985; Dr. Jan Peter Voute and Mrs. K. Rose Wood, interview with the author, Santa Fe, N.M., 3 January 1985. Both Dr. Voute and Mrs. Wood were colleagues of Dr. Hotopp in the health department.

[45]Marion Hotopp file in University of New Mexico Medical Center Library, Medical History Archives.

41

42

Figure 41. Dr. Margaret Cartwright (M.D., Woman's Medical College, Chicago, 1890) practiced in Albuquerque from 1908 to 1942. (Photo courtesy of BME.)

Figure 42. Dr. Ada Chevaillier (M.D., New York Eclectic Medical School, 1891) practiced five years in Albuquerque, then in Gallup from 1915 to 1941. (Photo courtesy of BME.)

43

Figure 43. Dr. Florence Janet Reid (M.D., College of Physicians and Surgeons, Keokuk, Iowa, 1896) was a tuberculosis specialist and practiced in Raton, Santa Fe, and Deming from 1912 to the early 1920s. (Photo courtesy of BME.)

Figure 44. Dr. Harriet R. Flanders (M.D., Tufts Medical College, 1908) was a Las Cruces physician from 1915 until 1922. (Photo courtesy of BME.)

44

45

Figure 45. Dr. Gertrude Light (M.D., Johns Hopkins, 1898) graduated in one of the early classes of Baltimore's famed Johns Hopkins University School of Medicine, then spent most of her career in Ranchos de Taos. She was there from 1922 into the 1940s. (Photo courtesy of BME.)
Figure 46. Dr. Sarah Coker (M.D., Woman's Medical College, Philadelphia, 1908) practiced in Albuquerque and Santa Fe in the teens and twenties. (Photo courtesy of BME.)

46

47

48

49

Figure 47. Dr. Evelyn Fisher Frisbie, ca. 1908. (Photo courtesy of BME.)
Figure 48. Albuquerque's Dr. Eleanor Adler practiced in the city from 1947 until the early 1980s. She was inspired to study medicine by her older brother, Stuart, but also by the example of a family friend, pioneer Pennsylvania woman doctor, Dr. Della Patterson Wetherby. In this 1912 photo, young Eleanor Adler (bothered by the sun) and a friend are preparing to go on a house call with Dr. Wetherby. (Photo courtesy of Dr. Eleanor Adler.)
Figure 49. Brooklyn Cottage Hospital, Dixon, New Mexico, ca. 1939. At one time, Dr. Sarah Bowen had this 28′ by 34′ building filled with 27 patients. (Photo courtesy of Dr. Virginia Milner.)

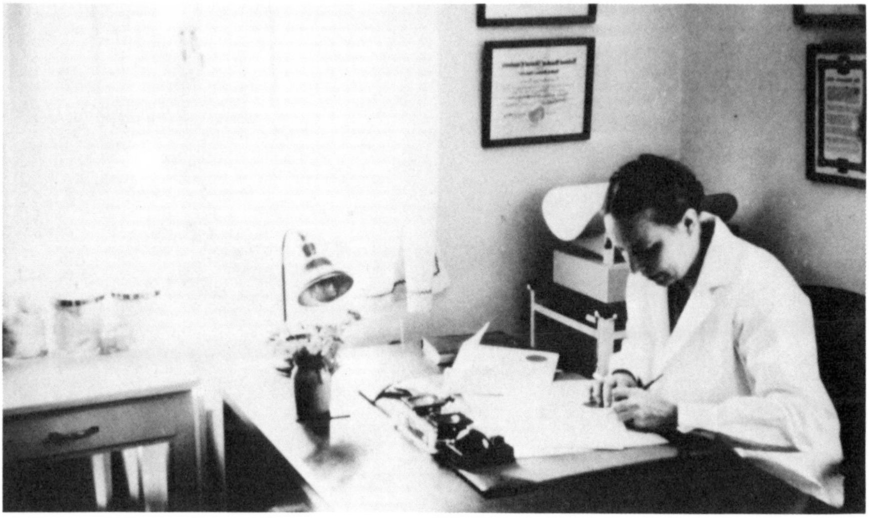

50

Figure 50. Dr. Sarah Bowen working at her desk at Embudo Hospital, ca. 1945. (Photo courtesy of Menaul Historical Library.)
Figure 51. For the women doctors of the Presbyterian mission in the Sangre de Cristo Mountains, a house call sometimes meant crossing the Rio Grande on a shaky bridge. This is Dr. Virginia Voorhies, black medical bag in hand, about 1940. (Photo courtesy of Dr. Virginia Milner.)
Figure 52. Or a house call (under good conditions) meant bumping along the dirt roads of the mountains with the ever real possibility of flat tires. This is Dr. Bowen with her chagrined back to the camera. (Photo courtesy of Dr. Virginia Milner.)

51

52

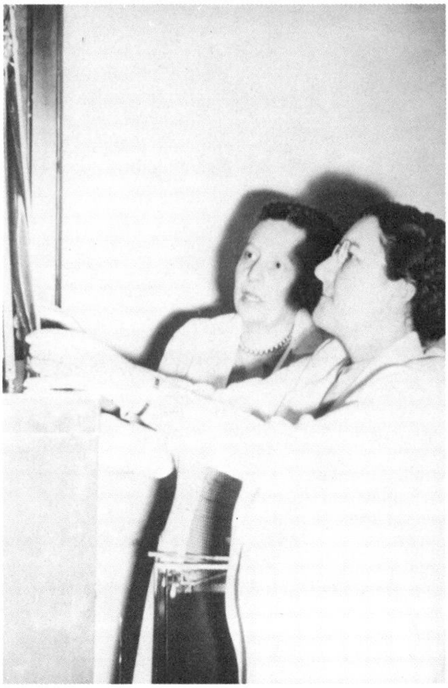

53

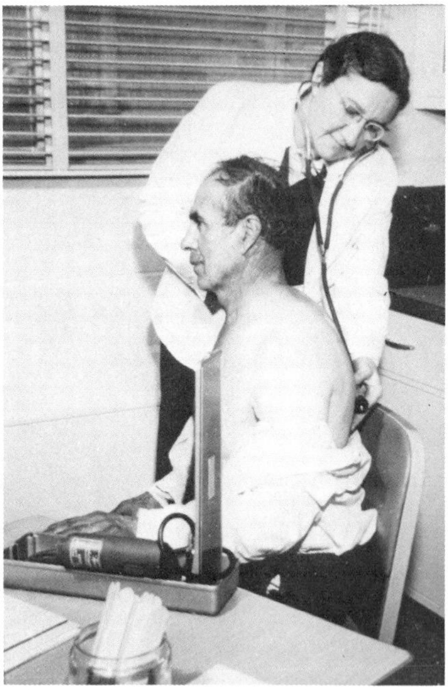

54

Figure 53. Drs. Edith Millican, front, and Sarah Bowen, rear, examining an X-ray, about 1950. (Photo courtesy of Menaul Historical Library.)

Figure 54. Dr. Edith Millican served in the Sangre de Cristo Mountains for more than thirty years. This photograph, taken around 1960, shows her in the Mora Valley Clinic she established. (Photo courtesy of Dr. Millican.)

Figure 55. Dr. Marion Hotopp, a photograph taken in retirement, around 1972. (Photo courtesy of State Archives.)

Figure 56. Dr. Walter Werner was one of the state's more prominent tuberculosis doctor-researchers. He practiced in Albuquerque from 1935 until his death in a plane crash in 1954. In this 1940s photo he is administering pneumothorax, artificially collapsing a patient's lung to allow it to rest. (Photo courtesy of UNM-MCL.)

55

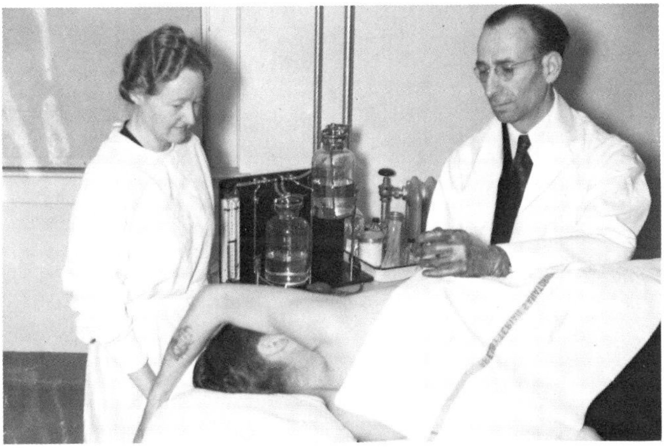

56

57

58

Figure 57. Dr. Carl Mulky, president of the New Mexico Medical Society, 1941–42, was a graduate of Chicago's Rush Medical College in 1900. He came to New Mexico seeking relief from his own case of tuberculosis and practiced more than thirty years in Albuquerque. (Photo courtesy of BME.)

Figure 58. Santa Fe's Dr. Robert O. Brown was one of the state's most highly respected internists. He, too, came to New Mexico with tuberculosis, but lived to practice 33 years in Santa Fe. In 1930–31, he was president of the New Mexico Medical Society. (Photo courtesy of BME.)

59

60

Figure 59. Dr. Harry A. Miller of Clovis (president of the New Mexico Medical Society, 1922–23) was one of the "characters" of the New Mexico medical community. Shown here around 1930 with his dog, One-Eyed-Pete (on whom he had performed unsuccessful ophthamological surgery), Dr. Miller amused the local boys by wrestling the pet bear he kept penned behind the old Santa Fe Hospital in Clovis. (Photo courtesy of High Plains Historical Foundation, Clovis.)

Figure 60. For more than thirty years, Dr. Owen Puckett was county health officer for Eddy County. He practiced in Hope, New Mexico, before moving to Carlsbad in 1925. (Photo courtesy of BME.)

61

62

Figure 61. Dr. Joaquin Garduño, who got his M.D. in 1913 from the National University in Mexico City, gave 44 years of his professional life to New Mexico. He practiced in Magdalena, Socorro, and Albuquerque. (Photo courtesy of BME.)

Figure 62. Dr. Eugene Fiske of Santa Fe was a leader among the state's physicians from his start in practice in 1917 until his death in 1962. He was president of the New Mexico Medical Society in 1938–39. (Photo courtesy of BME.)

63

64

Figure 63. A 1908 graduate of Syracuse University College of Medicine, Dr. J. W. Hannett came to Gallup, New Mexico as a railroad surgeon in 1919. Moving to Albuquerque in 1929, he was a leader of that city's medical community until his retirement in the early 1950s. Hannett was president of the New Mexico Medical Society, 1949–50. (Photo courtesy of BME.)
Figure 64. Dr. William H. Woolston came to Albuquerque from the faculty at Northwestern University in 1922. For the subsequent 35 years, he was one of New Mexico's most respected surgeons. (Photo courtesy of BME.)

65

Figure 65. A Health Department sponsored well-baby clinic in northern New Mexico in the 1940s. (Photo courtesy of State Archives.)

Figure 66. Dr. Stuart Adler, left, head of the Maternal and Infant Health division of the state board of health in the early 1940s, and Dr. Reynaldo DeVeaux of Taos at the Peñasco Clinic in 1943. (Photo courtesy of Dr. DeVeaux.)

Figure 67. A Mora County midwife before an adobe home in the 1940s. She is carrying the suitcase supplied her by the state health department containing obstetrical equipment and supplies to help her in her work. (Photo courtesy of State Archives.)

66

67

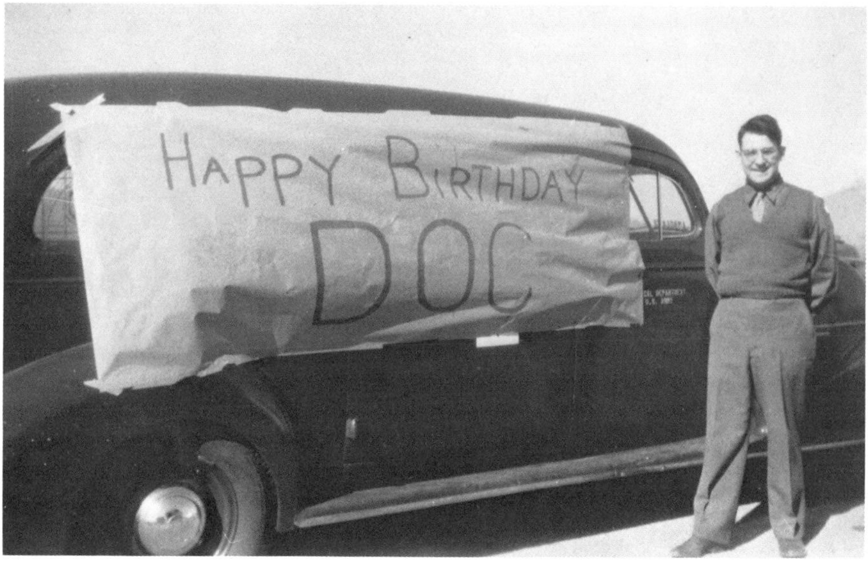

68

Figure 68. The Army brought to New Mexico many young specialists who decided to stay. Here Dr. Louis Levin, stationed at White Sands, New Mexico, in the mid-1940s, enjoys a birthday. Dr. Levin is still in practice in Albuquerque in 1986. (Photo courtesy of Dr. Levin.)

Figure 69. Drs. Stanley Leland, Robert C. Derbyshire, and I. J. Marshall (left to right) set good examples, taking their Salk polio vaccine sugar cubes in 1954. Drs. Derbyshire (1962–63) and Marshall (1950–51) served as president of the New Mexico Medical Society, and Dr. Leland headed the State Health Department. (Photo courtesy of State Archives.)

Figure 70. Perhaps the most widely known New Mexico physician of the twentieth century, Dr. Meldrum K. Wylder practiced in Albuquerque from 1903 until his death in 1962. He delivered and cared for thousands of babies in and around Albuquerque. (Photo courtesy of State Archives.)

69

70

71

72

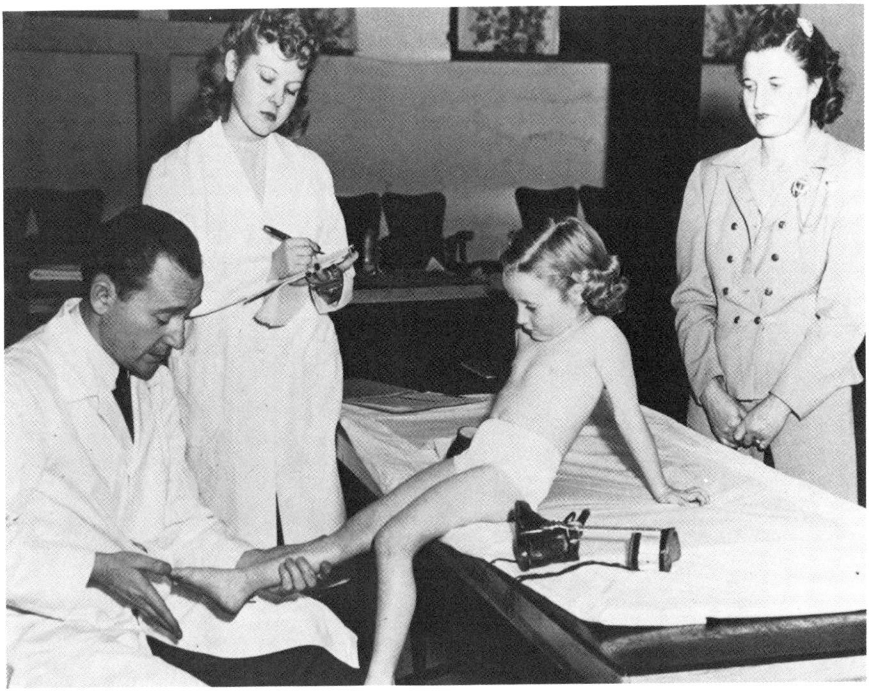

73

Figure 71. Christmas dinner at Taos's Holy Cross Hospital, ca. 1955. The physicians at the table with their wives are Drs. Al Rosen (left), Ashley Pond III (center), and Reynaldo DeVeaux (right). (Photo courtesy of Dr. DeVeaux.)

Figure 72. Dr. I. J. Marshall (left) and his brother Dr. U. S. "Steve" Marshall were both longtime Roswell physicians. This photo was taken at the 1981 ceremonies honoring Dr. I. J. Marshall on the occasion of his retirement as school physician at the New Mexico Military Institute. Major-General Gerald Childress, Superintendent of the school, rides in the center. (Photo courtesy of New Mexico Military Institute, Public Information Office.)

Figure 73. Dr. William Minear of the Carrie Tingley Hospital for Crippled Children in Hot Springs, New Mexico, examines a small patient in 1949. Dr. Minear continued his distinguished career in Albuquerque. (Photo courtesy of Dr. Minear.)

74

75

76

Figure 74. Five leaders of New Mexico's medical community in the 1950s and 1960s, all presidents of the state medical society. Front row, Dr. Earl Malone of Roswell (1955–56), left, and Dr. Stuart Adler of Albuquerque (1956–57), right. Back row, left to right: Dr. John Conway of Clovis (1954–1955), Dr. Sam Ziegler of Española (1957–58), and Dr. Lewis Overton of Albuquerque (1959–60). (Photo courtesy of UNM-MCL.)

Figure 75. Albuquerque Indian Hospital in early 1936, a little more than a year after its opening. The street running from lower left to upper right is Girard Boulevard. Lomas Boulevard did not yet exist. (Photo courtesy of Dr. Lawrence H. Wilkinson.)

Figure 76. A companion photo to the one opposite. This aerial photo, taken in 1966, shows the Indian Hospital at center flanked by Bernalillo County Medical Center. The new University of New Mexico School of Medicine is under construction behind BCMC. (Photo courtesy of Dr. Lawrence H. Wilkinson.)

77

Figure 77. Taos's Holy Cross Hospital, around 1945. The building had originally been constructed by Mabel Dodge Luhan as a home for her son, but was converted into a hospital in 1937. (Photo courtesy of Dr. Reynaldo DeVeaux.)

Figure 78. These two doctors together gave 74 years to Taos. Dr. Werner Onstine, right, practiced in the town from 1909 to 1913 and again from 1927 until his death in 1955, and Dr. Reynaldo DeVeaux, left, served the community from 1942 until his retirement in 1984. Nurse Bernadette Jennings stands between the doctors in this 1942 photo taken before the Questa Clinic. (Photo courtesy of Dr. DeVeaux.)

Figure 79. Dr. Reginald Fitz, founding dean of the University of New Mexico School of Medicine. (Photo courtesy of BME.)

78

79

80

81

82

Figure 80. Architects of the University of New Mexico School of Medicine, the University's Board of Regents in 1961. Front row, left to right: Judge Howard Bratton of Albuquerque; President Tom Popejoy of the University; Dr. Lawrence Wilkinson of Albuquerque; and Mrs. Dorothy Brandenburg of Taos. Rear, left is attorney Bryan Johnson of Corrales and, right, Thomas Roberts of Los Alamos. (Photo courtesy of Dr. Wilkinson.)

Figure 81. Dr. William R. Lovelace I (left) and Dr. William R. Lovelace II in the operating room at Bataan Hospital, 1957. At the time of this photo, "Uncle Doc" was 74 and Randy not quite 50. (Photo courtesy of Lovelace Foundation.)

Figure 82. Bataan Memorial Methodist Hospital (left) under construction in early 1952. The one-year-old Lovelace Clinic building is at right, and the Veterans Hospital is at the rear. Notice the "traffic" on Gibson Boulevard. (Photo courtesy of the Lovelace Foundation.)

83

84

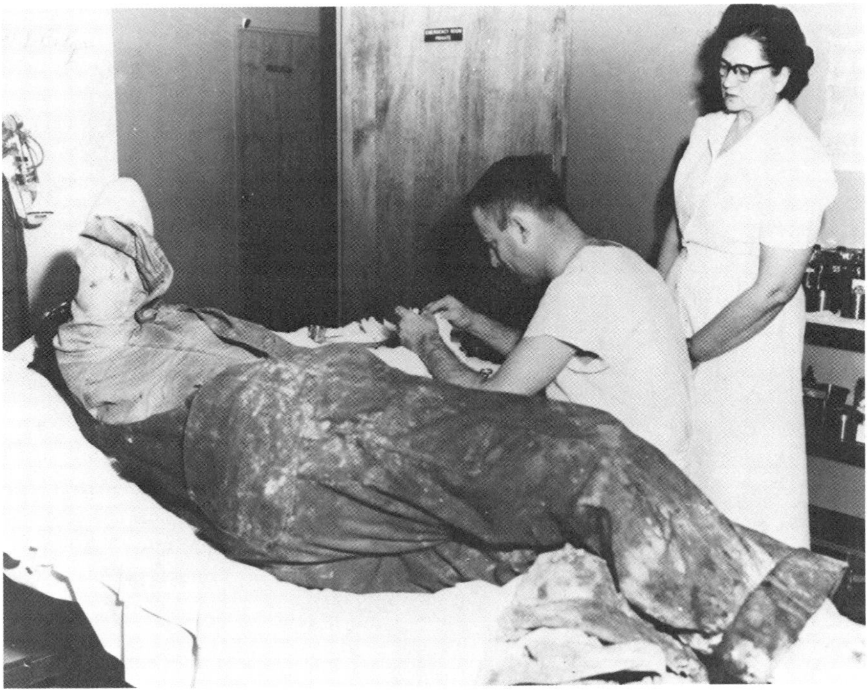

85

Figure 83. The original Board of Governors of the Lovelace Clinic after its reorganization in 1947. Left to right: Dr. H. L. "Jan" January, Dr. Edgar Lassetter, Dr. William R. Lovelace I, Dr. Lee Miles, and Dr. William R. Lovelace II. (Photo courtesy of the Lovelace Foundation.)

Figure 84. Mainstays of Albuquerque's Memorial Hospital in the early 1950s proudly displaying an award-winning professional meeting presentation on gall bladder disease. Standing, left to right, Drs. James W. Wiggins, Carl S. Williamson, and Fred H. Hanold. Kneeling, left, is Dr. Charles R. Beeson and, right, Dr. Lawrence H. Wilkinson. (Photo courtesy of Dr. Wilkinson.)

Figure 85. Oil field accident cases—this man has a hand injury—were part of the daily routine for Hobbs general surgeon, Dr. William E. Badger. Dr. Badger was president of the New Mexico Medical Society in 1961–62. (Photo courtesy of Dr. Badger.)

86

Figure 86. Three generations of New Mexico Medical Society leadership. Left, Ralph Marshall, Executive Director of the organization since 1949; center, Dr. Carl H. Gellenthien of Valmora, New Mexico, member of the society since 1927 and twice its president, 1944–45 and 1945–46; and, right, Randy Marshall, Associate Executive Director. (Photo courtesy of UNM-MCL.)

CHAPTER 6

Public-Health Services and New Mexico Doctors

THE MIDDLE PERIOD OF THIS HISTORY—FROM THE ATTAINment of statehood in 1912 to the Second World War—was largely a time of stabilization or consolidation, lacking the rapid movement and change of the previous and subsequent eras. It saw the elaboration or unfolding and then the leveling off and incipient decline of the state's sanatorium movement and tuberculosis industry. It also witnessed a significant shakeout of New Mexico's too-fat physician corps, a reduction of no less than a third within a decade or so. But, ultimately, the most significant development of those years was the birth of a public-health system. It can be argued that no other development of the past century has had a greater impact in affecting the general well-being of New Mexico society. Though the state was relatively slow in establishing a broad range of public-health services, and financial constraints have chronically limited their growth, one of the most comprehensive and effective, as well as innovative, public-health structures in the country had been built in New Mexico by the latter part of the twentieth century.

At the start of the twentieth century, New Mexico was still very much a frontier society in terms of its arrangements for the supervision and control of the public's health. A 1916 study, conducted under the auspices of the American Medical Association, compared public-health systems in the various states of the country and spelled out New Mexico's backwardness with stark candor: "It is unfortunate that a state with a population which now numbers nearly half a million should do nothing whatever for public health. It is the only state of which this can be said."[1]

The report's categorical assertion that "nothing whatever" had been done in the sphere of public health was only a very slight exaggeration. Throughout the latter years of the territorial period, New Mexico had a unified Board of Health and Medical Examiners, made up of reputable physicians from around the territory, but the activity of the Board had been restricted to the licensing of candidates to practice medicine. No funds were ever provided for any other activity of a public-health nature. Instead, when the Territorial Board of Health and Medical Examiners concerned itself at all with public health, it was content to make pious declarations of what the local counties should do for the public health, declarations that were promptly ignored and forgotten. The bland prose of a formal report written in 1918 by a surgeon of the United States Public Health Service summed up the Board's emptiness in clear terms:

> No other regulations [than those dealing with medical licensure] have ever been issued by the board under its authority, nor have investigations of nuisances, sources of filth, or causes of sickness been undertaken except in rare instances, as there were no funds with which to do so. In these instances it was necessary for the member concerned to bear his own expenses. . . . No records of public health activity are systematically kept by the board, and it has no office or clerical force for such a purpose.[2]

The point was curtly underlined in the Board's 1915 annual report to the governor, when its secretary, Dr. Walter E. Kaser of Las Vegas, noted:

> As no appropriation for health purposes is made by the state and the Board has no sources of revenue, naturally the activities of the Board as a Board of Health have been limited. No meetings as a Board of Health have been held in this year.[3]

Even when it was explicitly requested to investigate a public-health problem, the Board was forced to plead inadequacy. For example, in 1913,

[1]*American Medical Association Bulletin* 11 (1916):74.

[2]J. W. Kerr (M.D.), "Public Health Administration in New Mexico," *Public Health Reports* 33 (1918):1980–81. See, also, G. S. Luckett (M.D.), "Ten Years Ago," *Southwestern Medicine* 13 (1929):535.

[3]New Mexico, Board of Health and Medical Examiners, Annual Report to the Governor, 1915.

when it was asked by the Santa Fe railroad to certify as safe the drinking water supplies and ice it had to take on along its way through New Mexico, the Board secretary wrote to the railroad to declare that it lacked any way to execute that request. The only suggestion the Board could make was that its members might go out individually and inspect, take samples, and have water supplies examined by chemists and bacteriologists, but that procedure would require the railroad to pay ten dollars per day for the member's services plus his traveling expenses and the costs of the laboratory tests that were conducted.[4] Efforts made by the Board to pass the public-health buck to county authorities were also of little avail, for the great majority of New Mexico counties had little interest and still less money to invest in public-health work. The inadequacy of the counties was reflected in the problems encountered by the Board's secretary in 1915, when he sought to gather vital statistics for the state:

> A large portion of my letters of inquiry have gone without reply. Letters were written to each county clerk; to each county health officer; and to each city or town health officer. I was not even able to arrive at the names of a large proportion of the latter. The work done in the counties and cities . . . varies from none at all and no official in charge to really efficient work under discouraging circumstances. One county reports no county health officer at all because, forsooth, the county commissioners did not want to have any.[5]

As a consequence of this inattention, New Mexico, as late as the start of the First World War, remained something approaching a public-health officer's nightmare. Neglect of public sanitation was probably the most glaringly apparent problem among many. Milk supplies in the state were completely uncontrolled, and as a result, the milk was very often filthy and infected. No testing of dairy herds for tuberculosis or brucellosis existed, and mastitis was common. Nor was the labor force of the dairy industry subject to health controls of any sort. If a milker was not too sick to stand, he worked—even if he had diphtheria, typhoid, or whatever. Pasteurization of milk was an idea whose time had not yet come so far

[4]New Mexico, Board of Health and Medical Examiners, Minutes, 14 April 1913.

[5]New Mexico, Board of Health and Medical Examiners, Annual Report to the Governor, 1915.

as frontier New Mexico was concerned.[6] Nor were water supplies any better; rather, they ranged from the only moderately dangerous to the grossly unsafe. The well-water supplies of the state's larger cities were usually fairly safe, but all other sources of drinking water were at least worrisome. For example, water drawn from free-flowing surface supplies was very often contaminated, and much of it was nauseating and threatening to human health. Rural New Mexicans literally took their lives in their hands when they filled their drinking vessels, for most rural water sources were notoriously unsafe. Shallow village well-water and water dipped directly from irrigation ditches quenched the thirst of many New Mexicans, but often at a terrible price in human suffering. In the New Mexico of the early years of this century, chlorination or other disinfection of water supplies, even basic filtration, was nowhere practiced.

Sewage-disposal arrangements were similarly casual, even medieval. The few towns with sewer systems simply discharged their effluents, untreated, into the nearest stream, if one was handy, or into dry arroyos. In some places raw sewage was a utilizable resource, used for irrigating vegetable patches. Rural New Mexico, on the other hand, depended on the privy and on arrangements that would have been familiar to the Spanish colonists of the sixteenth century; and those premodern facilities were located and built without the slightest recognition of modern safety standards. Arrangements for garbage collection and other waste disposal ranged from the primitive to the nonexistent. No food-sanitation measures of any sort existed. Breeding places for the anopheles mosquito, the carrier of malaria, were abundant and no effort was made to eliminate or treat them. No public laboratory for chemical and bacteriological testing or other kinds of modern scientific investigation existed. There were no public-health nurses for health education and basic disease-prevention measures.

The bitter fruit of this public-health neglect was evident in the ill health

[6]Much of this summary of the public-health horrors of early twentieth-century New Mexico is drawn from "Public Health in New Mexico, 1919–1979," a chapter in a 1979 report, published by the state's Health and Environment Department, entitled *New Mexico: Fifty Years as a Vital Statistics Registration State, 1929–1979*, pp. 72–87, a useful introduction to the subject. More comprehensive and thorough on the entire subject of public-health development in New Mexico is Myrtle Greenfield, *A History of Public Health in New Mexico* (Albuquerque: University of New Mexico Press, 1962). The interested reader may also wish to consult the annual reports issued by the Department of Health, which, until 1950, were published in its journal, *The New Mexico Health Officer.*

of New Mexico's people. Although reliable figures do not exist—in the absence of any real Department of Health or effective Health Board, no agency existed to keep records regarding the public health—it is clear that New Mexico labored under a disease burden more severe than that of other states. For example, dysentery and diarrhea, the obvious concomitants of the poor sanitation suggested above, were major health problems and contributed significantly to the state's mortality rates. Almost all New Mexicans suffered, and sometimes died, from what was euphemistically called "summer complaint"; the label reflected the malady's special prominence during the warmer months (housefly season), but it was a specially potent threat to New Mexico's babies. The connection between these intestinal problems and the state's public-sanitation deficiencies was apparent, at least to some; but there was no agency to attack the root causes, and individual or local effort was inadequate. Diphtheria, typhoid fever, scarlet fever, poliomyelitis, and other communicable diseases spread easily through the state's communities in the absence of any barriers to their movement.[7] Malaria was a growing problem for many sections of New Mexico, especially in the Mesilla Valley, the middle Rio Grande region, and the Pecos and Española valleys, for there were no measures to control the mosquito carrier. This depressing litany could readily be extended, for a frightening potpourri of diseases threatened the people of New Mexico—commonplace things like pneumonias, measles, influenza, mumps, venereal diseases, and such, but also relatively exotic diseases like anthrax, undulant fever, smallpox, pellagra, and trachoma. Many of these were diseases which might have been controlled or even eradicated by public-health measures and technology already available at the turn of the century. There was a terrible irony in the situation: New Mexico liked to think of itself as a "salubrious El Dorado" in the territorial and early statehood period, but the sad reality was quite otherwise.

Part of the overall problem was the question of information about the health and health problems of New Mexico society. How much smallpox or diphtheria was there? How high was the infant mortality rate prior to statehood, and what were the major causes of that attrition? What was the maternal death rate among New Mexico women? Such basic questions

[7]Newspaper accounts, scattered public records, and the records of physicians and hospitals from the territorial and early statehood periods testify to the frightening outbreaks of epidemic disease that periodically swept New Mexico.

as these and most others dealing with New Mexico's health history prior to the 1920s cannot be answered because of the absence of vital statistics. Basic data, such as registration of births and deaths, disease morbidity and mortality, and the myriad other pieces of data necessary for evaluating the health of the territory and for planning strategies to improve it simply were not available.

Although New Mexico was at least a generation behind its sister states in the Union, pressure for the creation of a strong and effective Board of Public Health finally began to build in the first years of the twentieth century. Many different factors contributed to the growth of what might be called New Mexico's public-health movement. Prominent among them was the leadership and consistently strong advocacy of New Mexico's physicians for a modern state agency to supervise the public health. Before the turn of the century, the Territorial Medical Society was on record as supporting, in the most vigorous terms, the establishment of an effective Board of Public Health,[8] and individual doctors around New Mexico stood up in support of the proposal.[9] The virtual unanimity and conviction of the territory's physicians was a powerful determinant of public and legislative opinion on the issue. Probably more important, however, because much more tangible and visible, was the arrival in such large numbers of the "lungers." Certainly, the concern was produced by the presence within the New Mexico populace of so many tuberculars was a major factor in the citizenry's growing consciousness of public health. The "lungers" brought the issue from the more or less abstract realm into the real world, and many New Mexicans became alarmed at what they perceived as an immediate and growing danger. In witnessing what they took to be highly infectious people climbing off the trains daily—or being passed off on stretchers through lowered windows—even the most disinterested parties began to listen to the arguments of those who advocated state intervention to safeguard the public health.[10]

[8]New Mexico Medical Society, Minutes, 3 October 1892.

[9]See, for example, James A. Rolls (M.D.), "The Sanitary Needs of Santa Fe," *New Mexico Medical Journal* 5 (1909–10):202–6; Robert E. McBride (M.D.), "The New Mexico Medical Society: Some Duties and Opportunities," *New Mexico Medical Journal* 4, no. 2 (1908–9):10–15; "The Need of the Hour" (editorial), *New Mexico Medical Journal* 15 (1915–16):133–35.

[10]"Lungers" themselves, it should be noted, were among the most active supporters of the public-health movement. The guiding spirit of the New Mexico Public Health Association, a group formed in 1917 to spearhead the fight for an effective public-health system,

Yet even with a growing public consciousness of the importance of protective measures for public health, it still took the special circumstances of wartime and a major disease catastrophe to carry the day in winning for New Mexico its first public-health agency. For one thing, New Mexicans found to their chagrin that during the war their new state had missed out on federal-money grants, which were made available in connection with the exigencies of the war effort, because the state had no public-health machinery in place to administer the funds. Equally sobering was the hard evidence of substandard health conditions in the state, evidence provided by draft boards in the form of the results of U.S. Army physical examinations. Far too many New Mexico young men were rejected by Army doctors for physical conditions, and many of them, incidentally, were found to be suffering from incipient tuberculosis. The New Mexico rejection ratio was among the highest in the nation.[11]

Then came the tragic Spanish influenza epidemic of 1918, a natural disaster which proved the clincher in making the case for a state health agency. The flu thrust the public-health question onto the front pages of the newspapers, and finally, to its goal. As news of the international calamity began to claim an increasingly prominent place in the national press, many in faraway New Mexico reacted naively, even arrogantly, assuming that their state would be unaffected The *Santa Fe New Mexican*, for example, claimed that with "our salubrious . . . atmosphere" and the state's great distance from the nation's disease-ridden ports and big cities, there was "little likelihood that the Southwest will be visited by the epidemical malady."[12]

Contrary to such innocent expectations, the flu did arrive in the state in October 1918, immediately producing a full-scale emergency. Hundreds and then thousands of cases developed—eventually more than 15,000—

was John Tombs, a Canadian lawyer and businessman who had come to Albuquerque seeking relief from his tuberculosis. Clinton Anderson, later U.S. senator from New Mexico and an old "lunger" himself, cut his political teeth in the fight for a state Board of Health. See Greenfield, *History of Public Health in New Mexico*, pp. 14–21, 276–83.

[11]See United States, Medical Corps, Army, *Defects Found in Drafted Men: Statistical Information Compiled from Draft Records* (Washington: Government Printing Office, 1920), for a detailed study of this point.

[12]*Santa Fe New Mexican*, 28 September 1918, as cited in Richard Melzer, "A Dark and Terrible Moment: The Spanish Flu Epidemic of 1918 in New Mexico," *New Mexico Historical Review* 57 (1982):215. This essay is a solid account of the epidemic's history and impact on New Mexico society.

and many began to die. Final mortality associated with the epidemic reached 1,055, in an estimated total population of 350,000.[13] Measures to control and combat the disease, drummed up on the spur of the moment, proved completely inadequate in coping with its proportions. Though remarkable cooperation existed among the state's citizens, civil authorities, and private physicians and nurses, the machinery and organization to deal with a health problem of this magnitude was simply lacking. New Mexicans bitterly criticized state authorities for their unpreparedness and the futility of their efforts to stem the crisis, and the state's largest and most influential public-health interest group, Tombs's New Mexico Public Health Association, drove the point home:

> The outstanding feature of the situation was our absolute lack of health preparedness. . . . We will never know how many friends, relatives, and fellow citizens . . . were sacrificed as a result of the lack of an official health organization, linking up the counties and towns of our state for efficient health protection and the prevention of disease.[14]

The state's Board of Health and Medical Examiners clearly acknowledged its feebleness in its 1918 annual report to the governor:

> In this emergency the United States Public Health Service detailed Major Kerr of New York who, fortunately, at the time was engaged in making a public health survey of the state at the instance of the New Mexico Public Health Association, to assist this Board in meeting conditions. That is putting it not quite correctly, for this Board was in no position to render any service whatever and what public aid was given was given by the Public Health Service. . . . Our condition of helplessness and unpreparedness was deplorable.[15]

The public furor stimulated by the flu catastrophe finally moved the state legislature to act. The proponents of state health legislation took a bill drafted by experts in the U.S. Public Health Service, modified it slightly to fit New Mexico circumstances and political sensitivities, and pushed it through the legislature. Even with the special momentum afforded by the flu controversy, it was a difficult battle, and opposition in

[13]Ibid.:225.

[14]Cited in ibid.:229–30.

[15]New Mexico, Board of Health and Medical Examiners, Annual Report to the Governor, 1919.

the legislature was only slowly beaten down.[16] Funding for the new state agency, not surprisingly, was one of the major issues of the dispute, but advocates of the measure had already secured outside help to ease the birth pangs of the new board. With federal funds made available under the Rural Health Act of 1919, plus limited state money and money negotiated by Anderson from the Rockefeller Foundation, New Mexico's first real public-health agency was born on 25 April 1919.

The organizational development and establishment of programs and priorities by the new agency were painfully slow. The minutes of the very first, and brief, New Mexico Board of Health meeting, on 25 April 1919, show clearly the hesitancy and uncertainty of the new department before the challenges confronting it. With a limited budget and conflicting ideas about what it should and might seek to do, that first three-person Board of Public Health—made up of an enlightened Santa Fe woman from a politically influential family, Mrs. Adeline Otero-Warren; the medical director of Albuquerque's St. Joseph Sanatorium, Dr. Oliver T. Hyde; and the ubiquitous John Tombs—passed one resolution:

> to ask the Governor to apply to the Surgeon-General of the United States for the loan of an officer to organize the newly created Department of Health. A motion then prevailed that the Board take recess until called.[17]

In such modest, though prudent, fashion was public-health work inaugurated in New Mexico.

The creation of a state health department,[18] even tardily, was of course a major step forward, but the real effectiveness of the new agency was questionable for some time to come. Throughout the decade of the twenties, budget and staff limitations hamstrung health department operations, and it eventually took the powerful impact of the Great Depression

[16]The background and political machinations associated with passage of the state health department bill are summed up in a highly informative and charming letter written by Senator Anderson many years after the fact. Anderson was at the very center of the political battle, and his letter is printed in full in Greenfield, *History of Public Health in New Mexico*, pp. 276–83.

[17]James R. Scott (M.D.), "Twenty-five Years of Public Health in New Mexico, 1919–1944," *New Mexico Public Health Officer* 12 (1944):1.

[18]The new agency was initially called the Bureau of Public Health, and it has experienced a number of name changes over the years. However, it has always been the "State Health Department" in common parlance, even though that particular term has never formally applied.

and its national recovery programs to give real substance to public-health work in New Mexico. Nevertheless, a start was made when the new state agency formally opened its doors in 1919 with the arrival of Dr. Clifford E. Waller, a 1910 graduate of George Washington University School of Medicine and a public-health professional loaned to the state by the U.S. Public Health Service. Waller quickly developed a skeletal staff, composed largely of fellow officers from the federal service, and began the task of structuring the department and its programs. The work began literally at base zero, a fact that is reflected in the first three regulations, suggested by Dr. Waller and his staff and adopted by the State Board at its second meeting (20 August 1919): (1) "Regulations Governing the Reporting of Deaths and Births"—which, for the first time, made mandatory on a statewide basis the reporting of vital events; (2) "Regulations Governing the Disposal, Interment, Disinterment, and Transportation of the Dead"; and (3) "Regulations Governing the Reporting of Notifiable Diseases."[19]

The legislation establishing the health department had sought to create a system based on a relatively small central office in Santa Fe and a network of public-health units operating at the county level. County public-health officers were to be the front-line troopers of public-health work in New Mexico, with the central office in Santa Fe coordinating local work, supplying staff assistance and various kinds of technical support and expertise, and providing overall direction. The structure was devised to placate legislators, who, in opposing the agency's creation, had worried aloud about an army of state bureaucrats interfering and dictating to local authorities concerning what was best for them. Both elements of the structure—the Bureau of Public Health in Santa Fe and the local county-health offices—developed very slowly, with money being the chronic problem. For example, the budget for the entire operations of the Bureau of Public Health in Santa Fe was set at a penurious 16,700.66 dollars for the calendar year of 1921, a sum that was scarcely sufficient to get the doors open. It was enough to hire (at low wages) a grand total of four individuals, with each of them, not surprisingly, called upon to perform a wide range of duties. As an example, the state sanitary engineer, who was one of the "founding four," noted in one of his early reports that in addition to making food, milk, and water inspections and consulting on sewage disposal and mosquito control, he had also during the report year

[19]"Public Health in New Mexico, 1919–1979," in *New Mexico: Fifty Years as Vital Statistics*, p. 72.

represented the department at county budget hearings throughout the state; ordered, picked up, and moved in the furniture for his office; and assisted in a cesarean delivery.[20] Nor did the budget and staff strictures of the central office improve much, at least not until the thirties. After a decade of operation, in 1929 the total staff of the Bureau of Public Health had risen only to sixteen. Alongside a dozen clerks, stenographers, and laboratory helpers, there was a director of the agency (an M.D.), a chief of sanitary engineering and sanitation (an engineer with an M.S. degree), a chief of the state laboratory (an M.S. degree holder), and a registered nurse serving as chief of the Division of Child Hygiene and Public Health Nursing. And, although the Public Health Bureau's budget had risen to the lofty sum of 104,000 dollars, that sum was just less than the 107,152 dollars allocated to the Department of Game and Fish and light-years away from the 5,987,902 dollars spent by the Highway Commission.[21]

Similar problems limited the county end of public-health operations. From the very start, most counties around the state indicated their disinterest in creating effective local public-health units, or, more commonly, they expressed their financial inability to do so. Immediately after the new public-health law came in force in 1920, twenty-three New Mexico counties pleaded financial hardship and postponed indefinitely the inauguration of county-health operations. No more than five relatively prosperous counties—Bernalillo, Chaves, San Miguel, Santa Fe, and Union—established and funded county-health offices during that first year. Three others—Eddy, Torrance, and Valencia—joined the pioneer group in 1921, but the fragility or marginality of the county-health operations was clearly demonstrated when Torrance County closed down its health unit after less than a year in service. The county's coffers, never flush, had suffered with the drought of that year and the deferred payment of taxes by the depression-ridden railroad companies, so some of the county's services had to be suspended. The first thing to go was the infant county-health department. Financing was, by far, the most fundamental and persistent problem for local health units, and it involved an internal paradox of serious proportions. That seemingly insoluble paradox was spelled out in the first biennial report of the state health department director in 1922:

[20]Cited in ibid.

[21]It should also be noted that the State of New Mexico paid only about 40 percent of that total 104,000-dollar budget, with the rest contributed by the federal government, the Rockefeller Foundation, the Commonwealth Fund, and other donors.

Those counties which have been more progressive or more prosperous have been the first to adopt suggestions for improved health services. The less prosperous and less progressive counties will be the last to accept the benefits that science has to offer. Yet many of these latter are in greater need of such service because of the poverty, or ignorance, which contribute to ill health, the spread of infection, infant and maternal mortality, defective development of children and insanitary conditions of home and community.[22]

Outside agencies, such as the International Health Board of the Rockefeller Foundation, which gave ten thousand dollars to help pay the salaries of health officers for three particularly poor counties, and the U.S. Public Health Service, afforded assistance to the struggling health service in New Mexico, especially at the always precarious level of county operations, but the needs dwarfed the resources. With obvious reluctance, the state finally stepped in to help the local governments by passage of the Health Protection Fund in 1929. This legislation immediately made available money to assist the counties in their public-health responsibilities, but more importantly it established the principle of state aid to local governments for public-health purposes. Again New Mexico lagged behind the nation, for state assistance in local health work was well established throughout the rest of the country.[23] All such progress was relative, however, and subject to the vagaries of political and economic currents. When the depression struck New Mexico at the beginning of the 1930s, spending for public-health purposes was among the first programs to suffer. Public-health services quickly contracted, and as early as 1931 only six of the state's thirty-one counties preserved their trained, full-time health officer. The other twenty-five made do with expediencies, usually appointing a nominal county-health officer, since the state law of 1919 made the position mandatory; but in those counties, the titular County Health Officer was usually an appointed and unpaid or poorly paid private doctor, for whom public-health work was but a sideline to his private practice.[24] The hollowness of such arrangements was apparent in the health department director's 1932 report:

In Catron County with 3,282 people scattered over 7,042 square miles, the health

[22]First Biennial Report, cited in Scott, "Twenty-five Years of Public Health in New Mexico":4.

[23]New Mexico, Bureau of Public Health, Sixth Biennial Report, 1929–30, p. 11.

[24]New Mexico, Bureau of Public Health, Seventh Biennial Report, 1931–32, p. 14.

officer, the only doctor in the county, receives $600 a year and $100 for travel expenses. No sinecure![25]

Despite the essential unattractiveness of most of the county-health officer slots, there were those who for one reason or another coveted them, and thus political problems also bedeviled county public-health operations. Politics all too frequently intruded in both the staffing and direction of local health efforts, and at the expense of efficiency and even bare adequacy. For example, in 1932, in both Sandoval and Guadalupe counties serious outbreaks of epidemic disease—diphtheria in Sandoval and typhoid in Guadalupe—developed without the most elementary public-health measures available to cope with them. These notorious cases resulted in the removal from office of the county-health officers in those jurisdictions, each of whom was politically well connected (hence the job), but also entirely innocent of the basic principles of public-health campaigns to control communicable diseases and/or the energy and willingness to do the work.[26] Santa Fe officials and supporters of the public-health movement appealed throughout the 1920s and 1930s to county authorities for more regard to professional, as opposed to political, qualifications for the county-health officer slots, but it remained a constant battle.[27]

Given the range and dimensions of the problems confronting public-health authorities in New Mexico, it is surprising how much was accomplished in those first few years. A respectable start was accomplished in laying the foundations for a modern public-health establishment, but especially noteworthy progress was made in the spheres of modern sanitary engineering, public-health nursing, and the gathering of reliable health statistics. The reports of the health department throughout the 1920s and 1930s are replete with proud announcements that this or that municipality had, for example, just completed construction of a new, modern water-supply system or had just purchased a new waste-disposal system. The leadership and prodding of the health department's experts, in times

[25]Ibid.

[26]New Mexico, Bureau of Public Health, Second Biennial Report, 1923–24, p. ix.

[27]In 1933, when the Bernalillo County Commission dismissed county-health officer Dr. James R. Scott "for purportedly political reasons," the Bernalillo County Medical Society held a protest meeting to demonstrate its full support for Dr. Scott and its repugnance at the intrusion of politics in the sphere of public health. Dr. Scott held his job. Bernalillo County Medical Society, Minutes, 20 September 1933.

between delivery of babies via cesarean section, were central to that process, and indeed may be said to have inspired the start of a sanitary revolution, which eventually brought New Mexico into the twentieth century and contributed enormously to the well-being of its people.

Similarly, public-health nursing got a strong start in New Mexico during these decades and began to exert its beneficent influence on a wide variety of health conditions. When the Bureau of Public Health began operations in 1920, a grand total of four public-health nurses were at work in the state, mainly in the public school systems of the larger cities. Even within the tight money decade of the 1920s that figure expanded almost tenfold to thirty-five; and federal money, plus liberal grants from old institutional friends of the public-health movement, allowed still further expansion during the thirties. A 1930 donation from the Commonwealth Fund, for instance, made possible for the first time the assignment of public-health nurses to seventeen New Mexico counties too poor to afford such services. The significance of these nurses in extending medical care into remote communities around the state cannot be overstated. They provided a panoply of modern medical services to people who had never been exposed to them: an extensive range of health education programs; well-baby clinics; school inspection and inoculation work; maternity and infant-care clinics; and a host of other important services. Their courage and persistence in the face of sometimes daunting obstacles command for them a place of great respect in the history of health care in New Mexico.[28]

The third basic achievement of the early years of New Mexico's public-health system was the remarkable progress made in building a basic program of vital statistics. That task was essential in order to begin accurate identification and measurement and, hence, understanding of health conditions among the state's people. From extremely modest beginnings in the early 1920s—specifically, one registrar-bookkeeper-division manager and one clerk—the division of vital statistics grew into a critical component of the state's health complex. As early as 1929, New Mexico was admitted to the U.S. Census Bureau's official Birth and Death Registration Area listing, signifying the sophistication and efficiency of the state's information-gathering efforts in those basic areas. Again, outside

[28]For colorful and solid accounts of the work of those nurses in rural New Mexico in the 1930s, see Ruth Blackburn Huddleston, "New Mexico—'La Tierra de Mañana,'" *Public Health Nursing* 29 (1937):421–24; Helen James, "Nurse-of-the-Month," *Public Health Nursing* 26 (1934):616–17.

agencies were pivotal to the development of the service. Money, technical assistance, and personnel loaned to the state by the U.S. Children's Bureau, the American Public Health Association, the U.S. Census Bureau, and the Rockefeller Foundation undergirded the effort by state personnel to create modern statistical services. Alongside the registration of such vital events as births and deaths, the state's health department began to collect data in the 1920s on incidence of diseases (disease morbidity), causes of death, infant and maternal deaths, and much else, thereby establishing the essential informational framework for effective prevention and control strategies.

The information gathered by the primitive public-health apparatus of the 1920s afforded the first reliable insights into the state of New Mexico's health. The data collected emphasized the importance and impact of epidemic diseases in the state, but it also afforded the first hard information on the broad range of endemic health hazards. Table 8, although grossly inadequate by modern data-gathering standards, suggests the worrisomely broad range of health problems in New Mexico in the twenties. This elementary, but important, chore of collecting good data was a major step forward in helping to prepare the state's medical community for more effective warfare against New Mexico's health problems. Accurate data collection, for example, was the initial step in each of the two major public-health campaigns of the interwar period, one designed to arrest and then eradicate a spreading malaria menace in the state, and the other to reduce New Mexico's appallingly high infant-mortality rate. As the two major accomplishments of New Mexico's young public-health system, those two efforts deserve some special attention.

Doctors around the state in the first decades of this century grew increasingly conscious of the danger posed by malaria to the residents of New Mexico. There is a tendency to think of malaria as an exclusively tropical disease, but in fact the disease can exist anywhere that the mosquito vector carrying it can live. As a result, malaria in modern times has posed severe health problems in places so "unlikely" as Scandanavia and New York City. In post–World War I New Mexico, malaria was endemic in all the major river-valley complexes of the state and appeared to be spreading rapidly. It was generally a chronic, as opposed to acute, condition, sapping the vitality and weakening the constitutions of all its victims. Those whom it did not kill, it set up for other diseases. Although New Mexico doctors speculated that the disease was increasing in the state's populace, it took the energetic efforts of the public-health pioneers

Table 8
Disease Entities Reported to
State Health Authorities: 1923, 1924

	Number of Cases Reported	
Disease	1923	1924
Anthrax	0	1
Cancer	4	18
Chancroid	3	5
Chicken pox	414	577
Conjunctivitis	27	22
Diphtheria	1,161	510
Dysentery, amoebic	12	4
Encephalitis	3	2
German measles	5	4
Gonorrhea	257	307
Hookworm	2	2
Influenza	499	84
Malaria	15	13
Malta fever	1	0
Measles	1,056	4,267
Meningitis, cerebrospinal	2	9
Mumps	159	311
Parathyroid	0	9
Pellagra	4	5
Pneumonia	293	352
Poliomyelitis	2	6
Puerperal sepsis	4	8
Rabies in dogs	3	3
Scarlet fever	394	310
Septic sore throat	13	19
Smallpox	91	30
Syphilis	122	104
Tetanus	1	1
Trachoma	175	11 (whites)
Tuberculosis	763	1,094
Typhoid	359	487
Tularemia	0	4
Whooping cough	193	379
Vincent's angina	0	11

Source: New Mexico, Bureau of Public Health, Second Biennial Report, 1923–24, p. xix.

Note: This table should be viewed with caution. It suggests clearly the broad range of disease problems encountered in the state, but since it lists only cases *reported* to public-health authorities around the state, it at best hints at the real morbidity of the diseases listed.

of the 1920s to document the problem thoroughly. The initial statistics on the malaria question, gathered for the first time by public-health officials in the mid-1920s, gave precise dimensions to the problem and made it clear that the disease was a growing threat to New Mexico society, and not some kind of biological atavism that could be ignored and expected to go away. In fact, the data were sufficiently alarming that a formal declaration of a health emergency was made in 1927, at least so far as the Mesilla Valley was concerned, and the fight against the disease in that part of the state became a kind of test case for New Mexico as a whole. There was no money available to launch the campaign, but Governor Richard Dillon authorized the Bureau of Public Health to borrow money to get the campaign under way, and a malaria expert from the U.S. Public Health Service was sent to the state to help organize the program.[29] The borrowed funds served as seed-money to finance purchase of spraying equipment and chemical supplies, and the U.S. Public Health Service official, backed by his agency, represented the technical expertise essential for the work. Once again, outside money and experts provided the initial momentum behind public-health work in the state, but it was one of New Mexico's own, Dr. Charles W. Gerber of Las Cruces, who proved to be the driving force in the state's malaria eradication campaign.

Gerber was not a trained public-health professional at all, but rather a "country doctor" in the traditional sense of the term. He originally came to Las Cruces in 1901, possibly as a tubercular, and quickly established himself as one of the region's more successful private practitioners. A native New Yorker, he was familiar with the already well-developed public-health movement and public-health systems of the East, and quickly involved himself in trying to improve New Mexico's primitive public-health arrangements. He volunteered his services as a part-time county-health officer for Las Cruces during the period from 1907 to 1923, and through his unpaid work in that capacity and through his private practice, he became aware of the region's mounting malaria problem. When Doña Ana County created a full-time county-health office in 1923, Dr. Gerber

[29]For full details on the malaria problem in New Mexico and the campaign in the 1920s and 1930s to control it, see M. A. Barber, W. H. W. Komp, and C. H. King, "Malaria and the Malaria Danger in Certain Irrigated Regions of Southwestern United States," *Public Health Reports* 44 (1929):1300–1315; M. A. Barber and Louis R. Forbrich, "Malaria in the Irrigated Regions of New Mexico," *Public Health Reports* 48 (1933):610–23; C. W. Gerber (M.D.), "Summary of Malaria Control Work in Doña Ana County, New Mexico," *Southwestern Medicine* 15 (1931):370–75.

took the job of County Health Officer on a full-time basis and held that post until his retirement in 1947.

Gerber's first assignment as County Health Officer was to analyze and document the scope of the malaria problem in his county. Quickly convinced that the malady was on the verge of becoming a danger of the first magnitude to the public's health, he was intimately involved in the planning and initial implementation of the campaign to control the disease. Others planned the grand strategy, hustled the money, and organized the logistics and supplies of the effort; Gerber was the front-line soldier who actually did the fighting. In Doña Ana County he organized and coordinated a two-pronged attack on the disease, which involved treatment and extermination of the sickness in all those who suffered from it and those who carried it as well as the extermination of the mosquitoes that carried the disease from one victim to a new host. He organized and coordinated the work of all of the county's private physicians treating malaria patients, providing them with laboratory assistance, technical advice, and even quinine supplies for patients unable to afford the drug; and he personally treated a large number of patients unable to afford private care. That part of his program was important and involved large-scale logistical and paperwork problems, but it was his war on the mosquitoes that claimed the great bulk of his time and energies.

Gerber's basic approach to dealing with the burgeoning mosquito population of the Mesilla Valley and Doña Ana County, in general, was the already tested and effective procedure of spraying or dusting with chemical insecticides all possible breeding places of the insects and draining all low-lying land where water stood. His tactics were unexceptional, but his familiarity with the latest technology of mosquito warfare, probably gleaned through his U.S. Public Health Service advisors and his own personal study, was unusual. For example, Paris green, then still largely experimental, but a highly promising new insecticide, was regularly used by the crews under Dr. Gerber's supervision in dusting all of the region's mosquito breeding pools and ditches during breeding season. For eight months at a stretch, year in and year out, the doctor would personally pull on his wading boots and splash through the ditches and marshy areas of his county—catching and scientifically classifying mosquitoes, assisting the spraying crews, and evaluating the strengths and weaknesses of his project. The spraying program alone was gigantic in scope. According to the U.S. Public Health officer who helped Dr. Gerber to get started, it was one of the most extensive projects of its kind anywhere in the world.[30] His openness to innovation extended to some experiments now recognized as years ahead of their times. He was, for example, one of the Southwest's earliest bioengineers, for he enthusiastically supported one experiment which used the minnow *Gambusia affinis*, a notorious natural predator of mosquitoes and mosquito larvae, in an effort to control naturally the mosquitoes. Stocking the minnow "in every drain in lower Sierra and Doña Ana counties," Gerber watched with satisfaction as the then novel experiment contributed importantly to the reduction of mosquito numbers.[31] The trial with minnows ultimately proved successful enough to justify stocking drains and swamps all over New Mexico with the tiny predators. Marshy areas that could not be controlled by these methods became the object of massive drainage projects, and the small-town doctor was also successful in enlisting federal-government expertise and money in those efforts. Large federal grants and other forms of assistance were funneled into his district for his drainage programs—first through State Relief Administration Projects and, later, through the Work Projects Administration.[32]

The fruits of all this work were quickly evident. Within a very short time a steep decline in the mosquito population of the area was evident, and, more importantly, blood tests of Doña Ana County schoolchildren showed marked reductions in the number of children harboring the malarial parasite. Active cases of the disease declined steadily, and by the end of Gerber's tenure in the late 1940s, malaria was a negligible health problem for New Mexicans everywhere in the state. The morbidity of the disease had plummeted from the 447 *reported* cases of 1928 (and probably several thousand others unreported or subclinical) to only 13 in 1944, an obvious tribute to the efficacy of the work of the malaria fighters. There is probably little exaggeration in the judgment made in 1947 by Dr. James R. Scott, then state director of the Department of Public Health:

> The citizens of New Mexico should recognize the valiant and successful work carried on by Dr. Gerber, which has kept malaria from being a destructive menace to the areas of the Mesilla Valley, which were well on the way to becoming a

[30]Greenfield, *History of Public Health in New Mexico*, p. 33.
[31]New Mexico, Bureau of Public Health, Seventh Biennial Report, 1931–32, p. 24.
[32]Greenfield, *History of Public Health in New Mexico*, p. 33.

malaria ridden and scourged area when this quiet, scientific district health officer began his campaign in behalf of the farmers and residents of the Mesilla Valley.[33]

In 1949, the year of Dr. Gerber's death, there was a total of one malaria case reported in the state.[34]

The success of the campaign against malaria was a noteworthy achievement for New Mexico's young public-health corps, especially considering the agency's chronic staff and budget limitations. Much more difficult, because more complex, was the work begun in the 1920s to try to reduce the state's tragically high infant and maternal death rates. This effort to reduce the attrition of the state's babies and mothers is the single endeavor of the state's public-health authorities that is most often noted, and the campaign earned them the confidence and trust of the New Mexico populace as no other program has, before that time or since. In the absence of hard data, we can only speculate about the dimensions of the problem in territorial days. Given the frontier nature of New Mexico society and the feebleness of medical science, infant and maternal death rates must have been very high. The scanty information available from church registries, family letters and accounts, gravestones, and, here and there, physician and hospital records all suggest as much. The first even semireliable figures attempting to quantify the dimensions of these problems were calculated in 1929. In that year, state health department statistics indicated that the infant mortality rate for New Mexico—that is, the number of live babies who died before their first birthday—was an enormous 140 deaths per 1,000 live births.[35] For purposes of comparison, the average of the forty-eight states in that year was 68 deaths per 1,000, a figure more than doubled in New Mexico. (For additional perspective, the infant death rate for New Mexico in 1980 was around 14 per 1,000, which was ten times smaller than the 1929 figure.) This horror, called "the slaughter of the innocents" by the state's Director of Public Health in 1932,[36] became

[33]Scott, "Twenty-five Years of Public Health in New Mexico":54. Dr. Gerber's work was recognized and respected by his colleagues within the New Mexico medical community, for in 1935 he was elected president of the New Mexico Medical Society.

[34]New Mexico, State Department of Public Health, *Annual Report, 1949*, p. 17.

[35]This figure, incidentally, did *not* include the deaths of infants among New Mexico's Indian peoples. Those figures were not incorporated in the state statistics until 1943, and when they were, they made virtually no change in the statewide figures. See New Mexico, Department of Public Health, Annual Report, 1943, p. 80.

[36]New Mexico, Bureau of Public Health, Seventh Biennial Report, 1931–32, p. 6.

a major target of New Mexico's public-health professionals and private physicians in the four decades beginning with the twenties.[37]

From what did New Mexico's babies die? Before the problem could be scientifically attacked, that fundamental question had to be answered. There was no years-long, careful, and scholarly investigation of this question; the problem was far too urgent for that. Instead, there was quick and almost universal agreement on a complex of factors producing the carnage. Chief among them was the conviction, widely shared by both private practitioners and the public-health professionals, that inadequate medical attention at birth and in the critical first year of life was the major cause of infant deaths in New Mexico. Although physicians were reasonably well scattered across the state, including most of its rural areas where the loss of infants was especially high, there remained vast stretches of the state where access to a trained physician was very difficult, if not impossible. Distance alone was often a factor, given the dispersal of the state's populace across its more than 120,000 square miles of territory. And it ought be remembered that distance was a much more serious problem then than now, given the relative absence of modern, paved roads and swift, reliable means of all-weather travel. New Mexico was simply bigger in the 1920s and 1930s than today. Economic factors, too, very often limited access to regularly trained doctors. Although it is clear that extensive pro bono work, in some years up to 50 percent of a physician's total practice, was a fundamental part of New Mexico's medical tradition,[38] many would-be patients were reluctant to appeal to the physicians' sense of compassion and duty. Also, it would be less than

[37]There is no convenient summary of this important chapter in New Mexico's medical history. This quick summary is put together from official Bureau of Public Health reports of the 1920s and 1930s, miscellaneous articles bearing directly or indirectly on the topic, and an interview with Dr. Stuart W. Adler, director of the health department's Maternal and Child Health Division from 1941 to 1944. The interview, held in Albuquerque on 21 September 1982, was the very first in the New Mexico Oral History Project.

[38]Dr. Ashley Pond III, interview with the author, Taos, N.M., 5 September 1983; Dr. I. J. Marshall, interview with the author, Roswell, N.M., 15 August 1983; Dr. E. W. "Bud" Lander, interview with the author, Roswell, N.M., 19 August 1983; and Dr. Carl Gellenthien, interview with the author, Valmora, N.M., 18 December 1984. The account books of Dr. George W. Sammons of Farmington, New Mexico, held in the Farmington Historical Museum, show that in the year 1932 Dr. Sammons saw a total of 2,580 patients, billed a grand total of 4,895 dollars, and collected just 2,199 dollars, or 45 percent of the fees owed to him.

realistic to assume that the average physician's store of those qualities had no limits.

Additionally, cultural differences affected access or discouraged the effort to look to regular physicians for help. Especially among many of northern New Mexico's Spanish-American people, there was relatively little interest or confidence in "Anglo" medicine, particularly when a baby was about to be born. An anthropological study done in 1948, in the Ranchos de Taos community, emphasized the cultural traditions that discouraged resorting to regular M.D.s, particularly during childbirth:

> To the local mind pregnancy, labor, and childbirth are looked upon as natural functions of the body. The whole process of giving birth to a child is considered something decidedly different from physical pathology—as indeed it is—and it is put in a category by itself: motherhood. There is little or no notion of the necessity of medical supervision during the whole birth cycle, including the pre-natal period.[39]

It might also be noted that there was an especially strong reluctance among Spanish men, particularly in the traditional northern communities, to allow their women to be treated by male physicians.[40]

As a result of these factors and others, many New Mexico babies of the twenties and thirties were born without a doctor in attendance. Figures from the year 1925 testify to the dimensions of this reality: Of the 10,367 babies whose births in that year *were registered* by state officials, 40 percent (4,014) were delivered without the assistance of a doctor. Midwives (whose importance in this medical service will be discussed presently) delivered 2,207 babies, or 22 percent of the total; and 1,807 infants, 18 percent of the registered total, were delivered with only a relative, friend, or whomever in attendance.[41] The absence of trained

[39]Cited in Sister M. Michael Waters, "Culture in Relation to a Maternity Service," *Public Health Nursing* 42 (1950):69.

[40]Dr. Edith Millican, interview with the author, Albuquerque, N.M., 30 August 1983.

[41]New Mexico, Bureau of Public Health, Fourth Biennial Report, 1925–26, p. 32. These figures scarcely changed at all throughout the interwar years. In 1933 physicians delivered only 58 percent of all newborn babies registered with state authorities, while midwives and registered nurses delivered 29 percent and "others" 13 percent. (New Mexico, Bureau of Public Health, Eighth Biennial Report, 1933–34, pp. 16–17.) It might also be noted in passing that about one-third of the deaths in New Mexico during this period occurred without medical attendance and, thus, without any medical certification of the cause of death, which made death rates for the state listed by cause of death virtually meaningless. (New Mexico, Bureau of Public Health, Seventh Biennial Report, 1931–32, p. 4.)

physicians in such a large percentage of births undoubtedly contributed to the high infant mortality rate.

Closely related to this factor, of course, was the absence of adequate prenatal care for expectant mothers, a fact which also helped in boosting infant (and maternal) mortality rates. The same factors that restricted medical attendance at birth acted in intensified fashion to limit the number of expectant mothers who got reasonable prenatal care. If a mother-to-be could not get to a doctor for the delivery of her child for reasons of distance, cost, or whatever, she certainly would not visit one during the perfectly normal and natural period of expectancy leading up to it. Furthermore, many New Mexico physicians of the old school shared the widespread conviction that prenatal supervision was not necessary to the good health of both mother and baby, and they did not insist on it or even, in some cases, recommend it.[42]

Though many newborn babies in New Mexico died either at birth or during their first year of life as a result of conditions that trained physicians might have been able to handle, many others died as a result of disease entities or birth injuries that were beyond the competency of the era's doctors. Table 9, reproduced from health department statistics for the year 1928, shows the cause of death for 1,501 tiny New Mexicans whose deaths were reported to state officials. Table 9 provides important insights into the world of medicine in the late 1920s, with several things particularly noteworthy. First of all, no particular cause of death was available for 648 infant deaths in the report year, a whopping 43 percent of the total. So high a percentage often was a function of the limits of medical knowledge in 1928, but much more commonly it was a matter (as stressed above) of the lack of medical attention to the dying. Second, the modern-day reader may be struck by the relatively large number of deaths attributable to diseases no longer of consequence in our society—malaria, scarlet fever, diphtheria, rickets, and others—or those normally responsive to modern medical treatment—whooping cough, erysipelas, syphilis, intestinal obstructions, and the like. The progress in medical science and in therapeutics particularly, over the nearly six decades since the list was compiled, is obvious to contemporary readers. Third, the large number of deaths associated with prematurity, congenital problems of various sorts, or birth injuries is particularly evident, amounting to

[42]Lander, interview, Roswell, 19 August 1983.

Table 9
Infant Mortality, 1928

Cause of Death	Number	Cause of Death	Number
Malaria	1	Bronchitis	2
Measles	17	Broncho-pneumonia	94
Scarlet fever	1	Capillary bronchitis	1
Whooping cough	34	Lobar pneumonia	14
Diphtheria	3	Pneumonia (unspecified)	21
Influenza, pulmonary	8	Pulmonary congestion	2
Influenza (unspecified)	12	Other diseases of the respiratory system	1
Cholera nostras	1	Diseases of the pharynx and tonsils	1
Dysentery bacillary	2	Other diseases of the stomach	13
Dysentery (unspecified)	3	Diarrhea and enteritis	222
Erysipelas	2	Hernia	1
Anterior poliomyelitis	2	Intestinal obstruction	6
Chicken-pox	1	Acute nephritis	3
Mycoses	1	Congenital hydrocephalus	2
Tuberculosis: respiratory	1	Congenital cardiac malformation	22
Tuberculosis: C.N.S.	2	Congenital debility	78
Tuberculosis: intestinal	1	Congenital malformation	11
Syphilis	10	Premature birth	170
Rickets	1	Birth injury	31
Parathyroid disease	2	Diseases of early infancy	25
Thymus disease	4	Food poisoning	1
Other general diseases	2	Conflagration	1
Other general diseases	1	Accidental burns	2
Meningitis-simple	3	Accidental suffocation	3
Infantile convulsions	1	Accidental fall	1
Diseases of the ear	1	Auto accident	1
Diseases of the heart	1	Excessive heat	1
Disease of the nasal fossae	1	Ill-defined	2
Diseases of the larynx	1	Not specified or unknown	648
Diseases of the larynx (sic)	1		

Source: New Mexico, Bureau of Public Health, *Sixth Biennial Report, 1929–30,* p. 34.

314 deaths, or 21 percent of the total, a figure that has changed little over sixty years, at least in terms of the percentage of infant deaths.

But probably most striking of all from our perspective is the tragically high number of infants who died from gastrointestinal conditions. Diarrhea and enteritis alone claimed 222 New Mexico infants in 1928 (that we know about) before their first birthday, and probably a large fraction of the "not specified or unknown" as well. That figure, 15 percent of the total, constitutes the major difference between the 1920s and 1980s. A frighteningly large number of babies, most of them fundamentally healthy and strong, wasted away in horrible fashion as a result of gastrointestinal problems that could not be handled by the medicine of the day. The essence of the problem was the socioeconomic backwardness of so much of New Mexico, particularly the ignorance of the elementary precepts of modern sanitation among many of its people. Well into the 1930s and 1940s, for example, many New Mexico babies contracted fatal gastrointestinal disorders from the contaminated well water or irrigation-ditch water used as the basic water supply by their families. This cause of diarrheal or enteritic disease began to diminish only with the expansion of modern health education and sanitation improvements during the New Deal era and after. Sometimes, the fatal diseases were associated with nutritional problems or inadequacies within customary diets. On occasion, cultural traditions and perceptions played a part in adding to the death toll. At a public-health clinic in northern New Mexico, a nurse was told by a young woman whose baby was suffering from diarrhea, "We believe that you're supposed to leave the baby alone for three days, and often by that time, it cures itself."[43]

Much more important, however, than all the factors mentioned above was the spread of gastrointestinal diseases by houseflies. Into the 1930s and 1940s, common houseflies visited the poorly constructed privies of so many New Mexicans, then swept through the unscreened windows of others, spreading disease and death in their wake. Year in and year out, New Mexicans of all ages suffered from the "summer complaint" mentioned earlier here. By the early 1930s its incidence had been scientifically charted and its correlation with fly season well established, as the following chart shows.[44] Most New Mexicans survived their bouts with "summer complaint" with only moderate discomfort and unpleasantness,

[43]Waters, "Culture in Relation to a Maternity Service":71.

[44]New Mexico, Bureau of Public Health, Seventh Biennial Report, 1931–32, p. 8.

Chart 1
Deaths from Diarrhea and Enteritis (Under 2 Years)
During the Three Years—1929, 1930, 1931 by Months

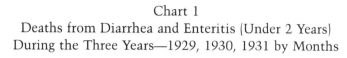

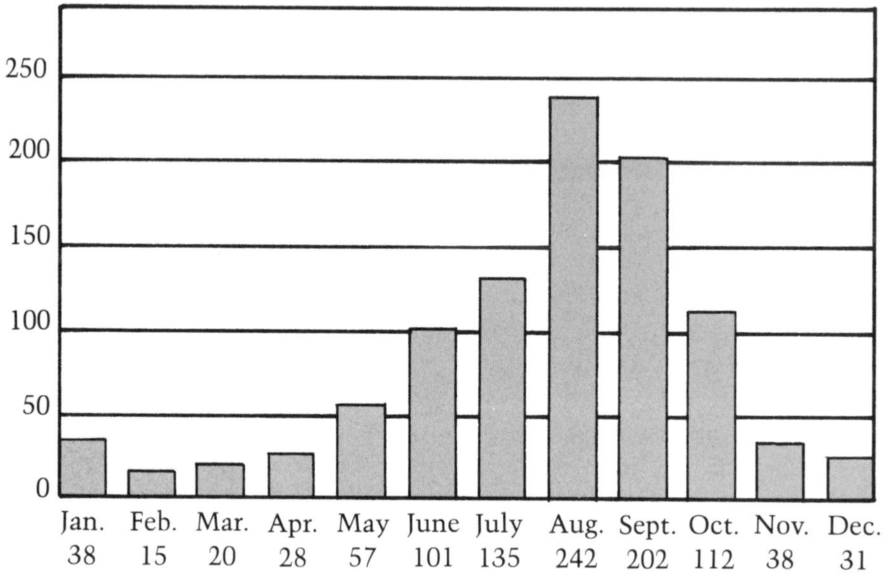

but for babies the ailment was all too often fatal. Even those babies who had the advantage of attention by physicians fared little better than those who had not, for modern medicines and support therapies were unavailable to the doctors of that era. One of them remembered:

In those days we did recognize the importance of giving IVs to some of our adult patients, but IV treatment wasn't common, and you didn't even *try* to give it to a baby. About all we could do was inject fluid under their skin and try to rehydrate them that way. We didn't know about electrolyte balance nor administering sodium or potassium, so a lot of them just died.[45]

Prevention, not treatment, was the basic key and the long-term solution to this grave problem, but successful preventive measures did not come easily or quickly. It eventually took a massive health-education campaign extending over three decades, and, just as importantly, the extension of modern sanitation facilities around the state, before the problem became

[45]Dr. Virginia Milner, interview with the author, Albuquerque, N.M., 18 October 1983.

essentially an unhappy memory. The installation of screened windows and doors, of flyproof privies, and of water and sewer pipes and systems were the prosaic means to that solution. The public-health doctors and other health professionals of New Mexico's Department of Health were strong advocates and educators pushing the necessity for sanitary reform as the key to alleviating the infant death problem, but that work was understood as a more or less long-term solution. Immediately, the health professionals set out to make high-quality obstetrical and pediatric care available to all New Mexicans, wherever they might live and whatever their economic circumstances. As indicated above, this was a major problem in New Mexico between the wars, and the state's developing public-health network sought to fill in some of the gaps. The strategy for broadening the range of modern maternity and child health services included three different lines of attack: (1) energetic expansion of public health nursing services, particularly into those areas where regular physicians were few in number; (2) the establishment of traveling clinics, in which public-health doctors and volunteer private physicians would hold maternal and child health clinics in areas desperately needing such services; and (3) the improvement of standards for the performance of midwives, who were so basic a part of the state's health-care-delivery system.

In 1920, when New Mexico's public-health work began, there was a grand total of four public-health nurses working in the entire state, with only one of them serving in rural areas, where the need for modern health care was so acute. Since nurses were significantly cheaper to hire than doctors, and since a public-health nursing specialty was already well developed within the profession, the infant Bureau of Public Health emphasized construction of a strong public-health nursing system as a major priority; public-health nurses were to be the cutting edge of its service to the state. Even so, expansion was slow, given the limited resources available to the effort. The four public-health nurses of 1920 grew to fourteen by the end of 1922, to thirty-five in 1930, and to fifty-eight in 1936.

Once again, private institutions and federal funding were central to the building of a public-health nursing system and assisted in shaping the structure and focus of its maternal and child health programs. The Sheppard-Towner Act of 1921 provided immediate federal assistance to help New Mexico get its public-health nursing system started, and it was directly involved in funding the state's maternal and child care work. Funds from this source were used to supplement meager county resources in hiring county-health nurses, and as early as 1922 this federal program made possible the employment of two field nurses, working directly under Santa Fe's control, whose exclusive assignment was maternal and child health care nursing. These Sheppard-Towner nurses were active throughout the 1920s and established the fundamental patterns of public-health work in those service areas. They visited and worked in individual counties for three months at a stretch, visiting in the homes of mothers with young infants, instructing local midwives, and giving basic physical examinations to young children. Their work involved the initial, "hands-on" thrust of public-health efforts to begin reduction of the infant and maternal death rates. One of the first public health reports emphasized the special nature of their work and its unique rewards:

> The most appealing phase of health work is maternal, infant, and school hygiene, for it is here that we come into most intimate contact with the home and have the greatest opportunity to influence the future generations of citizens. . . . There is little understanding of proper diets for infants and still less of preventive measures against communicable diseases. . . . Aside from the control of milk supplies in the towns and the eradication of flies, the reduction of infant mortality is largely a matter of education. To reach the mother who most needs this information, it is necessary to take the education to her, as she cannot come to the larger centers to get it. Here is where the public health nurse finds her greatest field.[46]

Individual counseling and other direct and individual services were the first priority of the Sheppard-Towner nurses, but general education efforts ran a close second. Their classes, presenting elementary principles of personal hygiene and preventive medicine, spanned all segments of New Mexico society and included Little Mothers Leagues for girls and Junior Health Leagues for boys of junior high school age, both sponsored by the health department. (As a matter of fact, junior high school children were special targets of the nurses' educational work because so many of them helped in caring for younger siblings at home and/or would have babies of their own in relatively short order. Also, since so many New Mexico young people ended their schooling at that level, it was a kind of last chance to reach them conveniently and in numbers.)[47]

Public-health nurses were the workhorses in the initial phases of the

[46]New Mexico, Bureau of Public Health, First Biennial Report, cited in Scott, "Twenty-five Years of Public Health in New Mexico":6.

[47]Dorothy A. Anderson, "Why New Mexico Nurses Cooperate in Maternity and Infancy Work," *American Journal of Public Health* 16 (1926):473–75.

campaign to reduce New Mexico's high infant and maternal mortality rates, but traveling clinics and demonstration programs also played an important part in the effort. County-health officers or personnel from the Santa Fe office planned and staffed such operations, but volunteer physicians from the private-practice community donated their time and services as well. These clinics would usually be held in remote communities, which were not often reached by private practitioners, and they customarily involved such things as prenatal examination of expectant mothers, counseling in infant nutrition, and well-baby care. However, these traveling clinics, designed for infant and maternity care services, usually expanded to include the whole range of modern medical services, since the needs were there and the nurses and doctors most often were not. A typical day at one of these clinics might include the infant and maternal work mentioned, but also a half-dozen or so tonsillectomies and adenoidectomies, the pulling of a few teeth, refraction of eyes and dispensing of glasses, the resetting of a fractured arm not growing correctly, and much else.[48] Such clinics were undoubtedly helpful in saving New Mexico babies and mothers, but certainly the most important dimension of the public-health campaign against infant and maternal deaths was the effort made to improve the caliber of service rendered by the state's large midwife community.

Long before modern medicine and scientifically trained practitioners became a factor in New Mexico health care, traditionally trained midwives, particularly in the numerous Spanish communities of the state, had claimed for themselves a central place in the region's medical culture. *Parteras* remained of basic importance across much of the state during the first half of the twentieth century, and, indeed, they have not been entirely displaced in some areas of the state to this day. Their prominence in the state's health-care delivery system is not hard to understand, given that complex of factors mentioned earlier—distance, economics, and cultural differences—which so distinctly colored the interaction between patients and doctors in New Mexico. The result was the statistics cited earlier in this chapter: In 1925 midwives delivered 22 percent of all *reported* babies and in 1929 around 29 percent, figures which undoubtedly underestimate their activity significantly. In particular parts of the state they totally dominated the obstetrics business. For example, in the largely Spanish and

[48]Ibid.:474.

rural county of Río Arriba, 48 percent of the live babies born to Spanish-speaking women were delivered by midwives and another 23 percent by neither physician nor midwife but presumably by relatives or friends. For Taos County, another heavily rural and predominantly Spanish region, the comparable figures for 1934 were 71 percent and 9 percent, respectively.

The range of skills and information among the midwives working in the state, and hence the caliber of their service, unfortunately varied across a broad spectrum. Many of them were solidly seasoned by years of practice and a great store of experience, but many others were not. Almost none of them had any formal education or training in the birthing experience, and there existed no formal supervision over them and their work. The consequences were predictable: Those areas with the largest number of babies delivered by midwives were the same areas with the highest infant and maternal death rates. Midwife practice was certainly not the sole explanation for the higher rates of those areas, but it was a factor in them. Too many of the traditional midwives were inattentive to the basics of prenatal care and the importance of cleanliness, and too few of them were competent to handle abnormal births and emergency situations. All of the traditional midwives should not be indicted with one, undifferentiating brush, for many of them performed a valuable service to their communities; but it was clear that any programmatic attack on New Mexico's high infant and maternal death rates would have to include the reality of midwife practice within its compass.

To their credit, New Mexico's health department officials, from the very inception of their work, recognized the realities of the situation and made the pragmatic decision to work *with* and not against the state's midwives, accepting them as indispensable partners in the regions' medical culture. That decision required considerable professional and political courage, for not all of the state's physicians were happy with a commitment of that sort. Influential members of the medical community, like Albuquerque physicians Meldrum K. Wylder and Ralph Mendelson among others, regretted any toleration of midwifery, complaining that no educational or remedial programs supervised by state authorities could ever raise the midwives as a group to acceptable standards.[49] Despite such criticism, health department officials stuck to their convictions, and from

[49]For Mendelson's views, see J. W. Amesse (M.D.), "Sources of Infant Mortality in the Western States," *Southwestern Medicine* 15 (1931):514. Dr. Wylder's skepticism is clear in his "Inferior Midwifery: A Case Report," *Southwestern Medicine* 20 (1936):178–79.

the 1920s through the 1950s programs designed to improve and regulate midwife practice were a major component of health department efforts to bring down the state's death rates for babies and new mothers.

The work began in 1922 with instructional programs started by a midwife consultant loaned the state by the U.S. Children's Bureau. (Her salary and the costs of her work, incidentally, were borne by the federal government.)[50] That solitary professional devised the basic procedures and programs for working with the state's midwives, a regimen which remained in place into the 1940s. Since the health department's initial estimates suggested that there were around eight hundred midwives practicing around the state, a figure consistently accepted all the way up to World War II,[51] the work of the midwife instructor began with a kind of pilot program focused on the five northern counties (San Miguel, Mora, Taos, Río Arriba, and Santa Fe) where midwifery was most common. Over the first decade or so of the program, the midwife specialist (several different federally employed registered nurses held the position) traipsed all across the five-county-core area, visiting in the homes of midwives to give personal instruction and consultation and also holding formal classes for small groups of them. (In the twelve months between 1 February 1925 and 1 February 1926, for example, Mrs. Agnes B. Courtney, a registered nurse on loan from the U.S. Children's Bureau, reported that she had located 198 midwives not previously identified, had made 367 visits to homes of midwives, and had held 301 formal classes for groups of midwives ranging in size from two or three up to a dozen.)[52] The pupils—who seem to have responded to the instruction, at worst, with resignation or, at best, with some degree of enthusiasm and gratitude—were taught standard obstetrical techniques, procedures for dealing with the most common complications encountered in the delivery of babies, and the fundamentals of care for the newborn, with emphasis always placed on the importance of cleanliness and on calling the doctor at the first sign of real difficulty.[53]

[50]New Mexico, Bureau of Public Health, Second Biennial Report, 1923–24, p. iv.

[51]New Mexico, Bureau of Public Health, Tenth Biennial Report, 1939–40, p. 19; Christine A. Heller, "Education in Nutrition as Part of the Maternal Health Program," *American Journal of Public Health* 32 (1942):1022.

[52]New Mexico, Bureau of Public Health, Third Biennial Report, 1925–26, pp. 18–20.

[53]Louise Wills, "Instruction of Midwives in San Miguel County," *Southwestern Medicine* 6 (1922):276–79; Margaret Tupper, "Maternal and Infant Hygiene in New Mexico," *Public Health Nurse* 14 (1922):191–94.

The instructional program, begun in northern New Mexico where the need was greatest, spread around the state by the end of the 1920s. The increasingly numerous public-health nurses of the state bore the brunt of the work, supervising midwife performance, consulting on the personal level, and holding formal classes using materials and a curriculum supplied by the central office in Santa Fe. In the early 1940s, certificates were issued to those who successfully completed the department's midwifery courses, and basic supplies were provided midwives on the department's "approved" list.[54] Also, in that period, a "midwife institute" was established in Las Vegas, a program which involved pulling together twenty to twenty-five midwives from the five surrounding counties two or three times during the year for "refresher courses" and what might be called advanced study.[55]

Slowly, but surely, the hard work of the health department personnel and the numerous private physicians around the state working with them began to pay dividends. By 1940 the 140-plus infant deaths per 1,000 live births of the 1920s had already fallen to 99.9, an encouraging sign of improvement even though the death rate was still twice the national average.[56] With the systematic extension of public-health programs throughout the state in the 1940s and 1950s and, equally important, the penetration of virtually the entire state by regular physicians traveling on decent roads and wielding new weapons like the sulfa drugs and penicillin, the infant and maternal death rate curves continued their happy plunge downward.[57] (See Figure 1 and Figure 2.) By 1979, when the national average stood at 13.0 infant deaths per 1,000 live births, the New Mexico figure was 14.2, actually a slight increase from the preceding year's figure.[58] That number was almost exactly *one-tenth* of the initial figures calculated in 1929.

The apostles of flyproof privies, pure-water supplies, and well-baby clinics first entered the world of New Mexico health care in the 1920s and 1930s, and very quickly they proved their usefulness to the state's society.

[54]Dr. Stuart Adler, interview with the author, Albuquerque, N.M., 21 September 1982.

[55]New Mexico, Department of Public Health, Annual Report, 1941, pp. 19–22.

[56]Scott, "Twenty-five Years of Public Health in New Mexico":63.

[57]New Mexico, Health and Environment Department, *New Mexico: Fifty Years as a Vital Statistics Registration State,* pp. 48, 53. It was the work of Dr. Marion Hotopp, mentioned in the preceding chapter, which was most instrumental in pushing through to completion this infant and maternity work begun in the twenties and thirties.

[58]Ibid., p. 48.

Figure 1
Infant Mortality Rate,
New Mexico Residents and United States, 1940–79

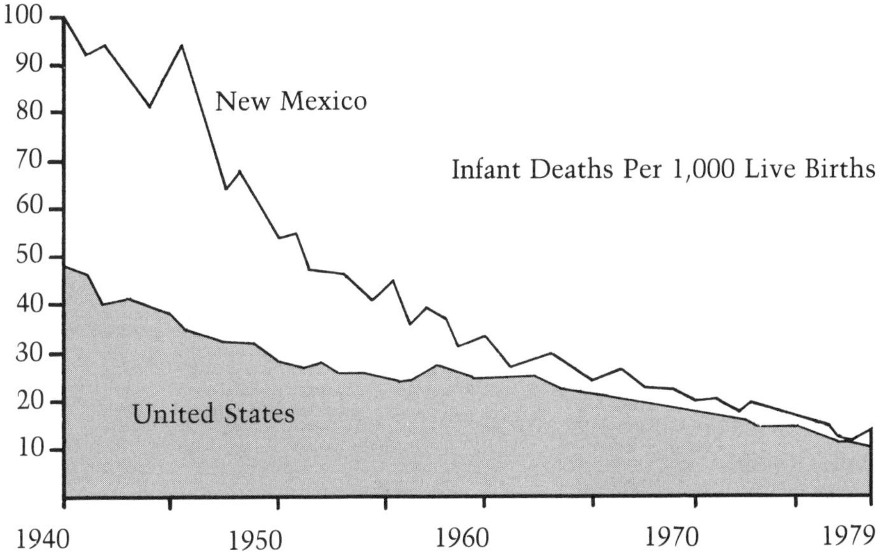

Figure 2
Maternal Mortality Rate,
New Mexico Residents and United States, 1940–79

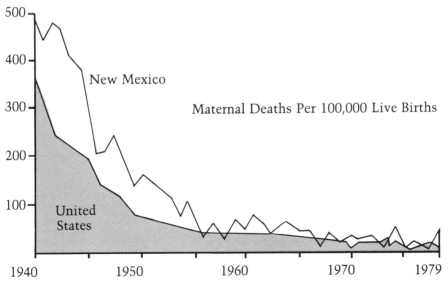

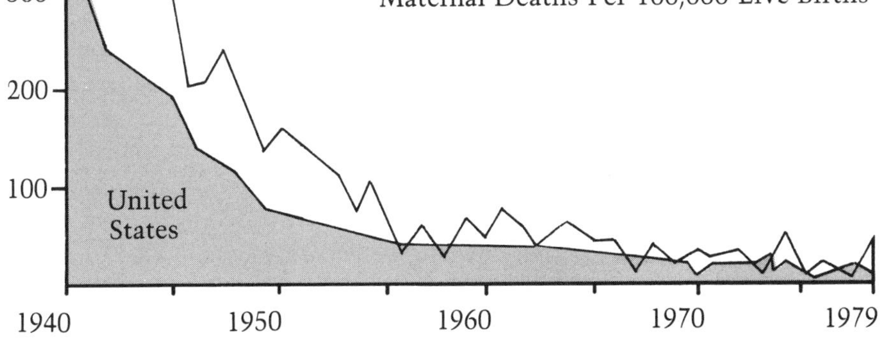

Within two decades, they were able to number among their accomplishments the banishment of the malaria threat to the state's peoples, the initiation of a broad-front campaign to bring in check "the slaughter of the innocents" around the state, and a number of less spectacular achievements. It was a remarkable start, given the limitations under which the health professionals worked, and strong foundations were laid for their successors of later decades.

This broad discussion of some of the significant developments in the world of New Mexico medicine between 1912 and 1941 would not be complete without at least brief reference to several major changes within the state's physician population during the same period. Important quantitative and, less clearly, qualitative changes took place. Most startling, superficially, was a major change in the supply of physicians in the state. Table 10 shows significant fluctuations in the numbers of M.D.s located in the state between 1912 and 1941 as well as in the physician-to-population ratio. Between 1912 and 1921, the number of doctors in the state continued the rise begun in the last years of the nineteenth century, and basically for the same reasons. "Lunger" physicians still found the state attractive, as did a number of doctors who were enticed by what they perceived to be the more promising opportunities of practice in a brand-new state. Still larger numbers of doctors came (as discussed in Chapter 2) because their weak credentials no longer guaranteed them the right to practice in other states, whereas the door remained open in New Mexico. The physician immigration proceeded at a pace faster than that of the general population, and the result was New Mexico's lowest ever physician-to-population ratio (until the 1970s); roughly, a one-to-seven hundred ratio was reached in the very early 1920s.

In the 1920s and 1930s, however, New Mexico's physician supply experienced sharp contraction. To a considerable degree, the reduction was part of a nationwide trend, for the great reform movement within American medical education at the turn of the century had resulted in fewer, but better-quality, medical schools that produced significantly smaller numbers of new doctors. Thus, in the twenties and thirties there were simply fewer new physicians entering the marketplace, while an older generation was dying out. In New Mexico, the number of new licensees fell still further as a result of a decline in the number of doctors coming to the state for health reasons. Of course, some "lunger" physicians continued to come—these decades saw the arrival in New Mexico of Drs.

Table 10
Physician Supply in New Mexico, 1912–41

Year	No. of M.D.s	State Population	Ratio M.D.s to Population
1886	99	131,895	1:1,332
1897	117	181,000	1:1,547
1902	166	206,000	1:1,241
1906	221	257,000	1:1,163
1909	367	308,000	1: 839
1912	429	350,000*	1: 816
1914	449	340,500	1: 761
1916	430	347,100	1: 807
1918	456	353,700	1: 776
1921	529	366,600	1: 693
1923	399 **	379,800	1: 952
1925	365	393,000	1:1,077
1927	357	406,200	1:1,138
1931	374	434,000	1:1,160
1934	393	467,000	1:1,188
1936	401	489,000	1:1,219
1938	419	511,000	1:1,220
1942	447 ***	531,818 (1940 census)	

Sources: *Polk's Medical and Surgical Directory*, 1886; *Flint's Medical and Surgical Directory*, 1897; *American Medical Directory*, all other years.

*This figure, proudly touted by New Mexico boosters at the time of statehood, is almost certainly too high. The true figure was probably closer to 335,000.

**The very large gap between the 1921 and 1923 figures almost surely exaggerates the physician loss of that two-year period, probably because of some change in statistics-gathering.

***This figure includes a large number of doctors who were residents of the state, but who were actually in military service in 1942.

Albert Lathrop, Harold "Monty" Mortimer, Carl Gellenthien, William E. Badger, Walter Werner, William Woolston, and (in 1942) Robert Derbyshire, among other prominent members of the state's medical profession—but fewer of them arrived than during the period from 1890 to 1920. New Mexico's reduction in the number of its doctors was also intensified by the passage of the new medical practice act in 1923, which made it much harder for poorly trained physicians to win licensure in the state.

After 1923, then, there was a large reduction in the number of doctors seeking license to practice in New Mexico. In the heyday of the medical exodus to New Mexico, during the period from 1906 to 1912, an average of ninety-nine new doctors per year had been licensed in the territory. There was a drop thereafter, but a still hefty number of forty-eight new licenses per year were issued during the period from 1913 to 1923. In the first ten years following the new medical-licensure reform of 1923, that number fell to twenty-three per year, one-quarter the average of two decades earlier, and it rose to higher than thirty-eight between 1934 and 1941. While fewer physicians were beginning practice in New Mexico in the 1920s and 1930s, the older generation of doctors already at work in the state was wasting away. Some of that decline was due to natural attrition, a factor especially pronounced in New Mexico since so many of the doctors who had arrived between 1890 and 1920 had been older men and/or ill. Some of the attrition was also produced by the departure from New Mexico of physicians for whom New Mexico had not worked out, for one reason or another, as the land of their dreams. Many simply retired or moved on to warmer and sunnier climes. Of the grand total of 529 physicians listed in New Mexico in the 1921 *American Medical Directory*, a full 281, or 53 percent, were no longer practicing in the state in 1927, just six years later.

The reduction, in and of itself, worked no real hardship on the New Mexico populace, for the ratio of one doctor for every twelve hundred people during the late 1930s was within an acceptable range, and indeed it was probably more satisfactory in many respects than the ratio of one doctor to roughly seven hundred people that marked the start of the 1920s. But the statewide figure masks some important regional disparities. Grouping the state's thirty-one counties into ten regional units provides a more accurate picture of the distribution of physicians within the state (based on 1940 statistics):

Bernalillo County	1:723
Santa Fe County	1:881

Doña Ana-Luna-Grant-Hidalgo	1:1,143
Chaves-Lea-Eddy	1:1,197
State Average	**1:1,234**
Quay-Curry-Roosevelt	1:1,281
Sierra-Catron-Socorro-Valencia	1:1,360
Torrance-Guadalupe-De Baca-Lincoln-Otero	1:1,465
Colfax-Union-Harding-Mora-San Miguel	1:1,512
San Juan-McKinley-Sandoval	1:1,763
Río Arriba-Taos	1:3,134

Just as in the territorial or pioneer period, there was a shortage of physicians in New Mexico's northern counties, when considered both in relation to the rest of the state and objectively. (See Map 5 and Map 6 for the distribution of physicians in 1940 by county and for physician-to-population ratios.) It was a particularly acute problem, for these were the state's poorest counties and those most in need of modern health care. This was, of course, the basic reason for the focus of so much of the new health department's work in northern New Mexico.

In addition to this regional maldistribution, there was an increasing tendency for physicians to desert the countryside and set up practices in the state's cities, as Table 11 shows. To a large degree the doctors were simply following the people to the cities, for New Mexico was becoming a more urban society during this period; yet the concentration of doctors in the cities and towns had taken place earlier and more intensely among the physicians than in the general populace. This growing abandonment of the countryside was an additional reason, of course, for the increasing importance of public-health professionals, especially the public-health nurses and county-health officers and their traveling clinics. The problem was also mitigated significantly by the willingness of doctors in the twenties and thirties, like their pioneer predecessors, to ride out into the countryside to reach the people who needed them. An "urban doctor," like Dr. Carroll Womack, living and practicing in Artesia in the 1930s, would drive the seventy miles west to Elk, New Mexico, to see a sick patient.[59] Dr. E. W. "Bud" Lander of Roswell poignantly remembers a

[59]Dr. Carroll L. Womack, interview with the author, Carlsbad, N.M., 12 March 1985. Almost all the doctors interviewed who first came to New Mexico in the 1920s and 1930s remember driving out into the countryside to see patients. See, especially, the interviews with Dr. Harold "Monty" Mortimer, Albuquerque, N.M., 21 September 1983, and Dr. Walter Stark, Las Vegas, N.M., 7 September 1983.

Map 5 NUMBER OF MEDICAL DOCTORS BY COUNTY, 1940

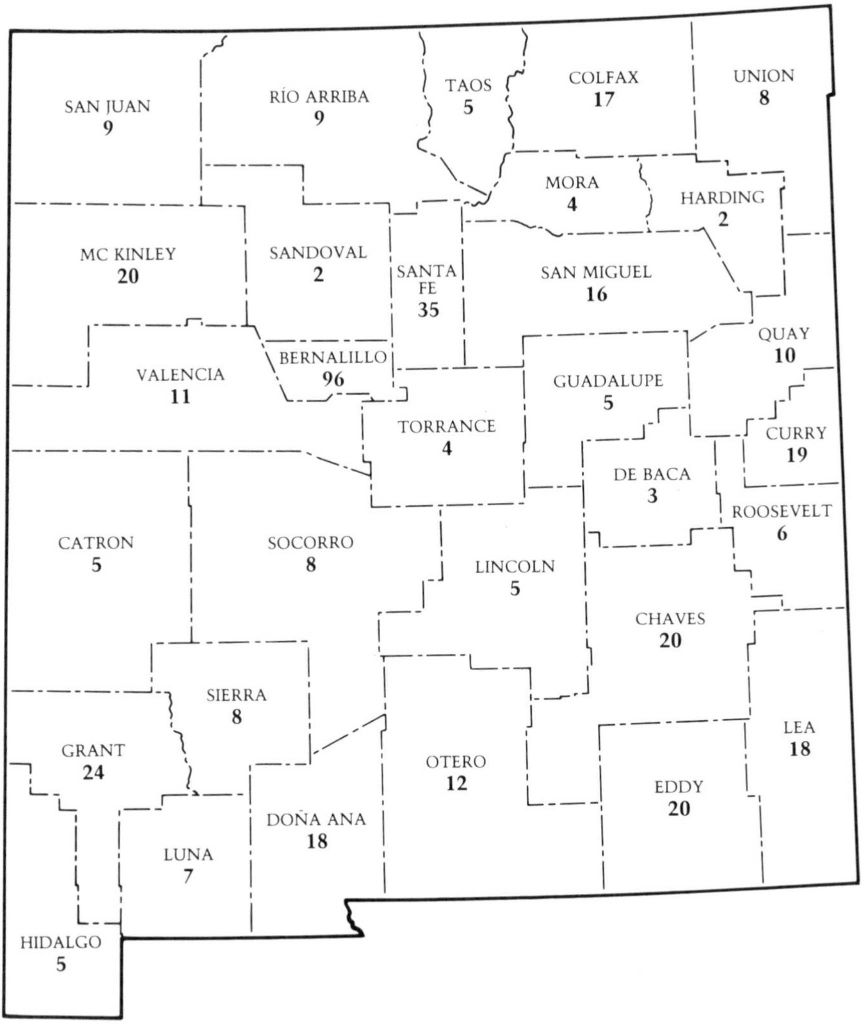

Map 6 RATIOS BY COUNTIES, MEDICAL DOCTORS TO POPULATION, 1940

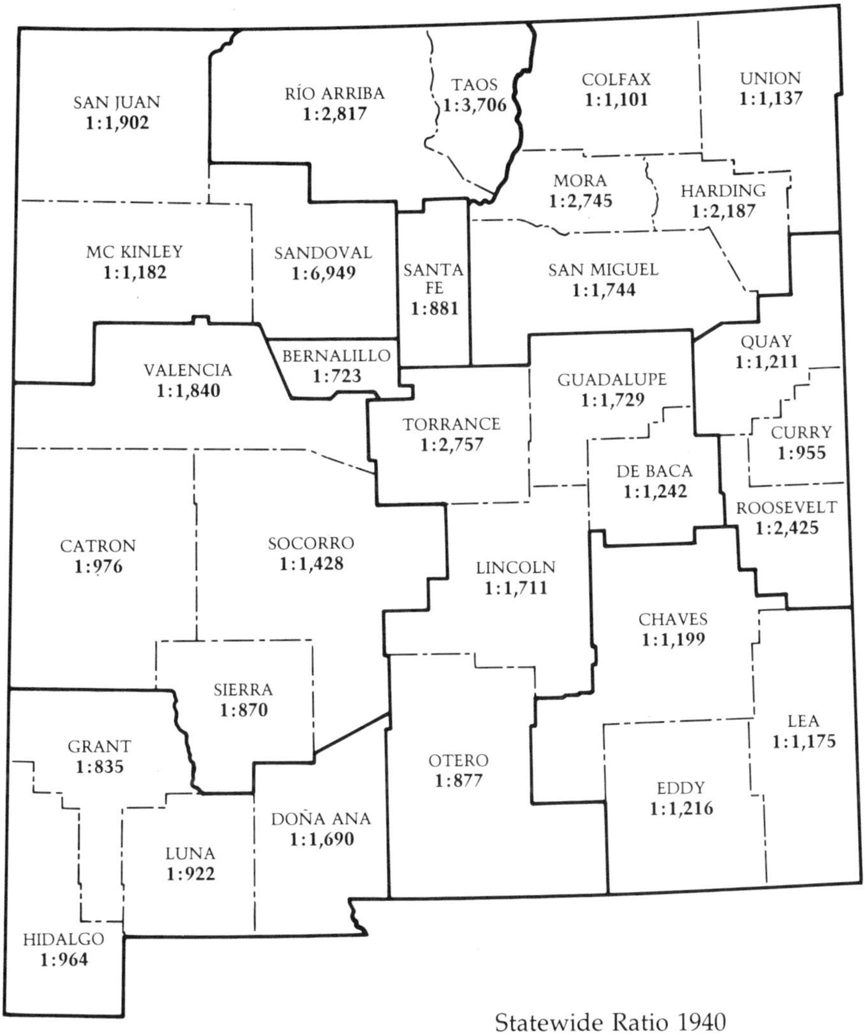

Statewide Ratio 1940
1:1,234 (one MD for every 1,234 people)

Table 11
Site of Physicians' Practice: 1912, 1940

1912		1940	
cities (5,000 and up)	104 (24%)	cities (7,500 and up)	161 (37%)
larger towns (1,500–5,000)	110 (26%)	larger towns (2,250–7,500)	114 (26%)
small towns (500–1,500)	87 (20%)	small towns (750–2,250)	85 (19%)
rural (fewer than 500)	130 (30%)	rural (fewer than 750)	79 (18%)

Source: *American Medical Directories* 3d ed. (1912) and 16th ed. (1940); U.S. Census figures for 1910 and 1940.

"country house call' which involved the first of the several thousand babies that he delivered over nearly fifty years of practice in Chaves County:

> In those days [1935] we had what were called "Okies" coming through here on their way to California. One night I got a call that a girl was having a baby in a tent under this cottonwood tree. When I arrived, this teenager about sixteen years old was having a stillborn, maybe a two or three pound baby, and breech, of course, but that didn't make any difference either. That was my first baby here, and they thanked me and I went on my way.[60]

Other statistics shed some light on the quality of New Mexico physicians during this middle period of the state's medical history. The data are suggestive only, but do hint that the doctors who came to New Mexico between 1912 and 1941 were at least as good as and perhaps somewhat better than their pioneer predecessors. For one thing, fewer among them had received their medical educations in the diploma mills ranging from bad to despicable, which so scarred the face of American medical education at the end of the nineteenth century. Table 12 lists the place of graduation for some 555 doctors who came to New Mexico during the period from 1912 to 1941.[61] It is different in several significant respects

[60]Lander, interview, Roswell, 19 August 1983.

[61]The Board of Medical Examiners issued a total of 1,071 licenses during the period, but many of those licensees, for one reason or another, never actually practiced in the state or practiced only a brief time before moving elsewhere.

Table 12
Medical Schools Attended by Physicians of the "Middle Period"

Rush Medical College, Chicago	28
University of Colorado	25
Baylor University	22
Northwestern University	22
University of Texas, Galveston	21
University of Illinois	20
University of Louisville	18
Tulane University, New Orleans	17
University of Tennessee, Memphis	13
University of Arkansas, Little Rock	13
Barnes Medical College, St. Louis	11
Vanderbilt University	11
St. Louis University	10
Jefferson Medical College, Philadelphia	10
Loyola University, Chicago	10
University of Nebraska	10
Memphis Hospital Medical College	9
Washington University, St. Louis	9
University of Michigan and Chicago College of Medicine	8 each
College of Medical Evangelists, Loma Linda, Calif.; Indiana University; and University of Oklahoma	7 each
Columbia University; University of Georgia; George Washington University; University of Kansas; Harvard; State University of Iowa; and Yale	6 each
University Medical College of Kansas City (Mo.); University of Nashville Medical Department; University of Buffalo; Creighton; Medical College of Virginia, Richmond	5 each
St. Louis College of Physicians and Surgeons; Chirurgical College of Philadelphia; Southern Methodist University; Baltimore Medical College; College of Physicians and Surgeons, Baltimore; University of Maryland; University of Minnesota; University of Alabama; and Kentucky School of Medicine, Louisville	4 each
University of Pennsylvania; Chattanooga Medical College; Hahnemann Medical College and Hospital, Chicago; Chicago Medical College; Miami Medical College, Cincinnati; Eclectic Medical College, Cincinnati; Emory, Atlanta; Southern Medical College, Atlanta; Central College of Physicians and Surgeons, Indianapolis; Indiana Medical College; and Keokuk College of Physicians and Surgeons	3 each
66 other schools, either one or two graduates	

from the similar list of schools attended by New Mexico's pioneer physicians (see Table 4, pp. 56–57). Most importantly, almost all the schools found in Table 12 were fully respectable institutions whose students had been exposed to the best of modern medical science and clinical training. Virtually gone (though not entirely, for some older physicians, who got medical degrees during the unreformed era, took licenses in New Mexico during this period) were schools like the Reform Medical College of Georgia (Macon, Georgia) and the St. Louis Hygienic College of Physician and Surgeons, which figured prominently on the earlier list. If graduation from modern medical schools was a legitimate measure, and surely it was, then New Mexico's doctors during the period from 1912 to 1941 were definitely a stronger group collectively than their predecessors.

Also new on the list was the emergence of schools in neighboring states as major suppliers of physicians for New Mexico. The University of Colorado, Baylor University, and the University of Texas, Galveston, all appear on the earlier list, but in positions much more modest than their eminence in Table 12. The flow to New Mexico of graduates from those schools is logical on geographical grounds, and it was somewhat delayed only by the time necessary for the maturation of those institutions. (Baylor's medical school, for instance, was not even founded until 1903; and neither the University of Colorado nor the University of Texas produced large numbers of medical graduates much before the turn of the century.) However, the rise of these new suppliers did not mean the complete displacement of New Mexico's earlier sources. Rush Medical College in Chicago heads both lists, and other Illinois schools fill the third, sixth, and fifteenth positions among the top twenty (Northwestern University, the University of Illinois, and Loyola University of Chicago, respectively). The Missouri and Kentucky schools so prominent as suppliers of New Mexico doctors in the pioneer era are still on the list, but at somewhat reduced levels of importance.

Table 13 and Map 7, which accompanies it, show the states where New Mexico doctors of the middle period received their medical degrees and may be compared with similar data for the pioneer period (see Map 4, p. 53 and Table 3, p. 54). Illinois, Missouri, and Tennessee retained their high rankings as major suppliers of New Mexico physicians (although Missouri's special prominence was much diminished), but they were joined on the list for the period from 1912 to 1941 by Texas and Colorado, total newcomers. More generally, Table 13 and Map 7 show the increasing ability of a maturing West to take care of its own needs, in this case through strong medical schools. In the pioneer period, only 29 of 586

Table 13
Location of Medical Schools Attended
by New Mexico Physicians, 1912–41

State	Number
Illinois	98
Texas	49
Missouri	49
Tennessee	44
Colorado	25
Kentucky	22
Pennsylvania	22
New York	21
Louisiana	19
Ohio	19
Nebraska	17
Maryland	15
Arkansas	15
Foreign	14
California	14
Georgia	13
Indiana	13
Michigan	13
Iowa	10
District of Columbia	8
Kansas	8
Oklahoma	7
Massachusetts	7
Minnesota, Virginia, Connecticut, and Alabama	6 each
North Carolina	3
South Carolina, Wisconsin, Vermont, New Hampshire, Mississippi, and Oregon	1 each
	555

Map 7 LOCATION OF MEDICAL SCHOOLS ATTENDED BY NEW MEXICO PHYSICIANS, 1912–1941

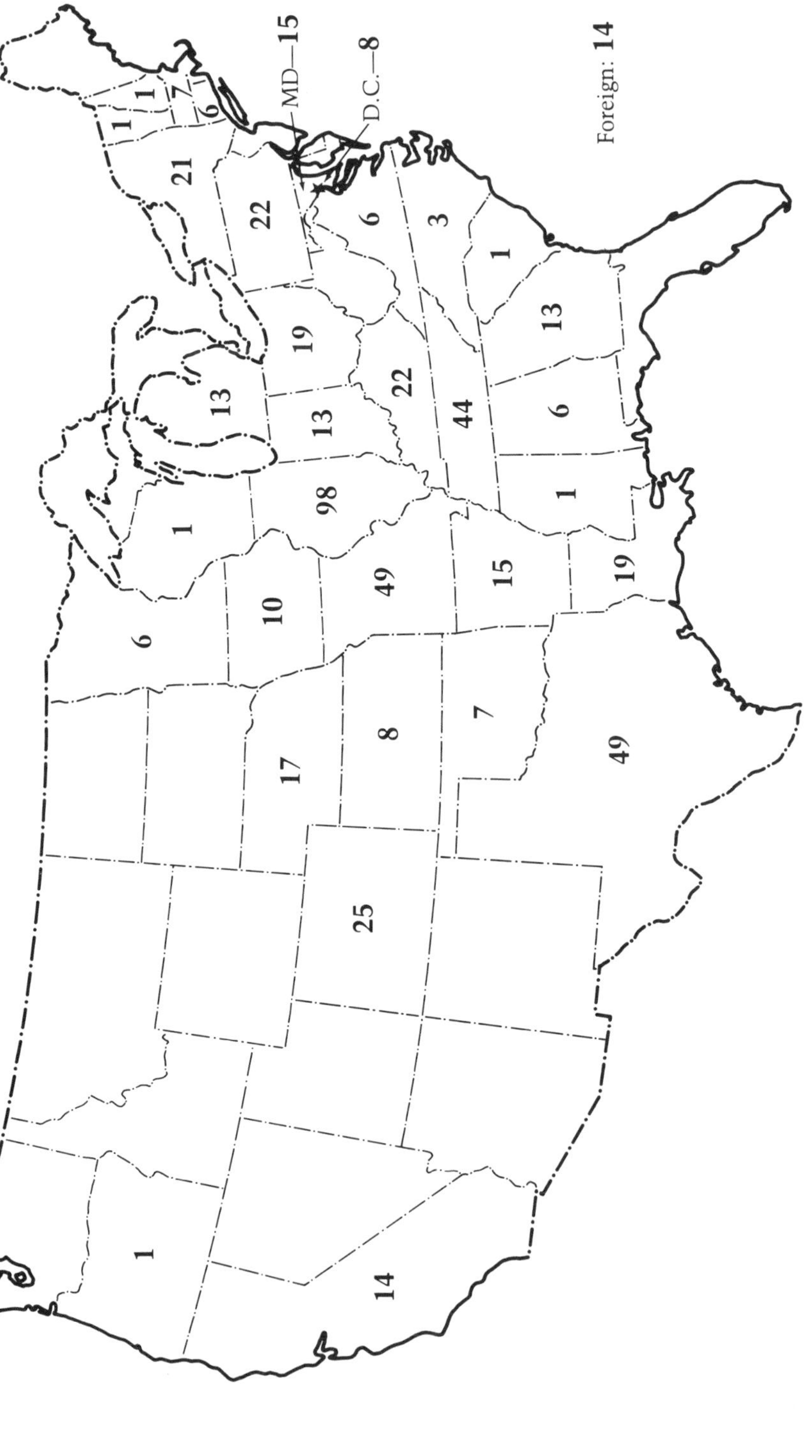

physicians practicing at some time or other in New Mexico, 5 percent of the total, received their degrees from schools west of the Ninety-fifth Meridian (roughly the eastern border of the Dakotas, Nebraska, Kansas, Oklahoma, and Texas); while in the later period, a total of 121 of 555, a full 22 percent, did so. New Mexico was growing less dependent on the East, but Chicago and St. Louis certainly retained their prominence as gateways to the West.

Two final points of statistical information about New Mexico's medical profession during the teens, twenties, and thirties should be mentioned. Over the twenty-nine years between 1912 and 1941, more and more young doctors fresh from medical school and internship (and perhaps some residency training) chose New Mexico as the place to start their careers. The trend is most obvious if the period is looked at on a decade-to-decade basis. From 1913 to 1922 only 15 percent of the physicians licensed in New Mexico were neophytes, that is, physicians who were three years or less from their medical-school graduation. That figure rose slightly to 21 percent between 1923 and 1932, and then soared to 51 percent from 1933 to 1941.[62] That change was achieved by an objective rise in the number of new doctors beginning their careers in New Mexico, but also by a sharp decline in the number of older doctors (ten years or more beyond medical school) arriving in the state. Presumably this decline—around twenty-five to thirty senior doctors per year set up practice in New Mexico from 1913 to 1922, and from 1932 to 1941 that figure had fallen to six to ten per year—was largely a matter of fewer tuberculous physicians coming to the state; but whatever the explanation the "mix" of new doctors in New Mexico grew younger year by year.[63] The significance of that change may be read variously: Younger, more energetic doctors with the most current information and skills were surely a positive addition to the New Mexico medical community, but the arrival of fewer experienced doctors, with the savvy produced by, in some cases, decades of practice, spelled a considerable loss.

Despite the significant turnover among New Mexico physicians during this period, and especially the large-scale shakeout that took place in the 1920s, there was a solid 50 percent of the total population of New Mexico doctors who stayed in place from year to year. Of all of the doctors practicing in the state in 1914, 51 percent were still there in 1921; 47 percent

[62]New Mexico, Board of Medical Examiners, Minutes, 1913–41.
[63]Ibid.

of those practicing in 1921 remained in 1927; 62 percent of those practicing in 1927 remained in 1934; and 54 percent of those practicing in 1934 remained in 1940. Thus, most New Mexicans could assume that once they had found a skilled and trusted family physician he would be there indefinitely in the future, whenever they needed him. This increasing stability was undoubtedly conducive to a higher level of care.

The fortunes of the New Mexico Medical Society rose and then fell with a thud during the decades between 1912 and 1941. It was a vigorously active and growing organization in the first part of the period, largely because of the gradually escalating struggle for better medical legislation in the state. When the doctors of the state felt the need for urgent and united action, as they did in the fight for a tighter licensure law, they looked to their medical society for leadership and gave it their support. In the early 1920s, roughly three-quarters of all the doctors in the state were members of the organization—298 of the state's 399 physicians were members in 1923—and county meetings and annual meetings of the society were well attended.[64] The momentum achieved was maintained through the mid-twenties by the efforts of a singularly enthusiastic and energetic secretary of the organization, Dr. Charles Yater of Roswell. Through exhortation—the pages of *Southwestern Medicine* are full of his pep talks to his colleagues—and untiring letter-writing campaigns, even combined with personal visitations, Dr. Yater kept the society's fires burning and its membership growing. (It was a case study of what one committed individual could do in terms of breathing real life into the institution, an object lesson that was lost until Ralph Marshall was hired as the society's executive secretary in 1949.) Dr. Yater midwived the birth or rebirth of several county societies as well, among them those of Grant County and Union County.

But with the departure of this organizational ramrod from the state in 1927 and the absence of major corporate business before the profession, the New Mexico Medical Society began to lose steam. The onset of the depression in 1929 increased the growing disinterest, diverting from the society some of the time and energy it might have claimed in better days.

[64]See the minutes of the state society's meetings, as printed in the *New Mexico Medical Journal* and, after 1919, in *Southwestern Medicine.* The good attendance and strong participation of the early twenties are further documented by the registrations ledger of the society's annual meetings, a volume held in the society's files in the New Mexico Medical History Archives.

Like other people during the depression years, doctors had to scrimp and scrape just to make a living, and relatively little time was left over for organizational activities.[65] In 1934, membership fell to a low of about 50 percent of the eligible doctors in the state, and participation at its meetings and in its work grew desultory. As early as 1929, before real lethargy set in, Dr. Franklin H. Crail of Las Vegas, president of the New Mexico Medical Society in 1929–30, was terribly candid in his presidential address regarding the unimportance of the society, in general, and the president's post, in particular:

What have its individual members been putting into this State Medical Society? I know that I have put practically nothing. This office was thrust upon me last year after I had gone home from the meeting, probably as a joke.[66]

The closest thing to a major issue facing New Mexico doctors of that period, aside from just making a living during the thirties, was the question of "state medicine." In New Mexico, the question took tangible form with the birth and extension of services by the state's health department. Where was the line properly drawn between private practice and the provision of medical services by the state from the public coffers? Initially, New Mexico's private-practice community was fully supportive of the new health department and its work, but it was not long before some of them grew suspicious of it. At the 1926 annual meeting of the state medical society, the Union County Medical Society presented a resolution that reflected its uneasiness about the growing dimenions of public-health services:

The Union County Medical Society fully appreciates the fact that the interest of the public in the prevention of disease and the promotion of health has been developed almost entirely through the discoveries and educational work of the medical profession. . . . The said Medical Society . . . believes the Board of Public

[65]Dr. V. Scott Johnson, interview with the author, Clovis, N.M., 31 May 1985. Dr. Johnson (as well as most of his colleagues who came to New Mexico in the thirties) remembers taking chickens, produce, and whatever else patients could afford to pay on account. Mrs. Johnson ruefully tells of one day hiring a high school boy to drive her, while her husband worked, as she made polite calls at a dozen or so farms in the Clovis vicinity, trying to collect something on account. She wound up the day a dollar in the hole—the sum she paid her chauffeur.

[66]F. H. Crail (M.D.), "Some Problems That Confront Practitioners in New Mexico," *Southwestern Medicine* 13 (1929):382.

Health should be required to bring before the Legislative Committee of the New Mexico Medical Society for consideration and action all matters of public health policy relating to the state as a whole, and that before proposing or undertaking any public health work restricted to a county and carried on by public funds it should first be submitted to the County Medical Society for consideration and action.[67]

Along with the growing concern about the scale and breadth of public-health activities and their possible impingement on the economic interests of private practitioners, there was opposition on philosophical grounds. In 1928, when Dr. George S. Luckett, director of the health department, asked the state medical society for its support in getting state money to fund more public-health nurses for its infant and maternal health programs, he encountered stiff opposition. Dr. Walter Gekler, one of Albuquerque's tuberculosis specialists, protested:

I am for public health work and no limit on the amount of expenditures, but when we get down to messing around in individual homes and encouraging people to lean on the Government, when we damage the morals of the citizen, we do worse than to cut his leg off. . . . I have no idea of throwing a monkey-wrench into the machinery of the public health department. I have never yet seen an organization that was as satisfactory as ours. The point I want to make is to be careful of keeping our balance and to keep these things, which seem to be increasing all the time, within bounds.[68]

Given the delicacy of the situation and the necessity for adjustments and compromise, good sense and considerable diplomacy were required of both sides and, with some minor exceptions, were found in good supply. A cordial, if slightly wary, relationship was established between the doctors of the public-health service and their colleagues in private practice, which provided a decent foundation for future cooperation between the two camps.

Neither the concern about the ostensible "dangers" of state medicine

[67]New Mexico Medical Society, Minutes, 44th Annual Meeting, 19–21 May 1926.

[68]New Mexico Medical Society, Minutes, 46th Annual Meeting, 10–12 May 1928. It should be noted that, despite the reservations expressed by Dr. Gekler and others, the motion of support of the health department passed unanimously.

nor anything else was sufficient to galvanize the New Mexico Medical Society to real activity in the thirties. It remained a low-key, loose, professional confederation, which was not yet a tightly organized, forceful, corporate spokesman and advocate for the medical profession. That change would come in the post–World War II period.

CHAPTER 7

Doctors of Medicine in the Modern Era

IN THE FOUR-PLUS DECADES FROM THE START OF THE SECOND World War to the mid-1980s, New Mexico medicine experienced change of fundamental dimensions. One major part of that process involved sweeping changes, even transformation, within the state's doctors of medicine community. The sheer number of M.D.s practicing in the state; the nature and caliber of their practices; the distribution of doctors around the state; the major institutions within which doctors worked and which oriented medical care generally in New Mexico; the organizational structure and cohesion of the medical profession; and much else was modified to such degree that an "old-time" physician of the 1930s would have had difficulty recognizing the much altered world of the eighties. Any effort to identify all those changes and summarize them reasonably within a few dozen pages is preordained to failure, for the complexity and heterogeneity of the period mock neat compartmentalization.

Nevertheless, five major changes or developments can be singled out for special examination, and through them the intricacies of the overall process may be suggested. First, there were enormous demographic changes in the state's M.D. population, and those developments radically affected health care delivery in the state. Second, there was a basic qualitative shift as well, with new, board-certified specialists rising to parity with the old general practitioners and then surpassing them, both in raw numbers and in influence. Third, the already well-established Lovelace Clinic, an Albuquerque institution with roots stretching back to the 1920s, was transformed in this period. Inspired by new leadership and a redefinition of its mission, it rose quickly in the late 1940s and 1950s to regional, and then national prominence. Fourth, in the early 1960s, a dream of many New Mexico physicians became reality with the establishment of a medical school at the University of New Mexico, and in short order the new institution claimed powerful influence within the state's medical community and health care delivery system generally. And, finally, the tide of change included the New Mexico Medical Society. The low-profile, casual organization of pre–World War II days was turned inside out. In the late 1940s and 1950s, it was fully professionalized and became for the first time in its history an effective, unifying force working on behalf of the profession. It not only afforded strong organization and direction for the state's physicians, but also it cooperated closely with an activist State Board of Medical Examiners in claiming for New Mexico a leadership role within the national medical community. It finally became the institution its founders envisioned a century earlier.

Despite Disraeli's famous warning—"There are lies, damned lies, and statistics"—statistical analysis does reveal interesting and important developments among New Mexico's modern era medical doctors. By far the most obvious change was their enormous increase in number. A grand total of 447 doctors resided in New Mexico at the start of the Second World War, and not all of them were actually in practice, serving the state's people. That number, for example, included retirees, physicians in government service or other restricted practices of one sort or another, and a handful of doctors involved in nonmedical pursuits. With so limited a number, it was possible for a professionally active (and curious) doctor to know personally the great majority of his colleagues practicing in the state. Forty years later, that had fundamentally changed, for no fewer than 2,522 physicians were listed in the New Mexico section of the 1985 edition of the AMA *Directory*.[1] This represented a 564-percent increase

[1]As with the figure cited for the start of World War II, not all those 2,522 doctors were in active practice. The number includes retired physicians; house officers and others in training situations of one sort or another; doctors engaged in research or teaching full time; M.D.s occupied in nonmedical careers (the famous photographer Eliot Porter of Santa Fe is one who comes immediately to mind); and so forth. The Health Resources Registry of the University of New Mexico School of Medicine estimated in mid-1985 that there were 2,308 M.D.s involved in some kind of medical practice in the state. However, in the statistics used in this chapter, the AMA *Directory* figure will be used to ensure comparability across

Table 14
Number of M.D.s in New Mexico, 1942–85

Year	No. of M.D.s	Total State Population	Ratio
1942	447	561,818	1:1,257
1950	504	681,187	1:1,352
1956	635	843,000 (est.)	1:1,328
1958	647	897,000 (est.)	1:1,386
1961	715	958,000 (est.)	1:1,339
1964	820	977,000 (est.)	1:1,192
1969	1,013	1,010,000 (est.)	1: 997
1973	1,348	1,104,000 (est.)	1: 819
1981	2,249	1,135,000 (est.)	1: 505
1985	2,522	1,424,000 (est.)	1: 565

Source: AMA *Directory* for years listed.

in slightly more than a four-decade period, a change of significant proportions. It was an increase which far outstripped the state's general population growth. New Mexico's 562,000 people of 1942 had grown to 1.4 million by mid-1984, an increase of 253 percent, but the state's supply of doctors of medicine had expanded at more than twice that pace. Nationally, the number of M.D.s in the country was growing rapidly—from 209,000 in 1950 to 502,000 in 1985, an increase of 240 percent—but New Mexico's physician boom in that same period (501 percent) dwarfed the national figure.[2] The pace of this physician boom in New Mexico is shown in Table 14. Growth was constant across the entire period, but it was most rapid during the 1970s. Between 1969 and 1981, the number of doctors of medicine in New Mexico more than doubled (a 122-percent increase), while the state's general population rose by a comparatively

the postwar period and with the pre–World War II period as well. The assumption is that though the *Directory*'s 1985 figure is probably at least 10 to 15 percent too high, a similar margin of error probably existed in its earlier calculations as well.

[2]United States, Department of Health and Human Services, *Health: United States, 1982* (Washington: Government Printing Office, 1983), p. 113.

modest 12 percent. (In the 1940s the physician supply grew 16 percent; in the 1950s, 42 percent; the same, 42 percent, in the 1960s; and in the period from 1980 to 1985, 12 percent.)

A number of factors explain this explosive growth in the numbers of doctors of medicine arriving in the state since the Second World War. First of all, physician supply nationally grew significantly in the period, outstripping the growth of the nation's general population by a factor of almost three. (As mentioned, between 1950 and 1985 the number of M.D.s in the country grew from 209,000 to 502,000, or 140 percent, while the nation's total population grew by 50 percent.) But while the numbers of physicians were increasing all around the country, New Mexico got far more than its share. This was partially a function of the Sunbelt's disproportionate growth in the period, but it was related to other factors as well. Certainly, the foundation and development of a medical school in the state (see pp. 309–28) contributed to the growth through the development and elaboration of its own staff and through its production of student-graduates, its enlistment of house officers in training programs, and the like. So, too, did the expansion of the federal government's presence in the state with military bases (and hospitals), research installations, Veterans Hospitals, and the like. Important as well was the growing attractiveness of much of the Rocky Mountain West to the ever larger numbers of Americans, young doctors of medicine among them, concerned about environmental pollution, high population densities, the annoyances of urban living, and a host of other "quality-of-life" concerns. The physical beauty and slower pace of life in New Mexico enticed many doctors and their families to the Land of Enchantment.

One of the major effects of this growth in physician supply was the radical alteration of the physician-patient ratio in the state, and, thus, indirectly at least, the availability of medical care. In the 1920s and 1930s, the physician-patient ratio in New Mexico had crept steadily higher to reach a figure of approximately 1 doctor for every 1,220 people in the state at the start of World War II. (See Table 10.) That ratio continued its slow climb higher (see Table 14) until the early 1960s, topping out at around 1 doctor of medicine for every 1,400 New Mexicans. That figure was markedly higher than the national average of 1 to 748 in 1960, and helps to explain the influx of physicians in New Mexico during the sixties and seventies. By comparison with that national average, New Mexico was significantly underserved by doctors throughout the first quarter-century after the war; not until the late 1970s or 1980s did the state's average approximate the national norm.[3]

As suggested in earlier chapters, it is deceptive to speak of "New Mexico" in throwing about figures of this sort. As in the pioneer and middle periods of New Mexico's modern history, significant distributional problems were concealed within the state's overall physician-to-population ratios. Map 8 shows the number of M.D.s resident in each of New Mexico's counties in 1960, and Map 9 the ratio of M.D.s to each county's population. Grouping the individual counties into regional blocs, as in earlier chapters, produces the following summary of physician distribution:

Los Alamos-Santa Fe	1:716
National Average	**1:748**
Bernalillo	1:849
State Average	**1:1,330**
Colfax-Union-Mora-Harding-San Miguel	1:1,507
Quay-Curry-Roosevelt	1:1,568
Chaves-Lea-Eddy	1:1,759
Grant-Hidalgo-Luna-Doña Ana	1:1,947
Valencia-Catron-Socorro-Sierra	1:2,248
Guadalupe-De Baca-Torrance-Lincoln-Otero	1:2,301
San Juan-McKinley-Sandoval	1:2,380
Río Arriba-Taos	1:2,508

These figures testify to the wide disparity within New Mexico in the availability of physicians in 1960. Medical doctors were roughly three times more readily available in the Los Alamos–Santa Fe complex or in Albuquerque as in northern or northwestern New Mexico. Furthermore, this grouping of the state's counties makes apparent New Mexico's relative physician shortage as of 1960. Only two areas of the state even approximated the national average in physician-population ratio; all other parts of the state were badly underserved. By 1980, when the number of M.D.s in the state had risen to about 2,000, the problem had become much less acute. (See Maps 10 and 11.) Significant numbers of doctors had moved into the underserved areas of the state, and the physician-to-population ratios in those regions had dropped far down. For example, in

[3]In 1980, when New Mexico's physician-to-population ratio stood at roughly 1 to 505, the national average was 1 to 514.

Map 8 NUMBER OF MEDICAL DOCTORS BY COUNTY, 1960

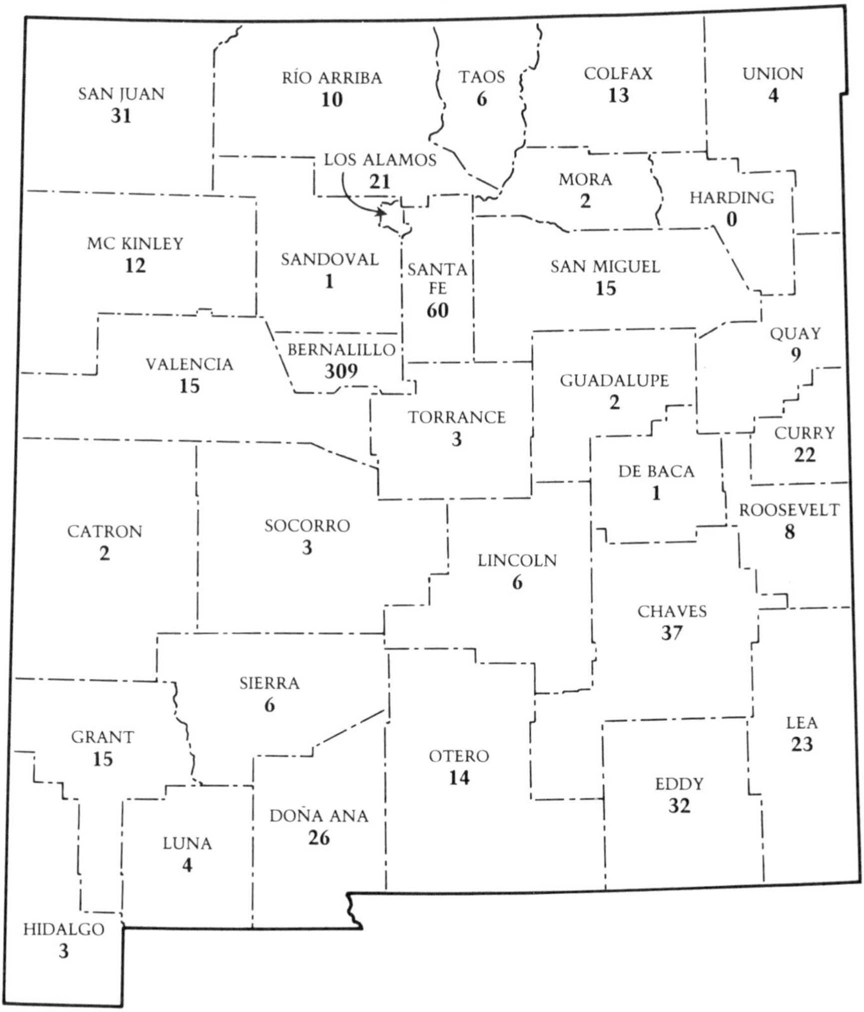

Map 9 RATIOS BY COUNTIES, MEDICAL DOCTORS TO POPULATION, 1960

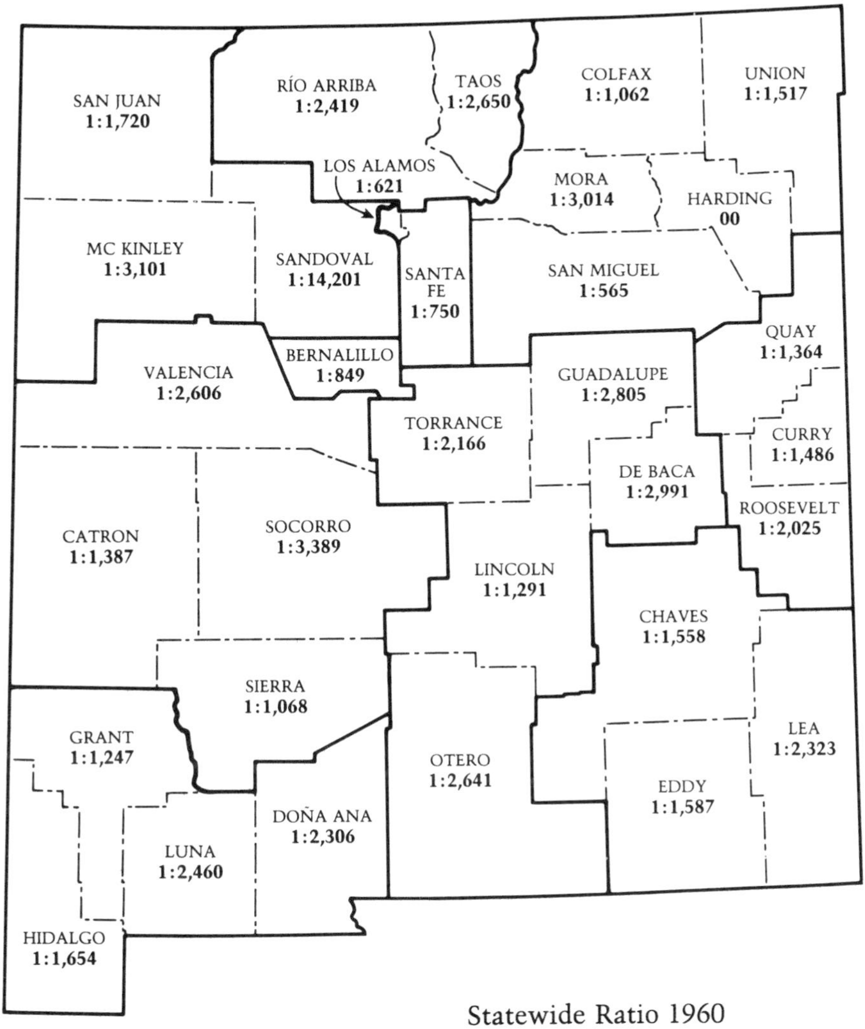

Statewide Ratio 1960
1:1,330 (one M.D. for every 1,330 people)

Map 10 NUMBER OF MEDICAL DOCTORS BY COUNTY, 1980

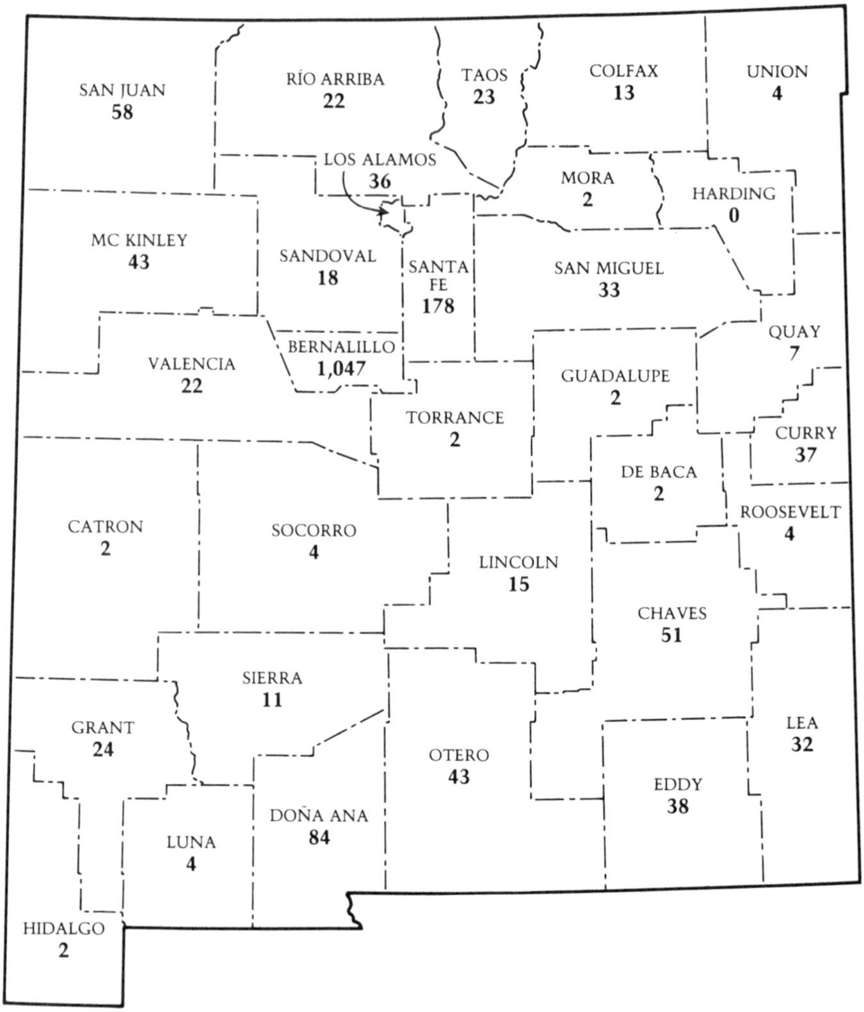

Map 11 RATIOS BY COUNTIES, MEDICAL DOCTORS TO POPULATION, 1980

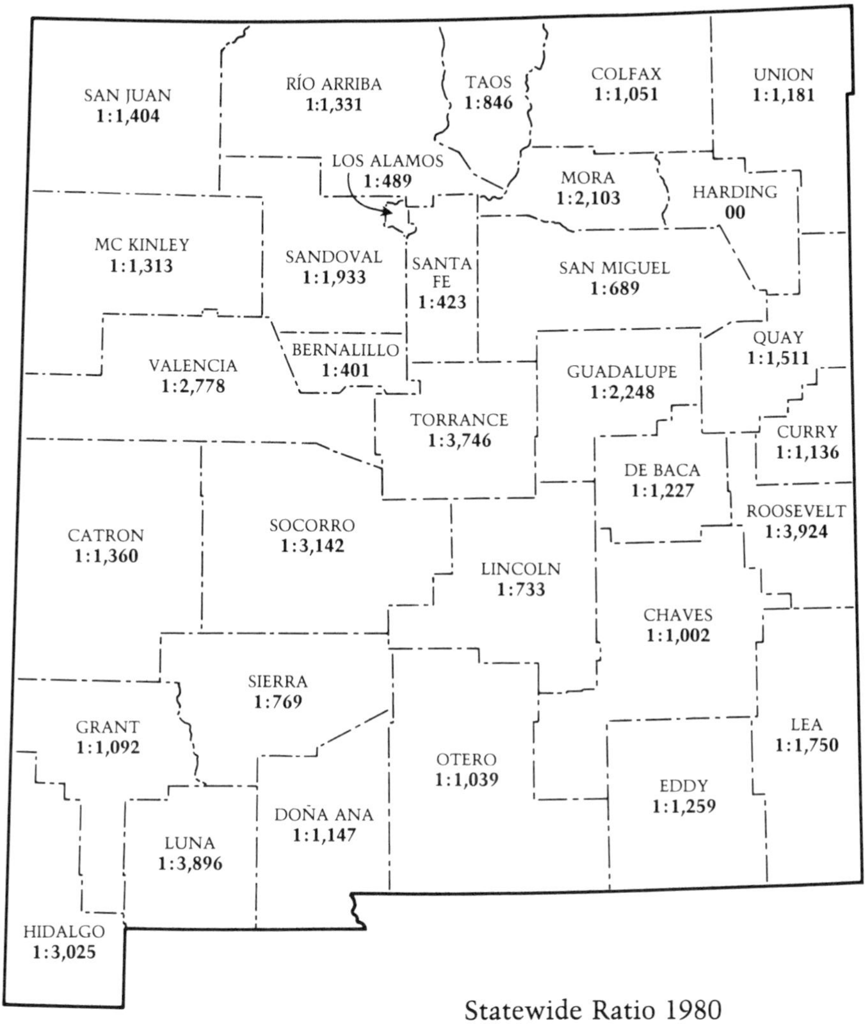

Statewide Ratio 1980
1:699 (one M.D. for every 699 people)

Table 15
Urban-Rural Mix of New Mexico Physicians

	1960		1980	
Cities (>10,000)	573 M.D.s	80.1%	1,623 M.D.s	87.0%
Towns (2–10,000)	92 M.D.s	12.9%	187 M.D.s	10.0%
Rural (<2,000)	50 M.D.s	7.0%	63 M.D.s	3.0%

1960 Río Arriba and Taos counties had only 1 physician (M.D.) for every 2,508 of their citizens, but by 1980 the ratio had fallen to 1 per 1,083. The counties of northeastern New Mexico had acquired new doctors in such numbers that their ratio had fallen from the 1960 level of 1 doctor serving 1,507 people to 1 per 893. Of course, pockets of the state remained underserved—primarily the extreme southwestern counties of Hidalgo and Luna and the Valencia-Socorro-Torrance triangle—but those problem areas were also being reduced by the mid-1980s.

The trend, first discernible in the 1930s, of physicians leaving the countryside and clustering in the state's cities and larger towns intensified in the postwar years, a phenomenon consistent with the increasing urbanization of the state (and nation) in general. Table 15 demonstrates the trend. This clustering of physicians in the state's cities and towns was less problematic than might at first be thought. By the sixties and seventies, most of New Mexico's people lived in its cities or close by, and the net of modern highways (and air transportation in emergencies) made access to medical care relatively easy for the rest. Physical access to medical care was a problem for only a handful of New Mexicans. The urbanization of New Mexico's M.D.s was particularly focused on Albuquerque, and the number of doctors in that city increased no less than fourteenfold during the years from 1940 to 1985. Its 94 doctors of the former year swelled to over 1,300 by the mid-1980s, and the Albuquerque community of physicians constituted 54 percent of the state's total by 1985. However, at least a dozen of the state's cities and towns developed sizable colonies of doctors in the sixties and seventies. Table 16 traces the growth of the M.D. community in fourteen New Mexico cities, and shows particularly rapid expansion in the years after 1969. By the 1980s the physician population in each of those cities was large enough and sufficiently differentiated to enable them to serve as medical-care hubs

Table 16
Physician Population in New Mexico Cities, 1940–1985

City	1940	1950	1961	1969	1979	1985
Alamogordo	3	4	14	15	35	32
Albuquerque	94	157	305	533	1,035	1,363
Carlsbad	14	21	24	28	31	50
Clovis	17	20	22	25	34	36
Española	4	4	5	6	19	25
Farmington	5	8	28	23	45	65
Gallup	14	11	11	12	37	61
Hobbs	10	11	16	17	27	46
Las Cruces	14	12	21	36	74	131
Las Vegas	15	15	13	22	29	26
Los Alamos	—	14	21	24	36	44
Roswell	18	27	35	35	50	69
Santa Fe	32	53	60	95	175	232
Silver City	13	13	9	17	20	33

Source: AMA *Directory* for the years listed.

for the rural areas surrounding them. Interestingly, this concentration of M.D.s in the state's cities had reached such levels by the late 1970s that something of a countercurrent set in. Young doctors chose, or found it expedient, to desert the cities, and places like Questa, Peñasco, Cimarron, and Jal got doctors for the first time ever or for the first time after years without one. Other small communities added a second or third doctor as part of this trend.

New Mexico's doctors of the modern period, those who came to the state during the Second World War or afterward, represented the gamut of American and even world medical education. Table 17 lists the top thirty medical-school producers of New Mexico physicians for the periods from 1942 to 1966 and from 1967 to 1985.[4] Significant changes took place

[4]The figures used in these rankings do *not* represent the total numbers of graduates from the respective schools who set up practice in New Mexico, but are based on a sample of 852 of the 1,442 physicians licensed by the state in the years from 1942 to 1966 and a

Table 17
Top Thirty Producers of New Mexico Physicians, 1942–85

1942–66		1967–85	
Univ. of Colorado	67	Univ. of New Mexico	209
Baylor Univ.	37	Univ. of Colorado	66
Univ. of Texas, Galveston	31	Univ. of Michigan	41
Northwestern Univ.	31	Northwestern Univ.	30
Univ. of Oklahoma	29	Washington Univ., St. Louis	30
Univ. of Indiana	21	Univ. of Kansas	29
Washington Univ., St. Louis	21	Univ. of Oklahoma	24
Ohio State Univ.	20	Univ. of Texas, Dallas	24
Univ. of Tennessee	20	Case Western Reserve Univ.	22
Univ. of Kansas	20	Univ. of Illinois	22
Harvard Univ.	18	Univ. of Pittsburgh	22
Univ. of Illinois	18	Harvard Univ.	21
St. Louis Univ.	17	State Univ. of NY, B'lyn	21
Tulane Univ.	17	Univ. of Texas, Galveston	21
Columbia Univ.	16	Univ. of Pennsylvania	20
Jefferson Medical Coll.	16	Univ. of Washington	20
Univ. of Minnesota	16	Baylor Univ.	19
Univ. of Texas, Dallas	15	Jefferson Medical Coll.	19
New York Univ.	15	Univ. of Tennessee	19
Univ. of Pennsylvania	15	Tulane Univ.	19
Univ. of Cincinnati	15	Univ. of Minnesota	18
Univ. of Michigan	15	Medical Coll. of Wisconsin	18
Univ. of Iowa	15	Univ. of Indiana	17
Case Western Reserve Univ.	13	St. Louis Univ.	17
Univ. of Maryland	13	New York Medical Coll.	17
Univ. of Louisville	13	Univ. of California, SF	16
Univ. of Chicago	11	Stanford Univ.	16
Hahnemann Med. Coll., Phil.	11	Ohio State Univ.	16
Johns Hopkins Univ.	11	Univ. of Wisconsin	15
State Univ. of NY, B'lyn	11	Univ. of Missouri	15
Total Sample	852		1,649

Sources: AMA *Directories*, 1942–85 (various), and files of the Board of Medical Examiners.

across the entire forty-three-year period. From the early 1940s to the mid-1960s, the medical schools of neighboring or nearby states played the dominant role in supplying physicians to New Mexico. The University of Colorado and the Texas schools at Houston (Baylor University) and Galveston (the University of Texas) retained positions of prominence first claimed in the twenties and thirties, and were joined by such other nearby institutions as the University of Oklahoma, the University of Kansas, and others. Midwestern schools that traditionally had played leading roles in funneling graduates to New Mexico—Northwestern University, Washington University (St. Louis), the University of Illinois, and St. Louis University—continued to send their graduates to New Mexico and were joined by the medical schools of Ohio State University and the University of Indiana. Less prominent were eastern or southern schools as major suppliers of New Mexico physicians in that period; only Harvard, the University of Tennessee, and a handful of others claim positions high up on the list.

In the period from 1967 to 1985, a major change took place, at least in the very top spot in the rankings. Not surprisingly, New Mexico's own medical school, the University of New Mexico School of Medicine, was the single largest producer of physicians for the state over that period. It graduated roughly one-eighth of all the doctors of medicine who set up practice in the state during that time, and that figure does not indicate the full impact of the school on the state's physician supply. It does not, for example, include the doctors attracted to the state by the medical school's residency programs, postdoctoral fellowships, and the like. Otherwise, the list for the 1967–85 period remained fundamentally the same as that of the 1942–66 era. Several schools rose to prominence as suppliers of New Mexico physicians for the first time in the later period—among them the University of Michigan, the Dallas branch of the University of Texas, Case Western Reserve University, the University of Pittsburgh, the University of Washington, and two California schools, the University of California, San Francisco, and Stanford University—but the continuity between the two periods is more striking than the changes.

If the medical-school alma maters of New Mexico's M.D.s of the modern period are retabulated in terms of the states where those physicians

sample of 1,649 of the estimated 4,507 licensed from 1967 through 1984. The samples were abstracted from the AMA *Directories* of the periods and from the files of the Board of Medical Examiners.

Table 18
States Where New Mexico Physicians Licensed in the Modern Era Earned Their Medical Degrees

State	No. Licensed, 1942–66 (Rank)	No. Licensed, 1967–85 (Rank)	Total (Rank)
New Mexico	0	209 (1)	209 (1)
New York	68 (3)	118 (2)	186 (2)
Texas	83 (1)	89 (4)	172 (3)
Illinois	79 (2)	89 (4)	168 (4)
Pennsylvania	55 (5)	99 (3)	154 (5)
Colorado	67 (4)	66 (7)	133 (6)
Missouri	40 (7)	62 (8)	102 (7)
Ohio	48 (6)	53 (10)	101 (8)
California	14	80 (6)	94 (9)
Michigan	21	62 (8)	83 (10)

received their medical degrees (see Table 18), a rather different picture emerges. The importance of the several medical schools located in New York State and Pennsylvania is underscored in that kind of tabulation, even though no single one among them claims "top-ten" ranking. The contribution of California's medical schools to the New Mexico medical profession is also clearer in this table than in the other, with eight different California schools combining to provide 94 New Mexico physicians, about 4 percent of the total 2,501 sample.

Perhaps most surprising of all is the increasingly large number of New Mexico's doctors of medicine who received their medical educations in foreign universities. Doctors with degrees from foreign medical schools were approximately a 3-percent minority of New Mexico's pioneer doctors, and slightly less than that—about 2.5 percent—in the twenties and thirties. That percentage jumped significantly among doctors newly licensed during the period from 1942 to 1966, with almost 7 percent of them (58 within the 852-physician sample) coming from foreign schools. That leap was just a harbinger of things to come, for in the period from 1967 to 1985 the percentage doubled again with approximately 16 percent of all M.D.s licensed in that period (257 of the 1,649-physician sample)

Table 19
Foreign Medical School Graduates Licensed in New Mexico, 1967–85

45	India
39	Mexico
30	Canada
13	United Kingdom
10	The Philippines
9	Argentina
8	Iran
6	Switzerland and Italy
5	Germany (West), Australia, Belgium, and Spain
4	Bolivia, Czechoslovakia, Thailand, Ireland, Nicaragua, and Lebanon
3	South Korea, South Africa, and Egypt
2	Sri Lanka, Taiwan, France, Hungary, the Netherlands, New Zealand, Peru, South Vietnam, and Yugoslavia
1	Austria, Chile, China, Colombia, Cuba, Denmark, Dominican Republic, Ecuador, Greece, Grenada, Guatemala, Hong Kong, Israel, Japan, Kenya, Poland, Rumania, Sweden, Turkey, USSR, and Zambia

having received their medical degrees in foreign schools. If lumped together and plugged into the list for the 1967–85 period of Table 17, foreign medical schools with a total of 257 graduates would easily claim first place in the rankings.

Table 19 classifies the 257 foreign medical graduates of the 1967–85 period in terms of where they received their degrees. In most cases, there is a high degree of correspondence between the country where the medical degree was earned and the nationality of the degree earner. In other words, almost all the 45 New Mexico doctors of medicine who earned their medical degrees in India were Indian nationals, the ten graduates of medical schools in the Philippines were Filipinos, and so forth. However, one conspicuous exception to this generalization was the 39 doctors listed in Table 19 as having received their degrees from Mexican medical schools.

Approximately one-quarter of them were Mexican nationals, but the other 75 percent were Americans who, in the sixties and seventies, sought their medical preparation in Old Mexico, most of them at the Universidad Autónoma de Guadalajara, in Jalisco, or the Universidad Autónoma de Ciudad Juárez. Similarly, some of the graduates of Canadian, United Kingdom, and European medical schools—perhaps 20 to 25 percent of them—were American nationals who took their medical education abroad, and then returned to their home country to practice.

The influx of foreign medical school graduates in New Mexico in the late sixties and seventies reflected a nationwide phenomenon. In 1979 foreign medical graduates constituted 21 percent of all physicians in the country, and despite some efforts to limit them, they were still 19 percent of all hospital house officers in this country in the 1982–83 training year.[5] These doctors of medicine who came to New Mexico to establish their careers seem to have blended without special difficulty into the mainstream of the state's medical community and to have been accepted readily by the people of the state. They established practices throughout New Mexico, but were particularly prominent in reducing physician shortages on the eastern plains of the state. For example, of the twenty-three new doctors of medicine who set up offices in Hobbs from 1975 to 1985, twelve were graduates of foreign medical schools—four from India, two from Argentina, and one each from Iran, Canada, Ireland, Mexico, the Philippines, and Zambia. Ten of the twenty-one new doctors in Clovis during roughly the same period were foreign medical graduates (from schools in Pakistan, Italy, Mexico, South Africa, Austria, India [two], Canada, South Vietnam, and Peru), and four of the six new doctors who chose Grants as the site of their practices were foreign medical graduates.

One final set of statistics provides critically important information regarding the changing face of New Mexico medicine in the postwar period. As new doctors began to move into the state during the late 1940s,

[5]The best short appraisal of the foreign medical graduate phenomenon of contemporary American medicine is Stephen S. Mick and Jacqueline Lowe Worobey, "Foreign Medical Graduates in the 1980s: Trends in Specialization," *American Journal of Public Health* 74 (1984):698–703. The statistics cited are found in this article on p. 698. See, also, Barry Stimmel, "The Impact of the Foreign Medical Graduate on Future Health Manpower Needs," *Bulletin of the New York Academy of Medicine* 56 (1980):631–42; R. A. Stevens, L. W. Goodman, and S. S. Mick, *The Alien Doctors: Foreign Medical Graduates in American Hospitals* (New York: Wiley-Interscience, 1978).

they reflected the general trend within American medicine away from the traditional family-doctor generalist and toward the more intensively trained specialist. The onrush of the specialists was a relatively rapid process and produced some fundamental rearrangement and adjustment within New Mexico medicine.

It is only a small exaggeration to say that specialization within New Mexico medicine began with the generation of doctors who came to the state during and immediately after World War II. Recognition must be granted to the score or so of physicians in the teens, twenties, and thirties who restricted their practices to tuberculosis, but with the exception of them and a handful of others, it is accurate to regard the large majority of New Mexico's pre–World War II doctors as general practitioners. Some of them, of course, preferred to concentrate their practices in particular fields where they had special interests or where they felt a special competence, but their practices still represented the gamut of general medicine. For instance, Albuquerque's Dr. P. G. Cornish, Jr., is remembered as a splendid surgeon, but he delivered thousands of babies as well. Dr. Robert McBride of Las Cruces was a gifted diagnostician, but could and would set a broken bone or sew up a severe laceration. In the larger towns a crude kind of differentiation of labor sometimes developed, but the specialist was relatively rare in New Mexico prior to the war. If certification by the recognized American boards is taken as the mark of who was truly qualified as a specialist and who was not—and in the postwar world board certification did increasingly carry that authority—a tiny 3.6 percent of New Mexico's doctors of medicine in 1939 could be called specialists. In that year, a grand total of sixteen of the state's doctors were board certified: three in internal medicine; two each in pediatrics, radiology, otolaryngology, and surgery; and one each in obstetrics-gynecology, ophthamology, orthopedic surgery, pathology, and psychiatry-neurology.[6] Throughout the state, there was not a single board-certified

[6]For the record those first sixteen specialists were: in internal medicine, Drs. Ralph Mendelson, Walter Werner, and LeRoy Peters, of all Albuquerque; in pediatrics, Drs. Stuart Adler and Meldrum Wylder of Albuquerque; in radiology, Drs. Erwin Johns and J. R. Van Atta of Albuquerque; in surgery, Drs. William Randolph Lovelace and William H. Thearle of Albuquerque; in otolaryngology, Drs. George Griswold of Roswell, and William C. Barton of Santa Fe; in obstetrics-gynecology, Dr. Lee Miles of Albuquerque; in ophthamology, Dr. Barton of Santa Fe; in orthopedic surgery, Dr. George Hensel of Hot Springs' Carrie Tingley Hospital; in pathology, Dr. Mark Beam of Albuquerque; and in psychiatry-neurology, Dr. John Myers of Albuquerque.

specialist in the fields of anesthesiology, dermatology, urology, or neurosurgery, among others. Predictably, the pioneer sixteen specialists were clustered in the cities: twelve of them lived and worked in Albuquerque, two in Santa Fe, and one each in Roswell and Hot Springs.[7]

The virtual absence of specialists in New Mexico prior to the Second World War was not quite so remarkable as may at first be thought, for the movement toward specialization within American medicine generally was new, essentially beginning in the interwar period. The specialty boards themselves were certainly new. The first of them, the American Board of Ophthamology, was only incorporated in 1917, and was followed by the American Board of Otolaryngology in 1924. Thirteen other boards were formed in the 1930s in such fields as surgery, radiology, pathology, and so on. With the exception of a few major cities, then, nowhere in the country had the shift toward specialization proceeded too far. That first *Directory of Medical Specialists*, published in 1940, listed 14,000 specialists, but the total physician population in the nation that year was approximately 180,000, so the percentage nationally of specialists was only about 8 percent. New Mexico's 3.6 percent looks less backward when compared with that standard.

Within the forty-five years from the start of the war to the mid-1980s, the mix within the state's physician corps between generalists and specialists changed radically. Table 20 shows the progressive increase of the specialists within the aggregate of New Mexico's doctors of medicine. Beginning in the late forties as a modest 13 percent of the state's regular physicians, and escalating steadily thereafter, the residency trained specialists rose to be the majority.[8] By the 1970s and 1980s, almost all of the state's new physicians had earned board certification as specialists, although the picture is clouded somewhat, at least statistically, by the strong emergence in the seventies of the new specialists called family practitioners. These new primary-care physicians, especially those who

[7]*Directory of Medical Specialists Certified by American Boards*, 1st ed. (New York: Columbia University Press, 1940), *passim*. This basic reference work published for the American Board of Medical Specialities has gone through twenty subsequent editions, with the most recent the 21st ed. (1983–84). It is the basic authority for my statistics regarding specialties.

[8]A sizable number of other New Mexico doctors of medicine were, in fact, practicing as specialists, although they lacked formal board certification. Thus, the figures cited in this section for specialists are conservative. The noncertified specialist, however, was much more common in the forties and fifties than later.

Table 20
Specialists Within the Total M.D. Population
of New Mexico, 1949–83

Year	No. of Specialists	No. of M.D.s in State	Percentage	National %
1949	67	504 (1950)	13.3%	15% (1950)
1955	161	635 (1956)	25.3%	
1961	249	715	34.8%	28% (1960)
1968	359	1,013 (1969)	35.4%	32% (1970)
1974	643	1,348 (1973)	47.7%	
1981	1,198	2,249	53.3%	53% (1980)
1983	1,531	2,375 (est.)	64.5%	53%

Source: *Directory of Medical Specialists Certified by American Boards* for each of the years listed.

practiced in rural New Mexico, were similar in the breadth of their practices to the general practitioners of the pre–World War II period, but with a critical difference: They were backed, not just in Albuquerque, but in all the larger cities and towns around the state, by a solid cadre of secondary- and even tertiary-care specialists. First in Albuquerque, and then in Santa Fe, Los Alamos, Roswell, and Las Cruces, sizable numbers of specialists hung out their shingles. Carlsbad, Farmington, Clovis, and Gallup soon followed, developing basic complements of board-certified specialists in the 1960s, and by the eighties towns so small as Shiprock or Ruidoso could boast their own specialists. The pace of the change in New Mexico was consistent with the development of the phenomenon nationally, as Table 20 also shows. In the 1980s, however, the statistics suggest a higher percentage of specialists in New Mexico than the national average, probably because of the younger age of New Mexico's physicians.[9]

[9]In 1983, 56 percent of New Mexico's nonfederal physicians were under forty-five years of age (and thus more likely to be board-certified practitioners), while nationally the comparable figures was 53 percent. Mary Ann Eiler, *Physician Characteristics and Distribution in the United States, 1983 Edition* (Chicago: American Medical Association, Survey and Data Resources, 1984), p. 75.

New Mexico medicine had matured with the times, and New Mexicans no longer looked beyond the perimeter of their home state for specialized care, except in a few unusual circumstance.

One of the institutional forces in New Mexico medicine which helped produce the shift from the age of the general practitioner to that of the specialist was Albuquerque's Lovelace Clinic. Of the sixteen board-certified specialists of 1939, no fewer than five (Drs. Adler, Johns, Lovelace, Thearle, and Miles) were members of the clinic's staff. Its significance in that process, however, was but one sign of its prominence generally within the New Mexico medical community. Indeed, it can be argued that with the University of New Mexico School of Medicine and the Presbyterian–St. Joseph hospital complex in Albuquerque the Lovelace Clinic (later Medical Center) has been one of the basic pivots of New Mexico medicine in the postwar age. Only the state medical society itself and the Board of Medical Examiners in Santa Fe, under the strong leadership of Dr. Robert C. Derbyshire, have come close to rivaling the Albuquerque institutions in exerting strong influence within New Mexico's world of medicine.

The Lovelace Clinic was born in the tuberculosis era of New Mexico history, for both of its founders came to the region to seek relief from their own cases of the disease. Twenty-two-year-old Dr. William Randolph Lovelace apparently contracted the disease in medical school or very shortly thereafter, and left his native Missouri for the high altitude and dry atmosphere of the Rocky Mountain West. He set up his initial practice as a frontier surgeon and country doctor in 1906 in Sunnyside (later Fort Sumner), New Mexico, and worked there for seven years before relocating to Albuquerque. Also in 1909, Dr. Edgar T. Lassetter came to the new state, stopping first at the army sanatorium in Fort Bayard. Dr. Lassetter had contracted pulmonary tuberculosis during military service in the Philippines during the Spanish-American War, but New Mexico's climate and the sanatorium regimen at Fort Bayard served him well. He recovered quickly and strongly, as had Dr. Lovelace, and moved to Albuquerque around 1920. The two physicians teamed in 1922, and the formation of their partnership is conventionally cited as the beginning of the Lovelace Clinic, although the name itself was not used until later in the decade. Dr. Lassetter, a skilled diagnostician and devoted family doctor, left most of the business aspects of the partnership to his more aggressive friend (and brother-in-law) Dr. Lovelace, but his strong commitment to patient care played an important part in the establishment of the clinic's reputation for excellence.

The decision to build a clinic upon the foundation of the Lovelace-Lassetter partnership was heavily influenced by the reputation and success of the famous Mayo Clinic of Rochester, Minnesota. In 1913, young Dr. Lovelace made the first of what became almost annual trips to that lodestar of group practice. For the frontier surgeon, the Mayo visits were a kind of continuing education process, and he spent much time in Rochester, observing and learning. He became personal friends with Drs. Will and Charlie Mayo and, as early as 1916, was initiated as a life member of the Surgeon's Club at Mayo.[10] He not only honed his surgical skills on the trips to Mayo, but also became a convinced apostle of the group-practice approach to medicine. He always acknowledged the Mayo exposure and example as a central influence in his life and work.

Group practice on the Mayo model was still a highly controversial issue within American medicine in the teens and twenties, despite the obvious success of the Mayo brothers.[11] Solo practice remained "the American way," and in an era almost obsessed with the fear of socialism and communism, the idea of cooperative efforts in medicine was unsettling and threatening to many.[12] The possible competitive advantages of the group practitioners also alarmed many doctors engaged in solo practice, and contributed fundamentally to the hostility that greeted the birth of most of the early clinics. Nevertheless, in the years after the First World War the clinic movement did gain steam, and Albuquerque's Lovelace Clinic joined Seattle's Mason Clinic, founded in 1920; the Cleveland Clinic (1921); the Santa Barbara Medical Clinic (1921); the Lahey Clinic in Boston (1923); and others as trailblazers in the group-practice movement within American medicine.

In its first two decades of existence, the Lovelace Clinic grew steadily, if not spectacularly. By national standards it remained relatively small, numbering no more than a dozen physicians by the start of the Second World War, but its influence was disproportionate. It was, for example,

[10]"William Randolph Lovelace I," archival file A–8, Lovelace Medical Center, Albuquerque, N.M.

[11]On this subject, see Starr, *Social Transformation of American Medicine*, pp. 209–15; Rosemary Stevens, *American Medicine and the Public Interest* (New Haven: Yale University Press, 1971), pp. 141ff.

[12]The title of a lead editorial in the *Journal of the American Medical Association* 76 (12 February 1921):452–53, suggests the anxiety: "Group Practice—A Menace or a Blessing?"

the largest single concentration of medical manpower and expertise for hundreds of miles around, and exercised a powerful influence over the practice and development of medicine throughout the Southwest. Housed on two floors of the First National Bank building in downtown Albuquerque, and linked solidly to nearby St. Joseph Hospital, the clinic became a potent force in both Albuquerque and state medicine. It reflected the ethos of its founders in focusing on serving a general, local practice, but it also increasingly acted as a specialty referral center for a broad portion of the Rocky Mountain region. Physicians throughout the state and beyond New Mexico came to know and respect the Albuquerque institution and its tradition of top-quality professional, but personalized, care. Many of the early staffers were Mayo-trained specialists, but all were expected to absorb the fundamentals of the Lovelace-Lassetter "family doc" style of practice.[13]

Throughout this period of foundation and consolidation, Dr. Lovelace was the dominant figure of this highly personalized institution. He directed the clinic and its personnel with a firm hand, focusing all of his considerable energies upon it. The clinic's telephone number literally rang at his home at night when the switchboard was shut down, and young doctors of the staff learned to expect his calls in the middle of the night: "Mrs. Ortega out in Alameda just called with a bellyache. Do you suppose you could take care of it?" (Dr. Robert Massey, former dean of the University of Connecticut School of Medicine and a Lovelace Clinic physician from 1951 to 1968, remembers accidentally going back to sleep after one such late-night call, then being awakened by the taxicab sent for him by Dr. Lovelace.)[14] Nothing at his clinic escaped Dr. Lovelace's personal attention. He supervised the ordering of supplies, worried about the quality of paper used as clinic stationery, and directed the placement of garbage receptacles on the clinic grounds—all while carrying a substantial surgical load well into his sixties.

Despite that level of commitment to the affairs of his clinic, Dr. Lovelace was an important contributor of his time and energy to his profession and his community. Over the sixty-plus years of his career, he filled many positions of responsibility and honor within his profession at all levels

[13]Interviews with longtime clinicians and professional and personal friends of Drs. Lovelace and Lassetter are unanimous in underscoring the special attentiveness of the founders toward their patients and their insistence on similar behavior by their staff colleagues.

[14]Dr. Robert U. Massey, interview with the author, Farmington, Conn., 4 January 1985.

of the medical world. In 1916, for instance, when he was still in his early thirties and still new in Albuquerque, he was honored by election as president of the Bernalillo County Medical Society. (This was, of course, *before* his decision to build a clinic.) In addition to serving more than two decades on the New Mexico Board of Medical Examiners, he was one of the founders of the Southwestern Surgical Congress, a member of the Founders' Group of the American Board of Surgery, and president of the International College of Surgeons, U.S. Section, in 1956. He also made time to give of his experience and good judgment to his community, most notably as Regent of the University of New Mexico for seven years, including two critically important years as the Board's president. Additionally, though never married himself, Dr. Lovelace welcomed the role of paterfamilias, devoting himself to his two cherished sisters and his brother and directing, to a considerable degree, the education and ambitions of his three nephews, two of whom became physicians on the Lovelace Clinic staff while the other became a prominent attorney in Albuquerque.[15]

As the Lovelace Clinic grew in size and influence, a yawning chasm developed between it and much of the rest of the Albuquerque medical community.[16] The division was fundamentally rooted in philosophical differences regarding styles of practice and the complex of factors alluded to earlier, but there was a keen personal edge in the Albuquerque split as well. For his part, Dr. Lovelace was strong-willed, even at times imperious, and markedly ambitious; he let no legitimate opportunity pass to advance himself and his clinic. Though essentially courtly and proper, he could also be brusque and cutting to the point of rudeness as well as fiercely unyielding (and unforgiving) in dealing with his foes. The leaders among the "downtown doctors"—surgeons P. G. Cornish, Jr., J. W. Hannett, and William H. "Uncle Billy" Woolston prominent among them—were equally strong characters, as emphatically confident of their own abilities (and rightly so) and the righteousness of their cause as Dr. Lovelace. They, too, were basically decent men of honorable motives, but they were just

[15]Dr. Edgar L. Lassetter (son of the founder), interview with the author, Albuquerque, N.M., 6 October 1985.

[16]In the 1950s a commonsense terminology developed to distinguish the two groups. The Lovelace staffers were, of course, "clinic people," the term faintly suggestive of dependent, controlled automatons, and their adversaries, "the downtown doctors," with the label indicating their focus in the staffs of the downtown hospitals, especially Presbyterian Hospital.

as intolerant and uncompromising once they had dug into their own adversarial position.

The effect was a fairly rigid separation of the Albuquerque medical community into mutually suspicious (and sometimes childishly disdainful) camps. The cleavage was intensified after 1952, when Bataan Memorial Methodist Hospital opened adjacent to the clinic in (then) the southeastern suburbs of the city. Prior to that time, a modicum of communication and cooperation between the two groups was enforced by the necessity of working shoulder to shoulder in St. Joseph Hospital and, to a lesser extent, Presbyterian Hospital; but that link was severed with the construction of the new hospital on land donated for the purpose by Dr. Lovelace.[17] Unfortunately, the local medical society contributed little to reducing the distance between the two factions, but, rather, was itself caught up in the fray. It became to considerable degree an instrument of the anti-Lovelace doctors, used to cudgel the clinic group when any opportunity presented itself. As early as 1929, Dr. Lovelace was forced to defend his behavior before a special committee of the county society on charges of unethical conduct, specifically of allowing (or causing?) his name to appear too prominently in the local papers.[18] He forced a grudging letter of vindication from the committee, but it was merely the first of a long series of disputes between the clinic and the county organization. The long and smoldering antipathy flared most dramatically in 1952 over charges of clinic "advertising," a chronic complaint of the downtown doctors.[19] The specific issue involved the nationally syndicated newspaper columnist Robert Ruark, who visited the clinic to see a friend undergoing diagnostic procedures, and wrote a series of articles hymning the praises of the Lovelace Clinic and its doctors.[20] (The fact that the articles eventually ran in some 160 American and Canadian newspapers made the offense more heinous.) Ruark quickly wrote a formal letter of disclaimer, insisting that the clinic's people had in no way inspired the articles—"it being a rather personal point of pride that nobody has ever

[17]Massey, interview, Farmington, Conn., 4 January 1985.

[18]Bernalillo County Medical Society, Minutes, 3 April 1929, in University of New Mexico Medical Center Library, History Archives, Albuquerque, N.M.

[19]They also objected unremittingly to the restrictive covenant written into the contract of every clinic physician. That clause forbade any physician who wanted to leave the clinic from practicing anywhere in Bernalillo County for a period of three years. It was finally eliminated in 1969.

[20]Robert Ruark File, Lovelace Medical Center, Albuquerque, N.M.

been able to *get* me to write anything on any subject that I did not feel deserving of publication"[21]—but the issue became a cause célèbre nonetheless. A petition carrying the names of nearly eighty local doctors called on the Bernalillo County Medical Society to censure the clinic collectively for its unethical behavior and to expel those deemed directly responsible for the affront.[22] The storm eventually blew over without such drastic consequences, except for the reinforcement of the legacy of ill will within the community. As late as 1973, a sizable minority of the clinic's medical staff would angrily call for a radical solution of the decades-old impasse. It moved for formal secession of the clinic's doctors from the county society and their incorporation as a separate group, called the Sandia Medical Society, which would be associated directly with the statewide organization.[23] At the end of the 1970s and in the early 1980s, new faces in leadership positions on both sides began the task of damping the fires, and new challenges to the medical establishment robbed the old rivalries of some of their ferocity. But the battles begun during the 1920s, in the halls of St. Joseph Hospital, have left their scars.

The character, dynamic, and basic structure of the Lovelace Clinic underwent fundamental change in 1946, with the addition of a third partner to the Lovelace-Lassetter duo. This was the charismatic Dr. William Randolph Lovelace II, or Randy, a nephew of the founders. (Young Dr. Lovelace's personality led people to comfortably call him Randy. The elder Dr. Lovelace was called "Uncle Doc," but not always out of affection or familiarity, for he was a somewhat austere and forbidding figure; rather, it was a label of convenience.) Randy Lovelace had been reared under the watchful eye of his physician-uncle and, indeed, spent lengthy stretches of his boyhood and adolescence within his uncle's Albuquerque home. Educated at Washington University in St. Louis, and then at Cornell and Harvard medical schools, Randy did his internship at Bellevue Hospital, then accepted his Uncle Doc's advice that he take a surgical fellowship at the Mayo Clinic in 1936.[24] During his ten years in Rochester—a decade interrupted for him by war service—Randy Lovelace established a brilliant

[21]Ibid.

[22]Dr. Albert Simms, interview with the author, Albuquerque, N.M., 17 and 18 May 1984.

[23]Lovelace Medical Center, Board of Governors, Clinic, Minutes, 9 January 1973.

[24]The best personal sketch of Randy Lovelace's life is Richard G. Elliott, "'On a Comet, Always': A Biography of Dr. W. Randolph Lovelace II," *New Mexico Quarterly* 36 (1966–67):351–87. This affectionate tribute to the man was done, after his death, at the request of the Lovelace institution's authorities.

record. He earned his M.S. degree in surgery, and was offered a staff position at the clinic as well as the lifelong friendship and respect of Dr. Charles W. "Chuck" Mayo. When he became head of a surgical section at Mayo in 1942, his aging uncle in Albuquerque was content, even though he hoped and expected that one day his nephew would return to New Mexico to run the Lovelace Clinic.

At Mayo, Randy Lovelace became interested in the work of Dr. Walter M. Boothby, one of the pioneers of aviation medicine. Dr. Lovelace had nurtured a love of flying since his youth, and during his Mayo years, he developed that interest both personally and professionally. In the late 1930s, when the air force turned to the Mayo staff for help in designing a high-altitude oxygen mask for aviators, it was Drs. Boothby and Lovelace, along with Dr. Arthur H. Bulbulian, who accepted the challenge. They produced what is known in the annals of aviation medicine as the "BLB mask," named after its inventors. A deceptively simple apparatus, the BLB mask was critical to the penetration of high altitudes by American aviation, and in 1940 Randy Lovelace was one of those honored with the coveted Collier Trophy, awarded annually for the greatest contribution to aviation during the preceding year. The mask fixed the name of the young surgeon in the rapidly developing field of aviation medicine, a reputation he reinforced during the war years with research on pulmonary physiology at high altitudes and at least one piece of old-fashioned derring-do. In June 1943, Major Lovelace jumped through the bomb-bay doors of a B-17, cruising at over forty thousand feet above the wheat fields of Washington State, to test bailout equipment and procedures at high altitudes. It was a bit of individual heroism that almost cost him his life and which brought him notice in newspaper stories across the nation as well as photos and stories in *Life* and *Look*. (It was also, incidentally, the first and only parachute jump that Randy Lovelace made in his life.)[25]

With significant accomplishments already under his belt and strong connections to prominent and powerful medical, military, and aviation circles, Randy Lovelace returned to the Mayo Clinic at the end of his military duty in 1945. His tenure there was brief and tragic, however, for in the summer of 1946, when an epidemic of polio struck Rochester, Randy and his wife Mary Lovelace lost both their young sons to the disease

[25]Files A–11 and A–13 through 16, "William Randolph Lovelace II," Lovelace Medical Center, Albuquerque, N.M.

within a six-week period, and the grieving family returned to Albuquerque to heal.

With Randy Lovelace's move to the Lovelace Clinic in 1946, as a full partner with his two uncles, the institution changed radically. Most obvious was its almost immediate physical expansion. The dozen physicians of 1946 grew to twenty-nine in less than five years and doubled again to more than sixty in the following decade—a 500 percent increase in fifteen years. Space and facilities in the downtown bank building were quickly inadequate, so planning began for a clinic building in the southeastern suburbs of town near the Veterans Hospital and Kirtland Air Force Base. The striking Lovelace Clinic Building, a four-story structure of modified pueblo style designed by the eminent Southwest architect John Gaw Meem, was formally opened in October 1950, and provided the institution with a modern and spacious facility appropriate to its rise to national prominence. Even before the clinic building was open, construction had begun on the Bataan Hospital, alluded to earlier, and the basic complex which was to become the Lovelace Medical Center began to take shape.[26]

The physical changes of the postwar period were accompanied by organizational changes of sweeping dimensions. Shortly after Randy Lovelace's return to Albuquerque in 1946, he and his uncles began to make specific plans for the conversion of the Lovelace Clinic partnership into an association of physicians based on the Mayo model and for the establishment of a Lovelace Foundation for Medical Education and Research, a nonprofit corporation. Drs. Lovelace I, Lassetter, and Lovelace II gave the name "Lovelace Clinic," and the goodwill associated with it, to the new foundation, plus all the physical assets, medical and research equipment, and the medical library which had belonged to them personally. Shortly after the Foundation's formal establishment, Dr. Lovelace I also gave it the large tract of land on which the Lovelace complex still stands.

The creation of the Foundation was largely the product of Randy's genius, reflecting his Mayo experience and his strong conviction about the need for such an institution in the Southwest. The nearest medical school at that time was 537 miles from Albuquerque; only one hospital in the area had residency and internship programs; there was only one nursing school within a radius of almost five hundred miles; and there were absolutely no facilities in the region to train medical technicians.

[26]The hospital, enlarged and modernized over the years, was purchased by Lovelace in 1969.

It was the founders' hope that the Foundation might fill some of these holes by serving as the educational and research focal point so badly needed. At the same time, Randy Lovelace intended the Foundation to concentrate its research in his beloved aviation, or aerospace, medicine, a critically important and underdeveloped field in a society pushing ever deeper into the heavens. It was not unreasonable to hope that the Lovelace center might become in time a kind of Southwest Mayo, a medical center deeply involved in the triad of medical care, education, and research. It was, of course, an old vision for the elder Dr. Lovelace.

In the period from 1946 to 1965, then, the modest, small-town group practice of the pre–World War II era was transformed into a modern and aggressive institution of considerable size, vitality, and ambition. The clinic not only expanded rapidly; it broadened its reputation as a specialty referral center while, at the same time, competing strongly for its local market. The hospital was pulled into closer partnership with the Lovelace operation, and rapid progress was also made in the educational mission directed by the Foundation. By 1965 various postdoctoral fellowship programs were in place; graduate programs were operating in conjunction with the University of New Mexico; five different paramedical training programs were under way; and among other educational endeavors, five approved residencies sponsored jointly by the Foundation and Bataan Hospital had been developed.

Perhaps most noteworthy, however, was the rapid creation at the Lovelace center of a staff with remarkable research capabilities and credentials. One of the special gifts of Randy Lovelace was his ability to attract colleagues of great ability who gave allegiance to his dream.[27] One such man was the brilliant physician, scientist, and administrator Dr. Clayton S. "Sam" White, who served as the backbone of Lovelace research work from the time of his recruitment by Randy Lovelace in 1947 until the mid-1970s. Dr. White, originally director of research for the Foundation and later its president, initiated a broad-based research program, which came in time to include work of a startling variety. Especially prominent was the Foundation's work in biophysics, particularly the biomedical aspects of high-energy blast waves and the effects of inhalation of fission products.

[27]Earl D. Johnson, interview with the author, Greenwich, Conn., 6 January 1985. Mr. Johnson, a prominent figure in aviation and defense circles, as president of General Dynamics among other things, was a personal friend of Randy Lovelace and a longtime trustee of the Lovelace Foundation.

In time, that work produced the Inhalation Toxicology Research Institute, a Lovelace subsidiary which by the 1980s had established a worldwide reputation in its field. In addition, clinical research projects in a variety of fields—among them radiation therapy, cardiopulmonary physiology, audiology, and lung-lavage techniques—have been a constant element within the Foundation's research thrust since its inception.

In the special field of aerospace medicine the Lovelace Foundation and Clinic won special renown in the 1950s and 1960s. From Randy Lovelace's (and Sam White's) personal interest in aviation medicine came Foundation programs concerned with the effects of flying on human life, and by the early 1950s the Foundation was already extensively involved in testing and collecting data on test pilots. In 1952, the Foundation arranged a groundbreaking symposium to plan and coordinate research on manned flights toward the top of the atmosphere, and the proceedings of that conference, published as *Physics and Medicine of the Upper Atmosphere,*[28] quickly became a classic in the field. The acknowledged expertise of the Albuquerque institution in aerospace medicine resulted in its selection in 1958 by the National Aeronautics and Space Administration (NASA) to devise the test protocol, and then to examine the first group of test-pilot candidates for Project Mercury, this country's first manned space-flight effort. The selection of the still fairly obscure Southwestern clinic[29] as the site of the medical testing of the first astronauts was a public-relations coup of the first magnitude for the Lovelace center, as well as a mark of the sophistication of New Mexico medicine.

As of the mid-1960s, then, the Albuquerque medical center was decisively "on the map" and growing in size and influence, but an era suddenly ended when Randy Lovelace was killed in a private plane crash in December 1965. He was not yet fifty-eight years old, and not long before, he had been appointed director of space medicine for NASA by President Lyndon Johnson. More importantly, it was clear that he had not yet exhausted his store of energy and ideas and had not yet tired of his extraordinary responsibilities. With his loss, the Albuquerque institution that he had done so much to shape was forced unexpectedly to shift gears. His Uncle Doc, at age eighty-two, could not be expected to bear the burden

[28]Clayton S. White, ed., *Physics and Medicine of the Upper Atmosphere* (Albuquerque: University of New Mexico Press, 1953).

[29]The "obscurity" of the Lovelace Clinic can easily be exaggerated. From the time of its reorganization in the late forties, it was a member of the "Big Six," the informal association of the nation's leading clinics, even though it was significantly smaller than the other five.

of leadership within the elaborate medical complex that he had founded—he died three years later, in 1968—and no special plans had been made for a changing of the guard. However, over the subsequent two or three years, leadership emerged to guide the Foundation and clinic through the trying times of the late 1960s and the 1970s. From within the house Dr. White provided strong and insightful leadership for the research and educational work of the Foundation, and two clinicians, first the radiologist Dr. Jack Grossman and then the otolaryngologist Dr. Donald Kilgore, capably steered the clinic through the period, a time made enormously more demanding by the revolutionary changes under way in the American health-care system. And an "outsider," New Mexico oilman, rancher, and businessman Robert O. Anderson, stepped forward as trustee, and then as chairman of the Board of Trustees of the Foundation, giving invaluable advice and assistance to the institution. His importance to the Lovelace center in the two decades following the deaths of the founders cannot be overestimated.

Despite the intense pressures of the time and the considerable anxiety over the institution's future directions, Lovelace weathered the challenges of this period of adjustment. Medicare and massive government intervention in the health-care system in general; rampant inflation and soaring interest costs; increased competition at all levels of the health-care spectrum; revolutionary changes in medical technology and skyrocketing costs; the challenges of marketing and prepaid health-care plans; and a host of other factors made for kaleidoscopic change in the years from 1965 forward. Lovelace considered and adjusted, picking its way carefully through the turbulent health-care environment. For instance, research at the Foundation shifted slowly but certainly from the previous heavy concentration on aerospace medicine to the broad and attractive field of bioenvironmental research—especially studies in inhalation toxicology, airborne pollutants, and biodynamics—while clinical programs in cancer diagnosis and therapy escalated. The clinic, under Dr. Kilgore's direction, experimented with satellite clinics, pioneered in the development of a health maintenance organization, and began internal reorganization to cope with the changed environment of medical practice. Dr. Kilgore was also one of the central figures in the most significant (and delicate) development of the period, the merger of the clinic and hospital in 1972 to form the Lovelace Center for the Health Sciences. (In 1977, all facilities were incorporated under the Foundation as the Lovelace Medical Center.)

Additional changes accompanied the selection of Dr. David J. Ottensmeyer, a neurosurgeon and modern physician-executive, to head the institution in 1976. Initiating new programs designed to strengthen the institution's competitive position and its responsiveness to the needs of a varied clientele, Dr. Ottensmeyer set the Lovelace institution on new paths. Internally, he directed administrative tightening and reform, launched major new equipment-purchasing and building-improvement programs, and elaborated a long-term financial-planning capability for the center. The satellite clinic program begun by his predecessor was pushed forward energetically, and Lovelace extended its physical presence around the state with the establishment of associated group practices in Roswell, Gallup, and Grants. Most interestingly of all, Dr. Ottensmeyer steered Lovelace capably through the latest major transition of its six-decade history. In a landmark agreement with Hospital Corporation of America (HCA), the Lovelace Medical Foundation became a joint-venture partner of the national health-industry giant. The unique partnership with HCA constituted a daring approach to strengthening the Foundation's traditional programs in medical education and in health-care research, and it made possible the complete rebuilding of the Lovelace health-care facilities at the main site in Albuquerque. It was a bold move, but one consistent—Dr. Ottensmeyer argued—with "the tradition of enterprise and innovation that have characterized Lovelace since the days of Randy Lovelace and Uncle Doc."[30] Building on that foundation, Lovelace stood poised to meet the challenges of the end of the twentieth century.

No single event in New Mexico's modern medical history has been more important than the decision in the late 1950s to build a medical school in the state. The institution created, the University of New Mexico School of Medicine (UNM-SOM), opened in 1964. It immediately became a powerful force for change and growth within the state's health-care system. Its influence quickly radiated out from the Albuquerque campus to the most distant corners of the state, and it can be argued that its development and remarkable success are among the most important achievements of postwar New Mexico society.

The decision to build a medical school within so poor a state as New Mexico came about through the interplay between national forces and developments within the state itself. On the national scene, the late 1940s and 1950s witnessed the steady spread and growth of the conviction that the United States was heading toward an acute physician shortage. The

[30]Lovelace Foundation, *Annual Report, 1984*, p. 2.

postwar "baby boom" produced a spike in the nation's population growth, and public demand for medical services escalated and threatened to increase in almost geometric proportions. Meanwhile, medical school production of new physicians around the country remained essentially static, producing growing anxiety about access to medical care in the future. Articles with titles that read "Doctor Shortage Coming," "Where Are Tomorrow's Doctors," "More Physician Are Needed," and "Who Shall Be Our Doctors?" were commonplace in the national media.[31] The Eisenhower administration began to press for federal programs to assist the expansion of medical manpower output, and even the corporate guardian of the medical profession, the American Medical Association (AMA), came to agree on the need for more doctors. At its 1960 annual meeting the AMA's House of Delegates accepted the recommendation of its Board of Trustees that the organization do all it could to expand existing medical schools and "to help to identify universities where new ones should be built . . . quickly."[32]

This growing national consensus on the need for more physicians provided the general matrix within which two particular forces in New Mexico began to push for the establishment of a medical school. One of them was the cadre of young specialists who had flocked to the state in the late 1940s and throughout the 1950s. Trained in residency programs coordinated closely by medical schools and faculties and not resigned to separation from the mainstream of modern medical thought, research, and practice the medical schools represented, these specialists became influential advocates of a medical school for the state in the 1950s. There were still some fierce individualists who sneered at the idea that a medical school was needed. In their minds, any good doctor could drive into the Gila Wilderness and amputate a leg by flashlight with a pocket-knife without needing to call for the help of some medical school professor.[33] But the newer generation of specialists was eager to link its practice to academic medicine.[34]

[31] *U.S. News and World Report,* November 9, 1959; *Time,* June 20, 1960; *Christian Century,* July 29, 1959; and *Commentary,* June 1957.

[32] *Journal of the American Medical Association* 174 (22 October 1960):1000.

[33] This colorful characterization is that of Professor Robert Loftfield, Professor of Biochemistry at UNM-SOM and the first Chairman of the Biochemistry Department at the school. Interview with the author, Albuquerque, N.M., 20 July 1984.

[34] In the more than ninety interviews I have made with New Mexico physicians over the last three years, there was consistent emphasis on this point. See, among others, the in-

They found a powerful, strategically placed ally in Tom L. Popejoy, president of the University of New Mexico. If any figure can be singled out and cited as "the father of the medical school," it is surely he. Popejoy became personally interested and involved in the medical school question through his work in the Western Interstate Commission for Higher Education (WICHE), a thirteen-state consortium he helped to organize in 1951. WICHE was designed to allow its member states to share their scarce educational resources and to coordinate their educational and manpower planning for the future.[35] Throughout the 1950s Popejoy served as one of WICHE's governing commissioners and kept close tabs on its programs, particularly the student exchange programs the organization coordinated. Through one of those exchange arrangements, students from the eight Western states lacking medical schools (New Mexico, Arizona, Nevada, Montana, Idaho, Wyoming, Alaska, and Hawaii) were given special status within the medical schools of the other five. The individual students paid only in-state tuition rates, and their home states made lump-sum compensation payments (initially $2,000 for each medical student) to the host schools. New Mexico made good use of those exchange opportunities, and between 1951 and 1968 sent just over 100 medical students to Western medical schools under the WICHE program, the majority (80 percent) to the University of Colorado School of Medicine. Its participation ranged from 20 to 30 students per year (spread over all four medical school classes) in the 1950s to a high of 43 in the 1960–61 school year.[36] In that busiest year of the program the WICHE exchange cost the state of New Mexico just $85,000; thus it was a cheap way for the state to help some of its residents get medical education without the enormous expense of providing a medical school.

Quickly, however, it became clear that the WICHE system was no long-term solution to the problem of too few doctors for New Mexico. For one thing, as the demand for places in medical schools increased, the host medical schools within the WICHE consortium could set aside fewer

terviews with Fred Hanold, M.D., Albuquerque, 8 October 1984; Robert Friedenberg, M.D., Albuquerque, 21 February 1984; Robert C. Derbyshire, M.D., Santa Fe, 9 October 1982; Lawrence Wilkinson, M.D., Albuquerque, 23 and 30 May 1984; and Lewis M. Overton, M.D., Albuquerque, 16 December 1983 and 10 January 1984.

[35]For a good basic summary of WICHE in general and the student exchange programs it developed in particular, see Dorothy P. Buck, *The WICHE Student Exchange Program, 1953 to 1970* (Boulder, Colo.: Western Interstate Commission for Higher Education, 1970).

[36]Ibid., pp. 24, 77–79.

spaces for the exchange students from other Western states. A "closing door" phenomenon was evident. In a letter to a powerful New Mexico state legislator, President Popejoy cited figures which emphasized the problem. In the school year 1959–60 only 168 out-of-state students were admitted for the 8,128 first-year places in the nation's state-supported medical schools, about 2 percent of the total, and the regional picture was similarly gloomy despite the WICHE arrangement. The five medical schools of California, for example, had already closed their doors to WICHE exchange students, and the four state-supported schools in Oregon, Washington, Utah, and Colorado were almost sure to follow.[37] Popejoy drew his figures and much of his argument from a grimly pessimistic WICHE staff study titled *The West's Medical Manpower Needs* (Boulder, Colorado: WICHE, 1960), which warned of dire shortages of physicians in the West by the 1970s. It is clear that study exerted critical influence upon President Popejoy. He was an active member of WICHE's Medical Advisory Committee, which directed the two-year-long study,[38] and was alarmed by the report's grim forecast for New Mexico.[39] More than any other single factor, it was the WICHE study that persuaded Popejoy of the necessity for acting boldly, despite the state's limited population and economic resources, to provide for its future physician and other health-care needs. The WICHE student exchange program had been useful as a stopgap measure, but that door, too, was closing. In addition, ten years of experience showed that the New Mexico residents who went off to school in Colorado or California were much more likely to set up their practices there than to return to New Mexico.[40]

Through 1959 and 1960, Tom Popejoy worked steadily toward establishment of a medical school at UNM, making his way carefully over the various hurdles to be negotiated and lining up the several constituencies

[37]Tom L. Popejoy to The Honorable Fabian Chavez, Senate Majority Leader, 13 February 1961, in UNM Medical Center Library, Medical History Archives, "UNM-SOM, Historical Archives."

[38]The other New Mexico members of the study committee were two influential physicians of the Lovelace Clinic staff, Drs. Randy Lovelace II and Robert U. Massey.

[39]"New Mexico's ratio of doctors to population is already lowest in the West and one of the lowest in the country and is almost certain to decline further by 1975" (p. 64).

[40]Of the 101 New Mexicans who left the state to study medicine as WICHE exchange students between 1953 and 1969, only 19 had returned to the state to set up their practices by 1970. Buck, *WICHE Student Exchange*, pp. 77–79. Among those who returned home to serve in their native states were such well-known physicians as Drs. P. G. Cornish III, Thomas H. Follingstad, Phillip U. Martinez, and John B. Roberts.

involved in the issue. He realized that the cost of the project was certain to be a major concern to many around the state and was therefore on the lookout for ways of reducing the financial strain associated with creation of a medical school. Through Dr. Ward Darley, Executive Director of the Association of American Medical Colleges,[41] President Popejoy learned that the W. K. Kellogg Foundation of Battle Creek, Michigan, was developing a grant-in-aid program to assist in the establishment of new medical schools in this country. The Foundation would provide seed money for planning and organizational purposes and to assist in the basic construction necessary for the establishment of new two-year schools of the basic medical sciences. Traditionally the first two years of medical school were focused on the study of the basic medical sciences, while the last two years were devoted to the clinical sciences, to "hands-on" learning in clinical settings. Since there was considerable attrition over the first two years of medical school, the logic of the two-year medical schools was straightforward: their graduates could transfer into the vacant spaces in the third-year classes of the full-scale four-year medical schools. In the late 1950s, two-year medical schools were already operating successfully at the state universities of both North and South Dakota and at Dartmouth University, so the concept itself was not new. Popejoy's preliminary discussions with the Kellogg authorities convinced him this outside money could be exploited to reduce the strain associated with start-up of a new two-year medical school in New Mexico,[42] hence he pushed ahead with planning for the school. In May of 1959, he won preliminary approval of the University's Board of Regents for detailed investigation of the subject, and a few months later successfully maneuvered the idea through the critical and potentially hostile Faculty Policy Committee.[43]

[41]Dr. Darley had served as a consultant to the WICHE Medical Advisory Committee mentioned above. He was already familiar to many New Mexico physicians and educators as a former Dean of the University of Colorado medical school and as one of the founding trustees of the Lovelace Medical Foundation. He was a crucial link to national sources of support and encouragement such as the AMA's Council on Medical Education and, of course, the Association of American Medical Colleges.

[42]Wilkinson, interview, Albuquerque, 30 May 1984 and University of New Mexico, Faculty Minutes, 12 April 1960. In the early 1960s the Kellogg Foundation served as financial midwife to three new two-year medical schools—UNM, Rutgers University, and the University of Connecticut—and assisted in the expansion of a fourth (Dartmouth). The University of New Mexico was the largest single beneficiary of its efforts, ultimately receiving more than 1.3 million dollars from the Foundation.

Simultaneously Popejoy enlisted the aid of influential figures within the New Mexico Medical Society, including its then president Dr. Lewis Overton of Albuquerque, Drs. Lawrence Wilkinson and Fred Hanold, also of Albuquerque, and Santa Fe's Dr. Robert Derbyshire, among others, to begin lobbying within that important constituency for the medical school.[44]

In mid-February 1960, a Liaison Committee formed of representatives of the Association of American Medical Colleges and the Council on Medical Education of the AMA visited Albuquerque at President Popejoy's invitation. They evaluated the potential for a medical school at UNM and urged approval of one. The external experts were impressed first of all with the strong commitment of the University itself to the proposal—faculty, administration, and board of regents—a result, of course, of President Popejoy's skillful handling of the issue within the university community.[45] Further, in language undoubtedly selected with care, the report alluded to "the apparent full support of the medical profession in the county and state."[46] There was, in fact, considerable opposition to the creation of a medical school, especially within the Albuquerque medical community, but it was largely muted and restricted to doctors' lounge and lockerroom grumblings.[47] Some doctors were fearful of the economic threat that a medical school and, eventually, a university hospital would pose. Others were simply jealous of the almost complete independence and elite status they possessed in the absence of a powerful medical school, and a larger number still were honestly worried about the cost to their poor state of a medical school. Officially, however, all these doubts and reservations were unexpressed, and at its annual May meeting in 1960 the New Mexico Medical Society went on record endorsing the creation of a two-year medical school at UNM.[48]

[43]Wilkinson, interview, Albuquerque, 30 May 1984. Many within the university, including its powerful former Graduate Dean and Academic Vice-President Dr. France V. Scholes, were fearful the financial requirements of a medical school would drain scarce resources away from the university's other programs.

[44]Overton, interview, Albuquerque, 10 January 1984, and others, and University of New Mexico, Faculty Minutes, 12 April 1960.

[45]The report of that liaison committee is conveniently summarized in a lengthy newspaper article, "Popejoy Cites Need of U. Med. School," in the 2 April 1960 edition of the *Albuquerque Journal.* The full report is available in UNM, Faculty Minutes, 12 April 1960.

[46]Ibid.

[47]Simms, Hanold, Wilkinson, and other interviews.

[48]New Mexico Medical Society, Annual Meeting, Minutes, 10 May 1960, as printed in *Rocky Mountain Medical Journal,* 57, no. 9 (1960):80.

With the University faculty and administration in line and the State Medical Society as an ally,[49] Popejoy turned his attention to the last two constituencies whose approval had to be won before the two-year medical school could become a reality, namely the University's Board of Regents and the state legislature. In his discussions with the Regents, Popejoy had a powerful and dedicated ally in Albuquerque surgeon Dr. Lawrence Wilkinson. Another in a long line of Texas-born and educated physicians to contribute importantly to New Mexico medicine, Dr. Wilkinson was a prominent member of that generation of ambitious young specialists who came to New Mexico just after the Second World War. Setting up his general surgery practice in 1948 at the old Santa Fe Railway Hospital at the invitation of a service friend, Dr. James Wiggins, then also on the railroad hospital staff, Dr. Wilkinson quickly established himself as a powerful and respected force in Albuquerque medicine. In 1959 Governor John Burroughs appointed him to the Board of Regents at the University of New Mexico, and in the critical year 1961 Dr. Wilkinson was president of that body. President Popejoy quickly enlisted the wholehearted support of the surgeon in the attempt to found a medical school, and Wilkinson did yeoman's work lobbying among his fellow physicians—"pleading in the hospital halls for the idea"—and as presiding officer of the University's oversight board.[50]

In dealing with the Board of Regents and later the state legislature, President Popejoy's trump card was the announcement in May 1960, by the Kellogg Foundation of a five-year 1.082-million-dollar grant to assist New Mexico in its endeavor to build a two-year medical school. More than half the grant was for the planning phases of the venture and for the first five years of its operational budget, including salaries of administrative and instructional personnel, and the remainder was dedicated toward construction of a basic medical sciences building.[51] The Kellogg

[49]The doubters within the medical community were so hushed that a few years later, President Robert P. Beaudette of the State Medical Society could assert, "The New Mexico Medical Society . . . is justifiably proud in having been the prime mover and influence in the establishment of the medical school." Robert P. Beaudette, M.D., "Presidential Address [to the Annual Meeting of the New Mexico Medical Society]," *Rocky Mountain Medical Journal* 63, no. 9 (1966):67.

[50]"Dr. Wilkinson: Key Man in Med School History," *Albuquerque Tribune*, 10 February 1971. For biographical material on Dr. Wilkinson, see his personal file in the UNM Medical Center Library Medical History Archives and the transcript of the Wilkinson interview.

[51]*Journal of the American Medical Association* 173 (4 June 1960):551–52.

money was the vitally needed start-up funds from the outside, which would enable New Mexico to begin without draining its own, limited resources. It was a key element in Popejoy's persuasion of the University regents and with the state's legislature, a skeptical body acutely concerned about the financial realities of the proposal.

Doubters abounded in both houses of the New Mexico legislature. Virtually no one questioned the desirability and utility of a medical school, but many questioned the capacity of the state to support one. The issue cut across party lines, and fiscal conservatives of both parties shook their heads and dug in their heels. They were encouraged in their opposition by representatives speaking for the other state institutions of higher learning who were anxious about the effects of so great a financial commitment on their own schools.[52] President Popejoy was aided enormously in discussions with the legislature by the commitment to the medical school of the powerful Speaker of the House of Representatives, the capable Roswell lawyer and future governor Jack M. Campbell. Campbell, concerned throughout his career with establishing a solid scientific and technological foundation for the future development of the state, became leader of the fight for the medical school in the legislature's lower house. (At one crucial juncture in the spring legislative session of 1961, he had to use his personal influence and persuasiveness to get a bill supporting the medical school from an absolutely deadlocked Appropriations Committee.) The Senate was also divided on the question, and only after Majority Leader Fabian Chavez of Santa Fe was convinced to support the proposal did an initial appropriation for $25,000 manage to squeak through that body.[53] Though the enthusiasm of the state legislature was hardly overwhelming, President Popejoy got what he wanted: the Santa Fe lawmakers and keepers of the state purse had agreed to support his two-year school.

From his diplomatic tour de force in winning approval for the basic sciences medical school, President Popejoy turned to the job of organizing it. He entrusted responsibility for that task to an Associate Dean at the University of Colorado College of Medicine, Dr. Reginald Fitz, whom

[52]Former Governor Jack M. Campell, interview with the author, Albuquerque, N.M., 25 October 1985.

[53]Appropriation Committees in both the House and Senate narrowly approved the expenditure for the medical school. Popejoy originally asked the legislature for a $100,000 appropriation, but settled for the lesser figure when the strength of the opposition became obvious.

Popejoy handpicked for the challenge of starting a medical school from scratch. Dr. Fitz proved a brilliantly successful choice for the job. He knew medical schools from the inside through years of exposure to them—both his father and grandfather had been deans of medicine at Harvard—and was well-connected nationally within the world of medicine. As a bonus, he was familiar with New Mexico and many New Mexicans from his years in Colorado. Most important of all, he had vision and inspired images of what might be in those with whom he worked. Looking back on the birth of the medical school two decades after the fact, his colleagues were unanimous in according Fitz great credit for the courage to dream.[54] Where they quite reasonably saw empty, unattractive mesa-land dotted with scrubby desert plants and tumbleweeds, he envisioned buildings and a bustling medical center, and he was able to communicate that excitement and special joy of being "present at the creation" to those whom he recruited for the experiment. His successor (once-removed) as Dean of the medical school, Dr. Leonard Napolitano, wryly summed up Fitz's special gift:

> He had a lot of the missionary in him and differed from most deans we had known. He was a remarkable judge of horse flesh in terms of the people he recruited. He had a vision and experience that was different from most of those he attracted in terms of what, inevitably, was going to come about. At that time, most of us had a much smaller vision. He'd have an architect come in and would say, "We're just long-range planning here, but this is what we think is going to transpire on north campus," and then he'd lay out the most extraordinary description of what was to be. Everybody thought he was smoking opium or something. But a significant portion of that has become a reality, in addition to some things that even he had not thought about.[55]

Arriving in Albuquerque in the summer of 1961, Dr. Fitz began the job of arranging physical facilities for the school and recruiting a faculty. The Kellogg grant provided a solid start toward construction of a modern basic sciences building, and that seed money was supplemented by federal government money of more than 3 million dollars under the Health Re-

[54]Interviews with Drs. Sidney Solomon, Albuquerque, N.M., 7 September 1984; Leonard Napolitano, Albuquerque, 12 September and 15 October 1984; Leroy McLaren, Albuquerque, 13 September 1984; Robert Anderson, Albuquerque, 5 September 1984; Thomas McConnell, Albuquerque, 22 August 1984; the Loftfield interview, cited earlier; and others.

[55]Napolitano, interview, Albuquerque, 12 September 1984.

search Facilities Act. Those funds, combined with a state investment of 1.6 million dollars, made the Basic Medical Sciences building a reality in relatively sort order (1967), but for the first years the new school had to make do with the facilities already on hand. Initially, all that were available were two recently purchased commercial buildings adjacent to the site of the projected new building. The larger of these was an old Seven-Up Company bottling plant, and the other had most recently been in use as the Exter-Tonella mortuary.[56] These structures were hastily remodeled, but Dean Fitz needed all the imagination he could muster in describing his physical plant to prospective faculty members.

Despite the constraints of his physical plant and the miscellaneous uncertainties inherent in the whole operation, Dean Fitz was remarkably successful in quickly assembling the nucleus of an excellent faculty. As anchors, he induced two distinguished scholar-physicians to join the new school. One was Dr. Solomon Papper, a nationally known nephrologist on the faculty of the Medical College of Virginia, who joined the organizing school in Albuquerque as its Chairman of the Department of Medicine, and the other was Dr. James S. Clarke, a member of the faculty at the UCLA Medical Center. Dr. Clarke, a figure of national repute in his field, became the new school's first Chairman of the Department of Surgery. Around Drs. Papper and Clarke, Dean Fitz assembled a stellar cast of ambitious, hard-driving young academicians—Ph.D.s and physicians who became the bedrock on which the UNM medical school was built. Robert Loftfield as head of biochemistry; Leroy McLaren and Joseph Scaletti in microbiology; and Sidney Solomon as chairman of physiology not only brought impeccable professional credentials and important ongoing research programs with them to the Albuquerque campus, but they remained committed to the dream. All were still on the faculty twenty years later. So, too, were the original "seconds-in-command" of the pathology and anatomy departments, Drs. Robert Anderson and Leonard Napolitano, serving in the mid-1980s as Chairman of Pathology and Dean of the Medical School, respectively. Dr. Robert S. Stone, the first chairman of pathology and Fitz's successor as dean of the school, contributed enormously to the infant institution then moved on to other professional

[56]Those two basic buildings—still in use, though several times remodeled—were supplemented by a handful of temporary structures for use as laboratories, classrooms, and other purposes. See University of New Mexico, *Annual Report, 1963/64*, "University of New Mexico School of Medicine Annual Report," pp. 4–5.

challenges, as did Dr. Aaron Ladman, first chairman of the department of anatomy. But the power of the dream conceived by Popejoy, Fitz, Wilkinson, and others is reflected in the remarkable continuity in place over a long period of time of so many of the original faculty members.[57] The success of the entire venture was due in large measure to the talent and dedication of the original faculty members.

Those first faculty who created the new school and, by their hard work, made it a success came to New Mexico for a variety of reasons, but two special ones stand out. The challenge of "making something from nothing," was a powerful inducement in the decision of many of them. On a dusty mesa graced by a bottling plant, a mortuary, some Butler buildings, and a high, blue sky, they were going to make a medical school. It was, when all was said and done, a nervy enterprise, but most of the original faculty members were young scholars just approaching their professional primes, and the challenge of starting from scratch appealed to them. For some of them the Albuquerque experiment was the opportunity to express their creative impulse, to be builders. There was a special excitement to the realization that, in the complete absence of "givens," whatever came to be would be one's own doing. Others came more simply at the call of opportunity. As they looked up the academic ladder in the institutions where they found themselves, impatience seized them, and the University of New Mexico became a quicker route to the top, to being one's own man, making one's own mistakes.[58]

More important still was the unique pedagogical approach projected for the new school. Dean Fitz, despite being literally reared in the halls of medical schools, was an academic reformer impatient with the conventions and traditions of medical education. He consciously set out to recruit reformers, men and women like himself dissatisfied with the status quo of medical schools. From the very beginning, the University of New Mexico School of Medicine was committed to innovation and experi-

[57]For detailed information regarding all these original faculty members, see their personal files in the UNM Medical Center Library's Medical History Archives and the interviews with Loftfield, McLaren, Solomon, Napolitano, Anderson, Dr. Walter Winslow (Albuquerque, N.M., 17 July 1984), Dr. Thomas McConnell (Albuquerque, 22 August 1984), Dr. Alice Cushing (Albuquerque, 10 July 1984), and others. See also Carolyn R. Tinker, "The Missionaries," *Salud* [a publication of the UNM Medical Center] Winter 1985, pp. 6–9.

[58]See the interviews with the early faculty members, all of whom acknowledged the importance of this psychology to greater or lesser degree. See particularly those with Loftfield, Napolitano, Winslow, and Anderson.

mentation in medical education. A few years after the school's opening, Dean Fitz and his Associate Dean, Dr. Robert S. Stone, described the latitude given the founders by University authorities:

> [The immediate assignment was] to establish a functioning school of the basic medical sciences which would, at an undetermined time, become a four-year, degree awarding School of Medicine. Beyond this primary assignment and responsibility, and the implicit necessity that the School meet accreditation standards and adhere to the academic, administrative, and fiscal regulations governing University operations, there were no restrictions.[59]

This freedom to rethink and restructure the process of medical education was probably the single most important element among the many operating to attract faculty members to the new school.[60] This was the most essential element in the excitement Dean Fitz and his cohorts were able to generate about the new school.

Fitz summarized the new pedagogical thinking of the New Mexico medical school innovators in clear terms:

> If the trend to broaden the base for scientific research by cutting across traditional disciplinary lines were essential to research, it should be accompanied by a similar movement in education. Within the setting of medical education, if interdisciplinary research were to be furthered, then the base for medical education should be interdisciplinary as well.[61]

The Western Reserve University School of Medicine had pioneered in medical school curriculum reform a decade earlier, and the New Mexico planners were quick to acknowledge their debt to the Ohio pioneers. But the new school in Albuquerque was going to be different from that model; it was going to begin as a fully interdisciplinary enterprise with the expectation that the flexibility and openness inherent in that approach would become the ethos of the institution. There was even consideration of eliminating traditional departmental structure in the new school.[62]

[59]Reginald H. Fitz, M.D., and Robert S. Stone, M.D., "New Medical Education in the Old Southwest," in Hans Popper, ed., *Trends in New Medical Schools* (New York and London: Grune and Stratton, 1967), p. 94.

[60]Again, one after another the interviews with the founders of the medical school support this judgment.

[61]Fitz and Stone, "New Medical Education," p. 95.

[62]Ibid.

As Fitz expected, the resolution to be different, to be cross-disciplinary in an organic way, proved attractive to many medical educators, especially the young to early middle-aged group referred to above. (It also frightened away some.) Much of the joy and satisfaction remembered by the founders from those early days stemmed from the brainstorming and intensive interaction required in devising the new curriculum. In small, informal groups they discused their ideas over lunch or sitting around a swimming pool or a poker table. The curriculum they produced did indeed reject the traditional compartmentalization of the program—with individual courses in anatomy, biochemistry, physiology, and so on—and instead embodied the integration of knowledge and effort they so prized. In what has come to be called the organ system or bloc system approach to medical education, individual subjects were presented and analyzed with the several basic medical sciences contributing their particular perspectives to the effort. A simple living thing like the erythrocyte or red blood cell, for example, could be examined in terms of its morphology, biochemistry, histology, physiology, and so forth, with the student being exposed to many of the fundamental principles, insights, and technologies of those disciplines in a concrete, "real world" context rather than as abstractions. At the macrocosmic level the approach could be applied to complex systems, such as the cardiovascular one, with the gross anatomy of the system studied prior to its interdisciplinary examination involving microscopic anatomy, physiology, biochemistry, and introductory clinical physiology.[63] The new approach had the added advantages of flexibility and "freshness," and students readily sensed and responded to the faculty's excitement in working with the new model.

As the physical facilities on north campus began to take shape and faculty recruitment accelerated, the builders of the medical school found another vitally important ally in Dr. Chester Kurtz and the Veterans Hospital in Albuquerque. The hospital had been founded in 1932 as a general hospital with a special focus on care of tuberculars and by the early 1960s had grown into a pillar of the New Mexico medical establishment, a 500-plus-bed institution twice the size of any other hospital in the state.[64] By the early 1960s, the Veterans Hospital had well-developed

[63]For a detailed explanation of the new curriculum, see ibid., pp. 96–100. For a delightful, lively description of it which captures the enthusiasm of its creators, see Loftfield, interview, Albuquerque, 20 July 1984.

[64]The single exception to this statement was the special case of the 1,150-bed New Mexico State Hospital in Las Vegas for the mentally ill.

residency programs in medicine and general surgery and, as per Veterans Administration regulations, had affiliated itself as a teaching hospital under the supervision of a Dean's Committee of the University of Colorado School of Medicine. In 1962, at a critical time in the development of the new basic sciences school at UNM, Dr. Chester Kurtz was appointed Hospital Director of the federal institution in Albuquerque. Dr. Kurtz, a 1927 graduate of Harvard's medical school, had spent nearly thirty years in the private practice of cardiology in Madison, Wisconsin, before joining the VA, and had served for more than a quarter-century on the faculty at the University of Wisconsin Medical School in Madison.[65] He understood medical schools from lengthy exposure to them and proved a vitally important friend to the organizing school in Albuquerque. Most directly, he helped the medical school planners build their staff by adding prospective faculty members to his staff at the VA Hospital, by "loaning" staff members already in place for teaching duties at the new school, and by facilitating the transfer of the VA Hospital and its teaching programs from the University of Colorado School of Medicine to the developing Albuquerque school. Without so sympathetic and experienced an ally, the organization of the UNM two-year school—and its later expansion to four years—would have been considerably more costly and difficult than it was.

The new medical school opened its doors in early September 1964, with twenty-four students, a handpicked group whom many faculty members remembered as a special group in more ways than one. They were not only first, but they were also an especially dedicated group. Some of them had been in a kind of suspended animation ever since the announcement in the early 1960s that a new, innovative medical school would be created by UNM. Many of them had been marking time, waiting for the opportunity.[66] With a faculty/student ratio of roughly one to one, those earliest students benefited from the personal attention of their professors and from the special electricity associated with the faculty's effort to put together and make work the new curriculum.[67] Very soon, however, anxieties began to develop within the new school. Specifically, the members

[65]Personal file, "Chester M. Kurtz" in UNM Medical Center Library, Medical History Archives and Chester M. Kurtz, M.D., interview with the author, Albuquerque, N.M., 4 October 1985.

[66]See particularly on this point the interviews with Loftfield, McConnell, and Kurtz.

[67]For the recollections of some of those first students, see Jean Hansen, "It Was the First Day of Classes," *Salud*, Winter 1985, pp. 3–5.

of that first class began to worry about the practicalities and details of transferring from the two-year school in New Mexico to a four-year school elsewhere, and the pioneer faculty members began to rethink the prospects and structure of the two-year school. Not just in New Mexico, but all across the nation a basic reevaluation of the viability and functionality of two-year basic medical sciences schools was already under way. The weaknesses of the two-year school concept were becoming apparent. In the first place, the two-year schools had difficulty competing for students with four-year ones, because the latter could guarantee greater security to their students. Second, the reevaluation made it clear that two-year medical schools contributed little toward attracting new physicians to a locale, since statistics showed that M.D.s tended to settle in states where they did their residencies and internships, not necessarily where they got their first two years of medical schooling. In addition, two-year schools had serious problems in building and expanding the resources available to them, since the alumni connection to the two-year schools where they started their medical educations was demonstrably weak. Finally, two-year basic science schools, which by definition had limited clinical programs, contributed little to the continuing education of practicing physicians and to the elevation of standards of local practice.[68]

From the very beginning there had been no confusion about the fact that the ultimate objective on north campus was a four-year medical school. All the various constituencies involved—the University, the state's physicians as represented by the state medical society, the legislature, and so forth—were committed to the idea that the two-year school should be preliminary to a full-scale one, but no one expected the transition to come so quickly as it did. Only a few months into the second year of operation of the two-year basic medical sciences school, discussion began concerning its expansion into a full four-year institution. Both national and local factors stimulated the discussion.[69] Nationally the consensus had grown rapidly in the early 1960s that, for the reasons described above, two-year medical schools should be expanded to four-year entities as

[68]On all these points see James M. Faulkner, *Opportunity for Medical Education in Idaho, Montana, Nevada, and Wyoming* (Boulder, Colo.: WICHE, 1964), pp. 46–49.

[69]The most thorough discussion available of the expansion issue is found in a position paper in which Dean Fitz spelled out the logic for transition to a four-year school: "Proposed Four-Year Program for the School of Medicine," submitted to the University faculty on 16 December 1965. University of New Mexico, Faculty Minutes, Agenda for Meeting of 16 December 1965, dated 10 December 1965.

rapidly as possible. This change of mind took tangible form in the rapid proliferation of federal government programs for the assistance of medical education in the 1960s and the expansion of existing ones. As examples, the Health Research Facilities Act of 1956 with its numerous extensions and expansions aided enormously in construction of the Basic Medical Sciences Building at UNM, the pivot around which the medical school revolved. It was followed by the Health Professions Educational Assistance Act of 1963, establishing a three-year program of matching federal grants for construction and rehabilitation of teaching facilities for medical and related professional schools and a six-year loan program for students; the extension and expansion in the early 1960s of the Hill-Burton Act, which made possible the enlargement and improvement of clinical facilities at the already existent Bernalillo County–Indian Hospital; the Mental Retardation Facilities and Community Mental Health Centers Construction Act of 1963, which funded development of the UNM Mental Health Center; and other pieces of federal government legislation which emphatically encouraged the transformation of New Mexico's two-year school. The impression was clear that New Mexico would be "penny-wise, but pound foolish" if it ignored these federal government inducements to expand.[70] There is little doubt, then, of the centrality of federal government policies and programs in accelerating markedly the pace of change in Albuquerque.

On campus, too, there was growing recognition that the objectives which had animated the birth of the two-year school could be achieved most expeditiously through a four-year, full medical school. It was more than just the growing anxiety of students facing the necessity for transferring. Faculty, too, quickly recognized the inherent limitations of the two-year concept and began an intensive campaign to persuade President Popejoy to push on to the four-year school.[71] This battle was readily won, and the approval of the legislature followed soon thereafter, with Gov-

[70]This argument (among others) is made in a letter from then Governor Jack M. Campbell to President Popejoy, dated 2 November 1965, in which the governor strongly encouraged Popejoy to approach the legislature for approval of the school's expansion. The UNM president was apparently hesitant because of his honest promises 4 1/2 years earlier that he did not expect expansion of the medical school for a considerable period of time. Letter, Gov. Jack M. Campbell, to Pres. Tom Popejoy, 2 November 1965, in UNM Medical Center Library, Medical History Archives, "UNM-SOM: Historical File."

[71]The Loftfield interview provides interesting details of the conversion of President Popejoy. (Interview, Albuquerque, 20 July 1984.)

ernor Campbell's office providing the legislative leadership and much of the backing.[72] It therefore developed that that first class admitted to the new two-year school of basic medical sciences at UNM in September 1964, never had to leave the campus at all. In June of 1968 nineteen of that class's original twenty-four members received their Doctor of Medicine degrees as the first products of the full-fledged University of New Mexico School of Medicine.

Over the first two decades of the school's operation, crises and problems were relatively few and manageable while achievements were noteworthy. There was a period of anxiety in late 1967 and early in 1968 when the founding dean Dr. Fitz stepped down from his post amidst growing criticism of his administrative style. He was the leader whose vision and confidence had done so much to get the experiment under way; naturally enough, uncertainty arose about how the school might fare without him.[73] The uneasiness intensified later that year when Dr. Solomon Papper, the highly respected Chairman of the Department of Medicine, also chose to leave the school. Dr. Papper had been prominent in criticism of the Fitz regime and found it expedient to leave himself soon after the naming of a new dean. The storm was weathered, however, partially as a result of the quiet, skillful leadership of Dr. Fitz's successor, Dr. Robert S. Stone, the original chairman of the school's Department of Pathology. Dr. Stone's five years as Dean (1968–73) were characterized by collegial leadership and strong, efficient administration, and when he left the school in 1973 to become Director of the National Institutes of Health his legacy to UNM-SOM, like that of his predecessor, was unquestionably solid and positive. The school's third Dean, Dr. Leonard Napolitano, was also one of the founding fathers, having come in 1964 as the second member of the school's anatomy department. Dean Napolitano was something of a maverick figure in the circles of medical education—a basic scientist, not an M.D., who headed a medical school—and was remarkable as well by the sheer length of his tenure. He succeeded Dr. Stone as Dean in 1973 and was still in place a dozen years later in the mid-eighties, this at a time when nationally the tenure of medical school deans stood at a half

[72]There were some in the legislature, however, who felt they had been deceived by the rapid change in the medical school. See the letter from State Senator Edmundo Delgado (Santa Fe) to Dean Robert S. Stone, UNM-SOM, 8 July 1969, held in UNM Medical Center Library, Medical History Archives, "UNM-SOM: Historical File."

[73]Fitz did get to see his first class graduate, but just barely. The first graduation ceremonies were in early June 1968, and his resignation was effective later than month.

dozen or so years. Dr. Napolitano proved specially adept at dealing with the state legislature, whose consistent support was central to the school's growth and expanding services, and was able to keep harmony within the house, providing firm, consistent direction for an institution restless with the energy of adolescence. Strong, constructive leadership, then, marked the first two decades of the new school's history.

So, too, did a tradition of innovation. Though the school adopted much of the basic structure and organization of traditional medical schools, it managed to preserve its openness to experimentation. This was reflected in a number of ways, most notably in an abiding interest in curriculum reform. The new approach to medical education fashioned by the founders in 1964—the organ system approach taught through a "bloc" organization and stressing the interrelatedness of medical knowledge—in time became something of a new convention itself. In the mid-1970s, then, interested faculty with the blessing of the school's administration and the tangible assistance, again, of the W. K. Kellogg Foundation began to develop a still newer approach to medical education they called the Primary Care Curriculum.[74] This approach stressed individual study and small tutorial groups in studying the basic medical sciences (instead of attendance at lectures) and exposed the student very early on to the daily routine and problems of patient care. (As early as the first year of medical school, Primary Care Curriculum students were working—for four months at a stretch—with physician preceptors outside Albuquerque.) This new program was formally inaugurated in 1979 and graduated its first students in 1983. Thus, from the end of the seventies, students entering UNM's School of Medicine had this optional approach to medical education, the choice reflecting the school's continuing commitment to making medical education fit the students and their objectives, not vice versa. The school also became a pioneer in expanding medical school opportunities for women and minority students, its record in those spheres outshining those of the very great majority of schools around the country.

At the end of two decades of operation, the UNM School of Medicine could cite a long list of solid achievements. If the school had been founded

[74]On the Primary Care Curriculum see Napolitano and Tinker, "The University of New Mexico School of Medicine":467; "Growing and Changing, 1964–1985," *Salud*, Winter 1985, p. 11; Charlotte Beyers, "Students Get a Taste of Practice Early in Training," *American Medical News*, 25 September 1981, pp. 33–34; and a description edited by one of its architects, Arthur Kaufman, M.D., ed., *Implementing Problem-Based Medical Education: Lessons from Successful Innovations* (New York: Springer, 1985).

fundamentally to produce physicians for doctor-short New Mexico, it had certainly fulfilled that objective. With fewer than twenty graduating classes, it had produced 837 M.D.s, 152 of whom had completed their postgraduate training and set up practice in New Mexico. (Others among that 837 were still outside the state in internship or residency training, but intending to return to New Mexico to practice.) More numerically important were the approximately 500 postgraduate fellows and former house officers practicing in the state who came to New Mexico to work in one or another of the training programs sponsored and supervised by the medical school. One can postulate a crude balance between the number of young M.D.s educated at the UNM-SOM who were lost to the state by going to practice elsewhere and the number of non-UNM M.D.s lured to the state by the medical school's sixteen residency programs and other house officer training opportunities. By 1980, as noted earlier in this chapter, New Mexico's supply of doctors was slightly better than the national average, and the medical school's contribution to that change is undeniable.

In addition to boosting the number of physicians in the state, the school also had great impact on the quality of practice as well. Though the standard of medical practice in New Mexico had always been higher than its weak economy and frontier character might have suggested—primarily as a function of the tuberculosis phenomenon—the young medical school quickly became the focus and vital stimulus for improving medical practice throughout the state. It played a major role in providing continuing education programs for the state's physician corps and generally established high expectations by example for the physicians of the region. Doctors around the state acknowledged its beneficent effect on the general level of medical practice statewide.[75] In addition, the medical school served as a referral center providing services not readily available in cities and towns scattered around the countryside. The Burn and Trauma Unit, established at UNM Hospital; the school's large and impressive Cancer Center; the Children's Psychiatic Hospital associated with the Bernalillo County Mental Health Center on the medical school campus; and the school's highly respected kidney transplant team were just some of the specialized services provided by the UNM-SOM as part of its multifaceted service to its New Mexico constituency.

[75]The ninety-plus interviews with physicians around New Mexico made as part of the preparation for this study are uniform on this point. See, as one example, the interview with Dr. Ashley Pond, Taos, N.M., 5 September 1983.

Nor did the school neglect its more general obligation to the world of medical scholarship at large, for, though much has been said here of its contributions to medical education, it has played an important role in medical research as well. Its active, on-going research programs have focused particularly in immunobiology, cell biology, arthritis and rheumatology studies, aging, cancer therapy, and the treatment of diabetes. One of its more promising programs involved the development and clinical testing of an insulin delivery system featuring an implantable pump controlled by an external, handheld device. Despite its distance from major "research corridors," the researchers of New Mexico's medical school remained true to the founders' dream twenty years ago that good teaching could not exist apart from good research. The commitment of those founders—to progressive medical education, innovative research, and top quaity health-care delivery—quickly made the improbable institution they created a central force in New Mexico medicine.

During this time of sweeping change in New Mexico medicine, the organization which spoke for doctors of medicine in the state was transformed, too. Throughout the first six decades of its existence, the New Mexico Medical Society had been a low-key, loosely organized, almost "clubby" association of the state's physicians. It had real tangibility only once in every year—when its annual meeting was held—and for the rest of the year its work and influence depended entirely on the energy and commitment of its officers. However well-intentioned these latter may have been, they were busy practitioners themselves and could hardly afford to take large chunks of time from their practices to devote to society work. Nor were they really expected to. It is clear that election to office within the society was more a badge of honor than anything else, a recognition of service and distinction within the world of practice. The officers of the state society, indeed the organization itself, were not really expected to do anything in particular. The annual gathering of the society provided opportunity enough to review matters of collegial concern and afforded a vehicle for joint action when circumstances demanded it. From time to time committees were appointed to study particular problems, but their charges were usually tightly circumscribed and their reports perfunctory, probably indicative of the level of their efforts. It is only a slight exaggeration to call the pre-WWII New Mexico Medical Society an invisible institution. It served some social and educational purposes and on occasion exerted modest political influence, but its effectiveness and meaningfulness in those early years were severely limited.

This insubstantiality of the organization is not surprising, for under the prevailing circumstances it could hardly have been otherwise. The size of New Mexico, the dispersal of physicians across it, and the relative primitiveness of early twentieth-century communications all made coordination and interaction among the state's physicians difficult. Just as important was the traditional free agent status of the doctor; in many respects he was the exemplar of early twentieth-century rugged individualism. Further, there were few obvious threats to the profession that might have precipitated joint action, and thus New Mexico physicians before World War II were little interested in investing time, energy, and money (always in short supply) in a dynamic state medical society. After the licensure worry of the century's early years had been satisfactorily resolved, the New Mexico Medical Society lapsed back into its perfunctory, largely ceremonial routines. The only issue that came close to shaking it from its torpor was the danger of state medicine that cropped up in the 1930s, but even that initially provoked relatively little response.

Several interlocking developments of the late 1940s shook the New Mexico Medical Society from its traditional inactivity and forced its reorganization. One was the rapidly rising number of doctors in the state. So long as New Mexico's physician population was small and stable, the casual, informal communication and coordination effected through the prewar medical society served the state's doctors reasonably well. However, many new doctors were introduced to New Mexico through military service during the war, and a sizable number of them decided to stay (or return) after it was over. They were reinforced by other young doctors whose start in private practice had been delayed by military service, and this influx of newcomers constituted a major change within New Mexico's physician community. But the change was more than mere numbers. Many of the new doctors were representatives of the "new wave" in medicine, namely the residency-trained specialists eager to claim leadership within the profession and slightly disdainful of the "country doctors" who still constituted the majority of the profession and dominated institutions like the New Mexico Medical Society. They were impatient with the inconsequentiality of the slow-paced, passive state society in New Mexico, especially since many of them during their training years in the East or Midwest had seen what could be achieved through efficiently organized and led medical societies. The impetus for change in the New Mexico Medical Society came to a large degree from this type of newcomer to the state.

Just as important, New Mexico's doctors of medicine and their colleagues across the nation were forced to take a new look at the structure of the medical profession and the future of the state's and country's health care systems by the "threat" in the late 1940s posed by national health insurance. Discussion of the question of national health insurance (which had immediately been labeled "socialized medicine" by the American Medical Association) had begun in the United States Congress in the 1930s, but it was the several Wagner–Murray–Dingell bills of the 1940s which first stimulated strong reaction by American doctors.[76] When President Harry S Truman announced his support of national health insurance in 1949 and made it part of his legislative program, the nation's doctors joined battle. The AMA, calling the proposal "regimentation" and "totalitarianism,"[77] was the chief instrument of physicians' opposition, but the national organization depended for its strength on the commitment of strong state societies. The campaign against socialized medicine, then, immediately required the reinvigoration of state societies like that in New Mexico. There was no longer to be room for nineteenth-century operations; tougher, more businesslike organizations were needed in the future.

The reorganization of the New Mexico Medical Society began in 1948 when a group of young reformers—Drs. Pardue Bunch of Artesia, Robert C. Derbyshire of Santa Fe, Leland Evans of Las Cruces, and John Conway of Clovis prominent among them—set out to force change within the state society.[78] Only one of them had been in New Mexico longer than a few years—Dr. Evans had come to Las Cruces in 1935—and all were inspired by their exposure in the states where they did their training to modern, efficient medical organization. They were prudent enough not to attempt to transplant eastern or midwestern models to the different circumstances of the Rocky Mountain West, but instead looked to New Mexico's neighbor to the north, the Colorado Medical Society, for guidance regarding what might work in New Mexico. In late 1948, a small

[76]On the battle against "socialized medicine" in the 1940s and 50s, see Stevens, *American Medicine and the Public Interest*, pp. 268–77, and James Gordon Burrow, *The American Medical Association: Voice of American Medicine* (Baltimore: Johns Hopkins University Press, 1963), pp. 329–35.

[77]Stevens, *American Medicine and the Public Interest*, p. 273.

[78]In addition to the printed sources cited and the records of the medical society, this account of the reorganization of the New Mexico Medical Society is based on the interviews held with Drs. Bunch and Derbyshire, plus those with Drs. I. J. Marshall and Stuart Adler and with Mr. Ralph Marshall.

delegation of the reformers visited the Denver offices of the Colorado organization to examine its structure and operations. They were quickly convinced that the Colorado society was a sound model and that it could be transplanted to New Mexico without serious modification.

In May 1949, the reformers presented their plan for reorganization to the society's House of Delegates meeting in Roswell. Dr. Bunch made their case in a report titled (somewhat misleadingly), "Features of the Colorado State Medical Society Public Relations Program Recommended for Adoption by the New Mexico Medical Society."[79] The reform program contained in that presentation was far broader than its title suggested and included five basic proposals, three concerning the structure of the New Mexico Medical Society and two dealing with its public relations needs. Foremost among the structural changes recommended was the proposal that the society hire a full-time Executive Secretary to establish and manage a full-time society business office. The reformers politely but firmly attacked the traditional organization of the institution, insisting that the time was past when the society could operate from the vestpocket of its president with its limited records and files stuffed in a cardboard box in its secretary's garage. The size of the profession in the state and the dimensions of its business demanded much more efficient arrangements and management. (Only a few years earlier, President Dr. Victor K. Adams of Raton had called for the hiring of an executive to manage the society's affairs and to establish "a full-time office where we could all drop in and receive information,"[80] but no action had followed his suggestion.) As the reform proposal envisioned it, the society's professional manager would be expected to supervise the routine duties of a central office, expand society services to individual members, develop an active public relations program, and "assist the American Medical Association in getting its educational work [combating 'socialized medicine'] in the state underway."[81] In addition to this basic structural change, the proposed reorganization also called for fundamental revision of the society's committee system to make it more central to the work of the

[79]A summary of that report is contained in the printed minutes of that meeting in *Rocky Mountain Medical Journal* 46 (1949):854 et seq. Dr. Bunch's original manuscript with his handwritten notes thereon is in the Bunch Papers, University of New Mexico Medical Center Library, Medical History Archives.

[80]*Rocky Mountain Medical Journal* 44 (1947):646.

[81]*Rocky Mountain Medical Journal* 46 (1949):854.

society and for the holding of training conferences for all newly elected state and county society officers.

The reorganization program advanced by Dr. Bunch and his colleagues made such sense—and its need was so apparent—that it encountered much less resistance than they had anticipated. They suspected that sheer conservatism or organizational inertia would lead some traditionalists to oppose the changes advanced, and they feared that longtime, veteran members of the society might resent the criticism of "their" institution made by the impatient newcomers. More worrisome still, they knew their reorganization proposals—particularly the establishment of a permanent office—would cost more money than the society was accustomed to spending and would require a significant increase in its dues. As late as 1949, the New Mexico Medical Society got along on a shoestring. Its total income in that last full year under its old organization was under $7,000 with the $20 per member annual dues providing almost all that sum.[82] To finance their reorganization plan, then, the reformers requested an immediate dues increase of 50 percent. By latter-day standards the sums involved were laughably small—an increase in annual dues from $20 to $30—but the psychological impact of the increase was great. (And the objective sum ought not be totally disregarded: it was a time when for many New Mexico physicians $10 represented five patient visits.) Nevertheless, the entire package, dues increase and all, moved through the House of Delegates with minimal opposition, and the reformers' reconstruction of the society was approved.[83]

It was clear to all involved that much of the success of this reformation would depend on the initiative and capability of the individual selected to run the new organization. After regional enquiries and consultation with the national office of the AMA, the Council of the New Mexico Medical Society decided to employ a not yet thirty-year-old business administration student at the University of Oklahoma, Ralph Marshall. Native to the Southwest (Arkansas and Oklahoma), Marshall spoke the language of the Society's leaders and was able to persuade them of his ability to handle the job despite his youth and inexperience. His only prior exposure to medical society administration came through his fiancée, who was secretary to the director of the Oklahoma State Medical

[82] *Rocky Mountain Medical Journal* 45 (1948):864.

[83] New Mexico Medical Society, Minutes, 67th Annual Meeting, 5–7 May 1949, Roswell, New Mexico.

Association,[84] but Marshall was confident that his business administration background, combined with his good judgment and ability to communicate and mediate among people, would enable him to master the job. He sold himself to the councillors of the society, and they hired him at $3,333 per year in the summer of 1949 as the first Executive Secretary (later Executive Director) of the New Mexico Medical Society. It proved to be an engagement of lasting consequence. In the centennial year of the New Mexico Medical Society (1986) its first Executive Director remained its only one—with Marshall celebrating thirty-seven years at that post, the longest tenure of any medical society executive in the country's history.

Beginning with a rented typewriter, one desk, and a telephone in the spare bedroom of the Marshall family home in Albuquerque, the New Mexico Medical Society in its new, more professional form quickly began to fulfill the high expectations of the reformers who had engineered its reorganization. In the very first full year of his tenure, 1950, Ralph Marshall persuaded that year's society president, Dr. I. J. Marshall of Roswell, to join him in extensive touring across the state. The idea was for the executive secretary and the society president to check the pulse of the physician community around the state by personally visiting every constituent county medical society and meeting as many individual doctors as possible. The rationale for the tour was straightforward and strongly laced with the common sense for which Ralph Marshall became noted: to be effective the state medical society had to establish close communication with the local, county societies. Through them it could learn what the state's physicians thought and how the statewide organization could serve them. This intimate relationship forged early on between the state office in Albuquerque and individual doctors around the state has been the hallmark and strength of the New Mexico Medical Society during its last 35 years. The yearly tours of the society's president in the company of its executive director required much of the men elected to the organization's presidency. No longer was that post merely honorific; for most of the incumbents it meant a year lost from practice, or something very close to it. It also required a great deal of stamina from them (and Mar-

[84]That fiancée with experience at a state medical society became Mrs. Ralph (Elaine) Marshall and proved an invaluable partner in getting the office of the New Mexico Medical Society started. Many of the interviewees questioned in preparation for this study emphasized her importance, particularly in the critical early years.

shall) and the understanding of their families. Nevertheless, the usefulness of the practice was quickly so evident that it became an accepted tradition of the society.

The organization's efficiency and responsiveness to the state's doctors was further enhanced by the construction of a strong committee system to handle the society's business. As mentioned earlier, the organization had employed committees and specially appointed ad hoc study groups from its earliest days, but with rare exceptions the committee system had not worked well. Physicians, like other busy professionals, were so preoccupied with their personal work, families, and purely local concerns, and communications within the state were still so difficult and time-consuming, that committee work most often was perfunctory and shallow.[85] Most important of all, the society's committees could not pretend to real effectiveness without the secretarial assistance of a central office and the data gathering and communications capability it could afford as well as the gentle prodding to get on with their work that sometimes was required. Since the reorganization in 1949, the committee structure of the New Mexico Medical Society has afforded the instrument through which its members could effectively shape the policies and behavior of the institution speaking for them. There have been numerous changes since 1949 in the way the society conducts its business, but the cornerstones of its work have remained the tight linkage established in the early fifties between the state office and the local societies and the organization's strong committee system.

In the third of a century since its reorganization, the New Mexico Medical Society has decisively taken the leadership role as corporate

[85]Dr. C. Pardue Bunch, interview with the author, Artesia, N.M., 4 June 1984, and Mr. Ralph Marshall, interview with the author, Albuquerque, N.M., 7 October 1982. In his 1951 presidential address to the society, Dr. Leland Evans of Las Cruces remembered the ineffectuality of the pre-1949 committees:

> Another factor which was most disturbing to many members was the complete inactivity of our committees prior to 1949. The reports of those committees would usually not require [in toto] over thirty minutes of the time allotted for the meeting of the House of Delegates. One could not sit in the House of Delegates session this morning without realizing what strides have been made and the vast amount of work now accomplished by our committees.

Leland S. Evans, M.D., "Better Public Relations Through Better Medical Service," *Rocky Mountain Medical Journal* 48 (1951):413.

spokesman and representative for the doctors of medicine of New Mexico. Its centrality to the profession is evident in the long list of issues, many of them complex and/or controversial, where the medical society has been a leading actor. As one example, it was the state society that orchestrated the response of New Mexico's physicians in the nationwide debate over compulsory health insurance from the end of the 1940s into the 1960s. Under the aegis of the state society, New Mexico's doctors of medicine formed their own insurance company, the New Mexico Physicians' Service, to write health insurance and to provide care for those unable to afford commercial health insurance. Instead of digging in their heels, denying any need for change within the traditional free enterprise structure of medicine in the state, New Mexico's doctors through this agency of their state society tried to make accommodations. They were among the pioneers in creating such arrangements, and their Physicians' Service company quickly became the largest in the state. It was finally phased out in the 1960s with the great expansion of federal government health programs and the state society's endorsement of the Blue Cross/Blue Shield health protection system.

Similarly, when the malpractice problem first began to threaten the medical profession in the 1960s and 1970s, the state medical society took the lead in seeking means to cope with the issue. As early as 1949—and as a part of the reform program adopted in that year—the state society had created a Board of Supervisors to act as a kind of grievance committee mediating between individual physicians and patients. (The Board also acted as an agency of internal discipline within the medical profession and performed an important service in control of problem cases within the physician community.) The loose, informal mediation of the 1950s and early 1960s took more concrete form in 1964 with creation of a Medical Review Commission, a tribunal composed of equal numbers of lawyers and physicians appointed by their respective state societies and presided over by a judge appointed by the State Supreme Court. Under this arrangement—which received extensive national publicity as "the New Mexico plan"—all charges of medical malpractice had first to be taken before this screening commission prior to any action within the regular courts system. By this procedure the medical profession was shielded from frivolous claims and pressure on the legal system was relieved, while consumer protection against demonstrable malpractice was ensured. Within two years of the establishment of this system, New Mexico dropped into the bottom five states of the nation in number of malpractice suits per population.[86] The state society also intervened in 1976, when the last commercial company writing medical malpractice insurance in the state decided to withdraw. The society created a physician-owned company, the New Mexico Physicians Mutual Liability Company, to provide coverage for doctors around the state, and that subsidiary quickly became a central element of the structure of the profession in New Mexico.

Since 1949, the state medical society has been active in other spheres as well. For example, it has energetically represented physicians' interests in dealing with both state and federal government welfare programs, providing the doctors with a counterweight to the massive power of the governmental bureaucracies. It spoke for the state's medical profession, as noted earlier in this chapter, in the discussions and planning that led to the foundation of the medical school at the University of New Mexico. From the late 1940s to the early 1970s, it was the state society which organized the recruitment of new physicians to practice in underserved, mostly rural areas of New Mexico. It also has been the central agency in legislative lobbying for the medical profession and in carrying out the increasingly important public relations efforts of the physician community. It has, in short, become the strong, efficient corporate force the reformers of the late 1940s hoped to build. Only two other institutions of the modern era approached it in authority and influence within the health sphere—the University of New Mexico School of Medicine, already discussed in these pages, and the state Board of Medical Examiners.

In the postwar era, New Mexico's Board of Medical Examiners suddenly emerged as a powerful agency for change within the state's medical community. Prior to 1952, the state board exercised some influence through its licensing authority, but in fact it had taken little initiative in seeking to improve the caliber of medical practice within the state. As a matter of fact, there is evidence that it had not always insisted on the letter of the medical practice law, which ostensibly guided its efforts, for the records indicate that some physicians were licensed despite their failure to meet the minimum standards specified in the legislation. It was, in short, a somewhat haphazard, casual organization, loosely run and not particularly vigorous in its supervisory responsibilities. Its leadership and continuity were vested in a secretary, but that executive position over time had become merely the part-time job of some Santa Fe physician content to keep the records. The agency had real tangibility only when it held its

[86]Ralph Marshall, interview, Albuquerque, N.M., 7 October 1982.

semi-annual, two-day meetings to review applicants for licensure. Beyond this limited work, the Board did nothing.

That tradition of inactivity was decisively broken in the years after 1952, when Santa Fe surgeon Dr. Robert C. Derbyshire was appointed Secretary of the Board. Dr. Derbyshire, a product of Virginia's Hampden-Sydney College, Johns Hopkins University School of Medicine, and residency training at the Mayo Clinic, initially came to New Mexico in 1942 to join the Lovelace Clinic. His choice of the Albuquerque institution was influenced by his interest in group practice, and his selection of New Mexico was dictated by his own case of pulmonary tuberculosis. He was in the last wave of "lunger" physicians who came west seeking health in the state's climes. After six years at the Lovelace Clinic and another two in Artesia, he moved to Santa Fe in 1950 and quickly established a successful practice in general surgery. In 1952, when the incumbent secretary of the Board of Medical Examiners resigned, Dr. Derbyshire was asked to take over the post. For the subsequent thirty-one years, he directed the activities of that state agency and transformed it into an agent of dynamic change within the medical community. Few, if any, individual doctors over the past century have had so great an impact on their profession as he, on both local and national scales.[87] Strong-willed and forceful, Dr. Derbyshire bent his considerable energies to the task of making the New Mexico medical community as capable and responsible as possible, and the state Board of Medical Examiners, working in close cooperation with the state medical society, was the vehicle of his work.

Under the leadership of this powerful figure, New Mexico's Board of Medical Examiners worked unrelentingly to improve the standard of practice in the state. It began by simple enforcement of the existing medical practice law, ending the sometimes lackadaisical performance of earlier days. Through the uncompromising eyes of its secretary, the Board carefully scrutinized the credentials of all applicants for licensure in New Mexico, a process which extended to professional investigation when circumstances suggested it. In addition, its written and oral examinations for licensure were improved, and the New Mexico board became a na-

[87]The ninety-plus doctors interviewed as part of the preparation for this study were unanimous in asserting his importance. The nickname "Derby" was the first response of the great majority of them when they were asked to identify the profession's most influential members during the span of their practice. Not all of them agreed with him in all the battles he waged over the past third of a century, but all acknowledged his importance and the constructiveness of his work.

tional leader in the development of the Federation Licensing Examination (FLEX), now used nationwide. (New Mexico was one of the first six states to adopt the FLEX exam, and Dr. Derbyshire individually was a dominant force nationally in the creation of this examination system.) The Board also began to exercise its disciplinary authority over already licensed physicians in cases where there was evidence of substandard practice or unprofessional behavior of whatever description. Working through the state medical society's Board of Supervisors when appropriate and with legal authorities when necessary, the Board of Medical Examiners for the first time in its history played a powerful role in the policing or oversight of the state's medical profession during the thirty years of Dr. Derbyshire's direction of it.

Within its overall campaign to improve the standard of medical practice in the state, the most revolutionary (and controversial) aspect of the Board's work was its effort to tie physicians' relicensure or recertification to compulsory continued education. As late as the 1970s, all required of a New Mexico physician intent on renewing his license "was to pay his annual license fee and stay out of jail."[88] Once a doctor had his license, it was his for life. New Mexico was not especially backward in this respect, for nowhere in the country were physicians required to present evidence of their continued competency or the currency of their knowledge and skills. The Oregon Medical Association in 1970 passed a regulation requiring its members to fulfill certain continuing educational standards to remain in good standing in that professional association, but nowhere in the country had the movement to demand continuing education taken more concrete form.

In 1969, a group within the New Mexico Medical Association, Dr. Derbyshire prominent within it, engineered the appointment of a Committee on Continuing Education to examine the question. The Santa Fean was appointed chairman of the group, but his commitment to reform was amply reinforced by other members of the committee—Dr. Robert S. Stone, dean of the university medical school, and Dr. Richard Angle, a prominent Santa Fe internist, among them. When the committee finished its study of the issue, it presented a report to the House of Delegates of the state society, asking it to sponsor legislation requiring evidence of continuing education courses for recertification. Not surprisingly, con-

[88]Dr. Robert C. Derbyshire, interview with Dr. Peter Olch and the author, Albuquerque, N.M., 8 October 1982.

siderable opposition to that proposal surfaced, for the state's physicians were being asked voluntarily to impose new demands on themselves and to increase the already growing external constraints on themselves and their practices. Nevertheless, the proposal passed and a draft law was presented the following year to the New Mexico state legislature with the blessing of the state medical society. It became law in 1971, and with it New Mexico became the first state in the nation to require continuing education of its doctors. (It is a reform measure since adopted by more than two dozen states around the nation.) In the original debate within the medical society on the question and ever since, there have been critics who grumbled about the emptiness or pointlessness of "Derby points"—the term used informally to denote the continuing education credits physicians must accumulate before relicensure—and there has been constant pressure to dilute or even eliminate the requirements, but the line has been held. In similar fashion, the Board of Medical Examiners led the campaign which resulted in 1976 in New Mexico's Impaired Physician's Act, or the "Sick Doctor statute," a law providing tighter, more effective means for control over physicians with problems. Here, too, although New Mexico was not first, it was among the first dozen or so states around the nation to devise such legislation.

With its tightly organized, smoothly functioning state medical society; its progressive, energetic Board of Medical Examiners; its young medical school already establishing a proud tradition; and its large and growing corps of sophisticated medical practitioners scattered around the state, New Mexico medicine was in solid position at the end of the twentieth century to greet the challenges of the twenty-first one. It had achieved that happy position and the confidence and respect of the New Mexico citizenry by a century of honorable service in the state. The Las Vegas pioneers of 1886 and the generations who came after them had built solid foundations for the young men and women who would strive to cope with the health needs of the future.

Appendix A

Letter from President M. W. Robbins, New Mexico Medical Society, to New Mexico Territory Governor Edmund G. Ross, 2 April 1887, regarding the need for reform of the Territorial Board of Medical Examiners:

To His Excellency E. G. Ross, Governor of New Mexico

In accordance with a vote of the New Mexico Medical Society taken April 2, 1887 after ample discussion of the subject at several meetings, and by two committees specially appointed in the circumstances, I have the honor to address you concerning the reorganization of the Board of Medical Examiners, and to forward herewith a copy of the resolutions adopted by the Society.

For several years past the members of this society have been cognizant of the fact that the statute regarding the practice of medicine in this territory has become well-nigh a dead letter and that the outlook of the Board upon the affairs connected with the statute was one of apathy. That our views may be justified, we make bold in the privacy of this letter to lay before you our opinions as to the present personal makeup of the Board and we are reinforced by similar opinions from distant parts of the Territory.

The present constitution of the Board is, as required by statute, four Regulars ("allopaths" in the statute—a term not used or recognized by the regular profession):

Dr. E. C. Henriques, Las Vegas
Dr. R. H. Longwill, Santa Fe
Dr. Louis Kennon, Silver City
Dr. W. A. Kittredge, Taos

two homeopaths:

Dr. J. M. Cunningham, Las Vegas
Dr. W. Eggert, Santa Fe

one eclectic

Dr. G. S. Easterday, Albuquerque.

We are satisfied that Dr. R. H. Longwill is not identified either with a lofty respect for the moral and intellectual standing of the medical profession nor yet with that zealous and philanthropic interest in the welfare of the citizens of this Territory that the conception and proper execution of such a statute reasonably demands. Whatever Dr. Louis Kennon's earlier qualifications may have been, there are certain reasons sufficiently well known generally to lead to the inference that his services in connection with the Board are hardly likely to be valuable. Dr. W. A. Kittredge of Taos appears to be lacking in any interest in the affairs borne upon by this statute, and, as we are informed, has not recently attended the meetings of the Board. Could substitutes for Drs. Easterday and Eggert be found in their respective schools, we should nominate them, but some search has failed to discover such in the Territory. We are heartily agreed that Drs. Henriques and Cunningham are desirable men to serve on the Board.

Competent legal advice has assured us that the statute, though clumsily framed, is valid and can be enforced. The experience of other states proves that the provisions of such laws can be put in action with the happiest results to the community, in that the people are protected from the ravages of pretenders or weaklings in the noble art of healing, while the educated and duly qualified members of the profession are stimulated to greater zeal in the maintenance of their standing as men of learning, and encouraged to have and hold a higher degree of that self-respect without which medicine as a vocation becomes a painful mockery.

A conscientious and energetic Board would not only examine applicants and issue certificates—as specified by statute—but would assume the duty of encouraging the prosecution of all offenders against these legal restrictions, a matter which has been wholly neglected except as far as the physicians of Las Vegas have several times endeavored to secure the conviction of such persons.

We would also call to your attention the fact that all the members of the present Board are "holding over"—their terms having expired—under Section 2554, and it is possible the Secretary of the Board has omitted to notify your Excellency thereof.

I remain, Honored Sir, very respectfully,
Your Obedient Servant,
M. W. Robbins, M.D, President
Francis H. Atkins, M.D., Secretary

Source: New Mexico Medical Society, Minutes, 2 April 1887.

Appendix B

Presidents of the New Mexico Medical Society

Las Vegas Medical Society

1882–1883	John H. Shout, Las Vegas
1883–1884	William H. Page, Las Vegas
1884–1885	William H. Page, Las Vegas

New Mexico Medical Society

1885–1886	William R. Tipton, Las Vegas
1886–1887	Myron W. Robbins, Las Vegas
1887–1888	Myron W. Robbins, Las Vegas
1888–1889	William R. Tipton, Las Vegas
1889–1890	E. C. Henriques, Las Vegas
1890–1891	Francis H. Atkins, Las Vegas
1891–1892	Francis H. Atkins, Las Vegas
1892–1893	James E. Wroth, Albuquerque
1893–1894	William R. Tipton, Las Vegas
1894–1895	George W. Harrison, Albuquerque
1895–1896	F. Marron y Alonso, Las Vegas
1896–1897	Charles G. Duncan, Socorro
1897–1898	John F. Pearce, Albuquerque
1898–1899	Samuel B. Swope, Deming

1899–1900	George S. Easterday, Albuquerque
1900–1901	John H. Sloan, Santa Fe
1901–1902	George W. Harrison, Albuquerque
1902–1903	Walter G. Hope, Albuquerque
1903–1904	George C. Bryan, Alamogordo
1904–1905	Edwin B. Shaw, Las Vegas
1905–1906	P. G. Cornish, Sr., Albuquerque
1906–1907	Thomas B. Hart, Raton
1907–1908	Robert E. McBride, Las Cruces
1908–1909	George K. Angle, Silver City
1909–1910	John W. Elder, Albuquerque
1910–1911	Francis T. B. Fest, Las Vegas
1911–1912	Robert L. Bradley, Roswell
1912–1913	LeRoy Peters, Silver City
1913–1914	Henry B. Kauffman, Albuquerque
1914–1915	William T. Joyner, Roswell
1915–1916	Evelyn F. Frisbie, Albuquerque
1916–1917	Clifford S. Losey, Las Vegas
1917–1918	John W. Kinsinger, Roswell
1918–1919	John W. Kinsinger, Roswell
1919–1920	Charles A. Frank, Albuquerque
1920–1921	Hugh V. Fall, Roswell
1921–1922	Chester Russell, Artesia
1922–1923	Harry A. Miller, Clovis
1923–1924	George S. McLandress, Albuquerque
1924–1925	John W. Stofer, Gallup
1925–1926	Dudley B. Williams, Santa Fe
1926–1927	Charles F. Beeson, Roswell
1927–1928	Carey B. Elliott, Raton
1928–1929	Thomas B. Martin, Taos
1929–1930	Franklin H. Crail, Las Vegas
1930–1931	Robert O. Brown, Santa Fe
1931–1932	Meldrum K. Wylder, Albuquerque
1932–1933	Fred D. Vickers, Deming
1933–1934	Henry A. Ingalls, Roswell
1934–1935	Charles F. Milligan, Clayton
1935–1936	Charles W. Gerber, Las Cruces
1936–1937	Mallory B. Culpepper, Carlsbad
1937–1938	George W. Jones, Clovis
1938–1939	Eugene W. Fiske, Santa Fe

1939–1940	George T. Colvard, Deming
1940–1941	William B. Cantrell, Hot Springs
1941–1942	Carl Mulky, Albuquerque
1942–1943	Wallace P. Martin, Clovis
1943–1944	J. E. J. Harris, Albuquerque
1944–1945	Carl H. Gellenthien, Valmora
1945–1946	Carl H. Gellenthien, Valmora
1946–1947	Charles A. Miller, Las Cruces
1947–1948	Victor K. Adams, Raton
1948–1949	Philip L. Travers, Santa Fe
1949–1950	J. W. Hannett, Albuquerque
1950–1951	I. J. Marshall, Roswell
1951–1952	Leland S. Evans, Las Cruces
1952–1953	Coy S. Stone, Hobbs
1953–1954	Albert S. Lathrop, Santa Fe
1954–1955	John F. Conway, Clovis
1955–1956	Earl L. Malone, Roswell
1956–1957	Stuart W. Adler, Albuquerque
1957–1958	Samuel R. Ziegler, Española
1958–1959	James C. Sedgwick, Las Cruces
1959–1960	Lewis M. Overton, Albuquerque
1960–1961	Allan L. Haynes, Clovis
1961–1962	William E. Badger, Hobbs
1962–1963	Robert C. Derbyshire, Santa Fe
1963–1964	C. Pardue Bunch, Artesia
1964–1965	Omar Legant, Albuquerque
1965–1966	Robert P. Beaudette, Raton
1966–1967	Tom L. Carr, Albuquerque
1967–1968	Emmit M. Jennings, Roswell
1968–1969	Earl B. Flanagan, Carlsbad
1969–1970	Hugh B. Woodward, Albuquerque
1970–1971	Harry D. Ellis, Santa Fe
1971–1972	Vaun T. Floyd, Albuquerque
1972–1973	Don Clark, Roswell
1973–1974	Armin T. Keil, Raton
1974–1975	U. G. Hodgin, Jr., Albuquerque
1975–1976	Robert E. Cutler, Española
1976–1977	Walter J. Hopkins, Picacho
1977–1978	Robert Zone, Santa Fe
1978–1979	William C. Gorman, Albuquerque

1979–1980	Robert Wilbee, Las Cruces
1980–1981	John D. Abrums, Albuquerque
1981–1982	Ashley Pond III, Taos
1982–1983	Douglas C. Layman, Albuquerque
1983–1984	William Liakos, Roswell
1984–1985	W. Marion Jordan, Albuquerque
1985–1986	William A. Boehm, Alamogordo

Appendix C

Interviews Within the Oral History Project of the New Mexico Medical History Program

1982

1. Stuart W. Adler, M.D., Albuquerque, 21 September
2. Ralph Marshall, Albuquerque, 7 October
3. Robert C. Derbyshire, M.D., Santa Fe (interviewed in Albuquerque), 9 October

1983

4. I. J. Marshall, M.D., Roswell, 15 August
5. Joe P. Williams, M.D., Roswell, 17 August
6. E. W. "Bud" Lander, M.D., Roswell, 19 August
7. Edith F. Millican, M.D., Embudo and Cleveland (interviewed in Albuquerque), 30 August
8. Michel Pijoan, M.D., Española (interviewed in Albuquerque), 1 September
9. Demarious C. Badger, M.D., Hobbs (interviewed in Albuquerque), 2 September
10. William E. Badger, M.D., Hobbs (interviewed in Albuquerque), 2 September
11. Ashley Pond III, M.D., Taos, 5 September

12. Walter Stark, M.D., Las Vegas, 7 September
13. James C. Sedgwick, M.D., Las Cruces and Albuquerque (interviewed in Albuquerque), 19 September
14. Harold M. Mortimer, M.D., Las Vegas (interviewed in Albuquerque), 21 September
15. William Sedgwick, M.D., Las Cruces, 4 October
16. Andrew M. Babey, M.D., Las Cruces, 5 October
17. Lloyd Foster, M.D., Reserve, 7 October
18. Virginia V. Milner, M.D., Embudo and Albuquerque (interviewed in Albuquerque), 18 October
19. Albert W. Egenhofer, M.D., Santa Fe, 20 October
20. Jose Maldonado, M.D., Santa Fe, 21 October
21. Victor E. Berchtold, M.D., Santa Fe, 27 October
22. Joe A. Domingues, D.O., Taos, 1 November
23. Elizabeth Budlong, RN, Ranchos de Taos, 2 November
24. Reynaldo DeVeaux, M.D., Taos, 3 November
25. U. S. "Steve" Marshall, M.D., Roswell, 15 November
26. A. N. Spencer, M.D., Carrizozo (interviewed in Ruidoso), 17 November
27. Robert J. Saul, M.D., Mountainair, 18 November
28. P. G. Cornish III, M.D., Albuquerque, 21 November
29. Louis M. Pavletich, M.D., Raton, 30 November
30. Milton Floersheim, M.D., Raton, 1 December
31. John J. Johnson, M.D., Las Vegas, 6 December
32. Samuel R. Ziegler, M.D., Española, 13 December
33. Lewis M. Overton, M.D., Albuquerque, 16 December

1984

34. Robert Friedenberg, M.D., Albuquerque, 21 February
35. Alvin H. Follingstad, M.D., Albuquerque, 14 March
36. Howard B. Peck, M.D., Albuquerque, 21 March
37. Lucy McMurray, M.D., Albuquerque, 28 March
38. Earl L. Malone, M.D., Roswell, 6 April
39. Junius A. Evans, M.D., Las Vegas and Roswell (interviewed in Roswell), 8 April
40. Bert Kempers, M.D., Albuquerque, 11 April
41. Eleanor Adler, M.D., Albuquerque, 18 April
42. L. G. Rice, Jr., M.D., Albuquerque, 9 May
43. Albert G. Simms II, M.D., Albuquerque, 17 May
44. James W. Wiggins, M.D., Albuquerque, 21 May

45. Lawrence Wilkinson, M.D., Albuquerque, 23 May
46. C. Pardue Bunch, M.D., Artesia, 4 June
47. William J. Hossley, M.D., Deming, 6 June
48. Alice H. Cushing, M.D., Albuquerque, 10 July
49. Walter W. Winslow, M.D., Albuquerque, 17 July
50. Robert B. Loftfield, Ph.D., Albuquerque, 20 July
51. William R. Hardy, M.D., Albuquerque, 23 July
52. Thomas McConnell, M.D., Albuquerque, 22 August
53. Robert E. Anderson, M.D., Albuquerque, 5 September
54. Sidney Solomon, Ph.D., Albuquerque, 7 September
55. Leonard Napolitano, Ph.D., Albuquerque, 12 September
56. Leroy McLaren, Ph.D., Albuquerque, 13 September
57. John J. Corcoran, M.D., Albuquerque, 17 September
58. Louis Levin, M.D., Albuquerque, 19 September
59. H. Richard Landmann, M.D., Santa Fe, 27 September
60. Oliver S. Cramer, M.D., Albuquerque, 3 October
61. Fred Hanold, M.D., Albuquerque, 8 October
62. Rodger MacQuigg, M.D., Albuquerque, 10 October
63. Bergere Kenney, M.D., Santa Fe, 17 October
64. Angus McKinnon, M.D., Albuquerque, 25 October
65. Carl H. Gellenthien, M.D., Valmora, 18 December

1985

66. Robert U. Massey, M.D., Albuquerque (interviewed in Farmington, Conn.), 4 January
67. Arthur Fischer, M.D., Las Cruces and Albuquerque (interviewed in Albuquerque), 21 January
68. A. H. Schwichtenberg, M.D., Albuquerque, 20 February
69. William L. Minear, M.D., Ph.D., Hot Springs and Albuquerque (interviewed in Albuquerque), 8 March
70. A. Clay Gwinn, M.D., Albuquerque and Carlsbad (interviewed in Carlsbad), 11 March
71. Carroll L. Womack, M.D., Artesia and Carlsbad (interviewed in Carlsbad), 12 March
72. Catherine Armstrong-Seward, M.D., Carlsbad, 13 March
73. Allan L. Haynes, M.D., Clovis, 15 March
74. Thomas L. Chiffelle, M.D., Albuquerque, 23 March
75. V. Scott Johnson, M.D., Clovis, 31 May
76. Martin B. Goodwin, M.D., Clovis, 1 June

77. Charles F. Fishback, M.D., Albuquerque, 4 June
78. David J. Ottensmeyer, M.D., Albuquerque, 23 August
79. Carol K. Smith, M.D., Santa Fe, 11 September
80. Murray M. Friedman, M.D., Santa Fe, 27 September
81. Chester M. Kurtz, M.D., Albuquerque, 4 October
82. Ulrich C. Luft, M.D., Ph.D., Albuquerque, 11 October
83. Clayton S. White, M.D., Albuquerque, 14 October
84. Donald E. Kilgore, Jr., M.D., Albuquerque, 18 November
85. Anne Fox, RN, Santa Fe, 29 December

N.B.: Many of these interviews were completed over more than one day. The date listed is that of the interview's start.

Bibliography

I. Primary Sources: Archives

Alamogordo, New Mexico.

- A. International Space Hall of Fame.
  1. Papers relating to Dr. William Randolph Lovelace II, primarily newspaper clippings, magazine articles, and some personal correspondence; memorabilia.

Albuquerque, New Mexico.

- A. Albuquerque Public Library, Main Library.
  1. Newspaper clipping folders on health and medical subjects.
- B. Lovelace Foundation for Medical Education and Research.
  1. Board of Trustees. Minutes, 1947–81. Includes accompanying documentation submitted to the Board, including reports, correspondence, financial data, and so forth.
  2. Lovelace Clinic. Board of Governors. Minutes, 1952–82. Includes correspondence of the Board, departmental reports, and other internal documentation.
  3. Personnel files, including files on Drs. William Randolph Lovelace I, William Randolph Lovelace II, Clayton S. White, Donald E. Kilgore, Jr., David J. Ottensmeyer, and many others.
  4. Miscellaneous files.
- C. Menaul Historical Library, Menaul School.
  1. Virginia Voorhies Milner, M.D., Diary, 1939–41.

2. Miscellaneous files, including those on Sarah Bowen, M.D.; Edith Millican, M.D.; Virginia Voorhies Milner, M.D.; Brooklyn Cottage Hospital; Embudo Presbyterian Hospital; and others.

D. University of New Mexico. Zimmerman Library. Archives.
1. Minutes, Faculty of the University of New Mexico, 1957–66.
2. Minutes, Regents, 1958–67.

E. University of New Mexico. Zimmerman Library. Special Collections.
1. University of New Mexico. Annual Reports, 1957–80.

F. University of New Mexico. Medical Center Library. Medical History Archives.
1. Bernalillo County Medical Society. Minutes, 7 April 1915–7 November 1945.
2. Bunch Papers. Personal and professional papers of Dr. C. Pardue Bunch (1913–85), Artesia, New Mexico; particularly strong in materials dealing with the affairs of the New Mexico Medical Society. (Dr. Bunch was its president in 1963–64, longtime Speaker of its House of Delegates, and active on many committees.)
3. Greenfield Papers. Personal and professional papers of Miss Myrtle Greenfield, Director of the State Public Health Laboratory in Albuquerque from 1920 to 1956.
4. Las Vegas Medical Society. Constitution. January 1882.
5. ———. Minutes, 1882–86.
6. New Mexico Medical Society. Annual Meeting. Minutes, 1886–1983.
7. ———. [Annual Meetings] Registration Ledger. 1925–42, 1944.
8. Physician files. Biographical and professional files on more than 200 New Mexico physicians, including all those included within the Oral History Project (see Appendix C) and more than 125 others.
9. University of New Mexico School of Medicine. Historical files, including scattered correspondence, budget data, faculty information, newspaper clippings, and so forth.

Farmington, New Mexico.

A. Farmington Historical Museum.
1. Sammons Papers. Professional papers of Dr. George W. Sammons (1874–1952), including account books, prescription formulary, and some patient records.

Fort Stanton, New Mexico.

A. New Mexico State Hospital and Training School.
1. Scattered historical holdings, including patient registry, 1909–38; memorabilia.

Las Cruces, New Mexico.

A. New Mexico State University Library. Rio Grande Collection.
1. Materials on Las Cruces physicians, especially Dr. Robert E. McBride (1873–1947), tuberculosis sanatoria of the area, and hospitals of the city.

Las Vegas, New Mexico.

A. Thomas C. Donnelly Library of New Mexico Highlands University.
  1. Miscellaneous health and medical related materials, including newspaper clippings, magazine articles, and public information reports regarding the New Mexico State Hospital, Las Vegas
B. New Mexico State Hospital. Library.
  1. File folders regarding the institution's history.

Raton, New Mexico.
A. Arthur Johnson Memorial [City] Library.
  1. File folders regarding health and medical matters in the city, including a partial list of the city's physicians, 1922–66.
B. Miner's Hospital
  1. Scattered historical records.

Roswell, New Mexico.
A. Chaves County Historical Museum.
  1. Galloway Papers. Professional papers of Dr. David Galloway (1859–1944), limited to article reprints and photographs.
B. New Mexico Military Institute. Public Information Office.
  1. Materials, including photographs, relating to Drs. I. J. and Steve Marshall.
C. St. Mary's Hospital.
  1. Patient ledgers and miscellaneous correspondence, 1916–51.

Santa Fe, New Mexico.
A. New Mexico. Board of Medical Examiners.
  1. Physician files, 1902–present. File folders on all physicians licensed for practice in New Mexico, including personal data, educational background, professional history, and the like. Incomplete for the early years of the century.
  2. Historical folders, regarding licensure refusal, professional disciplinary matters, and miscellaneous correspondence, 1895–1924.
B. New Mexico. Health and Environment Department. Vital Statistics Division.
  1. Notifiable Diseases, 1922–47. Six ledger volumes, divided by county.
C. New Mexico. Museum of New Mexico, History Library. Photo Archives.
  1. Photographs of New Mexico physicians, health institutions, public health activities, and so forth.
D. New Mexico. State Records Center and Archives.
  1. Board of Medical Examiners. Annual Reports to the Governor. 1903–18; 1923–30; 1955; 1959–80.
  2. ———. Minutes. 1 December 1902–20 November 1979. (A microfilm copy of these minutes is held in the University of New Mexico Medical Center Library, Medical History Archives.)
  3. ———. Register (of all physicians licensed by the Board). 3 volumes. 1902–68.
  4. Shuler Papers. Personal and professional papers of Dr. James J. Shuler

(1858–1916) of Raton, New Mexico, including ledger books and some patient records, but largely focused on Dr. Shuler's political career.

E. St. Vincent's Hospital. Library.

1. Santa Fe County Medical Society. Minutes. 27 March 1909–9 January 1923. (A complete copy of these minutes is held in the University of New Mexico Medical Center Library, Medical History Archives.)
2. Hospital records (scattered) and photographs.

Taos, New Mexico.

A. Holy Cross Hospital.

1. Limited historical materials regarding the institution's history, mostly newspaper clippings, and partial files regarding hospital staff.

Valmora, New Mexico.

A. Valmora Sanatorium.

1. Memorabilia, scrapbooks of newspaper clippings and magazine articles, professional article reprints, patient ledger, and other materials regarding the institution and its staff.

II. Primary Sources: Published Matter

American Board of Medical Specialties. *Directory of Medical Specialists Certified by American Boards.* 1st edition (1940) through 22nd edition (1985–86).

American Medical Association. *American Medical Directory.* Volume 1 (1906) through Volume 29 (1985).

———. Center for Health Services Research and Development. *Directory of Women Physicians in the United States.* Chicago: American Medical Association, 1979.

Chatterton, A. L., comp. *Flint's Medical and Surgical Directory of the United States and Canada.* New York: J. B. Flint and Co., 1897.

Eiler, Mary Ann. *Physician Characteristics and Distribution in the United States, 1983.* Chicago: American Medical Association, 1984.

Lovelace Foundation for Medical Education and Research. *Annual Report, 1950* through *Annual Report, 1983.* Published annually by the Foundation in Albuquerque.

New Mexico. Bureau of Public Health. *Biennial Report, 1921–1922* (Santa Fe: Bureau of Public Health, 1923) through *Biennial Report, 1939–1940* (Santa Fe: Bureau of Public Health, 1941). Appeared thereafter as *Annual Report,* 1941–present.

New Mexico. Health and Environment Department. *New Mexico: Fifty Years as a Vital Statistics Registration State, 1929–1979.* Santa Fe, N.M.: Health and Environment Department, 1980.

Polk's Medical and Surgical Directory of the United States. 1st edition, 1886; 7th edition, 1902; and 12th edition, 1912–13.

United States. Army. Medical Corps. *Defects Found in Drafted Men: Statistical*

Information Compiled from Draft Records. Washington: Government Printing Office, 1920.

———. Department of Health and Human Services. *Health: United States, 1982.* Washington: Government Printing Office, 1983.

III. Books and Articles

Adams, Victor K., M.D. "The Medical Pioneers." *New Mexico Magazine* 28, no. 5 (1950):15, 35, 37.

Adler, Stuart W., M.D. "Biography of a Society." *Rocky Mountain Medical Journal* 64, no. 12 (1967):33–38.

———. "Southwestern Medical Center." *New Mexico Magazine* 28, no. 2 (1950):22–23, 42–43.

Albuquerque Civic Council. *Sunshine and Health in Albuquerque.* Albuquerque: Albuquerque Civic Council, 1932.

Amesse, J. W., M.D. "Sources of Infant Mortality in the Western States." *Southwestern Medicine* 15 (1931):511–14.

Anderson, Dorothy R. "Adventures in New Mexico." *Public Health Nurse* 19 (1927):346–47.

———. "Why New Mexico Nurses Cooperate in Maternity and Infancy Work." *American Journal of Public Health* 16 (1926):473–75.

Anderson, George B., ed. *History of New Mexico: Its Resources and Peoples.* 2 vols. Los Angeles: Pacific Publishing Co., 1907.

Appel, D. M., M.D. "The Army Hospital and Sanatorium for the Treatment of Pulmonary Tuberculosis, at Fort Bayard, New Mexico." *Journal of the American Medical Association* 39 (29 November 1902):1373–79.

———. "United States General Hospital for Tuberculosis at Fort Bayard, New Mexico." *Journal of the American Medical Association* 35 (1900):1003–5.

Arguello, Jose P. "Pioneer Researcher, Country Doctor." *New Mexico Highlands University Magazine* 9, no. 2 (1984):4–8.

Baker, Samuel L. "Physician Licensure Laws in the United States, 1865–1915." *Journal of the History of Medicine and Allied Sciences* 39 (1984):173–97.

Balcomb, Kenneth C. *A Boy's Albuquerque, 1898–1912.* Albuquerque: University of New Mexico Press, 1980.

Barber, M. A., and Louis R. Forbrich. "Malaria in the Irrigated Regions of New Mexico." *Public Health Reports* 48 (1933):610–23.

Barber, M. A., W. H. W. Komp, and C. H. King. "Malaria and the Malaria Danger in Certain Irrigated Regions of Southwestern United States." *Public Health Reports* 44 (1929):1300–1315.

Beaudette, Robert P., M.D. "Presidential Address [to the Annual Meeting of the New Mexico Medical Society]." *Rocky Mountain Medical Journal* 63, no. 9 (1966):67–68.

Beimer, Dorothy S. *Hovels, Haciendas, and House Calls: The Life of Carl H. Gellenthien, M.D.* Santa Fe, N.M.: Sunstone Press, 1985.

Berger, M. L. "The Influence of the Automobile on Rural Health Care, 1900–1929." *Journal of the History of Medicine and Allied Sciences* 28 (1973):319–35.

Beyers, Charlotte. "Students Get a Taste of Practice Early in Training." *American Medical News*, 25 September 1981, 33–34.

Bodemer, C. W. "Medicine in Nineteenth Century Montana." *Rocky Mountain Medical Journal* 76, no. 2 (1979):66–71.

Bordley, James, and A. M. Harvey. *Two Centuries of American Medicine, 1776–1976.* Philadelphia: Saunders, 1976.

Breeden, James O. "The Health of Early Texas: The Military Frontier." *Southwestern Historical Quarterly* 80 (1977):357–98.

———. "Medicine in the West: An Introduction." *Journal of the West* 21, no. 3 (1982):3–4.

Brieger, Gerd. "Health and Disease on the Western Frontier: A Bicentennial Appreciation." *Western Journal of Medicine* 125 (1976):28–35.

———. *Medical America in the Nineteenth Century.* Baltimore: Johns Hopkins University Press, 1972.

———. "Medical Education in the Far West." *Journal of the West* 21, no. 3 (1982):42–48.

Buck, Carl E. *Health Survey of the State of New Mexico.* Santa Fe, N.M.: Bureau of Public Health, 1934.

Buck, Dorothy P. *The WICHE Student Exchange Program, 1953 to 1970.* Boulder, Colo.: Western Interstate Commission for Higher Education, 1970.

Bullock, Alice. "Medicine Man to the Medicine Men." *New Mexico Magazine* 32, no. 8 (1954):29, 55–56.

———. "Memories of Doc Hobbs." *Impact, The Albuquerque Journal Magazine* 4, no. 9 (1980):10–11.

Bullock, Earl S., M.D., and Charles T. Sands, M.D. "Twelve Years of Pulmonary Tuberculosis Treatment in the West." *Journal of the American Medical Association* 52 (19 June 1909):1973–80.

Bunch, George P., M.D. "New Mexico Medical Society, Roots and Foundation." *New Mexico Medical Society Newsletter* 2, no. 7 (1982):5.

Burroughs, Jean, ed. *Roosevelt County History and Heritage.* Portales, N.M.: Bishop Printing Co., 1975.

Burrow, James Gordon. *The American Medical Association: Voice of American Medicine.* Baltimore: Johns Hopkins University Press, 1963.

———. *Organized Medicine in the Progressive Era: The Move Toward Monopoly.* Baltimore and London: Johns Hopkins University Press, 1977.

Cameron, Virginia, and Esmond R. Long. *Tuberculosis Medical Research: National Tuberculosis Association, 1904–1955.* New York: National Tuberculosis Association, 1959.

Carrington, Paul M., M.D. "The Climate of New Mexico, Nature's Sanatorium for Consumptives." *New York Medical Journal* 86, no. 1 (1907):1–10.

Cecil, Russell L., ed. *A Textbook of Medicine by American Authors.* Philadelphia and London: W. B. Saunders and Co., 1927.

Chauvenet, Beatrice. "For Your Health's Sake." *New Mexico Magazine* 30, no. 4 (1952):13–15, 52–55.

———. *Hewett and Friends: A Biography of Santa Fe's Vibrant Era.* Santa Fe, N.M.: Museum of New Mexico Press, 1983.

Clapesattle, Helen. *Dr. Webb of Colorado Springs.* Boulder, Colo.: Colorado Associated Universities Press, 1984.

Clarke, Walter. *Syphilis in New Mexico.* Santa Fe, N.M.: New Mexico Tuberculosis Association, 1934.

Clayton, Delia Jenkins. "Pioneer History of Eddy County Hospitals, 1890–1977" in *Eddy County, New Mexico, to 1981.* Carlsbad, N.M.: Southwestern New Mexico Historical Society, 1982.

"Comparison of Public Health Activities Between New Mexico and Arizona." *Southwestern Medicine* 10 (1926):312–13.

Comroe, Julius H., Jr. "T.B. or Not T.B.?: The Treatment of Tuberculosis." *American Review of Respiratory Disease* 117 (1978):378–89.

Crail, Franklin H., M.D. "Some Problems That Confront Practitioners in New Mexico." *Southwestern Medicine* 13 (1929):379–82.

DeMark, Judith L. "Chasing the Cure—A History of Healthseekers to Albuquerque, 1902–1940." *Journal of the West* 21, no. 3 (1982):49–58.

Derbyshire, Robert C., M.D. *Medical Licensure and Discipline in the United States.* Baltimore: Johns Hopkins University Press, 1969.

———. "Threats to Medical Standards." *Rocky Mountain Medical Journal* 60, no. 9 (1963):23–26.

"Diphtheria in New Mexico." *Southwestern Medicine* 11 (1927):38.

Douthirt, Cranford H., M.D. "Report on Pneumonia Control Program in New Mexico." *New Mexico Health Officer* 10 , no. 3 (1942):42.

Dowling, Harry F. *Fighting Infection: Conquests of the Twentieth Century.* Cambridge, Mass.: Harvard University Press, 1977.

Duffy, John W. *The Healers: A History of American Medicine.* Urbana, Ill.: University of Illinois Press, 1979.

———. "Medicine in the West: An Historical Overview." *Journal of the West* 21, no. 3 (1982):5–14.

Dunlop, Richard. *Doctors of the American Frontier.* Garden City, N.Y.: Doubleday, 1965.

———. "Spanish Doctors in the Old Southwest." *Today's Health* 41, no. 2 (1963):44–47, 81–83.

Ealy, Ruth R. "Medical Missionary." *New Mexico Magazine* 32, no. 3 (1954):16–17, 38–39, 42–43, and 32, no. 4 (1954):22, 39.

———. *Water in a Thirsty Land.* Pittsburgh: n.p., 1955.

Elliott, Carey B., M.D. "Pioneers in the Medical History of New Mexico." *Southwestern Medicine* 11 (1927):264–68.

Elliott, Richard G. "'On a Comet, Always': A Biography of Dr. W. Randolph Lovelace II." *New Mexico Quarterly* 36 (1966–67):351–87.

Evans, Leland S., M.D. "Better Public Relations Through Better Medical Service." *Rocky Mountain Medical Journal* 48 (1951):413–16.

Faulkner, James M. *Opportunity for Medical Education in Idaho, Montana, Nevada, and Wyoming.* Boulder, Colo.: Western Interstate Commission for Higher Education, 1964.

Fergusson, Erna. *Albuquerque.* Albuquerque: Merle Armitage Editions, 1947.

———. *Our Southwest.* New York: Alfred Knopf, 1940.

Fest, Francis T. B., M.D. "The Consumptive's Holy Grail." *New Mexico Medical Journal* 5, no. 5 (1909–10):115–20.

———. "Eine neue Operation zur Heilung der Incontenentia bei Frauen." *Der Frauenarzt* 10 (1895):193–201.

"First Methodist Hospital Nothing Like Today's," *Albuquerque Tribune,* 24 May 1967.

Fitz, Reginald H., M.D., and Robert S. Stone, M.D. "New Medical Education in the Old Southwest" in Hans Popper, ed., *Trends in New Medical Schools* (New York and London: Grune and Stratton, 1967):94–100.

Fitzpatrick, George. "Here's Health." *New Mexico Magazine* 32, no. 2 (1954):11–13, 34–35, 42.

Flexner, Abraham. *Medical Education in the United States and Canada: A Report to the Carnegie Foundation for the Advancement of Teaching.* New York: Carnegie Foundation, 1910.

Forssen, John A., ed. *Petticoat and Stethoscope: A Montana Legend.* Missoula, Mont.: Bitterroot Litho, 1978.

Frisbie, Evelyn F., M.D. "Gonorrhea in the Female." *New Mexico Medical Journal* 7 (1911–12):128–32.

———. "Obstetrical Anesthesia and Analgesia." *New Mexico Medical Journal* 16, no. 3 (1916):77–81.

———. "Some of Our Problems in the Southwest." *New Mexico Medical Journal* 17, no. 1 (1916):5–16.

Gale, Godfrey, M.D., and Norman C. DeLarue, M.D. "Surgical History of Pulmonary Tuberculosis: The Rise and Fall of Various Technical Procedures." *Canadian Journal of Surgery* 12 (1969):381–88.

Gellenthien, Carl H., M.D. "Rx Climate." *New Mexico Magazine* 27, no. 6 (1949):16–17, 47.

Gerber, Charles W., M.D. "Summary of Malaria Control Work in Doña Ana County, New Mexico." *Southwestern Medicine* 15 (1931):370–75.

Gilbert, Jesse R., M.D. "Some Experience with Guaiacol and Ichthyol as a Local Antiseptic." *New Mexico Medical Journal* 6 (1910–11):274–75.

Gittings, Clyde L. "Arizona's Reputation as a Health Spa." *Arizona Medicine* 40 (1983):150–53.

Goddard, Roy F., M.D., Stanley J. Leland, M.D., and John C. Cobb. "A Review of Infant Mortality in New Mexico and the Bordering Mexican States." *Southwestern Medicine* 42 (1961):168–72, 215–20, 272–75.

Greenfield, Myrtle. *A History of Public Health in New Mexico.* Albuquerque: University of New Mexico Press, 1962.

Gregg, Josiah. *Commerce of the Prairies.* Edited by Milo Milton Quaife. Lincoln, Neb.: University of Nebraska Press, 1967.

Hall, T. B. *Medicine on the Santa Fe Trail.* Dayton, Ohio: Morningside Bookshop, 1971.

Hannemann, Judith. "Birth of the Colorado Medical Society." *Rocky Mountain Medical Journal* 68, no. 4 (1971):25–31.

Hannett, J. W., M.D. "The Public Health Officer and the Average Doctor." *New Mexico Health Officer* 18, nos. 1 and 2 (1950):3–4.

Hansen, Jean. "It Was the First Day of Class." *Salud,* Winter 1985:3–5.

Harrison, Will. "Anything But Medicine." *Southwestern Medicine* 44 (1963): 252–54.

Heller, Christine A. "Education in Nutrition as Part of the Maternal Health Program [in New Mexico]." *American Journal of Public Health* 32 (1942):1021–24.

"High Country Haven: Army Air Forces Convalescent Hospital in Albuquerque." *New Mexico Magazine* 23, no. 1 (1945):15–19.

Hope, Walter G., M.D. "Reminiscences of Medical Men and Matters in Albuquerque." *New Mexico Medical Journal* 10 (1912–13):156–58.

Hoyt, Henry F., M.D. *A Frontier Doctor.* Boston and New York: Houghton Mifflin Co., 1929.

Huddleston, Ruth B. "New Mexico—La Tierra de Manana." *Public Health Nursing* 29 (1937):421–24.

Hurley, Charles. "Where Miracles Are Routine." *New Mexico Magazine* 30, no. 2 (1952):21–23, 34, 36.

Hurt, Amy P. "Desert Sanctuary." *New Mexico Magazine* 28, no. 6 (1950):19, 42–44.

An Illustrated History of New Mexico. Chicago: Lewis Publishing Co., 1895.

Ivey, T. N. "Medicine in the Pioneer West, 1850 to 1900." *North Carolina Medical Journal* 26 (1965):161–65.

Jacobs, Philip P., comp. *The Campaign Against Tuberculosis in the United States.* New York: National Association for the Study and Prevention of Tuberculosis, 1908.

James, Helen. "Nurse-of-the-Month." *Public Health Nursing* 26 (1934):616–17.

Japp, Phyllis M. "Pioneer Medicines: Doctors, Nostrums, and Folk Cures." *Journal of the West* 21, no. 3 (1982):15–22.

Johnson, Bobby H. "Doctors, Druggists, and Dentists in the Oklahoma Territory, 1889–1907." *Arizona and the West* 19 (1977):121–34.

Johnson, Byron A., and Robert K. Dauner, eds. *Early Albuquerque: A Photographic History, 1870–1918.* Albuquerque: Albuquerque Journal and Albuquerque Museum, 1981.

Jones, Billy M. *Health-Seekers in the Southwest, 1817–1900.* Norman, Okla.: University of Oklahoma Press, 1967.

Karolevitz, R. F. *Doctors of the Old West: A Pictorial History of Medicine on the Frontier.* Seattle: Superior Publishing Co., 1967.

Kaufman, Arthur, M.D. *Implementing Problem-Based Medical Education: Lessons from Successful Innovations.* New York: Springer, 1985.

Kaufman, Martin, Stuart Galishoff, and Todd Savitt, eds. *Dictionary of American Medical Biography.* 2 vols. Westport, Conn.: Greenwood Press, 1984.

Keers, R. Y. *Pulmonary Tuberculosis: A Journey Down the Centuries.* London: Baillière Tindall, 1978.

Kellogg, George M., M.D. "New Mexico as a Health Resort." *Journal of the American Medical Association* 27 (12 September 1896):582–84.

Kennedy, J. W. "Early Medical Conditions in Arizona." *Arizona Medicine* 29 (1972):582–85, 655–57.

Kerr, J. W., M.D. "Public Health Administration in New Mexico." *Public Health Reports* 33 (1918):1979–81.

Kimball, Clark, and Marcus J. Smith, M.D. *The Hospital at the End of the Santa Fe Trail: A Pictorial History of St. Vincent Hospital, Santa Fe, New Mexico.* Santa Fe, N.M.: Rydal Press, 1977.

Kyner, J. L. "Doctor Josiah Gregg, Scientist of the Southwest, Portrayer of the Santa Fe Trail." *Journal of the American Medical Association* 224 (2 April 1973):101–5.

Laws, J. W., M.D. "Observations of a Country Physician." *New Mexico Medical Journal* 13 (1914–15):88–92.

Lawson, Hampden C. "The Early Medical Schools of Kentucky." *Bulletin of the History of Medicine* 24 (1950):168–75.

Lea County Genealogical Society. *Then and Now—Lea County Families.* Lovington, N.M.: Lea County Genealogical Society, 1979.

Lee, J. G. "Spanish Medicine on the Old Frontier." *Arizona Medicine* 22 (1965):448–53.

Litoff, Judy Barrett. *American Midwives, 1860 to the Present.* Westport, Conn.: Greenwood Press, 1978.

Long, Esmond R., M.D. "Tuberculosis in Modern Society." *Bulletin of the History of Medicine* 27 (1953):301–19.

Loveridge, Arthur N. *A Man Who Knew How to Live Among His Fellow Men: A Graphic Life Story of Chester T. French.* Boulder, Colo.: Old Trails Publishers, 1965.

Luckett, G. S., M.D. "Ten Years Ago." *Southwestern Medicine* 13 (1929):534–38.

Lundwall, Helen J., ed. *Pioneering in Territorial Silver City: H. B. Ailman's Recollections of Silver City and the Southwest, 1871–1892.* Albuquerque: University of New Mexico Press, 1983.

Marshall, Ralph. "The First Lady President of a State Medical Society." *Rocky Mountain Medical Journal* 59, no. 11 (1962):35–36.

Martin, Anna Y. "Hope for the Mentally Ill." *New Mexico Magazine* 32, no. 7 (1954):30–31, 52–53.

Masten, H. B., M.D. "New Mexico as a Health Resort." *New York Medical Journal* 76 (1902):414–17.

Mayes, C. M., M.D. "The Indigent Consumptive Proposition." *New Mexico Medical Journal* 5, no. 2 (1909–10):18–19.

Mayo, Charles W., M.D. *Mayo: The Story of My Family and My Career.* New York: Doubleday and Co., Inc., 1968.

McBride, Robert E., M.D. "The New Mexico Medical Society: Some Duties and Responsibilities." *New Mexico Medical Journal* 4, no. 2 (1908–9):10–15.

McKay, J. A. "Rural Medicine at the Turn of the Century." *Medical Opinion and Review* 6 (1970):84–93.

McKee, John DeWitt. "Help for the Handicapped." *New Mexico Magazine* 37, no. 6 (1959):20–21, 49.

Means, Florence Crannell. *Sagebrush Surgeon.* New York: Friendship Press, 1956.

Melick, Dermont W., M.D. "Surgical Therapy of Pulmonary Tuberculosis—A Rare Necessity of the 1980s: An Historical Review." *Arizona Medicine* 40 (1983):158–59.

Melzer, Richard. "A Dark and Terrible Moment: The Spanish Flu Epidemic of 1918 in New Mexico." *New Mexico Historical Review* 57 (1982):213–36.

Mendelson, Ralph W., M.D. *I Lost a King.* New York: Vantage Press, 1964.

Mick, Stephen S., and Jacqueline Lowe Worobey. "Foreign Medical Graduates in the 1980s: Trends in Specialization." *American Journal of Public Health* 74 (1984):698–703.

Middleton, R. P. "Highlights of Early Surgery in Utah." *Rocky Mountain Medical Journal* 64, no. 1 (1967):33–40.

Montana Medical Association. *First One Hundred Years: Being a Review of the Beginnings, Growth, and Development of the Montana Medical Association in Commemoration of Its Centennial Year.* Missoula, Mont.: Bitterroot Litho, 1978.

Mumey, Nolie, M.D. "Medicine in Colorado During the Primitive and Formative Years." *Rocky Mountain Medical Journal* 68, no. 4 (1971):1–23.

Murphey, Walter T., M.D. "A Plea for a More Extensive Use of Tuberculin in the Treatment of Tuberculosis." *New Mexico Medical Journal* 15 (1915–16):121–26.

Nahm, Milton C. *Las Vegas and Uncle Joe: The New Mexico I Remember.* Norman, Okla.: University of Oklahoma Press, 1964.

Napolitano, Leonard, and Carolyn R. Tinker. "The University of New Mexico School of Medicine." *Western Journal of Medicine* 140 (1984):465–70.

Olch, Peter D., M.D. "Medicine in the Indian-Fighting Army, 1866–1890." *Journal of the West* 21, no. 3 (1982):32–41.

Osler, William, M.D. *The Principles and Practice of Medicine.* 3rd ed. New York: D. Appleton and Co., 1898.

Pageant of Progress, the Carlsbad Story. Carlsbad, N.M.: Carlsbad Chamber of Commerce, n.d. (1972).

Palmieri, Anthony, and Daniel J. Hammond. "Drug Therapy at a Frontier Fort Hospital: Fort Laramie, Wyoming Territory, 1870–1889." *Pharmacy History* 21, no. 1 (1979):35–44.

Patterson, E. B. *Sagebrush Doctors and Health Conditions of Northeastern Nevada from Aboriginal Times to 1972.* Springville, Utah: Art City Publishing Co., 1972.

Perkins, J. S., M.D. "How To Do Clean Surgery at Small Cost." *Transactions of the Rocky Mountain Inter-State Medical Association* 3 (1901):116–24.

Perrigo, Lynn. *Gateway to Glorieta: A History of Las Vegas, New Mexico.* Boulder, Colo.: Pruett Publishing Co., 1982.

Peters, LeRoy S., M.D. "Changing Concepts of Tuberculosis During Twenty-Five Years." *Southwestern Medicine* 24 (1940):46–48.

———. "New Mexico Medicine." *New Mexico Quarterly Review* 11 (1941): 322–29.

———. "What New Mexico Needs Most in Tuberculosis Legislation." *New Mexico Medical Journal* 15 (1915–16):229–33.

———. "What Next in Medicine?" *Southwestern Medicine* 22 (1938):429–31.

Peters, LeRoy S., M.D., and Earl S. Bullock, M.D. "Artificial Pneumothorax in the Treatment of Pulmonary Tuberculosis." *New Mexico Medical Journal* 9 (1912–13):95–97.

Peters, LeRoy S., M.D., and P. G. Cornish, Jr., M.D. "The Cauterization of Adhesions by Closed Pneumolysis After the Jacobaeus-Unverricht Method." *Southwestern Medicine* 15 (1931):61–64.

Pizer, I. H. "Medical Aspects of the Westward Migrations, 1830–1860." *Bulletin of the Medical Library Association* 53 (1965):1–14.

Price, George Bacon. *Gaining Health in the West (Colorado, New Mexico, Arizona).* New York: B. W. Huebsch, 1907.

"Public Health in New Mexico." *Southwestern Medicine* 9 (1925):362.

Quebbeman, Frances E. *Medicine in Territorial Arizona.* Phoenix: Arizona Historical Foundation, 1966.

Raynor, T. E. "Country Doctor." *New Mexico Magazine* 34, no. 4 (1956):22, 56–57.

Redman, Jack Curry, M.D. "Medical Education Milestone in New Mexico." *Southwestern Medicine* 41 (1960):399–400.

Reeder, John D. "Faywood—A New Era." *New Mexico Magazine* 60, no. 3 (1982):50–56.

"The 'Rest Cure' for Tuberculosis." *The Herald of the Well Country* 1, no. 5 (1915):6.

Rhoades, E. R., and D. B. Bullock. "Medicine in Southwestern Oklahoma Before Statehood." *Journal of the Oklahoma State Medical Association* 64 (1971):497–503 and 65 (1972):65–73.

Robbins, Cathy, "Health Services: History," *The New Mexico Independent,* 12 August 1977.

Rogers, Frank B. "The Rise and Decline of the Altitude Therapy of Tuberculosis." *Bulletin of the History of Medicine* 43 (1969):1–16.

Rolls, James G., M.D. "The Sanitary Needs of Santa Fe." *New Mexico Medical Journal* 5, no. 8 (1909–10):202–6.

Romero, Leo M. "The Quest for Educational Opportunity: Access to Legal and Medical Education in New Mexico." *New Mexico Historical Review* 53 (1978):337–46.

Rothstein, William G. *American Physicians in the Nineteenth Century: From Sects to Science.* Baltimore: Johns Hopkins University Press,1972.

Rude, J. C. "Medicine in Texas." *Texas Medicine* 63 (1967):48–122.

Samet, J. M., Charles R. Key, Daniel Kutvirt, and Charles L. Wiggins. "Respiratory Disease Mortality in New Mexico's American Indians and Hispanics." *American Journal of Public Health* 70 (1980):492–97.

Saylor, Dennis E. *Songs in the Night: The Story of Marian Van Deventer.* Lomita, Cal.: Palos Verdes Book Co., 1980.

Schofield, J. R. *New and Expanded Medical Schools, Mid-Century to the 1980s.* San Francisco: Jossey-Bass Publishers, 1984.

Schulman, Sam, and Anne M. Smith. *Health and Disease in Northern New Mexico: A Research Report.* Boulder, Colo.: Institute of Behavioral Science, 1962.

Scott, James R., M.D. "The County Health Unit." *Southwestern Medicine* 15 (1931):366–69.

———. "Twenty-five Years of Public Health in New Mexico, 1919–1944." *New Mexico Health Officer* 12 (1944):1–81.

Sedgwick, James C., M.D. "Adherence to Principle Versus Conceding to Expediency." *Rocky Mountain Medical Journal* 56, no. 7 (1959):29–32.

Sethman, H. T., ed. *A Century of Colorado Medicine, 1871–1971.* Denver: Colorado Medical Society, 1971.

Shane, Karen. "New Mexico: Salubrious El Dorado." *New Mexico Historical Review* 56 (1981):387–99.

Shortle, Abraham G., M.D. "Artificial Pneumothorax." *New Mexico Medical Journal* 9 (1912–13):98–101.

———. "Home Treatment Versus Sanitarium Treatment of Tuberculosis." *New Mexico Medical Journal* 5 (1909–10):221–24.

———. "Treatment of Pulmonary Hemorrhage." *New Mexico Medical Journal* 15 (1915):86–92.

Shryock, Richard H. *Medical Licensing in America, 1650–1965.* Baltimore: Johns Hopkins University Press, 1967.

———. *National Tuberculosis Association, 1904–1954: A Study of the Voluntary Health Movement in the United States.* New York: National Tuberculosis Association, 1957.

———. "Women in American Medicine." *Journal of the American Medical Women's Association* 5 (1950):371–79.

Sigerist, Henry A. *A History of Medicine.* 2 vols. New York: Oxford University Press, 1951, 1961.

Simmons, Marc. "New Mexico's Smallpox Epidemic of 1789–1791." *New Mexico Historical Review* 41 (1966):319–24.

"Smallpox in New Mexico." *Southwestern Medicine* 10 (1926):127.

Smith, Marcus J., M.D. "The First Hundred Years." *Newsletter* (*New Mexico Medical Society*) 2, no. 8 (1982):3.

———. "The Rocky Mountain Medical Association and New Mexico Territorial Society." *Newsletter* (*New Mexico Medical Society*) 24, no. 1 (1981):2.

Smith, Toby. "They Were Called Lungers." *Albuquerque Journal,* 16 March 1980.

Spriggs, E. A. "Rest and Exercise in Pulmonary Tuberculosis: A Study of Fashions in Treatment." *Tubercle* 41 (1960):455–62.

Starr, Paul. *The Social Transformation of American Medicine.* New York: Basic Books, Inc., 1982.

Stevens, A. D. "Arizona's History of Surgery." *Arizona Medicine* 21 (1964):36–39, 177–79, 394–96, 548–50, 705–9.

———. "Arizona's Medical Memories." *Arizona Medicine* 23 (1966):279–82, 743–46 and 24 (1967):1112–13.

———. "Arizona's Territorial Tales." *Arizona Medicine* 29 (1972):727–28.

———. "Medical Fees of an Earlier Era." *Arizona Medicine* 31 (1974):286–87.

Stevens, R. A., L. W. Goodman, and S. S. Mick. *The Alien Doctors: Foreign Medical Graduates in American Hospitals.* New York: Wiley-Interscience, 1978.

Stevens, Rosemary. *American Medicine and the Public Interest.* New Haven: Yale University Press, 1971.

Stimmel, Barry. "The Impact of the Foreign Medical Graduates on Future Health Manpower Needs." *Bulletin of the New York Academy of Medicine* 56 (1980):631–42.

Sweet, Ernest A., M.D. "Interstate Migration of Tuberculous Persons, Its Bearing on the Public Health, with Special Reference to the States of Texas and New Mexico." *Public Health Reports* 30 (1915):1059–91, 1147–73, 1225–55.

Szasz, Ferenc. "Francis Schlatter: The Healer of the Southwest." *New Mexico Historical Review* 54 (1979):89–104.

Thompson, Howard, M.D. "Pioneer Practice in the Southwest." *Southwestern Medicine* 1 (1917):46–48.

Thurman, Ruth. "Here's Health!" *New Mexico Magazine* 21, no. 3 (1943):17–19.
Tinker, Carolyn R. "The Missionaries." *Salud*, Winter 1985:4–6.
Trewhitt, Hank. "Atomic Medicine." *New Mexico Magazine* 28, no. 8 (1950):22–23, 50–52.
Tupper, Margaret. "Maternal and Infant Hygiene in New Mexico." *Public Health Nurse* 14 (1922):191–94.
"Typhoid in New Mexico." *Southwestern Medicine* 11 (1927):511.
van der Eerden, M. Lucia. *Maternity Care in a Spanish-American Community of New Mexico [Ranchos de Taos]*. Washington: Catholic University Press, 1948.
Van Doren, Wilma. "Indian Clinic." *New Mexico Magazine* 36, no. 8 (1958):26–27, 46.
Van Druff, Strawcy. "Miracle Waters." *New Mexico Magazine* 27, no. 12 (1949):22–23, 42–43.
Vickers, Fred D., M.D. "Artificial Pneumothorax." *Southwestern Medicine* 11 (1927):443–48.
Waksman, Selman A. *The Conquest of Tuberculosis*. Berkeley, Cal.: University of California Press, 1964.
Walmsley, Myrtle. *I Remember, I Remember Truchas the Way It Was, 1936–1956*. Albuquerque: Menual Historical Library, 1981.
Waters, M. Michael. "Culture in Relation to a Maternity Service." *Public Health Nursing* 42 (1950):68–72.
Waxham, F. E., M.D. "Impressions of Albuquerque, New Mexico as a Health Resort." *Chicago Clinical Review* 1 (1892–93):433–35.
Werner, Walter I. "The Problem of Tuberculosis in New Mexico." *Southwestern Medicine* 24 (1940):404–8.
Western Interstate Commission for Higher Education. *Meeting the West's Health Manpower Needs*. Boulder, Colo.: WICHE, 1960.
———. *The West's Medical Manpower Needs*. 2nd edition, with revised data. Boulder, Colo.: WICHE, 1960.
White, Clayton S., M.D., ed. *Physics and Medicine of the Upper Atmosphere*. Albuquerque: University of New Mexico Press, 1953.
Whitmore, M. V. "Early Medical Conditions in Arizona." *Arizona Medicine* 29 (1972):655–57.
Wills, Louise. "Instruction of Midwives in San Miguel County." *Southwestern Medicine* 6 (1922):276–79.
———. "Isolated New Mexico." *Public Health Nurse* 14 (1922):291–93.
Wilson, J. G. "Investigation of Diarrheal Diseases in New Mexico." *Southwestern Medicine* 11 (1927):61–64.
Wilson, Julius Lane, M.D. "The Daily Sanatorium Routine Was the Treatment." *American Lung Association Bulletin* 68, no. 2 (1982):7–10.
———. "Pikes Peak or Bust: An Historical Note on the Search for Health in the Rockies." *Rocky Mountain Medical Journal* 64, no. 9 (1967):58–62.

———. "The Western Frontier and Climate Therapy." *The Journal-Lancet* 86 (1966):564–67.

Wilson, Stephany. "The Passing of an Era: Presbyterian Sanatorium Coming Down." *Inside: The Presbyterian Hospital Center Magazine* 1, no. 2 (1967):2–6.

Woodham, Marion. *A History of Presbyterian Hospital 1908 to 1976, with an Update Through 1979.* Albuquerque: Presbyterian Hospital Center, 1980.

Woods, Betty. "Medicine Water." *New Mexico Magazine* 18, no. 3 (1940):12–13.

Wroth, James H., M.D. "The Climate of New Mexico as Viewed by the Medical Fraternity There." *Transactions of the American Climatological Association* 7 (1890):285–90.

Wylder, Meldrum K., M.D. "Childhood Tuberculosis: Discussed with Special Reference to Preventive Measures." *Southwestern Medicine* 18 (1934):120–23.

———. "Inferior Midwifery: A Case Report." *Southwestern Medicine* 20 (1936):178–79.

———. *Rio Grande Medicine Man.* Santa Fe, N.M.: Rydal Press, 1958.

Yater, C. M., M.D. "Therapetitic [*sic*] Notes—Status of Tuberculosis in the City of Roswell." *New Mexico Medical Journal* 5 (1909–10):270–72.

IV. Newspapers and Others Periodicals

Albuquerque Journal, 1903–81.

Albuquerque Tribune, 1938–80.

Journal of the American Medical Association, 1883–1984.

Las Vegas (N.M.) Daily Optic, 1881–1904.

New Mexico Health Officer, 1942–59.

New Mexico Magazine, 1922–82.

New Mexico Medical Journal, 1905–17.

Rocky Mountain Medical Journal, 1903–72.

Southwestern Medicine, 1917–44.

V. Interviews

(See Appendix C for a complete list of the interviews held within the New Mexico Medical History Oral History Project. Those interviews are not listed again here.)

Aberle, Sophie, M.D. Interview with the author. Albuquerque, N.M., 26 August 1984.

Adler, Scott, M.D. Interview with the author. Albuquerque, N.M., 3 September 1982.

Aragon, Mrs. Jake (daughter of Las Cruces physician Dr. Bruce Lane). Interview with the author. Las Cruces, N.M., 5 October 1983.

Brinegar, Mrs. Earlene (daughter of Santa Fe physician Dr. Earl LeGrande Ward). Albuquerque, N.M., 12 November 1984.

Campbell, Governor Jack. Interview with the author. Albuquerque, N.M., 25 October 1985.
Chauvenet, Mrs. Beatrice. Interview with the author. Albuquerque, N.M., 1 October 1984.
Dornacker, John. Interview with the author. Albuquerque, N.M., 3 February 1985.
Escudero, Richard (longtime employee at New Mexico State Hospital, Las Vegas). Interview with the author. Las Vegas, N.M., 7 September 1982.
Hennigar, Mrs. Carl (daughter of Wagon Mound physician Dr. J. H. Steele). Interview with the author. Raton, N.M., 29 November 1983.
Korte, Fred (longtime employee at New Mexico State Hospital, Las Vegas). Interview with the author. Las Vegas, N.M., 7 September 1983.
Nohl, Mrs. Margaret (daughter of Albuquerque surgeon Dr. J. W. Hannett). Interview with the author. Albuquerque, N.M., 1 August 1984.
Savage, George. Interview with the author. Albuquerque, N.M., 28 January 1985.
Sisk, Mrs. Arthur Hope (daughter of pioneer Albuquerque physician Dr. Walter G. Hope). Interview with the author. Albuquerque, N.M., 4 April 1984.
Voute, Jan Pieter, M.D. Interview with the author. Santa Fe, N.M., 3 January 1986.
Wood, K. Rose. Interview with the author. Santa Fe, N.M., 3 January 1986.

VI. Unpublished Material

Adler, Mildred S. "Early Military Medicine in New Mexico." Typescript, no date, in University of New Mexico Medical Center Library, Medical History Archives.
Beimer, Dorothy S. "Hovels, Haciendas, and House Calls." Typescript, 1981, in University of New Mexico Medical Center, Medical History Archives.
———. "Pioneer Physicians in Las Vegas, New Mexico, 1880–1911." Typescript, November 1976, in University of New Mexico Medical Center Library, Medical History Archives.
Dellinger, Maxine. "The History of Abdominal Surgery in New Mexico." Typescript, August 1960, in University of New Mexico Medical Center Library, Medical History Archives.
DeMark, Judith L. "Evelyn Fisher Frisbie: Pioneer New Mexico Physician." Typescript, 1977, in possession of the author.
Evans, Leland S., M.D. "History of the Doña Ana County Medical Society." Typescript, early 1970s(?), in University of New Mexico Medical Center Library, Medical History Archives.
Foote, Cheryl J. "Mission Teacher of the Southwest: Alice Blake of Trementina, New Mexico." Typescript, 1982, in possession of the author.
Johnson, Judith R. "Health Seekers to Albuquerque, 1880–1940." M.A. thesis, University of New Mexico, 1983.
———. "History of St. Joseph Hospital, Albuquerque, New Mexico." Typescript, March 1977, in possession of the author.

———. "A Study of Two Hospitals in Albuquerque from 1902 to 1945." Typescript, no date, in possession of the author.

Taylor, Thomas D. "The Economic Impact of the University of New Mexico School of Medicine on Albuquerque, New Mexico, 1963–1969." Thesis, Southwestern Graduate School of Banking, 1970. (Copy in University of New Mexico Medical Center Library, Medical History Archives.)

Index